MAKING DEVELOPMENT WORK

World Bank Series on Evaluation and Development

Robert Picciotto, Series Editor

Evaluation and Development:
The Institutional Dimension
edited by Robert Picciotto and Eduardo Wiesner

Involuntary Resettlement:
Comparative Perspectives
edited by Robert Picciotto, Warren van Wicklin,
and Edward Rice

Evaluation and Poverty Reduction
edited by Osvaldo N. Feinstein and Robert Picciotto

Making Development Work:
Development Learning in a World of Poverty and Wealth
edited by Nagy Hanna and Robert Picciotto

Managing a Global Resource:
Challenges of Forest Conservation and Development
edited by Uma Lele

MAKING DEVELOPMENT WORK

Development Learning in a World of Poverty and Wealth

World Bank Series on
Evaluation and Development

Volume 4

edited by
Nagy Hanna and **Robert Picciotto**

Transaction Publishers
New Brunswick (U.S.A.) and London (U.K.)

Library of Congress Catalog Number: 2001052296
ISBN: 0-7658-0118-3 (cloth); 0-7658-0915-X (paper)
Printed in the United States of America

Library of Congress Cataloging-in-Publication Data

Making development work : development learning in a world of poverty
and wealth/ Nagy Hanna and Robert Picciotto, editors
     p. cm. — (World Bank series on evaluation and development ; v. 4)
    Includes bibliographical references and index.
    ISBN 0-7658-0118-3 (cloth : alk. paper) — ISBN 0-7658-0915-X (pbk. : alk.
paper)
    1. Developing countries—Economic policy—Citizen participation.
2. Poverty—Developing countries. 3. Democracy—Developing countries.
I. Hanna, Nagy. II. Picciotto, Robert. III. Series.

HC59.7 .M2539 2002
338.9'009172'4—dc21

2001052296

Contents

Part 3: Focus on Results

Part 4: Partnerships: Local and Global

Part 5: Synthesis

Acknowledgments

This book has benefited from the contributions of staff of the Operations Evaluation Department of the World Bank, The Institute of Development Studies, the Overseas Development Institute, and Oxford Policy Management. Special thanks are due to to Keith Bezanson and Robert Chamber of IDS, to Simon Maxwell and Mick Foster of ODI, and to William Branson of Princeton University and Gregory Ingram of OED.

Valuable advice and comments on specific chapters were provided by Ramgopal Agarwala, Carl Dahlman, Shantayanan Devarajan, Ishac Diwan, David Dollar, Marco Ferroni, Alan Harold Gelb, Geoffrey B. Lamb, Pierre Landell-Mills, John Page, Anthony J. Pellegrini, Guillermo Perry, Guy Pfeffermann, Ian C. Porter, Neil D. Roger, Nemat Talaat Shafik, William E. Stevenson, Michael Walton, and John Eriksson. Special thanks to Ashoka Mody for his comments on the overall book.

Meta de Coquereaumont edited the manuscript. Parveen Moses provided production support. The book was produced by the Partnerships and Knowledge group of OED under the direction of Osvaldo Feinstein.

Introduction

Robert Picciotto

World poverty has increased and growth prospects have dimmed for developing countries during the last decade, despite the gains from technological change and more open trade. In response to this overarching development
challenge, the World Bank launched the Comprehensive Development Framework (CDF) in January 1999. It has evoked considerable interest and debate
throughout the development community.

The basic elements of the proposed development compact are not new.
But their joint articulation as a framework to guide development assistance is.
The papers in this volume examine development experience and prospects
through the lens of the CDF principles:

- *A long-term, holistic approach*. Because binding development constraints are
  structural and social, they cannot be overcome quickly and require a strategic
  vision of societal change in addition to economic stabilization and sound macroeconomic management.
- *Local ownership*. Experience suggests that policy and institutional reforms cannot be imported or imposed; for reforms and investments to be sustainable,
  countries must take ownership.
- *Focus on results*. Development activities must be guided and judged by results,
  not by intentions or inputs.
- *Partnership*. Government, the private sector, civil society, and development
  agencies need to work together to achieve coherence and a judicious division of
  labor.

The World Bank's *1999 Annual Review of Development Effectiveness* examined World Bank operational performance in light of these principles.[1]
This volume presents more varied perspectives on the challenges involved in
implementing CDF principles. It identifies promising approaches for devel-

oping countries and aid agencies as they seek new modes of comprehensive and balanced development.

The Evolution of the Holistic Approach

Chapter 1 provides a historical backdrop for a newly emerging consensus on development and sets the stage for the rest of the volume. Nagy Hanna and Ramgopal Agarwala explore the meaning of the CDF principles, showing how they differ significantly from the practices of the "planning" and "adjustment" eras. They trace some of the precursors to the CDF and collect research and evaluative evidence in support of the paradigm shift.

In chapter 2, Simon Maxwell and Tim Conway look at multisectoral and integrated approaches to development planning and draw lessons for a renewed emphasis on long-term and comprehensive development strategies. They draw on experience with target-based planning. Common pitfalls, they believe, can be avoided by substituting a learning process approach for blueprint planning. It is better to start small, develop short- to medium-term goals, pitch ambitious but realistic targets, develop capacity and credibility through action, promote partnerships, avoid central integration, and build on initial success to address increasingly complex problems.

Local Ownership

Next, the focus of the volume shifts to country ownership of development policies and programs. In chapter 3, William Branson and Nagy Hanna discuss the limits of conditionality. They propose a broader view of conditionality as an evolving and learning process in support of a policy compact for achieving long-term objectives. It would be designed to ensure mutual commitment by aid agencies and countries and provide sufficient room and flexibility for the country to design, phase, and adapt its reforms. These proposals are grounded in a recent evaluation of higher-impact adjustment lending and recent empirical evidence on successful adjustment lending.

Chapter 4 is based on extensive research by James Blackburn, Robert Chambers, and John Gaventa that draws lessons for making participation an integral part of development. They stress policy consultation with the poor and a wide range of civil society actors. In scaling up participation to national levels, they counsel against rapid change, inflexible procedures, and fickle involvement. They suggest that mainstreaming participation requires profound changes in aid agencies: adopting flexible approaches, nurturing collaborative attitudes, and improving the capacity of different stakeholders to own and share. Finally, they explore the potential of participatory monitoring and evaluation and highlight the importance of enabling environments for popular participation.

In chapter 5, Richard Crook and James Manor present a state-of-the-art review of democratic decentralization. They suggest that democratic decentralization best supports holistic development when power and resources are devolved to elected bodies at intermediate levels—districts, counties, municipalities. Democratic decentralization holds promise for promoting partnership among government agencies, civil society, and grassroots communities. It can make government processes more visible and intelligible to ordinary people and more open to local access, influence, and accountability. The chapter further examines the enabling conditions for democratic decentralization, options for fiscal decentralization, and the role of safety nets for the poor. Much more learning is needed to realize the potential of democratic decentralization for development.

Chapter 6 deals with the cognitive and motivational aspects of autonomy-compatible development assistance—the intellectual basis for engendering ownership and helping others help themselves. David Ellerman examines the paradox of autonomy-compatible intervention by drawing on a rich body of multidisciplinary literature seldom consulted by development professionals. Helpers (aid agencies) have to start where the doers (countries) are. They have to see through the doers' eyes. Paternalistic benevolence is ineffective. Doers must be in the driver's seat. He examines the consequences of helpers transmitting knowledge to passive doers: loss of ownership and self-confidence, cognitive dependency, and moral hazard. Within development organizations, he argues for an open learning model and for promoting internal debate.

In chapter 7, Nagy Hanna introduces lessons from the United Nations Development Programme Long-Term Perspective Studies and from the World Bank's evaluation of key diagnostic and advisory tools. He asks why it has been so difficult to promote intellectual partnership and local capacity building. Development assistance agencies tend to reify and impose their own frameworks instead of adapting their models to variable and complex realities. They also ignore the need for developing countries to self-diagnose and self-evaluate, learn from each other, and adapt global best practices. The chapter concludes with implications for the design of new client-centered development assistance tools that would move beyond blueprints, mobilize local learning, build on local knowledge, and engender local ownership.

Achieving Results

Chapters 8 through 10 examine approaches and instruments used by aid agencies. In chapter 8, Mike Foster and Felix Naschold explore medium-term expenditure frameworks and sectorwide approaches to development cooperation that focus on donor-government partnership in the budget process. They draw lessons from early efforts to achieve an integrated approach to expenditure management that is owned by government and focused on achieving results. From the recent experiences of Ghana, Rwanda, and Uganda, Foster and Naschold conclude that a comprehensive framework becomes meaningful only when it forces choices among priorities and sequencing within realistic budget constraints.

In chapter 9, Stephen Jones and Andrew Lawson further examine the experience with sectorwide approaches and the reasons for mixed progress. They find several preconditions for progress: effective leadership, commitment to the process in the ministry of finance and at the political level, broad consensus between government and donors on key sector policies, and macroeconomic and political stability. Jones and Lawson also examine experience with medium-term expenditure framework initiatives. They conclude with a preliminary assessment of strategies for scaling up from project-based planning to sector approaches and for adapting these strategies to country conditions.

In chapter 10, James Fox applies the CDF to the U.S. Agency for International Development's (USAID) experience—an example from bilateral aid. He looks at a number of countries and programs where development outcomes are conclusive. These include some conspicuous successes—assistance to the Republic of Korea, family planning, agricultural research, university training, and smallpox eradication. He concludes that USAID's decentralization of authority to local country missions helped adapt programs to local conditions. New knowledge and technology were critical to success in most cases. The need for a long-term focus is evident from all the cases. But the search for holistic and long-term strategies should not distract from timely investment in windows of opportunity. Quality of implementation is at least as critical as quality of vision. There are risks in partnership approaches when efforts to coordinate lead to least common denominator approaches. Results orientation is a critical success factor.

Partnerships and Global Governance

In chapter 11, Maxwell and Conway look at the forms and practices of partnership in different fields, including business and law as well as development assistance. They argue that aid agencies must be explicit about the kinds of partnerships they seek with countries and the kinds of strategic selectivity they will exercise. Partnership should be treated as an organic process, in which mutual trust is built over time. It should be based on monitorable and mutual accountability.

In chapter 12, Marco Ferroni argues that globalization trends and aid effectiveness call for a transboundary way of looking at development and aid.

Many of the crises on today's global agenda can be traced to an undersupply of international public goods. Issue-oriented transboundary networks are emerging. Ferroni suggests that greater attention to global concerns would help improve development effectiveness by strengthening partnership and processes of cooperation. He suggests strengthening the interface between national and international public goods programs and national capacity-building efforts.

Synthesis

In the final chapter, Nagy Hanna pulls together the lessons of development experience at sectoral, national, and international levels. Drawing on the perspectives of earlier chapters, he outlines key tensions and challenges between short and long term, comprehensiveness and selectivity, ownership and conditionality, speed and broad-based ownership, the need to focus on and scale-up results and poor local evaluation capacity and accountability records, and enhanced country focus and increasing globalization. He advocates that the one-size-fits-all current mentality be replaced by client empowerment and learning by doing. This is a challenging agenda: the old development assistance culture is firmly rooted in blueprint planning and operational practices. Changing these practices will take time. We'd better start right away.

Note

1. Operations Evaluation Department. 1999. *1999 Annual Review of Development Effectiveness*. Washington, DC: World Bank.

Part 1

Long-Term
Holistic Approaches

1

Toward a Comprehensive Development Strategy

Nagy Hanna and *Ramgopal Agarwala*

Globalization has raised the bar for developing countries to compete and grow. But while it amplifies the risks from increased instability in earnings and employment and increased stress on institutions and communities, it also increases the rewards of connecting to the world. The growth rewards are not automatic, however. Developing countries can thrive in the new global economy if they are able to combine economic openness with a clear domestic investment strategy and effective institutions for governance, conflict management, and inclusion. Complementary policies and institutions are needed to promote strategies that develop and deploy each country's resources and capabilities.

The successful experiences of East Asian countries provide some pointers: investing in human capital, reducing structural inequality, and developing coherent long-term visions, science and technology institutions, and export promotion, among others. Institutions of governance, negotiation, coordination, and regulation, as well as mechanisms of social protection, will be increasingly important for coping with global turbulence and countering the widening inequality that openness can bring (Rodrik 2000). But there are no blueprints. Countries have to fashion their own strategies in a fast-changing global marketplace, starting from very different initial conditions.

The Comprehensive Development Framework (CDF) responds to this changing global environment by promoting more effective development assistance through national processes and institutions that address and manage the new opportunities and risks arising from the global environment (OED

3

1998a). Just as modern businesses set their goals in line with the external environment, market competition, and core competencies, each developing country needs to take a long view of its potential and aspirations and to take account of its regional context and global factors. This suggests moving beyond the current fragmented, short-term, and project-based development framework to one that emphasizes the interactions among policies, investments, and institutions, and their dynamics over the long term.

Globalization will require developing nations to reach out to international partners to manage changes beyond their sole control—in trade, finance, and environment—and promote global public goods and global governance mechanisms that are equitable and supportive of development. And because democratic decentralization can be an essential part of the enabling environment for development, the forces of democracy and decentralization must guide development assistance. This also suggests an institution-building approach shaped by the learning of local stakeholders and open to participation by the poor. Finally, development cooperation must emphasize learning and information sharing—within countries and among aid partners—as key ingredients for holistic development, empowerment, ownership, partnership, and managing for results.

Toward a New Consensus

The CDF reflects a growing consensus on the key ingredients for development effectiveness through a more comprehensive and participatory approach than during the "planning era" of the 1960s and 1970s or the "adjustment era" of the 1980s and 1990s. Like all new paradigms, however, it is embryonic and the tools for implementation are still being developed. This volume looks at the experience of aid agencies and developing countries through the lens of the CDF and distills key lessons and promising practices to guide the implementation of the CDF principles.

Focus on Macroeconomic Concerns

By the late 1960s the limitations of central planning were becoming obvious (Faber and Seers 1972). Without proper attention to macroeconomic balances, development plans in many countries ran into serious balance of payments and inflation problems, while industries that had developed behind the protective shield of high tariffs and import controls led to negative value added.

With the energy crises of the 1970s, economic distortions increased in many developing countries, forcing attention to be redirected from investment planning to macroeconomic adjustment. The changes in incentive systems unleashed by energy price boosts, inflation, exchange rate fluctuations, and rising interest rates in the global economy pushed price distortions to the fore of the development debate. By the early 1980s the limits of government and the potential of markets had been fully recognized in developed countries, and there was a new "consensus" about the central role of economic stabilization, liberalization, and privatization—the so-called "Washington consensus" (Williamson 1990).

The Washington Consensus

The debt crisis of the 1980s left many developing countries with no choice but to follow the Washington Consensus, to access the resources of the IMF and the World Bank. Highly indebted countries sought respite from their massive foreign obligations by following orthodox macroeconomic policies and dismantling protectionist structures. This brand of development became popular with the collapse of the central planning systems of Latin America and Eastern Europe. "Its appeal was helped by its self-assured tone (the consensus), its prescriptive orientation, its directional message and its origin in Washington, the capital of the victorious empire" (Naim 2000, p. 90). In fact, the Washington consensus served as a simplifier of what was, and continues to be, an overwhelmingly diverse and complex reality. Policymakers faced increasingly complex and sometimes politically impossible challenges and their resistance to adopting radical policy measures was derided as ignorance or lack of political will.

By the late 1980s neglect of the social dimensions of adjustment programs was becoming evident. It also became apparent that it was not just the social dimensions of adjustment that were in question but the economic dimensions as well. In most countries with adjustment programs, growth of income, saving, investment, and even exports were slower than expected. The power of vested interests and the increasingly evident governance dysfunction proved too strong to be tackled by the traditional policy conditions under adjustment lending. Institutions emerged as a key missing dimension of the Washington consensus.

The Washington consensus had also ignored the consequences of globalization, especially in the financial sphere (Naim 2000; Stiglitz 1998; OED 1998a). The East Asian financial crisis made clear that the adjustment era had paid too little attention to public and corporate governance, financial institutions, and social insurance mechanisms. With globalization, participatory political institutions have become critical for forging the political consensus needed to undertake policy reforms and to bridge the tensions between market forces and social needs (Rodrik 2000).

New Focus on Ownership

A World Bank report on sub-Saharan Africa acknowledged in the late 1980s the problems of adjustment lending and weak governance and called for greater attention to social, ecological, and institutional issues (Ohiohenuan 1998). It argued for a more holistic approach to development, one that goes beyond economic issues and includes political, sociological, and cultural aspects of development for sustainable growth. The report also cautioned against donor-directed development as a substitute for government-directed development and against a blueprint policy package approach as a substitute for a blueprint planning approach. It highlighted the importance of long-term perspectives and endogeneity in development programs.

Similarly, a common theme of World Bank evaluation reports of the 1990s has been the importance of ownership for success in investment and adjustment lending and in analytical and advisory services. A 1995 Country Assistance Review of Ghana noted the disappointments in almost all areas of development and proposed a more comprehensive approach (Box 1.1).

Increasingly, the Development Assistance Committee (DAC) of the Organization for Economic Co-operation and Development also called for taking a comprehensive approach to development and putting the country in the driver's seat. The preamble to the DAC's development strategy for the twenty-first century lays down the "basic principle" that "locally owned country development strategies and targets should emerge from an open and collaborative dialogue . . . in ways that respect and encourage strong local commitment, participation, capacity development and ownership" (OECD 1996, p. 14).

Taking a similar approach, the United Nations Development Assistance Framework (United Nations Secretary General 1997) envisages a framework for formulating each country assistance program with "common objectives and timeframe." Its conceptual and operational underpinnings were developed by a team of the UN Development Group, which recommended that the framework become a strategic instrument for programming the United Nation's development assistance and setting out areas for collective United Nations action, both grounded in the country context. The Development Assistance Framework would integrate global conferences and conventions with national priorities, taking a holistic approach and strengthening the links between peace and development. It would be results driven, focusing on impact and outcomes that ultimately can be measured and reported. In time, the UN expected this framework to become an instrument for coordinating all external assistance in the areas covered. It was also expected to promote consensus building and partnership. Finally, it would strengthen monitoring and evaluation for both accountability and management needs.

Box 1.1
Learning from Ghana's Economic Recovery Program—
A Precursor of the CDF

It is now more than ten years since Ghana launched its far-reaching but "gradualist" Economic Reform Program. The World Bank Group has lent more than $2 billion since 1984, more than $1 billion of it for adjustment operations. In the 1980s, against a background of highly strained relations and mutual mistrust, the Bank succeeded, by and large, in establishing excellent Bank-country relations and a true sense of partnership with a core group of Ghanaian officials. These officials were believed to be responsible for preparing and implementing the reform program and for sustaining the reforms since 1983, despite a setback in 1992.

Unlike the experience in many adjusting countries, the stabilization objectives were achieved simultaneously with increased real public expenditures, especially on social services and public investment. This win-win outcome facilitated the pursuit of adjustment with a human face.

The World Bank's country evaluation (OED 1995) suggests that fiscal problems have resurfaced since 1992 and the move toward greater democracy. There is a long agenda of unfinished adjustment. Despite the relative success of the stabilization program, the evaluation suggests that performance has been disappointing in private-sector development, public enterprise restructuring, civil service reform, expenditure control, agricultural development, educational achievement, environmental control, and institutional development. Progress in privatization is also believed to have been slow, despite some important new measures since 1994.

Current efforts in Ghana to implement the CDF represent a continuity of efforts at learning from experience in the Bank. The lessons from past experience and learning led OED (1995) to make the following recommendations in its evaluation:

- Focus strategy on sustainability, institutional development, and economic governance;
- Develop a more strategic and longer-term Bank strategy;
- Build on Bank comparative advantages;
- Reach out and listen to broader constituencies within and outside Ghana;
- Beware of downsides of aid dependency;
- Develop new aid coordination policies and practices;

- Change the skill mix of staff to better meet skill requirements of the strategy;
- Reassess the mix of staff between headquarters and country offices.

The evaluation recommends that the future strategy should be based on a shared vision of the kind of society that the government and the people wish to bring about. The evaluation draws attention to the words of a senior Ghanaian official: "When we know what we want and take the initiative, things go okay. But when the World Bank takes the initiative, things don't work so well."

Elements of the New Consensus

Building on this new way of thinking about development, World Bank President James D. Wolfensohn warned in 1999 that if the Bank and other development partners continued along the present path, the battle against poverty would not be won. He proposed a new CDF with the following distinguishing features:

- A development strategy has to incorporate not only the economic dimensions but also governance and human and social dimensions.
- The country has to be in the driver's seat in formulating and implementing its development strategy. Because a country is more than its government, a country-led strategy has to involve all the stakeholders, including the private sector and civil society. This dimension was largely absent from the government-led strategy formulation of the 1950s and 1960s.
- Donors and multilateral institutions should concentrate on their areas of comparative advantage in partnership with the country.
- Success in development assistance has to be judged by progress on the bottom line of poverty reduction and sustainable growth rather than progress on investment (as in the planning era) or on compliance with policy conditionality (as in the adjustment era).

The principles of the CDF differ from those of the planning and adjustment eras (Table 1.1). The CDF seeks to balance the three I's of development: investment, incentives, and institutions. The planning era focused on investment and neglected incentives and institutions; the adjustment era focused on incentives and neglected investment and institutions. The CDF thus adds a new emphasis on institutions—economic and social governance, rule of law, financial systems, and social capital—while also emphasizing the interdependence of investments, incentives, and institutions.

TABLE 1.1
Three Development Paradigms

Planning	Adjustment	CDF
• Pervasive market failures • Government-led development	• Pervasive government failures • Market-led development	• Joint public-private-civil society failures • Country-led development through local partnerships
• Centrally driven, detailed blueprints	• Short-term adjustments	• Long-term vision, social learning process
• Investment-led development • Resource allocation by administrative fiat	• Incentive-led development, with investments and institutions following	• Investment, incentives, and institutions considered jointly
• Dominance of planners and engineers	• Dominance of economists and financial experts	• Multidisciplinary approach
• Resource gap filled by donors	• Resource envelope determined by donors	• Country-driven aid coordination based on comparative advantages
• Donor-placed foreign experts	• Donor-imposed policies	• Donor-provided advisory assistance to empower stakeholders with options
• Marginal role for monitoring and evaluation	• Donor-driven monitoring of policy implementation	• Participatory monitoring and evaluation to enhance learning and adaptation

Long-Term View

Development is essentially about transforming society and its institutions (Stiglitz 1998, 2000). A development strategy should set forth a vision for the transformation of institutions and the nurturing of new social capital and capabilities. It should also identify the barriers and catalysts for change and set a framework for implementation. A long-term vision is the key to consistency and coherence in the development effort.

The transformation is a long process. There is no quick fix. Developing a broad-based and inclusive national consensus on development takes time, particularly in societies fraught with social divisions and inequities. Developing and transforming institutions takes even longer. Pressures to shortcut the social learning processes and to impose blueprints from above or outside must be resisted. The experience of transition economies suggests that the shock therapy approach has failed where institutions have been weak (Stiglitz 2000).

Developing countries have little control over an increasingly volatile external environment. Hence, the CDF is more like a compass than a map or blueprint. No blueprint can anticipate the dynamics, risks, and shocks along the way. Solutions are conditioned by national history and social capital. A development strategy needs to open up opportunities and facilitate experimentation, identify areas of dynamic comparative advantage, and build new competencies. In this context, projects become policy instruments and vehicles for social learning.

Holistic and Balanced

Economic development can be seen as a process of expanding human freedom, taking account of social and economic institutions, legal frameworks, governance, social capital, and culture (Sen and Wolfensohn 1999). It seeks freedom from starvation, from undernourishment, from illiteracy, from preventable disease, and from premature death. It also seeks freedom of political participation and social association. These linked freedoms are both the primary ends and the principal means of development.

Achieving development objectives thus requires more balanced attention to social as well as economic development—a balance of growth and poverty reduction concerns. Social development, an end in itself, is also essential for sustained economic development, while economic policies that ignore social dimensions, such as adjustment policies that increase unemployment and tear at the social fabric, are not sustainable. World Bank evaluations suggest that "the best hope for promoting growth and reducing poverty" comes from an "integrated approach that combines macroeconomic stabilization and structural adjustment with appropriately tailored public expenditure in social sectors, mechanisms to upgrade skills and institution capabilities, and safety-net policies offers" (Jayarajah 1996).

Poverty is multidimensional and location specific, and therefore poverty reduction efforts should be directed at several fronts (Kanbur and Squire 1999). Poverty goes beyond income and consumption to health and education, risk and vulnerability, and a sense of powerlessness. A World Bank evaluation of the health sector in India highlights the importance of addressing intersectoral linkages, seeing a need for "more focus on determinants of health status that are outside the traditional confines of the formal medical care system—transport, communications, environment, pollution, and health education are examples" (OED 1997b). Hence, holistic development should focus on empowerment through participating in programs and decisionmaking, security through reducing vulnerability and establishing safety nets, and opportunity through sustaining growth and investing in human capital.

The highly successful Sri Lanka Karunagela and Second Rural Development Project used such an integrated approach. The first attempt at multisectoral planning for an entire district in Sri Lanka, it had subcomponents in agriculture, adjustment, finance, transport, water and sanitation, power, education, health, and monitoring and evaluation. Sixteen more projects have been implemented, and another four are planned, building on the multisectoral integrated approach and existing institutions, correcting earlier failures to include beneficiaries, and focusing more on poverty alleviation.

Recent research suggests that many ingredients contribute to sustainable development and that they interact to create poverty traps or virtuous circles (Dollar 1999; World Bank 2000). Hence, there is a need to identify bottlenecks and address binding structural constraints such as governance and institutions. These tasks have often been postponed—even though governance and institutional quality are excellent predictors of growth—as donors went after easier targets (Wolfensohn 1999).

Ownership and Social Learning

Ownership as a key to success has been a regular theme in evaluations (Johnston and Wasty 1993). The success of both investment and adjustment operations has been strongly associated with borrower ownership and beneficiary participation. Hirschman (1992), Putnam (1993), Fukuyama (1995), and others have argued that the success of a market economy cannot be understood through narrow economic incentives; norms, institutions, social capital, and trust play critical roles. Social transformation requires change-oriented social institutions, whose emergence often weakens traditional relationships. The danger arises when this process of destruction occurs before new organizational and social capital are created. Social and organizational capital cannot be created overnight or handed over from outside. They must be created gradually, from within. Thus the pace of change and the pattern of reforms must match each country's ability to create such capital.

Rodrik (2000, pp. 40–41) makes a strong case for a home-grown strategy:

> The lesson of the 20th century is that successful development requires markets underpinned by solid public institutions. Today's advanced industrial countries— the United States, Western European nations, Japan—owe their success to having evolved their own specific workable models of mixed economy. While these societies are alike in the emphasis they place on private property, sound money, and

the rule of law, they are dissimilar in many other areas; their practices in the areas of labor-market relations, social insurance, corporate governance, product-market regulation, and taxation differ substantially. All these models are in constant evolution, and none is without its problems. . . .

What is true of today's advanced countries is also true of developing countries. Economic development ultimately derives from a home-grown strategy, and not from the world market. Policy makers in developing countries should avoid fads, put globalization in perspective, and focus on domestic institution building. They should have more confidence in themselves and in domestic institution building, and place less faith on the global economy and blueprints emanating therefrom.

To be sustainable, development models, policies, and institutions must be owned, not imposed. World Bank evaluation studies have repeatedly emphasized that lack of ownership has severely compromised development effectiveness (OED 1999b; Shah 1998; Girishankar 1999). Complex projects have performed poorly, mainly because they were prepared by outsiders, failed to engage stakeholders, exceeded local implementation capacity, and thus did not engender borrower commitment. Evaluation lessons indicate that borrower ownership is not a given; it must be earned. Development as transformation affects both what we do and how we do it. It argues for openness, partnership, and participation. A change in mindset is central to development, but the change cannot be forced from outside or ordered by a small elite group. Transformation must come from within.

Change is often threatening. Participatory processes ensure that concerns and anxieties are not only heard, but also addressed, thus dissipating resistance to change. Creating the capacity for participation and social learning so that countries can forge their own development strategies through active and transparent debate needs to take center stage. Operations Evaluation Department findings suggest that "ownership of Bank assistance needs to occur at several levels: Bank staff, senior government officials involved in negotiations, civil servants concerned with implementation, the intended beneficiaries and those indirectly affected by an intervention" (OED 1999b).

Decentralization is spreading throughout the world, in response to growing forces of democracy and popular movements (World Bank 1999). Devising successful decentralization is a complex process, as it involves risk. Yet this process is critical to development. Over time, decentralized systems should allow for a more wide-ranging sense of ownership of policies and programs, as lower-level bureaucrats, accountable to elected officials, move to higher posts, bringing an enthusiasm for the consensual and responsive modes of governance that tend to develop in decentralized systems. Decentralization also holds considerable promise for partnerships between local government institutions and civil society and grassroots communities.

Partnership and Development Cooperation

Spurred by global economic and political change, development cooperation is undergoing fundamental changes in rationale, strategy, and mode of
operation (Picciotto 1999; Gwin 1999). Globalization has replaced super-
power geopolitics as a driving force in development assistance. Globalization
has intensified concerns about increasing inequality and volatility, as well as
a host of transnational problems. In this changing context, industrial countries
seek competent partners in the developing world, while developing countries
look to international institutions in which they have a voice to manage the
global economy in ways that foster stability and equitable outcomes.

This is generating change in the rationale for development assistance.
Major shifts in strategy are in store, from special treatment to accelerated
integration of developing countries into the global economy and the shared
management of problems arising from rapid integration. Aid is increasingly
viewed as a source of knowledge and a catalyst for deriving sustainable and
equitable benefits from greater openness.

In a related shift in perspective, effectiveness and selectivity (in allocating
aid in response to performance) have replaced the notion of aid as entitlement
(Gwin 1999). Aid is also increasingly seen as a means of providing international public goods that benefit and require the involvement of developing
countries.

Recent studies have concluded that there is an urgent need for a country-
led partnership approach to development assistance (OED1999a). But while
there is a growing commitment to expand partnership and integrate development efforts, conflicting interests among donors and barriers to progress within
countries should not be underestimated. Mechanisms for coordination have
multiplied, and the development assistance system is fragmented and a particularly onerous burden for poor and weak countries. To avoid duplication
and overlap, evaluations suggest that the Bank team up rather than "compete"
with private foundations and development assistance agencies with a long
tradition of grant giving (OED 1998b) by forging strategic alliances and a
consensus on policy objectives and criteria for involvement (Corarrubing
1996). They recommend that the Bank play a supporting role in areas where
it does not have a comparative advantage (Girishankar 1999)—for example,
concentrating on mainstreaming programs while relying on other agencies to
pilot and demonstrate new approaches. Evaluation findings also highlight the
need for active internal and external involvement by management and a well-
staffed country office for ensuring effective coordination at the sectoral and
implementation levels (Kreimer et al. 1998; OED 1999a).

Focus on Results, Learning, and Accountability

A focus on development results is a growing priority in response to demands by citizens of donor and developing countries for transparent and accountable development assistance. The aid business has focused on inputs, financial commitments and disbursements, and supply-driven technical assistance. A recurrent theme of evaluation reports is poor monitoring of development operations and the need for better performance indicators to manage projects and strategies (Johnston 1999). One evaluation study suggests that the Bank's main failings were due to the difficulty in reaching objectives using "plans" rather than "results" for assessing the quality of management (Van Wicklin 1998).

However, concern for development results and effectiveness is growing, spurred by stagnant aid flows and rising poverty. International development goals have been set, and the need to keep score has been established. Recent changes in the political environment in many developing countries are also shaping results-based approaches to development: the drive for greater public transparency, the expanded role of legislatures, and the increasing involvement of civil society.

A focus on results and on development as a learning process implies an enhanced role for monitoring and evaluation and other mechanisms for generating and sharing knowledge at all levels of participation within the country and among development partners. An extensive evaluation literature provides ample evidence of the crucial impact of monitoring and evaluation on performance, learning, and development effectiveness.

Evaluation findings also suggest that focusing on the ultimate goals of expenditure reform right from the start is important for proper selection of expenditure instruments and for better implementation (Datta-Mitra 1997). A recent evaluation of public expenditure reviews concludes that their focus on monitoring and control of inputs rather than outputs and outcomes prevents them from adequately assessing public sector performance in the delivery of public services (Shah 1998).

Institutional Alternatives

The view of development as a holistic, long-term, social learning process calls for institutional experimentation across a rich array of institutions. A consistent theme of evaluation findings for almost twenty years has been that institutions matter and that institutional innovation is a key to progress (OED 1997a). From an extensive literature about the potentials and limits of governments, markets, and civil organizations, it is possible to construct a hierarchy of participation and market features in line with the nature of the goods produced (Picciotto 1999). The problems of poverty and development call for blending such capabilities and for partnerships among institutions at the local, national, and global levels.

Managing adjustment in an increasingly demanding global economy requires that societies develop their own institutional innovations for dealing with conflicts and reaching consensus on policy reforms (Rodrik 2000). In particular, globalization—and integration of developing countries into the global economy—calls for innovation in institutions for conflict management and social insurance. Such institutions legitimize a market economy by improving stability and social cohesion. Economic history also suggests that desirable institutional arrangements vary not only across countries, but also within countries over time. The best performers are countries that have liberalized gradually, tailoring their reform programs to institutional preconditions. Conditionality ought to leave room for development policies that diverge from the orthodoxies of the day (Rodrik 2000). Whatever shape the evolving architecture of the global economy takes, it should allow developing countries to experiment with institutional arrangements and reform strategies, based on local practices and needs.

Learning to Implement the CDF

The task before the supporters of the CDF is to learn from the experience of the planning and adjustment eras. They will need to design a process of implementation that avoids the mistakes of the past and a set of tools, skills, and processes appropriate for the emerging paradigm. It is vital that the CDF be applied as a learning process, not a rigid blueprint. The pilot program for implementing the CDF principles in twelve countries—increasingly extended to others who are preparing poverty reduction strategy papers—should focus testing and learning on areas where new tools, processes, and approaches are especially critical. The following chapters identify the challenges—and the areas in which learning is needed most

Like any new paradigm, the CDF calls for retooling, adaptation, and innovation. "Led by a new paradigm, scientists adopt new instruments and look in new places. Even more important, during [paradigm shifts] scientists see new and different things when looking with familiar instruments in places they have looked before" (Kuhn 1970). Current tools and processes have been shaped by a mechanistic, technocratic, control-oriented, and supply-driven paradigm. In adopting the new paradigm, experts may not find ready-made tools and standard solutions at hand; they will have to see through a new lens, craft new tools, and learn new ways as they proceed.

Finally, the CDF calls for a new role for development experts—one that challenges traditional norms and assumptions of technocratic expertise and professional effectiveness. It calls for new professional competencies, defined less by techniques and more by capacity building and action learning with clients.

References

Corarrubing, Alvaro. 1996. "Lending for Electric Power in Sub-Saharan Africa." Washington, D.C.: World Bank.

Datta-Mitra, Jayati. 1997. "Fiscal Management of Adjustment Lending." Washington, D.C.: World Bank.

Dollar, David. 1999. "The Comprehensive Development Framework and Recent Development Research." Washington, D.C.: World Bank, Development Economics Development Research Group.

Faber, Michael L.O., and Dudley Seers. 1972. *The Crisis in Planning*. London: Chatto and Windus, for Sussex University Press.

Fukuyama, F. 1995. *Trust: The Social Virtues and the Creation of Prosperity*. New York: Free Press.

Girishankar, N. 1999. "Civil Service Reform: A Review of World Bank Assistance." Washington, D.C.: World Bank.

Gwin, C. 1999. "The New Development Cooperation Paradigm." In *ODC Viewpoint*. Washington, D.C.: Overseas Development Council.

Hirschman, A.O. 1992. *Rival Views of Market Society*. Cambridge, MA: Harvard University Press.

Jayarajah, C. 1996. *Social Dimensions of Adjustment: World Bank Experience 1980–93*. Washington, D.C.: World Bank.

Johnson, J., and Sulaiman Wasty. 1993. *Borrower Ownership of Adjustment Programs and the Political Economy of Reform*. World Bank Discussion Paper 199. Washington, D.C.: World Bank.

Johnston, Timothy. 1999. "Health, Nutrition and Population." Washington, D.C.: World Bank.

Kanbur, Ravi, and Lyn Squire. 1999. "The Evolution of Thinking about Poverty: Exploring the Interactions." Background Paper, *World Development Report 2000/2001*. Washington, D.C.: World Bank.

Kreimer, A., J. Eriksson, R. Muscat, M. Arnold, and C. Scott. 1998. "The World Bank's Experience with Post-Conflict Reconstruction." Washington, D.C.: World Bank.

Kuhn, Thomas S. 1970. *The Structure of Scientific Revolution*. Vol. II. Chicago, IL: University of Chicago Press.

Naim, Moises. 2000. "Washington Consensus or Washington Confusion." *Foreign Policy* (Spring).

OECD (Organisation for Economic Co-operation and Development), DAC (Development Assistance Committee). 1996. *Shaping the 21st Century: The Contribution of Development Cooperation*. Paris, France.

OED (Operations Evaluation Department). 1995. "Ghana: Country Assistance Review." Report No. 14547. Washington, D.C.: World Bank.

———. 1997a. *Annual Review of Development Effectiveness*. Washington, D.C.: World Bank.

———. 1997b. "A Comparative Review of Health Sector Reform in Four States: An Operational Perspective." Washington, D.C.: World Bank.

———1997c. "World Bank Activities in the Health Sector in India." Washington, D.C.: World Bank.

———. 1998a. *Annual Review of Development Effectiveness.* Washington, D.C.: World Bank.

———. 1998b. "Process Review of World Bank Grant Programs." Washington, D.C.: World Bank.

———. 1999a. "Review of Aid Coordination and the Role of the World Bank." Washington, D.C.: World Bank.

———. 1999b. *The World Bank and Agricultural Sector in Kenya,* Washington, D.C. World Bank.

Ohiohenuan, Lily. 1998. "Synthesis of Lessons of Experience from National Long-Term Perspective Studies." United Nations Development Programme, Entebbe, Uganda.

Picciotto, R. 1999. *"Poverty Reduction and Institutional Change."* The 1999 Inaugural Wolf Lecture. Santa Monica, CA, Rand Graduate School.

Putnam, R. 1993. "Education and Social Capital." NBER Working Paper 7121. Cambridge, MA: National Bureau of Economic Research.

Rodrik, Dani. 2000. "Development Strategies for the Next Century." Paper presented at the Annual World Bank Conference on Development Economics, April 8. Washington D.C.: World Bank.

Sen, Amartya, and James D. Wolfensohn. 1999. "Development: A Coin with Two Sides." *International Herald Tribune,* May.

Shah, Anwar. 1998. "Public Expenditure Review." Washington D.C.: World Bank.

Stiglitz, Joseph E. 1998. "Towards a New Paradigm for Development: Strategies, Policies, and Processes." 1998 Prebisch Lecture, United Nations Conference on Trade and Development, October 19, Geneva, Switzerland.

———. 2000. "Whither Reform? Ten Years of the Transition." In Boris Pleskovic and Joseph E. Stiglitz, eds., *Annual World Bank Conference on Development Economics 1999.* Washington, D.C.: World Bank.

United Nations Secretary General. 1997. *Renewing the United Nations: A Programme for Reform.* Geneva, Switzerland.

Van Wicklin, W. 1998. "Recent Experience with Involuntary Resettlement: Overview." Washington, D.C.: World Bank.

Williamson, John. 1990. "What Washington Means by Policy Reform." In John Williamson, ed., *Latin American Adjustment: How Much has Happened?* Washington, D.C.: Institute for International Economics.

Wolfensohn, James. D. 1999. "A Proposal for a Comprehensive Development Framework (A Discussion Draft)." Washington, D.C.: World Bank, Office of the President.

World Bank. 1997. *World Development Report 1997: The State in a Changing World.* New York: Oxford University Press.

———. 1999. *World Development Report 1998/99: Knowledge for Development.* New York: Oxford University Press.

———. 2000. *Quality of Growth.* New York: Oxford University Press.

2

Comprehensive Approaches:
Lessons from the Past

Simon Maxwell and *Tim Conway*

The Comprehensive Development Framework (CDF)—and its implementation through Poverty Reduction Strategy Papers (PRSPs)—emphasizes a long-term, holistic, and strategic approach that is also participatory, flexible, and carefully sequenced (see Chap. 1 and Box 2.1). This chapter looks at experience with multisectoral, holistic planning in integrated rural development, river basin management, and multisectoral approaches to nutrition, national food security, and poverty reduction. This review highlights many common problems, some of which resonate with the CDF: ambitious goals, overemphasis on data collection at the expense of implementation, imposition of new administrative structures, political naivete about the scope for genuine consensus, poor quality dialogue between donors and recipients, and weak linkage between planning and implementation.

There are ways forward, however, that can inform the CDF:

- Replace blueprint planning with adaptive process planning;
- Substitute flexible, task-based approaches for role-based hierarchies;
- Start small, build in a bias to action, avoid complex new bureaucracies, and train staff in multidisciplinary work;
- Focus on setting clear, short-term goals and use targets in moderation and with an appreciation of local realities.

Box 2.1
The Approach to Planning in the CDF

"I believe that unless we think of having all the basic prerequisites, say over a 20 year timeframe, we will endanger and sometimes ruin the effectiveness of individual projects and programs which we undertake with our clients. Clearly, not all the objectives can be approached simultaneously. The framework should not become a straightjacket. We need the flexibility to adjust to the varied conditions of each country. There will be a need for setting priorities, for phasing action based on financial and human capacity and on necessary sequencing to get to our objectives. . . .

What is new is an attempt to view our efforts within a long-term, holistic, and strategic approach, where all the component parts are brought together. Such development should, in our judgement, be a participatory process, as transparent and as accountable as possible within the political climate prevailing in each country. This is not a return to central planning . . . "

Source: Wolfensohn 1999 (pp. 7–8, 30–31).

Planning is Discredited — Requiring New Approaches

We have been here before.[1] Indeed, if "here" means full-scale multicultural or comprehensive planning, we have been here before with notably unsuccessful results. As Maxwell remarked in 1997 (p. 515)[2]:

> The death of planning is widely advertised; and it is not surprising that this should be so. The pretensions of planning to objectivity and impartiality have long been questioned. Current conventional wisdom privileges the market over the state and disparages the jobs that planners do, like setting targets, allocating resources, or even designing projects. Further, the philosophical tide has turned, away from concepts familiar to planners, like order, sequence and predictability, toward other, less manageable constructs, like variability, risk and diversity.

Planning means two different things, depending on context. First, it can refer to broad objectives and directions of changes. This can cover sectoral planning, multisectoral or thematic planning (food security, poverty reduction), or national, macroeconomic planning (five-year plans or centrally planned economies).[3] A second meaning of planning is narrower, and refers to tools and mechanics of implementation.

Both types of planning are central to the work of development agencies such as the World Bank, whose role is defined primarily by its "responsibility for the structural and social aspects of development" (Wolfensohn 1999, p. 3).[4] In both broad usage (government regulation and direction of economic and social change) and narrow usage (design, implementation, and management of integrated systems of productive or social infrastructure), planning has undergone numerous crises of identity and conscience. Since the late 1970s the underlying global trend has been away from directive planning toward enabling planning (World Bank 1996a).

While planning failures occur in rich as well as poor states, failures are more likely, and their effects more serious, in the developing world, where the state typically

- has more limited information and analytical capacity, and so faces greater problems in identifying best-choice solutions to complex problems;
- displays more rigid demarcation between planning functions;
- is less subject to checks (either by regulatory state bodies or by civil society) on misguided or self-serving planning; and
- is more dependent on coercive than on institutional means of enforcing its will in the face of opposition to planning decisions.

These problems may be exacerbated by a failure of donor discipline in coordinating development aid. In many poor and aid-dependent countries, the state itself has been marginalized by the independent project planning processes of donors. Sometimes donors see this as a logical solution to the problems of working through weak or corrupt state structures. This "solution" is largely illusory, however, since improvements will be sustained in the long term only if implemented through improved government structures. When multiple donors pursue independent approaches, the result is limited or even counterproductive (Box 2.2).

World Bank President James Wolfensohn's emphasis on participation, flexibility, and sequencing suggests that the World Bank is well aware of the problems posed by the idea of planning (see Box 2.1). Lessons from the past provide pointers that governments and others can use to help make the CDF work. Below we illustrate these lessons through several examples.

Lessons of Experience with Comprehensive Planning

Many of the lessons from previous attempts at multisectoral, holistic planning can be summarized as the challenge of how to shift from a role culture to a task culture, or from a blueprint approach to a process approach. Our case studies provide suggestions for practical action to be taken by program managers and policymakers. Supplementary to Davies' (1994) concern for minimal bureaucratic soundness are eleven specific lessons on planning, implementation, and evaluation and public relations (adapted from Maxwell 1997):

Box 2.2
Need for Partnership in Planning: Donors
and the Education Sector in Cambodia

Between 1989 and 1994 the Swedish International Development Co-operation Agency (SIDA) pursued its humanitarian and development objectives in Cambodia by funding the projects of multilateral agencies and international NGOs. At one point SIDA provided support for the development of primary education by funding both UNICEF and the Asian Development Bank. These two agencies subsequently pushed for different approaches to education sector planning, resulting in a public division between donors and a retrenchment of attitudes in the Ministry of Education, Youth, and Sports. Having made grants to both organizations, SIDA was caught in the frustrating position of having "unintentionally supported different, and to a large extent conflicting, approaches to educational development in Cambodia" (Bernander et al. 1995, p. 149). In general, "too much, and sometimes conflicting, donor pressure on the Ministry has led to a reaction, by which the Government is likely to take a much more conservative stand, and be less open to reform." While the problems of the education ministry cannot be blamed entirely on poor donor planning, the lack of partner ownership of sectoral planning can be seen to have further retarded the development of the sector.

On Planning
- Articulate a clear long-term vision to structure goals and activity planning.
- Set specific short-term goals and work toward them. Focus on the task.
- Train the team to work together, with training in communication, conflict-resolution, and multidisciplinary skills.
- Build team cohesion through collaborative fieldwork and participative leadership.
- Stay close to the customer and build in participation.

On Implementation
- Build in a bias to action. Start small and grow.
- Take risks and innovate. Embrace error.
- Downgrade overt integration. Apply integrated planning but independent implementation.

On Evaluation and Public Relations
- Build in constant iteration between planning, execution, and evaluation. Be flexible.
- Monitor progress. Be publicly accountable for targets.
- Raise the profile of the topic. Raise consciousness.

Integrated Rural Development

From the late 1970s donors and governments broadened their understanding of rural problems. The solution was seen to lie in a multipronged approach to interlocking problems: although varying widely, most approaches combined interventions to raise agricultural productivity (inputs, irrigation and advice) with improvements in health care, education, and access to credit (Kleemeier, 1988).

The planning and organizational problems of integrated rural development (at least in its first incarnation) have been a common theme of the literature.[5] A good example is the review by Crener (1984), which lists seven reasons for failure, two of which clearly concern planning:

- Projects were too rigid, due to an overly idealized view of the economic, political, and institutional environment.
- Neither newly created nor existing structures fostered effective and efficient project management.

Birgegard's 1987 analysis reached a similar diagnosis (pp. 6–7). He points out that the characteristics of the integrated rural development (IRD) task require management that is:

> flexible, adaptable, willing to experiment, to learn and to accept mistakes. Managers need to have bargaining and negotiating skills to reconcile conflicting interests [and] placate influential demands at different levels . . . and have the ability to explore and to understand the dynamic informal processes between conflicting interests in the project environment. . . . Sadly, the "control-oriented," compartmentalized government bureaucracies with centralized decision making hardly match the prerequisites of effective management of [integrated rural development] projects.

Several problems surface in these analyses, and in many others on the same theme.[6] Crener (1984) offers one set of solutions, in the form of five general principles for a new-style IRD planning approach:

- Simple or medium-term interventions on an initially limited scale at the outset.
- Constant interaction among planning, execution, and evaluation.
- Dynamic analysis and more in-depth comprehension of the milieu.
- Increased participation by target groups in decision-making, implementation, and evaluation.
- Diversification and strengthening of the support given to local capacity for institutional organization.

These five principles encapsulate the new approach to rural development planning, styled "process approaches" in contrast to earlier "blueprint" models. Blueprint planning uses technical specialists to devise a scientific plan in the capital city, which is then implemented according to a rigid timetable; process planning is bottom up in nature, organic, flexible, and action oriented. Chambers has summarized the differences between blueprint and process approaches (Box 2.3).

Box 2.3
Blueprint and Process Approaches in IRD Planning

	Blueprint	**Learning Process**
Idea Originates In	Capital city	Village
First Steps	Data collection and plan	Awareness and action
Design	Static, by experts	Evolving, people involved
Supporting Organization	Existing, or built top down	Built bottom up, with lateral spread
Main Resources	Central funds and technicians	Local people and their assets
Staff Development	Classroom, didactic	Field-based action learning
Implementation	Rapid, widespread	Gradual, local, at people's pace
Management Focus	Spending budgets, completing projects on time	Sustained improvement and performance
Content of Action	Standardized	Diverse
Communication	Vertical: orders down, reports up	Lateral: mutual learning and sharing experience
Leadership	Positional, changing	Personal, sustained
Evaluation	External, intermittent	Internal, continuous
Error	Buried	Embraced
Effects	Dependency creating	Empowering
Associated With	Normal professionalism	New professionalism

Source: Chambers 1993 (p. 12), adapted from Korten (1980).

River Basin Development Planning and Management

River basin planning can be seen as a special case of IRD. River basins, as natural systems with clear physical boundaries, would seem to be logical candidates for geographically defined planning authorities with jurisdiction over interlinked issues of forest management, agriculture, fishing, river navigation, and water supply for human and industrial consumption. Since the Tennessee Valley Authority was established in the United States in 1933, "multipurpose," "integrated," or "holistic" river basin planning has been used throughout the developed and developing world for a variety of reasons. In the Philippines (Koppel 1987) and Mexico, river basin planning was introduced to promote decentralized rural development; in Africa, central governments have seen it as a way of circumventing local administrative structures that are "stagnant, corrupt, or difficult" (Adams 1992, cited in Barrow 1998, pp. 176–77).

Although there are differences of opinion on some points, the lessons of integrated or holistic river basin planning can be summarized in several points:

- Formal politics does not appear to strongly influence performance. Management structures and styles seem to explain why some schemes work and some fail, regardless of whether the national system is characterized as a democracy or one-party rule.
- Lack of baseline data and adequate monitoring leads to decisions based on false assumptions.
- Single basin authorities tend to be either ineffective relative to established line departments or too effective, ignoring national rules and regulations (as in Kenya).
- History is important: where there is a legacy of failures with river basin planning approaches, planners may be better off with another system rather than attempting to reform deeply discredited river basin planning institutions.
- Strong river basin planning institutions—especially national institutions that monitor projects and mediate between regional and national interests—can prevent some of the problems that arise from donor insistence on bilateral negotiation on projects (multiple conditionalities).
- Participatory mechanisms are essential to ensure that development does not harm the interests of local stakeholders, such as smallholder farmers or artisanal fishers (Barrow 1998).

The prescription emerging from a review of river basin planning schemes is to apply a sensitive multidisciplinary approach in order to integrate the needs of numerous local and national stakeholders; adopt a flexible, adaptive process approach to deal with inevitable unforeseen problems; consult with and encourage participation of the private sector (for funding and for identifying economic interests); and ensure community participation to hold administrators accountable to local communities. Authorities with responsibility for coordinating the work of existing regional, national, commercial, and private organizations may be more effective than stand-alone all-encompassing bodies.

Multisectoral Nutrition Planning

Large-scale multisectoral nutrition planning underwent a boom in the 1970s. In reviewing experiences with multisectoral nutrition planning, Field (1987, 23ff) identified seven "intellectual flaws" that "derailed" the approach.[7]

- Planners who were largely oblivious to problems of implementation, ignoring that it is "an inherently pluralistic, often conflictual process that is uncertain, even precarious . . . "
- Programmatic features that were "devastating to effective implementation," with ambitious goals, long chains of causality, and multiple decision points.
- Organizational overload, with a "premium placed on inter-ministerial coordination [that] was neither realistic, desirable, nor necessary."
- Naiveté about political economy and illusions about technocratic omnipotence.
- Political conservatism and disregard of broader social, economic, and political relationships.
- Neglect of wider development linkages.
- An identity crisis deriving from the absence of a sectoral home.

Field identified several lessons for multisectoral nutrition planning. These included introducing a process dimension to nutrition planning, with increased emphasis on beneficiary participation and "backward mapping"; downgrading the importance of formal planning; emphasizing the need for simplicity and for subordinating analysis to action; and focusing on the implementing role of sectoral ministries. This list is similar to the lessons of the IRD process model, except that it applies the lessons to questions of national planning rather than to project implementation.

National Food Security Planning

National food security planning has suffered from numerous organizational difficulties. The evaluation literature has identified these as, among others: communication problems between government departments; difficulties of donor coordination on food security; the quality of dialogue between governments and donors; the difficulty donors face in integrating instruments in pursuit of food security; and the institutional problems in linking relief and development in food security planning (Belshaw 1990; Maxwell 1991; Kennes 1990; Davies 1994). As with IRD, the attempt to provide a comprehensive solution for food security has run up against constraints of capacity, flexibility, and sustainability.

How, then, can the ideal of promoting food security as an "organizing principle" (Hindle 1990) be put into practice? The UN Food and Agriculture Organization has pioneered planning methods involving workshop sessions to develop and analyze multiple criteria for ranking and choosing food security interventions (Huddleston 1990). More generally, an approach to food security planning has been proposed (Maxwell 1990, p. 6) that draws on the lessons of experience and emphasizes:

- Integrated planning, but independent implementation (no super ministries).
- Importance of a bias to action over planning (start small and grow).
- Value of risk-taking and innovation (pilot projects).
- Importance of explicitly addressing the need for new modes of organization in multidisciplinary team work (task cultures, not role cultures).

These, again, are familiar themes. Davies (1994) suggests caution, however, citing Moore (1993) to the effect that many African countries may need to (re)create a public service that meets minimal Weberian requirements for competence and accountability before adopting more complex systems. Davies concludes, "Overcoming institutional constraints . . . may therefore necessitate the establishment of a minimal level of apparently old style bureaucracies before these can then be reformed to respond to the complex needs of linking relief and development" (p. 52).

Poverty Planning

A wave of work on poverty followed the publication of the *World Development Report 1990: Poverty* (World Bank 1990), including a large number of poverty assessments and poverty reduction strategies. A 1994 review of World Bank work in sub-Saharan Africa identified two areas of weakness that are relevant to planning issues (IDS/IUED 1994).

The first was a lack of interdisciplinary analysis of poverty, particularly of political and social analysis. The poverty assessments reviewed had concentrated on collecting economic (consumption) data and had neglected analysis of underlying social processes. Toye and Jackson (1996, pp. 58–59) concluded that "the analysis of the process of poverty . . . has been the major weak point of the Bank's poverty assessment efforts to date . . . it is a critical area of weakness, given the boldness and ambition of the new poverty agenda."

The second weakness was a lack of linkage between poverty assessments and other instruments of planning and policy. Poverty reduction strategies were designed to influence policy across the board, but then often seemed to have little influence. Toye and Jackson noted that "there seems to be little connection between the processes of preparing the new Poverty Assessments and other tasks of country documentation, including the preparation of Public Expenditure Reviews . . . without any particular sensitivity to the logical links between the attempt to achieve a new antipoverty emphasis in country policies and the implications of this for changes in their public expenditure management" (p. 60).

Implicit in these criticisms is a model of preparing poverty assessments that entrusts the task to a small group that may not consult as widely as it should and whose report is thrown into a competitive arena with other sectoral or thematic special interests.

A World Bank task force report was remarkably frank about the difficulties of integrating poverty assessments into country assistance strategies and lending programs, and concluded that although poverty assessments "have done a reasonably good job of identifying the policy and strategy options that will assist the poor to become more active participants in the growth process, these options, typically, are not being reflected in the Bank's assistance strategies or operations" (World Bank 1996b, p. 102).

Among the reasons cited for the shortcomings are inadequate information; complacent attitudes by governments; a willingness by Bank management to compromise on poverty in the interest of good country relations; and—important for our purposes—a tendency to base operational decisions more on sectoral interests and less on the understanding that poverty reduction requires "a multisectoral, integrated approach" (World Bank 1996b, p. 110).

The solutions offered by the task force (World Bank 1996b, pp. 111–12; emphasis added) are to strengthen links among the poverty assessment, the country assistance strategy, and the lending program, and to achieve this by:

- Establishing poverty reduction as the pervasive organizing principle, "through the *leadership* of managers and the actions of staff."
- Establishing a strengthened *process* for preparing country assistance strategies, working with country teams, governments, donors, and other stakeholders.
- Introducing *procedures* requiring country business plans to detail how the poverty reduction strategy will feed into the Bank's work program.
- Providing new *training* and *incentives* for staff.
- *Monitoring* how well a new poverty strategy is being implemented.

Industrial Organization

A final example of comprehensive planning comes from "post-Fordist" industrial organization, characterized by a move from repetitive production line routines to more flexible and responsive team work. Many of the precepts of new approaches to development planning—process planning, participation, a bias to action, and decentralization—are familiar to students of what Murray (1992) calls the "new managerialism."[8] It is interesting, for example, to compare Chambers' description of process planning (see Box 2.3) with a description of contrasting corporate cultures (Box 2.4); the two are entirely complementary.

Many of these precepts emerge from a long-standing literature on organizational culture and structure. Handy (1985, Chap. 7), for example, classified organizational cultures as *power, role, task,* or *person* cultures.[9] In development administration there is often a need to change traditional "role cultures" (characterized by hierarchical relationships and the prevalence of rules) into more innovative "task cultures" (in which teams come together with minimal hierarchy to engage in particular tasks). A task culture is particularly suitable for collaborative development assistance of the kind envisioned by the CDF.

The teamwork found in task cultures has generated much literature of its own. Bradford and Cohen (1997) identify the ideal working environment as one in which team members share a commitment to an overarching goal; pursue open, expressive, and supportive relationships; share decisions, where possible, by consensus; and look for supportive rather than authoritarian leadership. This description echoes the partnership theme of the CDF.

The great challenge for corporate and other organizations is how to move from one culture to another and how to thrive in rapidly changing environments (hence the popularity of books such as Peters' 1987 *Thriving on Chaos*). Change is not easy, however; it often takes a crisis to drive change forward. Managers are advised to build "change coalitions" and to offer "quick wins" to reinforce desire for change (Plant 1995; Kotter 1996). It is interesting to speculate what the "quick wins" might be in the case of the CDF.

The Role of Targets

Targets are now a prominent feature of development discourse.[10] Many targets adopted at UN conferences provide the basis for planning in governments and donor agencies. For example, selection of targets drawn together by the Development Assistance Committee of the Organisation for Economic Co-operation and Development as international development goals (DAC 1996) have in turn influenced national policy statements. There are also increasing pressures to have the countries' PRSPs shaped and driven by these International Development targets.

Are targets a good idea? The United Nations Development Programme (UNDP) argues in favor, citing the World Summit for Children of 1990, which "helped raise general awareness. . . . Low cost and cost-effective actions [made] it possible to achieve the goals by restructuring budgets rather than by making big increases in spending. Monitoring was also vital. . . . Up-to-date information [is] widely used to assess progress and mobilize and maintain support" (UNDP 1997, p. 111).

A contrary view sees international targets as oversimplifying and overgeneralizing complex problems.[11] "They distort public expenditure priorities, both because they misrepresent the problem and because they privi-

---

Box 2.4
Contrasting Approaches to Corporate Organization and Planning

Mechanistic	Organic
Closed Systems	**Open System**
• Adapting	• Adaptive
• Internally oriented	• Interplay of internal and external
• Passive consumers	• User-centered
• Arms-length suppliers	• Close, long-term supplier relations
• Competitive	• Collaborative networks
Planning	**Strategy**
• Pre-planning	• Feedback from action
• Concentrated at center	• Participatory process
• Detailed targets	• Adjustable range of targets
• Imposed by center	within constraints consensus
Organization	**Network**
• Multilayered pyramid	• Flat hierarchies
• Vertical flow of information	• Horizontal connectedness through
and command	project teams, task forces, matrix
• Unitary segmented organization	methods, decomposed system
• Departmental specialization	functional redundancy or duplication
• Role culture	• Task culture
• Organograms and job descriptions	• Clusters and project goals
• Centralization of operating	• Workplace autonomy
• Responsibility and rules and manuals	• Management role: boundary manage-
• Management role: planning, command,	ment system adjustment, enabling,
coordination, control, organization	supporting, educating, monitoring
as instrument	• Organization as learning
Labor	**Staff**
• Labor as cost	• Labor as asset
• Incentives through pay	• Incentives through quality of work
• Strict hierarchies	• Less inequality
• Rate for the job	• Incremental pay
• Taylorized: fragmented, deskilled	• Lower turnover
division of labor between mental	• Multiskilling—requisite variety
and manual	and group working

Source: Murray 1992 p. 81.

lege some sectors at the expense of others. Monitoring progress is extremely expensive and detracts from action on the ground. And the political benefits, though appreciable at first, may rapidly be lost if targets are not achieved" (Maxwell 1996c, 1998, p. 79). Poverty provides a good illustration, because it is a multidimensional concept with a large subjective element. An income or consumption measure of poverty may fail to capture important aspects of poverty, including deficiencies of access to health, education, and other services; social exclusion; powerlessness; lack of autonomy; and loss of self-esteem.[12]

In planning to meet targets, multidimensionality does not matter if alternative indicators are closely correlated so that any one can stand as a proxy for the others. Thus, low income might not capture the full reality of poverty, but it might serve adequately to identify the poor and to measure the extent of their deprivation. Unfortunately, it is hard to defend the assumption that this is the case. In some cases of multiple deprivation all the indicators agree; in other circumstances they clearly do not. This matters because one objection to target-based planning is that targets distort policy and ignore context.

Do Targets Distort Policy?

There is always a risk that a single-minded pursuit of targets will result in the distortion of policy at various levels. Some sectors are privileged above others. Those that have been the subject of an international conference are likely to benefit from target-driven increases in resources. Those that are less fortunate are likely to become the orphans of public expenditure reviews. The DAC targets are a case in point. They have become hegemonic in international discourse, even though they are deliberately selective. It is not clear why the nutrition goals of the World Summit for Children or the International Conference on Nutrition were not incorporated, for example (WFS 1996, p. 1; UNICEF 1990; FAO and WHO 1992). Leaving these out would not matter if everything were strongly correlated to everything else—but this is rarely the case.

What is the Opportunity Cost of Monitoring Progress?

In a liberalized economy, public expenditure is the main instrument of economic policy, and the public expenditure process is the main arena for arbitration between competing policy priorities. Monitoring progress toward targets is itself a public expenditure and therefore has an opportunity cost; how high a cost depends on the complexity of the targets. Simple-sounding targets may be difficult to measure. In halving dollar-a-day poverty, for example, what assumptions are to be made about purchasing power, variability in prices, the valuation of subsistence production, seasonal or other variations in income, or intrahousehold distribution? These are not trivial problems.[13]

These difficulties are multiplied if the targets are broadened to include nonmonetary aspects.[14] Some people have argued that participatory methods can cut through the complexity, give a higher priority to people's own perceptions, and cut costs. Participatory methods are certainly ethically attractive and greatly enrich analysis, but their very diversity makes it difficult to aggregate their findings and, thus, difficult to use them to monitor international targets.[15]

Leaving aside the feasibility or desirability of deriving generalizable explanations,[16] we are still left with a problem. If targets work, they do so because progress toward them can be monitored. But monitoring is expensive, and the more subtle the targets, the more expensive monitoring is likely to be. This cost must be measured in the time of scarce professionals as well as in money. Measurement may become the dominant activity of policymakers: the DAC targets and the follow-up to the World Food Summit increased the workload for statisticians and advisers in the development ministries of OECD countries. The investment in information may not be matched by investment in action, with a "missing link" between analysis and response (Buchanan-Smith and Davies 1995).

Can Unrealistic Targets Destroy Political Momentum?

A final question concerns the political value of targets. The justification for targets is that they can mobilize and sustain political support for actions to help the poor. This they clearly do. The use of the DAC targets has been impressive, for example, in the UK White Paper on development and in the political discourse that surrounds it.

Management texts remind us that teams thrive on goals that are SMART (stretching, measurable, agreed, recorded, and time-limited; Leigh and Maynard 1995, p. 220). In private and public sector organizations, targets are in common use to motivate employees and monitor progress (Leigh and Maynard 1995, p. 52). The DAC targets appear to succeed as SMART goals—with a qualification regarding the degree to which they are agreed. The wording of the core DAC target for poverty reduction is stronger than the wording of the international conference (the 1995 Copenhagen Social Summit) from which it was derived, which merely stated that countries would define and work toward poverty targets. In this sense the more specific DAC target for poverty reduction is not "agreed" to by the governments of the developing world, who will have to carry the main burden of implementation.

Targets may also fail because they appear to be unrealistic and set too far in the future. Goals should be stretching, so it is acceptable that they may initially appear unrealistic. If targets appear to be hopelessly ambitious, however, planners will fail to mobilize the support required to transform aspirations into outcomes. Shorter horizons are more effective: the private sector, for example, generally aims to reduce two- or three-year deadlines to practical, incremental steps in order to generate commitment and action (Leigh and Maynard 1995, pp. 62 and 64).

It is thus hard not to be a little cynical about the current enthusiasm for ambitious development targets. Many past targets have been disturbingly aspirational and have not been met. The DAC targets run the same risk. A twenty-year time horizon is part of the problem. Most of the civil servants who devised these targets, and most of the politicians who use them, will not still be active in 2015.

Lessons for Target-Based Planning

A target-based approach to development planning is like the curate's egg: excellent in parts. The translation of SMART targets from management theory to international development has many political attractions, galvanizing opinion and concentrating minds. But not all targets are SMART, and a certain cynicism is understandable when the same targets reappear at regular intervals. Targets are reductionist, may distort spending plans, can be expensive to monitor, and entail political risks if not met. Those whose job it is to devise targets should think hard about appropriate time horizons (five years maximum?) and ambitions (stretching, but not to the breaking point).

The development community should also acknowledge that targets (particularly international targets) have only a tenuous connection to national planning. In assisting national processes, donors should be guided by an epistemology that recognizes the diversity and complexity of real-world situations and that builds on the knowledge, insights, and ideas of local partners.

The very number of national action plans engendered by international conferences now poses real problems for planners in developing countries (despite the considerable overlap between plans for different purposes). National action plans, in keeping with SMART principles, exhibit a top-down approach. There is a need to temper this approach with a more open, participatory process planning approach, in which poverty features prominently, but with no requirement that any given international target will feature at all.

Conclusions: Lessons for the Comprehensive Development Framework

Failures of multisectoral planning occur in the large and professionally trained bureaucracies of the advanced economies, where planners are subject to the scrutiny of organized civil society (community or environmental groups, business associations, and a free press).[17] It should not then be surprising that planning failures are common in the developing world, where states are often underendowed with material and human capital and lack good social and economic information on which to base planning decisions, and where civil society may lack the security or institutions to challenge state planning prescriptions.

There are thus strong arguments for new approaches to planning, approaches in which disciplinary perspectives, actors, and sectors behave in a more integrated (or holistic) manner and in which targets are used to monitor and drive performance. Yet these approaches are not without problems. The lessons from earlier attempts at holistic planning tell us that:

- Planning needs to move from a blueprint to an adaptive process approach, one that acknowledges that reality is complex and information imperfect and that planning will have to be flexible enough to account for changing circumstances.
- Complex, ambitious efforts at multisector or multiagency planning have tended to fail. In holistic approaches to planning it is better to start small, achieve initial successes that establish credibility and enthusiasm, and then expand in stages. The actors involved need to develop clear, short- to medium-term goals; allocate tasks to meet these goals; and build on these successes to address more complex problems (Maxwell 1997, p. 524).
- Tempting though it may be, it is best to avoid delegating responsibility for integrated planning problems to separate super institutions created specifically for the task. Experience suggests that these are either ineffectual in the short term (unable to assert themselves in relationships with established line structures and local government) or unproductive and unsustainable in the long term (failing to influence the practices of parallel mainstream structures and sustained only by donor funds). This is especially likely when, as in the case of IRD or river basin development, integrated planning bodies take the form of regional structures that attempt to claim (but in fact often merely duplicate) the responsibilities of regional departments of national ministries. New bodies should instead be given responsibility for coordinating the relevant elements of existing organizations.
- Even with these more limited goals, it is necessary to rein in ambition. Integrated implementation is often too complex and cumbersome for existing structures. It is better to agree on a comprehensive analysis of the problem and, on this basis, on a division of tasks among the various organizations involved. These contributions to the overall goal, agreed among partners, should be semi-independent (although sequencing will require some tasks to be implemented before others can begin). Integrated planning institutions should see their primary role as encouraging cross-ministerial analysis and obtaining agreement on the division of labor to tackle intersectoral problems. This is encapsulated in the advice to planners to pursue "integrated planning but not integrated implementation" (Maxwell 1997, p. 522).
- There can be problems with this approach too: it predisposes those involved toward perceiving intersectoral planning as a series of clearly defined steps (analysis, division of tasks, implementation by existing authorities according to this agreed plan), when it should more properly be seen as a continuous and

recursive process. It is necessary to institutionalize the process of coordinated planning, with successive rounds of analysis, allocation of tasks, implementation, and evaluation driven by the coordinating body. This approach requires both regular interministerial meetings and improvements in routine communication between different government institutions. Independent "policing" bodies—perhaps a committee reporting directly to the prime minister's office, as in river basin planning in the Philippines, or a capable local grassroots organization—can be used to oversee progress in both interministerial and central-local coordination.

- In pursuing integration in planning, it is necessary to invest effort in changing the work culture of the organizations involved. Most governments or development assistance agencies can be categorized as role cultures, based on clearly demarcated duties reflecting technical or statutory specializations. Interorganizational partnerships formed to address intersectoral problems require a move away from a rigid role culture in the direction of a team-based, objectives-oriented task culture.

There is some overlap between these prescriptions and those that emerge from a review of the precepts of target-based planning. Targets can serve as the locus for national ownership of policy and donor coordination. But as top-down influences on the planning and policy process, targets can also distort decision-making. The most influential targets tend to be determined at the international level. There is a danger that as national governments and the country managers of bilateral and multilateral agencies try to incorporate these targets in their planning processes, agreement on goals (essential for coordination and integrated planning) will slip into blueprint planning. It is necessary to remember that:

- The use of global targets based on measurable indicators can obscure national and local variations around a global problem. Targets will be most useful if they are derived or operationalized in a consultative or participatory manner: ownership of the analysis both improves the quality of that analysis and strengthens commitment to the targets that emerge from it.
- Actions chosen because they are most likely to result in desirable changes are not always exactly the same as the actions most likely to result in *measurable* changes. There is a danger that a one-size-fits-all application of targets can bias planning decisions away from actions likely to result in desirable change to actions likely to result in measurable change. Emphasis on targets may then divert limited resources into measurement rather than action.
- Donors using targets to guide the work they execute in partnership with governments need to walk a careful path. They need to use targets to drive action, but must simultaneously remain open to the possibility that targets may be inappropriate or immeasurable—or may come to be so in the future. Targets should be pitched to encourage all partners to strive harder for essential improvements, but not pitched at an unattainable level, which will discourage efforts. Targets need to be based on a realistic appraisal of the likelihood that they might be achieved.

It is possible from both the literature and experience to synthesize some "dos and don'ts" for the CDF and its counterpart—the PRSPs. These are summarized in Box 2.5.

Box 2.5 Do's and Don'ts for the Comprehensive Development Framework	
Do	**Don't**
• Encourage a broad-based debate in the country. • Expect the government to develop a strategic development vision. • Talk to the government about areas of agreement and disagreement. • Set SMART targets. • Reinforce government leadership (for example, through the Ministry of Finance). • Invest in training and capacity building. • Find ways to disburse quickly. • Revise plans frequently. • Build two-way accountability.	• Be naïve about the expression of a single national consensus. A statement of consensus is a necessary condition for the initiation of donor cooperation, but this consensus will always be contested and subject to change in the future. • Expect to agree with every word. • Impose rigid conditionalities. • Simply replicate international targets, without local adaptation. • Develop piecemeal plans with sectoral ministries. • Make unrealistic demands for data, accounts, and the like. • Insist on the perfect plan before starting to implement. • Insist on a rigid logical framework. • Set performance standards for recipients, without also setting performance standards for donors

Notes

1. This section draws on Maxwell (1997).
2. See also Scott (1998) and, for an extreme position, Escobar (1992).
3. The slightly old-fashioned use of the word *planning* in a national macroeconomic context—where today it is more likely that *policy* or *management* would be used

instead—can be seen in the entry under "Planning" in *The New Palgrave Dictionary of Economics* (Vohra 1987, pp. 885–891), or in the chapter headings that fall under–"Planning and Resource Management" in Volume II of the *Handbook of Development Economics* (Chenery and Srinivasan 1989). Multisectoral planning refers to thematic objectives and plans that cut across traditional sectors and established ministries.

4. Wolfensohn (1999) uses this definition of the Bank's work to distinguish it from the International Monetary Fund, whose primary role is macroeconomic stabilization and surveillance.
5. See, for example, Korten (1980); Korten and Klauss (1984); Gwyer and Morris (1984); Rondinelli (1983); and Chambers (1993).
6. See bibliography in Birgegard (1987), especially footnote 2.
7. Despite disagreement on details, others concur with the main points of this diagnosis, especially for the large-scale multisectoral systems analysis projects of the 1970s (Berg et al. 1990; Levinson 1995).
8. See also Peters (1987).
9. See also Moris (1989), reproduced in Maxwell (1997, pp. 517–18).
10. This section draws on elements of Maxwell (1998).
11. Reductionism is, of course, a general problem in development research; see Chambers (1997, p. 42).
12. See, for example, UNDP (1997, pp. 15–16); Baulch (1996a); Chambers (1983); and Shaffer (1996).
13. See Hanmer, Pyatt, and White (1997, Section 8.3) for a review of "problematic" money-metric poverty assessments in sub-Saharan Africa.
14. See, for example, Oppenheim and Harker (1996) and CESIS (1997), cited in Maxwell (1998).
15. Compare Chambers (1997) and Baulch (1996b, pp. 39–40).
16. Baulch (1996b) accepts that participatory methods yield diverse pictures of poverty and dismisses them because no replicable answers emerge. The proponents of poverty reduction assessments argue that this is a core strength, that there *are* no simple answers, and that policy needs to avoid reductionism and adapt to the complex reality on the ground (Chambers 1997), an approach I have dubbed "post-modern" (Maxwell 1996b).
17. In the United Kingdom, for example, there has in recent years been more attention to the lack of "joined-up thinking" about issues of poverty and social exclusion (see Oppenheim 1998).

References

Adedeji, Adebayo, Devaki Jain, and Mary McCowan. 1998. "External Inputs for the Development of the United Nations Development Assistance Framework (UNDAF): Report of the High-level Team of Experts." September 30.

Asamoa-Baah, Anarfi, and Paul Smithson. 1999. "Donors and the Ministry of Health: New Partnerships in Ghana." WHO Discussion Paper 8. Geneva, Switzerland: World Health Organization.

Barrow, Christopher J. 1998. "River Basin Planning and Management: A Critical Review." *World Development* 26 (1): pp. 171–86.

Baulch, Bob. 1996a. "Poverty, Policy and Aid." Editor's introduction to special issue of *IDS Bulletin* 27 (1).

— — —. 1996b. "Neglected Trade-offs in Poverty Measurement." Special issue of *IDS Bulletin* 27 (1).

Belshaw, D. 1990. "Food Strategy Formulation and Development Planning in Ethiopia." *IDS Bulletin* 21.

Berg, Elliot Associates. 1990. *Adjustment Postponed: Economic Policy Reform in Senegal in the 1980s*. Bethesda, MD: Development Alternatives Inc.

Birgegard, L-E. 1987. "A Review of Experiences with Integrated Rural Development." Issue Paper 3. Swedish University of Agricultural Sciences, International Rural Development Centre, Uppsala, Sweden.

Bradford, D.L., and A.R. Cohen. 1997. *Managing for Excellence: The Leadership Guide to Developing High Performance in Contemporary Organisations*. New York: Wiley.

Buchanan-Smith, M., and S. Davies. 1995. *Famine Early Warning and Response — The Missing Link*. London, U.K.: IT Publications.

Chambers, Robert. 1983. *Rural Development: Putting the Last First*. Harlow, U.K.: Longman Scientific and Technical.

— — —. 1993. *Challenging the Professions: Frontiers for Rural Development*. London, U.K.: IT Publications.

— — —. 1997. *Whose Reality Counts? Putting the Last First*. London, U.K.: IT Publications.

Chenery, Hollis, and T.N. Srinivasan, eds. 1989. *Handbook of Development Economics* Vol. II. Amsterdam: North Holland.

Crener, M.A. 1984. *Integrated Rural Development: State of the Art Review*. Ottawa, Canada: CIDA.

DAC (Development Assistance Committee) 1996. *Shaping the 21st Century: The Contribution of Development Co-operation*. Paris, France: Organisation for Economic Co-operation and Development.

Davies, S. 1994. "Public Institutions, People, and Famine Mitigation." *IDS Bulletin* 25: pp. 46–54.

Escobar, Arturo. 1992. "Planning." In Wolfgang Sachs, ed. *The Development Dictionary: A Guide to Knowledge as Power*. London, U.K.: Zed Books.

FAO (Food and Agriculture Organization) and WHO (World Health Organization). 1992. International Conference on Nutrition, "World Declaration and Plan of Action for Nutrition," Rome, Italy.

Field, J.O. 1987. "Multi-Sectoral Nutrition Planning: A Post-Mortem." *Food Policy 12:* 15–29, in Food and Nutrition Bulletin, Cambridge, MA.

Gwyer, D.G., and J.C.H. Morriss. 1984. "Some Findings from Key ODA Evaluations in Selected Sectors: Natural Resources." In B.E. Cracknell, ed., *The Evaluation of Aid Projects and Programmes*. London, U.K.: ODA.

Handy, C.B. 1985. *Understanding Organisations* (3rd ed.). Harmondsworth: Penguin.

Hanmer, Lucia, G. Pyatt, and H. White. 1997. *Poverty in Sub-Saharan Africa*. The Hague: Institute of Social Studies.

Hindle, R. 1990. "The World Bank Approach to Food Security Analysis." *IDS Bulletin* 21: pp. 62–66.

Huddlestone, B. 1990. "FAO's Overall Approach and Methodology for Formulating National Food Security Programmes in Developing Countries." *IDS Bulletin* 21: pp. 72–80.

IDS (Institute of Development Studies) and IUED. 1994. "Poverty Assessments and Public Expenditure: A Study for the SPA Working Group on Poverty and Social Policy." Sussex: IDS.

Kennes, W. 1990. "The European Community and Food Security." *IDS Bulletin* 26: pp. 67–71.

Kleemeier, L. 1988. "Integrated Rural Development in Tanzania." *Public Administration and Development* 8: pp. 67–73.

Koppel, B. 1987. "Does Integrated Area Development Work? Insights from the Bicol River Basin Development Program." *World Development* 15 (2): pp. 205–20.

Korten, D. 1980. "Community Organisation and Rural Development: A Learning Process Approach." *Public Administration Review*. Malden, MA: Blackwell.

Korten, D., and R. Klauss, eds. 1984. *People-Centered Development*. West Hartford, CT: Kumarion Press.

Kotter, John P. 1996. *Leading Change*. Boston, MA: Harvard Business School Press.

Leigh, A., and M. Maynard. 1995. *Leading Your Team: How to Involve and Inspire Teams*. London, U.K.: Nicholas Brealey.

Levinson, F. James. 1995. "Multi-Sectoral Nutrition Planning: A Synthesis of Experience." In P. Pinstrup-Anderson et al., eds. 1995. *Child Growth and Nutrition in Developing Countries: Priorities for Action*. Ithaca, NY: Cornell University Press.

Maxwell, Simon. 1990. "Food Security in Developing Countries." *IDS Bulletin* 21.

— — —. 1991. "National Food Security Planing: First Thoughts from Sudan." In *To Cure All Hunger: Food Policy and Food Security in Sudan*. London, U.K.: IT Publications.

— — —. 1996a. "The Use of Matrix Scoring to Identify Systemic Issues in Country Programme Evaluation." *Development in Practice* 7 (4): pp. 408–15.

— — —. 1996b. "Food Security: A Post-modern Approach." *Food Policy* 21 (2): pp. 155–70.

— — —. 1996c. "A Food Charter for the Millennium." *Appropriate Technology* 23 (2).

— — —. 1997. "Implementing the World Food Summit Plan of Action: Organisational Issues in Multi-sectoral Planning." *Food Policy* 22 (6): pp. 515–31.

— — —. 1998. "International Targets for Poverty Reduction and Food Security: A Mildly Skeptical but Resolutely Pragmatic View with a Call for Greater Subsidiarity." *Canadian Journal of Development Studies* 19: pp. 77–96.

Moore, M. 1993. "Competition and Pluralism in Public Bureaucracies." *IDS Bulletin* 23.

Moris, J. 1989. "What Organisation Theory Has to Offer Third World Agricultural Managers." Mimeo.

Murray, R. 1992. "Towards a Flexible State." *IDS Bulletin* 23: pp. 78–89.

Oppenheim, Carey. 1998. "Changing the Storyline." *Manchester Guardian,* April 1: pp. 6–7.

Oppenheim, C., and L. Harker. 1996. *Poverty: The Facts*. London, U.K.: Child Poverty Action Group.

Peters, T.J. 1987. *Thriving on Chaos*. London, U.K.: Pan Books.

Plant, Roger. 1995. *Managing Change and Making It Stick*. New York: Harper Collins.

Rondinelli, D. 1983. *Development Projects as Policy Experiments*. London, U.K.: Methuen.

Schaffer, P. 1996 "Beneath the Poverty Debate: Some Issues." Special issue of *IDS Bulletin* 27 (1).

Scott, James C. 1998. *Seeing Like a State: How Certain Schemes to Improve the Human Condition Have Failed*. New Haven, CT: Yale University Press.

Toye, J., and C. Jackson. 1996. "Public Expenditure Policy and Poverty Reduction: Has the World Bank Got It Right?" *IDS Bulletin* 27 (1).

UNDP (United Nations Development Programme). 1997. *Human Development Report 1997*. New York: Oxford University Press.

UNICEF (United Nations Children's Fund). 1990. *The State of the World's Children*. New York: OUP / UNICEF.

Vohra, Rajiv. 1987. "Planning." In John Eatwell, Murray Milgate, and Peter Newman, eds., *The New Palgrave: A Dictionary of Economics*. London, U.K.: Macmillan.

WFS (World Food Summit). 1996. *Rome Declaration on World Food Security and World Food Summit Plan of Action*. Rome, Italy: World Food Summit, November.

Wolfensohn, James D. 1999. "A Proposal for a Comprehensive Development Framework (a discussion draft)." Memo to the Board, Management, and Staff of the World Bank Group, January 21, Washington, D.C.

World Bank. 1990. *World Development Report 1990: Poverty*. New York: Oxford University Press.

———. 1996a. *World Development Report 1996: From Plan to Market*. New York: Oxford University Press.

———. 1996b. Taking Action to Reduce Poverty in Sub-Saharan Africa: An Overview. Washington, D.C.

Part 2

Local Ownership

3

Conditionality and Policy Learning

William Branson and *Nagy Hanna*

What is the role of policy conditionality within the context of the Comprehensive Development Framework (CDF)? Traditionally, conditionality has been perceived as a blueprint package of policy conditions attached to tranche releases of single loans. We propose a broader view of conditionality as a policy learning process, based on mutual commitment to the achievement of sustainable development policy objectives. In such a context, the World Bank and its development assistance partners would act as enabling agencies in support of country-owned reforms, leaving significant room for the country to determine the means and timing of policy changes according to political economy considerations and local policy learning.

Several factors present the opportunity to rethink conditionality as an instrument of policy reform: the declining relevance of geopolitical considerations in development assistance, international efforts to reduce indebtedness among poor developing countries, improvements of macroeconomic policies in many countries, and recent research findings on aid effectiveness (Collier et al. 1997). There is growing consensus that the relationship between donors and aid recipients must move toward partnership, that country ownership is essential to sustainable policy improvement, and that traditional conditionality has often been misused and overused.

Within such a collaborative framework, conditionality is best understood as a credible indicator of commitment by the Bank and its partners to support a mutually agreed reform process. This conception of conditionality contrasts with the use of coercive conditions to force externally designed policy changes on unwilling governments. It represents a transparent and explicit understanding of sustained external support for programs formulated by the country with wide participation by the private sector and civil society—in cooperation with external partners. The reform programs would be owned by the country and conditionality would define the parameters of external support.

This chapter first examines conditionality as a mutual commitment and learning process. It proposes different forms of conditionality tailored to countries at different levels of ownership and phases of a long-term reform process: ex-post tranching for established reformers with a track record, floating tranches for credible reformers aiming to establish a track record, regular tranching, and an experimental single up-front tranche or continued Bank engagement through advisory and technical assistance for new or less credible reformers. Next, the authors explore the links between conditionality, ownership, and participation, and propose ways to asses ownership and tailor conditionality to increased ownership and participation. The core of this chapter is the empirical evidence of successful adjustment lending: higher impact adjustment lending, reevaluation of the Dollar and Svenson (1998) data on the political economy of reform, and ten country case studies of aid and reform in Africa. The chapter concludes with the recent proposals to streamline conditionality at the International Monetary Fund (IMF), which move towards the new modalities proposed here.

This chapter does not address issues related to the policy content of conditionality or the overall nature and validity of the specific economic reform. Other chapters (4, 5, 6, and 7) suggest ways to enhance the validity, appropriateness, and sustainability of such reforms, particularly institutional reforms. Chapter 7 argues against the dominance of prepackaged blueprints and universal best practices for policy and institutional reforms. Conditionality must leave room for local knowledge, local experimentation, and institutional diversity. However, moving beyond blueprints has profound implications for the World Bank, the IMF, and other development assistance agencies (Chaps. 6, 7, and 13).

Conditionality as a Mutual Commitment Mechanism

Conditionality is widely viewed as an attempt to generate policy change in return for grants or loans, as expressed in Killick, Gunatilaka, and Marr (1998, pp. 10–11):

> In its relevant sense, a condition, according to the Oxford English Dictionary, is something demanded or required as a prerequisite to the granting or performing of something else: a stipulation. . . . " A condition attached to a loan or grant sets out a requirement for action of some sort by the recipient government without which assistance will not be granted or continued. . . . What is implied here is a distinction between "pro forma" and "hard core" conditionality. . . . Hard core conditionality . . . consists of actions, or promises of actions, made only at the insistence of the lender.

Killick, Gunatilaka, and Marr define "hard core" conditionality as coercion. They contrast such conditionality and borrower ownership by asking the question: "If the country owns the program, why is conditionality needed?" The answer advanced in this chapter is that conditionality, appropriately developed and adapted, can nurture domestic ownership of reform over time. It supplements rather than supplants country-based efforts. The rationale for this new concept of conditionality is outlined by Stiglitz (1998, p. 11):

> This much seems clear: effective change cannot be imposed from outside. Rather than encouraging recipients to develop their analytical capacities, the process of imposing conditionalities undermines both the incentives to acquire those capacities and recipients' confidence in their ability to use them.

From this perspective, effective conditionality can be used as an instrument of mutual accountability. Rather than imposing a position on borrowers, the Bank and its partners commit themselves to lend under certain jointly determined conditions. External assistance agencies commit themselves to provide external advisory and financial support through conditionality, while the borrowing government commits itself through ownership of programs it has designed in consultation with its partners. In this sense, conditionality is a compact for poverty reduction and policy reform.

Four Forms of Conditionality

New-style conditionality goes well beyond the rigid concepts that have lost credibility among borrowers and lenders alike. It can be ex post, with continued lending based on continued and anticipated progress toward broadly shared development objectives rather than tied to increasingly detailed and specific reform conditions. Reform-minded governments can proceed with reform with explicit assurances of continued external support. External lenders can support ongoing reform based on actions already taken, with appropriate safeguards against potential policy reversal. This form of ex-post conditionality is consistent with the collective action principles of reciprocity that underlie trust in repeated games associated with reputation development under neo-institutional models of cooperation.

In another form of conditionality the borrowing government receives an initial tranche, based on meeting clear selectivity criteria, and the lender commits to further tranches as reforms continue. Timing is determined at the discretion of the recipient government. Countries borrowing under this form of floating tranche, developed under the Higher Impact Adjustment Lending (HIAL) initiative in sub-Saharan Africa, have performed relatively well (OED 1999).

A third form of adaptable conditionality involves multiple tranches for agreed policy reforms initiated by the government. It combines rigor with sustained lender commitment to financial support for an ongoing reform process. This option is appropriate for a new government beginning a reform process. Switching to one of the more flexible forms may be considered by joint agreement as the reform proceeds.

The fourth form would involve a country with a government not yet ready for reform. The lender would maintain contact and policy dialogue, offer advice and technical assistance, and commit to support if the government can commit to reform. The country could also be a candidate for an experimental single tranche credit extended to a potential reformer with the understanding that additional lending will follow actual reform. This should pilot local policy (particularly institutional reform) innovations and provide room for demonstration and learning.

All of these scenarios are consistent with adaptable conditionality. As countries progress, they could move up to higher forms of conditionality. A country just beginning reform would move from form four to three, but with a commitment by the donor to move toward form two and then one as the process continues. This prospective sequencing should strengthen the movement toward mutual commitment.

Conditionality as a sign of commitment of external support adds to the credibility of domestic reform programs, particularly for the private sector and civil society. Externally, adaptable conditionality can shorten the foreign investment pauses associated with reforms. Thus, conditionality as commitment would be part of a virtuous circle in which donor involvement contributes to the success and credibility of sustained growth and poverty reduction.

Conditionality as a Process

Most studies treat conditionality as a one-off event—a set of specific conditions set by external lenders for a particular loan. This static view sees conditionality and its results as tied to single loans rather than as part of a relationship, a view implicitly shared by Killick, Gunatilaka, and Marr (1998) and Dollar and Svensson (1998), whose unit of account is the loan. Our analysis reorganizes the Dollar and Svensson data to make the country the unit of account, setting the relationship within a long-term horizon, and acknowledging the information available from repeated lending. As shown later, the data demonstrate that conditionality can work when pursued within a longer-term framework.

In this new approach, conditionality forms part of an ongoing process through which the borrower and external partner develop and nurture mutual trust and commitment as the reform program proceeds. Under the CDF, policy reform is a dynamic, flexible concept—not a one-time resetting of policy matrices or a fixed set of institutional changes. The World Bank commits to support the reform process and the country commits to continuing along the path. In the ongoing dialogue between the Bank and the country, the path toward broad reform goals is altered as new information about the effectiveness of reforms and the economic environment facing the country materializes. Local knowledge and experimentation are allowed, even encouraged, to supplement and adapt best practices in policy reform (Chap. 7). Allowance is also made for changes in the country's preference for the sequence and pace of reform—for example, to ensure social cohesion and broad-based ownership of the reform process.

Conditionality as the Bank's or donors' commitment evolves over time. As the reform process deepens, conditions become increasingly flexible. This is akin to the relationship between a commercial bank and its customers. As long as the customer remains a credible performer, the credit line continues and perhaps increases. Such a long-term approach to policy reform avoids the uncertainties and disruptive practices of stop-go disbursements. It also captures the information and policy learning gained from a long-term relationship.

Conditionality, Ownership, and Participation

Broad participation in the cooperative development of a program strengthens commitment on both sides. With broad support, the government can make its ownership more credible. With more credible country ownership, more flexible forms of conditionality are appropriate. The government may request assistance in developing participation through, for example, seminars for a wide range of participants, including members of parliament and the press. Equally, cooperation with local research organizations can help develop policy knowledge and contribute to ownership through participation of local researchers and officials (Chaps. 5 and 8).

Assessing country ownership can be difficult, but it is key to the design of flexible conditionality and of strategies to build ownership over time (World Bank 1999). Johnson and Wasty (1993) offer a methodology for assessing borrower ownership based on four factors: the locus of initiative in formulating the reform, intellectual conviction among key policymakers, political will as expressed by top leaders, and efforts to build consensus among constituencies. This method focuses on key political leaders. While such "political entrepreneurs" are needed to capture opportunities for change, this approach may be appropriate where changes require sustained institutional effort to implement.

Two complementary tools for ownership assessment are stakeholder analysis and reform readiness analysis. Stakeholder analysis is used to acquire an understanding of the influence and interests of stakeholders and to involve each stakeholder group in subsequent stages of policy work. This tool also has its limitations: it often fails to assess the incentive and capacity of those affected by policy change to reorganize themselves as a political force. For radical policy reform the tool cannot reveal interest groups that are ready to push the reform forward, as the nature of the change and its likely outcome are beyond a society's experience. Reform readiness analysis tries to look behind the positions of actors to get to the underlying basis for those positions and to illuminate institutional arrangements that affect the ability of various actors to influence policy decisions or implementation. This tool demands detailed knowledge of a proposed reform and of the political situation surrounding it.

Most promising is to use these tools to identify ways for the government and external partners to build broad ownership over time, not simply to make a "go" or "no go" decision. Analytical work can be disseminated to potential beneficiaries to mobilize their support. Sequencing of reforms could build support by achieving early gains. Participatory and other political processes can help build ownership for subsequent reforms. The Bank and other partners can combine country knowledge with expertise about what has worked in other countries in reform areas of interest to the country. Monitoring of performance and policy impact can also contribute to policy learning, flexible conditionality, and broad ownership.

Finally, the reform process is likely to vary across sectors. Partners need to develop a clearer sense of the dynamics and specificity of ownership and vested interests likely to govern each sector. For example, reforming governance and institutions in the health and education sectors has proved to be complex and demanding, as these sectors involve many stakeholders, strong vested interests, and diverse contextual factors (Nelson, forthcoming).

The consultative aspects of the CDF process should give the policy reform targets increased legitimacy, because targets would be mutually agreed and nationally owned. Conditionality is part of the dialogue between the Bank and countries, not an alternative to such a dialogue. Increased ownership would justify greater flexibility in conditionality design and phasing: if there is consensus about the broad objectives and directions, there is less justification for imposing a rigid view on means and detailed conditions (Hopkins et al. 1999).

This approach to evaluating conditionality, ownership, and partnership combines economic and management concepts. The economist's view of development emphasizes the need to align incentives and institute measures to ameliorate imperfect markets (Hopkins et al. 1999). It recognizes that there are conflicts of interest and principal-agent problems. The CDF, by contrast, is primarily a management tool to ensure that everyone is on board with agreed development objectives. Combining the two views in complementary fashion is likely to yield the best results.

Empirical Evidence on Successful Adjustment Lending

Three sets of recent evidence support the view of conditionality as a long-term commitment process and highlight the superior performance of adaptive conditionality: the recent OED (1999) evaluation of HIAL, a re-evaluation of the Dollar and Svensson (1998) data using the country as the unit of observation, and a recent series of country studies on "Aid and Reform in Africa" (Devarajan, Dollar, and Holmgren 2001).

The HIAL Study

After nearly two decades of adjustment lending in Africa, the consensus in the Bank was that it had not achieved high rates of economic growth nor reduced poverty (OED 1997b, 1993; World Bank 1996; Elbadawi 1992). OED's (1997b) study of adjustment lending to sub-Saharan Africa during fiscal 1980–96 concluded that even in the best performing countries improvements in GDP growth have not been large enough to reduce poverty. A 1996 review of adjustment lending from 1980 through 1992 (World Bank 1996) found that the three strongest determinants of failure of adjustment lending were poor macroeconomic management, domestic political shocks, and too many loan conditions. While the first two are not under the control of the Bank, appropriate use of tranching and conditionality was thought to be a key to a successful operation.

The sub-Saharan Africa Region at the World Bank formed a working group in 1995 to develop recommendations for improving adjustment-lending results. The working group identified poor compliance with conditionality and weakness in the design of adjustment lending as key issues. Their recommendations were to enhance the results of adjustment lending by applying greater country selectivity and improving the design of adjustment lending by allowing for floating tranches. In particular, by introducing floating tranching of conditions, HIAL let governments decide when to meet conditions (that were generally sectoral) and draw on the tranche. Several HIAL programs had an initial tranche based on selection criteria, generally related to macroeconomic stabilization, followed by floating tranches. During fiscal 1997, HIAL lending to sub-Saharan Africa exceeded $1.5 billion, through fourteen operations in thirteen countries.

According to the HIAL working group, six factors should go into an assessment of country commitment and stakeholder participation and should be incorporated systematically into decisions on adjustment lending:

- Assessment of the country's track record on implementation of reform;
- Willingness of the government to draft its own Letter of Development Policy and adjustment program;
- Quality of national support for reforms;
- Fit between the country's official statements and the context of the proposed reforms;
- Fit between government tax and spending policy and the content of the proposed reforms; and
- Extent of desirable "lock-in" actions to be completed before negotiation of an adjustment lending.

Four criteria were used to assess whether the Bank has in fact been selective in approving HIAL operations: compliance track record with agreed-on policy conditionality (OED 1997b), the Bank's country performance ratings, measurement of program ownership, and debt sustainability. The HIAL countries' performance at the time of selection was not significantly different from that of other sub-Saharan Africa countries except on prior country performance ratings, where HIAL countries were marginally better.

A primary indication of borrower ownership is willingness to draft its own Letter of Development Policy, which states government policy in specific areas supported by adjustment lending. Letters of Development Policy were drafted by the government in seven cases, jointly by government and the Bank in two cases, and by the Bank alone in five cases. IMF guidelines are similar, "to ensure ownership of the policy framework paper, the authorities should be encouraged to initiate its drafting" (IMF 2001). All thirteen HIAL countries were implementing an IMF program at the time the HIAL operation was approved.

The quality of national support for the economic reform matters under the HIAL program. Governments are more likely to buy into adjustment lending conditions for operations that promote a participatory process and increased ownership of reform programs. For example, to increase support for HIAL, operations were prepared in broad consultation with civil society, the rationale for reforms was explained to a wide audience, and government was encouraged to present reform plans to the public—processes that constitute one of the pillars of the CDF. Engaging civil society in projects and programs leads to better design and implementation results and usually greater effectiveness, including more local ownership. Governments consulted stakeholders in nine of the thirteen HIAL countries. This approach fostered transparency and ownership and reduced some of the negative sentiment about adjustment.

HIAL was also meant to improve adjustment lending program design by matching financial assistance to needs and providing smoother resource flows through flexible disbursement and fewer, more appropriate conditions. HIAL operations averaged about half the number of conditions on adjustment lending to sub-Saharan Africa from 1980 to 1993.

Prior to HIAL, two-tranche adjustment loans were the rule, three-tranche operations were less frequent, and single-tranche operations were rare. HIAL introduced floating tranche mechanisms and promoted single-tranche operations as an alternative in particular circumstances.[1] Of the twenty-one HIAL operations in fiscal 1996–98, nine had floating tranches (from one to five tranches) and five were single-tranche operations. Thus about two-thirds of the operations have adopted tranching innovations. The new tranching arrangements increased ownership by giving governments increased freedom in the timing of reforms. The larger number and smaller size of tranches, together with more flexible timing, reduced pressure on the Bank to disburse when conditions were not fully met.

While HIAL operations support macroeconomic and sectoral policies that promote growth and efficient resource allocation, both essential for poverty reduction, they also address social concerns more directly. The majority of HIAL operations aim to reorient public spending toward infrastructure and basic services for the poor or to eliminate distortions that disadvantage the poor. According to World Bank Poverty Board criteria, eleven of the fourteen fiscal 1996–97 HIAL operations were "poverty focused." Specific social sector conditionality was included in a significant number of HIAL operations.

The recent OED (1999) study "Higher Impact Adjustment Lending: Initial Evaluation" (the HIAL study) concluded that the HIAL group of countries performed better than other IDA countries in policy outcomes and economic impacts because of greater selectivity in lending and more flexibility in disbursement. HIAL countries performed better than comparators (IDA countries in sub-Saharan Africa and elsewhere) in fiscal adjustment, exchange and interest rate policy, and structural reforms. Better results were also achieved in economic growth, inflation, current account balance, foreign exchange reserves, and debt sustainability. The HIAL share of poverty-focused operations is higher relative to the comparators. While social sector expenditures as a share of GDP have, on average, decreased slightly in HIAL countries, interpretation of these results must take into account the short time since the start of HIAL and the many gaps in social expenditure data.

Reevaluation of Assessing Aid

Assessing Aid (World Bank,1998; Dollar and Svensson 1998) indicated the importance of political economy variables in predicting success or failure using OED ratings.[2] These authors conclude: "These results have clear implications for how to manage policy-based lending. They suggest that the role of

TABLE 3.1

	Conditionality, Policy Outcomes, and Impact under HIAL, Fiscal 1996–98						Change from 1993–95 to 1996–98						
Country	Number of Board Effectiveness Conditions	Number of Post-Effectiveness Conditions	Total No. of Conditions	Tranching Mechanism	Average No. of Post-Effectiveness Conditions	Primary Balance (Percent of GDP)	Inflation	Real Effective Exchange Rate (1990 = 100)	Current Account Balance	Interest Rate Differential	Non-Gold Reserves	Gross Domestic Investment	Real Per Capita GDP Growth
Chad SAC I	13	N/A	13	1regular	N/A								
Chad SAC II	23	N/A	23	1 regular	N/A	5.5	-7.4	-2.7	2.7	..	..	3.0	7.0
Madagascar	13	N/A	13	1 regular	N/A	1.7	-21.6	7.1	3.0	..	17.7	1.1	2.2
Niger	15	N/A	15	1 regular	N/A	2.7	-11.6	-3.4	0.2	6.8	-9.9	4.2	0.4
Malawi	1	3	4	1 regular + 1 floating	3	8.8	-26.0	12.0	5.3	-2.7	4.7	-0.5	2.8
Cameroon SAC II	10	15	25	1 regular + 2 floating	7.5	5.2	-9.0	-5.3	2.0	..	..	1.4	5.8
Tanzania	8	19	27	1 regular +4 floating	4.75	4.0	-10.7	32.4	9.6	-18.7	11.2	-1.9	2.6
Cote d'Ivoire	6	11	17	1 regular +5 floating	2.2	2.9	-10.4	-5.2	1.8	8.1	5.8	3.9	3.3
Priv. Sect. Adj. Cr.													
Kenya	4	11	15	2 regular	11	-0.3	-15.5	12.8	-1.5	13.4	1.0	-0.7	1.0
Mozambique	32	5	37	2 regular	5	5.2	-33.4	9.2	18.0	..	..	-5.6	1.8
Zambia	2	11	24	2 regular	11	0.8	-64.0	9.1	1.8	44.2	-5.6	2.3	6.9
Uganda/SAC III	6	13	19	2 regular 2 floating	4.33	2.0	-6.5	4.6	2.3	3.1	3.3	0.7	-1.9
Cameroon SAC III	11	25	36	2 regular +4 floating	5	5.2	-9.0	-5.3	2.0	..	..	1.4	5.8

TABLE 3.1 *continued*

Uganda/Educ. Sect. Adj.	14	31	45	3 regular	15.5	2.0	-6.5	4.6	2.3	3.1	3.3	0.7	-1.9
Mali	1	17	18	3 regular +2 floating	4.25	2.4	-9.4	-6.3	3.9	2.4	5.1	1.1	2.8
Mauritania	3	11	14	3 regular +2 floating	2.75	5.4	-3.6	-4.5	8.5	..	..	-3.3	0.1
Cote d'Ivoire	6	31	37	4 regular +1 floating	7.75	2.9	-10.4	-5.2	1.8	8.1	5.8	3.9	3.3
Transp. Sect. Adj. Cr.													
Ghana	9	N/A	9	1 regular	N/A	1.1	-5.5	12.8	2.3	5.8	-	1.8	0.2
Cape Verde	9	5	14	2 regular	5	13.5	0.0	1.4	4.8	..	..	1.1	-0.7
Guinea	17	8	25	2 regular	8	-8.5	-2.7	-2.7	1.8	1.4	-	-0.8	0.4
Senegal	13	6	19	2 regular	6	2.8	-11	-8	2.6	7.2	7.8	2.7	3.4
Average	9.77	14.50	24.00		7.13								
Standard Deviation	8.28	9.51	11.24		3.71								
Mode	6	11	37		5								

adjustment lending is to identify reformers not to create them" (Dollar and Svensson 1998, p. 4). The results are based on probit regressions predicting the probability of success of an adjustment loan using political economy variables for the country receiving the loan, variables under control of the Bank, and dummy variables for geographic location. The unit of analysis is the loan, so no account could be taken of multiple loans to individual countries.

The authors of this chapter hypothesize that past success or failure could be used to predict subsequent success and thus to select and design adjustment loans. Earlier OED cross-country evaluations of adjustment lending (Jayarajah, Baird, and Branson 1994; Jayarajah, Branson, and Sen 1996) reported on many cases of multiple adjustment loans. A frequency distribution of all adjustment loans evaluated for the period 1979–98 by loans per country shows that 27 percent of countries had just one adjustment loan and 27 percent had five or more. Thus, for a high proportion of countries there was prior information on success or failure in adjustment lending.

The patterns of success or failure on OED ratings for countries with five or more adjustment loans are consistent with the interpretation of conditionality as commitment instrument and learning process. Additional probit regressions were estimated by adding to the Dollar and Svensson data set a variable that captures—for each adjustment program—the performance of any previous adjustment loan, with a view to explaining the performance (satisfactory or unsatisfactory OED rating) of adjustment programs. The coefficients of the variables capturing the effect of previous adjustment loans on the current one have the expected positive sign and are highly significant, implying that past success, as measured by OED ratings, is a better predictor of current success than any of the other variables. A project's likelihood of success is 10 percent higher when preceded by at least one satisfactory adjustment loan and 21.5 percent higher when preceded by a series of successful projects. These findings suggest that there is information in past success that Bank staff could use to forecast current outcomes.

These results are hardly definitive. The OED ratings summarize a wide range of information about past loans that is difficult to quantify for regression analysis. But they do support the concept of conditionality as a long-term commitment and learning device. A string of successful ratings, and the information that underlies them, could support increasing the flexibility of conditionality. The successes indicate increasing local ownership of the program and a deepening of policy learning by the country, a signal that the Bank can move toward ex-post conditionality.

The *Assessing Aid* analysis was conducted for adjustment lending using the traditional form of conditionality. Information from past performance and learning might be used even more effectively if conditionality were more flexible and tailored to the evolving reform process and the long-term relationship between the Bank and the country.

Aid and Reform in Africa: Case Studies

Earlier analyses (Dollar and Svensson 1998, for example), and much of the recent literature, relied on cross-country regressions that suggested that policy formulation depends primarily on domestic political factors and that aid has had no effect on average on the quality of macroeconomic policies (World Bank 1998; ODI 1998). But the average relationship disguised the fact that aid supported policy reforms in some cases and poor policies in others. It hid a much richer story about when and how reforms can take place.

A recent study of aid and policy reform in ten countries in Africa (Devarajan, Dollar, and Holmgren 2001) reveals that aid can make a difference, provided that conditionality is compatible with country ownership. Policy is driven primarily by domestic political economy issues and often induced by crises. In general, donors have not been selective but have provided the same reform package everywhere and at all phases of reform. Donors often failed to distinguish between first-generation reforms, which may be undertaken by a small circle of reformers, and second-generation reforms—such as improving civil service performance—which demand adaptation, broad ownership, and sustained support.

Perhaps the most important lessons come from the reformers—Ghana and Uganda in this case study series. First, institutions are important to the success and sustainability of reforms, along with technocrats, leadership, and the way society organizes interest groups. Second, the timing and mix of financial and nonfinancial services are critical to different phases of reform. Before reform, knowledge assistance and policy dialogue are often useful if demand-driven and adapted to local conditions. Policy learning has to take place at a country's pace, and knowledge transfer should support local learning and capacity building. In this phase, "pressure to lend" from the Bank and donors could have perverse effects if it leaves no space for learning and if financial aid lets countries defer reforms. In a rapid reform phase, conditional aid finance can support a deepening of reform commitments, increasing the benefits of reform, reducing the tendency for backsliding, and signaling the seriousness of reform to civil society and the private sector. But even during rapid reform it is more important to build commitment for the broad directions while allowing for flexibility and adaptation in implementation. These findings are consistent with our view that policy reform is a learning process and that conditionality and other instruments should be compatible with autonomy and ownership.

A disturbing finding of the case studies is the tendency for aid to decline and for donors to become increasingly prescriptive and rigid (conditionality covering more scope, in more detail) with reformers, once good policies are in place. Donors tend to attach their money to a specific policy package—not to a relationship of mutual commitment and policy learning. Devarajan, Dollar, and Holmgren (2001) thus speculate that conditional assistance should have quickly outlived its usefulness, as continued use of conditionality would undermine government credibility as a reformer and limit local participation in policymaking. But this should not be the case if conditionality is viewed as a long-term commitment and learning process, with progressively flexible conditionality used for credible reformers who could sustain and deepen the transformation of their economies and societies over time. In this context, the reform process is perceived as locally managed and continuously adapted, while donors allocate their aid selectively in support of long-term commitment by reformers.

Recent Proposals at the IMF

This chapter has so far focused on the experience and results of the World Bank's conditionality, but the arguments for reforming conditionality apply to the IMF as well. Conditionality is a key aspect of the IMF's involvement with its member countries. It is the link between approval and continuation of the IMF financing and implementation of specified elements of economic policy by the country receiving this financing.

Recently, the IMF has initiated an internal review to streamline and focus conditionality, to give greater scope for national ownership (IMF, 2001). According to this review, the IMF has increased the scope of its conditionality since the early 1990s, as it became increasingly engaged with the structural issues of the heavily indebted countries, the transition economies, and the Asian Crisis countries. The Washington Consensus has also been augmented to incorporate structural and institutional conditions that underpin growth and policymaking in a market economy.

The change in policy content accompanied a change in the modalities of monitoring and policy reviews. As many structural reforms take considerable time to implement and produce results, structural benchmarks became increasingly important to map out a series of steps toward an overall policy result. The growing comprehensiveness of policy reviews and the proliferation of structural benchmarks in turn led to ambiguity about the boundaries of IMF conditionality and raised concerns about short-circuiting national decision making and micromanaging the reform. Concerns have also been raised about whether IMF-supported reform programs have exceeded authorities' ability to rally political support for a multitude of policy changes at one time, and to implement such reforms. Overly invasive conditionality may have thus undermined ownership, galvanized domestic opposition, and reduced the authorities' focus on what is essential.

The emerging proposals for streamlining the Fund's conditionality are to:

- Curtail the scope of policies included under conditionality;
- Reduce the detail of conditions;
- Coordinate more closely with the World Bank, so that each can focus conditionality in its core expertise; and
- Focus on broad policy results, and leave room for local policymakers to fashion the specific actions to achieve those results.

These proposals are consistent with the findings of this chapter. IMF experience also points to the common drift of donors towards blueprints and intrusive conditionality, well beyond their areas of expertise. The new Poverty Reduction Strategy Paper process should facilitate such reforms in the IMF's design of conditionality, help refocus the Bank's and IMF's conditionality on their core areas of expertise, avoid cross-conditionality, and promote new modalities for conditionality.

Conclusion

This chapter proposes a new view of conditionality as a process of signaling and nurturing mutual commitment between lender and borrowing country—a policy compact—in place of conditionality that coerces borrowers to take actions. Because other stakeholders are involved, the risks of coercion implicit in a secret negotiation between a hard-pressed borrower and a powerful lender are reduced. Equally, transparency and participation should minimize the risks of shirking or policy reversals. The design of conditionality should be supportive of ownership and a symmetrical relationship between the borrower and the Bank that implies mutual accountability for results. It should take a long-term view of reform.

Thus understood, current donor practices in designing conditionality, adjustment lending, and technical assistance instruments should be reformed. Conditionality must be made flexible and must be combined with capacity building and policy learning to level the playing field in the relationship. Ongoing and credible reformers should have the option of ex-post conditionality, with lending based on past actions and the expectation that the reform process will continue. The country proceeds with reforms with the expectation that lending will continue. In a successful relationship, both expectations are fulfilled. Credible new reformers might have floating tranche loans, as in the HIAL approach in Africa. Essentially, the country decides the sequence of reform and sectoral tranche release. Conditionality would also be increasingly flexible as the country increases its ownership of the program and as the reform process tackles the more complex institutional change.

Acknowledgment

The authors gratefully acknowledge excellent research assistance and comments from Federico Mini and William Battaile. They also acknowledge the contribution of Fareed Hasan to the HIAL study. The conclusions of this research are consistent with some of the proposals made in parallel by Leandro, Schafer, and Frontini (1999).

Notes

1. Single tranche operations were selected in cases where the track record of reform was still limited, or where the information base on the country was rudimentary. Single tranche operations are expected to be embedded in a longer-term reform program. For instance, HIAL programs in Chad, Madagascar, and Niger envisaged a series of single tranche operations rather than a one-time event.
2. Dollar and Svensson (1998) argued that whether or not a country has an adjustment program is not a very good predictor of who actually reforms. On the other hand, a few political economy factors—political stability, democracy, social division, and leader's time in power—can successfully predict the outcome of adjustment lending 75 percent of the time.

References

Collier, P., et al. September 1997. "Redesigning Conditionality." *World Development* 25: pp. 1399–407.

Devarajan, Shanta, David Dollar, and Torgny Holmgren, eds. 2001 "Aid and Reform in Africa: Lessons from Ten Case Studies." Washington, D.C.: World Bank.

Dollar, David, and Jakob Svensson. 1998. "What Explains the Success or Failure of Structural Adjustment Programs?" Washington, D.C.: World Bank Policy Research Working Paper 1938.

Elbadawi, I.A. 1992. "World Bank Adjustment Lending and Economic Performance in Sub-Saharan Africa in the 1980s: A Comparison of Early Adjusters, Late Adjusters and Non-Adjusters." World Bank Policy Research Working Paper 1001. Washington, D.C.

Hopkins, Raul, et al. 1999. "Conditionality and the Comprehensive Development Framework." *Journal of International Development*, UK, 9: 507–16, June 1997.

IMF. 2001. "Conditionality in Fund-Supported Programs: Overview." Conditionality@IMF.org. http://www.imf.org/external/np/pdr/cond/2001/eng/overview/index.htm

Jayarajah, C., W. Branson, and B. Sen. 1994. *Social Dimensions of Adjustment: World Bank Experience, 1980–93*. Washington, D.C.: World Bank, Operations Evaluation Department.

Jayarajah, C., Mark Baird and William Branson. 1996. "Structural and Sectoral Adjustment Operations: World Bank Experience, 1980–92." Washington, D.C.: World Bank, Operations Evaluation Department.

Johnson, J., and Sulaiman Wasty. 1993. *Borrower Ownership of Adjustment Programs and the Political Economy of Reform*. World Bank Discussion Paper 199. Washington, D.C.

Killick, T., Ramani Gunatilaka, and Ana Marr. 1998. *Aid and the Political Economy of Policy Change*. London, U.K.: Routledge, Overseas Development Institute.

Leandro, Jose, J. Schafer, and G. Frontini. 1999. "Towards a More Effective Conditionality: An Operational Framework." World Development, Vol. 27. No. 2, pp. 285–299. Pergamon/Elsevier Science Ltd., U.K.

Nelson, Joan. 1999. *Reforming Health and Education: The World Bank, The IDB, and Complex Institutional Change*. Overseas Development Council, Washington, D.C.

OED (Operations Evaluation Department). 1993. "Adjustment in Sub-Saharan Africa: Selected Findings from OED Evaluations." Report 12155. Washington, D.C.: World Bank.

— — —. 1995a. "Higher Impact Adjustment Lending. Report of the Working Group to the SPA Plenary, October 1995." Washington, D.C.: World Bank, Office of the Chief Economist, Africa Region.

— — —. 1995b. "The Social Impact of Adjustment Operations: An Overview." Report 14776. Washington, D.C.: World Bank.

— — —. 1997a. "Lessons of Fiscal Adjustment: Selected Proceedings from a World Bank Seminar." Washington, D.C.: World Bank.

— — —. 1997b. "Adjustment Lending in Sub-Saharan Africa: An Update." Report 16594. Washington, D.C.: World Bank.

— — —. 1999. "Higher-Impact Adjustment Lending (HIAL): Initial Evaluation." Report 19797. Washington, D.C.: World Bank.

ODI (Overseas Development Institute). 1998. *Aid and the Political Economy of Policy Change*. Washington, D.C.

Rodrik, Dani. 1999. Paper prepared for the International Monitory Fund Conference on Second-Generation Reforms. Washington, D.C., November 8–9, 1999.

Stiglitz, Joseph E. 1998. "Towards a New Paradigm for Development: Strategies, Policies and Processes." Geneva, Switzerland, Prebisch Lecture, UNCTAD, October 19.

World Bank. 1996. "Portfolio Improvement Program: Review of Adjustment Operations." Washington, D.C.: Office of the Vice President, Development Economics, and Chief Economist.

— — —. 1998. *Assessing Aid: What Works, What Doesn't, and Why*. Washington, D.C.

— — —. 1999. "Assessing Borrower Ownership Using Reform Readiness Analysis." PREM Note 25. Washington, D.C.: Poverty Reduction and Economic Management Network, Economic Policy Group.

4

Mainstreaming Participation
in Development

James Blackburn, Robert Chambers, and *John Gaventa*

Efforts in the past decade to bring participation to center stage in development have yielded a rich harvest of learning, much of it now echoed in the guiding principles of ownership and partnership in the Comprehensive Development Framework (CDF), the Poverty Reduction Strategy Papers (PRSPs), and similar frameworks of the Development Assistance Committee and United Nations (Chap. 1). Participation is about building ownership from the bottom up.

It has been known for some time that strong participation on the ground by primary stakeholders boosts project performance. More recently, participation has shown promise in several areas outside the project framework: for informing national policymakers (Norton and Stephens 1995; Robb 1999; Holland and Blackburn 1998), for planning and implementing large-scale government programs (Thompson 1995), and for encouraging good—and often local—governance (Gaventa and Valderrama 1999). This has made clear the need for better partnerships with secondary stakeholders—not just for more ownership by primary stakeholders—as participation goes to scale.

But what is participation, exactly? We define it as a process through which primary stakeholders influence and share control of their development initiatives, decisions, and resources (Tandon and Cordeiro 1998, building on World Bank 1994.) Mainstreaming participation means adopting the "institutional reforms and innovations necessary to enable full and systematic incorporation of participatory methodologies into the work of the institution so that meaningful primary stakeholder participation becomes a regular part of a project and policy development, implementation and evaluation" (Long 1999, p. 11). Scaling up participation means increasing the number of participants, the areas participating, or the number of activities included. It means involving people throughout the development process in a way that empowers (Gaventa 1998). The challenge is to expand without undermining quality.

This chapter explores the challenge of broadening ownership in the design and implementation of comprehensive development strategies. It draws lessons from recent experience with participatory poverty assessments: government should take ownership early, nongovernmental organizations (NGOs) and government should forge partnerships, and poverty assessments should inform actions by all levels of governments. It examines the challenge of scaling up participation and draws lessons for governments: against procedural inflexibility and rushing to scale and for promoting champions, alliances, continuity, and attitudinal change. It draws lessons for donors: make the management framework flexible, improve collaboration to avoid consultation fatigue, build the capacity of weaker stakeholders, and create organizational cultures that support participation. Participatory monitoring and evaluation is singled out as a new key to learning and ownership. Finally, the chapter argues for policies and initiatives that create enabling environments for participation. It cautions against too much reliance on top-down approaches and suggests the district as an optimal level for holistic programs. Decentralization, democracy, and diversity—the "three Ds"—open the way to a holistic approach, reducing the need for coordination higher up. This chapter concludes that none of these lessons offers an instant solution and that all entail long-term commitment and much learning.

Policy Consultations with the Poor

The use of participatory research, specifically participatory rural appraisal,[1] to make national policymakers more aware of how the poor really live began on a large-scale in the mid–1990s. One of the most interesting developments has been the gradual institutionalization of World Bank-promoted country-level participatory poverty assessments—a complement to the Bank's conventional poverty assessments. Several analysts have argued that participatory poverty assessments reveal more about the dynamics of poverty and its multiple dimensions than conventional survey-based economistic studies do (Booth et al. 1998; Brocklesby and Holland 1998; Robb 1999). To date, more than one hundred participatory poverty assessments have been carried out, the largest number in Africa.

But so far participation has been limited in most participatory poverty assessments and participatory sectoral studies to consulting multiple stakeholders on policy design—and this is not the same as ownership (Chap. 7).

Effective ownership means involving primary and secondary stakeholders in every stage of the policy cycle (NGO Working Group on the World Bank 1999). Recent participatory poverty assessment experience, especially in Uganda, shows how the influence of such assessments can be extended beyond consultation to build cross-partner in-country ownership into policy design. Networks of governmental, nongovernmental, and other organizations committed to bringing the voices of the poor to the ears of policymakers now exist in many countries and could provide informed advice on implementing comprehensive development strategies for poverty reduction.

Importance of Involving Government

Though it is difficult to trace policy effects back to causes, participatory poverty assessments seem to have a greater effect on policy when governments have greater ownership. In Zambia, government officials were included from the early stages of the poverty assessment process, leading to changes in sectoral balances and higher priority for rural road construction and maintenance (Milimo, Norton, and Owen 1998). In Lesotho, government ownership increased when participatory poverty assessment results were included in the government action plan. In Argentina, although the specific policy changes have not been documented, ownership has been important in modifying monitoring and evaluation indicators of social programs (Robb 1999). In a participatory sectoral study of education in The Gambia, early involvement of government officials in research proved important in modifying education policy—increasing the number of female teachers and reducing tuition fees by 50 percent in secondary schools (Kane, Bruce, and O'Reilly de Brun 1998).

Involving a Wide Range of Civil Society Actors

Civil society actors have been involved at different stages of the participatory poverty assessment in different ways. In Zambia, the inclusion of a cross-section of stakeholders created a shared feeling of ownership of the process and the action plan (Robb 1999). In Lesotho, NGOs and the World Bank worked on the action plan together, and the government received extensive support from both. South Africa made a concerted effort to build stakeholder ownership into every stage of the research process, from design and methodology to management, facilitation, and synthesis (Attwood and May 1998).

These kinds of partnerships require that more powerful partners cede control to weaker partners. Only then can the weaker partners be the main owners. This sort of involvement requires time and commitment. The idea is to view participatory poverty assessments as a learning process in which capacities—of government, NGOs, and development agency staff—are built.

A Learning Curve of Innovations

Participatory poverty assessment methods have evolved through cycles of innovation, learning, and change. Participatory rural appraisal methods were introduced in the Ghana participatory poverty assessment of 1993 (Dogbe 1998) and further developed in Zambia that same year (Milimo, Norton, and Owen 1998) and in Mozambique in 1994 (Owen 1998). While earlier participatory poverty assessments had been seeded and sustained principally by donors, the South African assessment, introduced in 1995, was owned and managed by South Africans. The process was managed by a South African consultancy firm—Data Research Africa—and overseen by a management committee of representatives from academia, NGOs, and the private sector. Organizations and individuals were selected for fieldwork after a transparent, competitive process. The outcome of their work was a report of groundbreaking insight and authority—one that included the voices of poor people (May 1998).

The Bangladesh participatory poverty assessment also engaged the poor—this time in focus groups separated by gender and by urban and rural residence. Participants voiced needs that workers had not anticipated. The second priority of "doables" for poor urban women, for example, was a place where they could wash in private.

The participatory poverty assessment in Shinyanga in Tanzania also broke ground by being regional rather than national, by involving district government staff as facilitators, by engaging participants intensively—with three weeks of training and three weeks of residence in each community—and by working on participatory follow up (Shinyanga Human Development Report Project 1998).

The Uganda Participatory Poverty Assessment Process:
A Model for the Future?

Initially funded by donors, the Uganda participatory poverty assessment process is owned and managed—and championed—by the government. A committee of donor and NGO representatives, chaired by a government staffer, oversees and coordinates it. The initial timespan is three years, longer than any previous participatory poverty assessment. Before beginning, field workers underwent thorough training in which they learned lessons from the experience in other countries. Three people in each of nine districts—two from government and one from an NGO—make up the core teams. Feedback is given to the district level and to district planning, as well as to the center. Ongoing participatory monitoring and evaluation in communities have been built in.

The participatory poverty assessment unit has more policy influence than previous units because of its location within the Ministry of Finance. Sectoral ministries seek advice and feedback from the unit for their policies and proposals, in a process that has already influenced a policy change in line with poor people's priorities for water services. Policy in agriculture, taxation, and education is also being discussed, and there is potential for further policy influence on the budget process. While it is too early to draw firm conclusions, the participatory poverty assessment process in Uganda seems to be a useful case study for governments and donors committed to reducing poverty in ways that are sensitive to the realities and priorities of poor people.

Lessons for Governments

Participatory poverty assessments have the potential to influence all sectors of the CDF by informing and influencing policies, providing feedback on implementation, enhancing awareness and commitment among donors and beneficiaries, and encouraging and strengthening champions of the poor. These influences will be stronger and more sustainable if the process includes ongoing participatory monitoring and evaluation.

Five lessons and conclusions stand out:

- *Government should take ownership—early.* Most of the first participatory poverty assessments were owned largely by donors. In South Africa, for example, the assessment was owned by South Africans, but the process took place almost entirely outside government and transfer of ownership and commitment to government was never complete.
- *NGOs and government should forge partnerships.* When a government is committed to participatory antipoverty policies, it should be in the driver's seat. Patterns and possibilities will vary, but one promising approach is to have an NGO staff member work in a government office (as in Uganda).
- *Participatory poverty assessment should be a part of government.* The South African participatory poverty assessment became an orphan when its government home, the Reconstruction and Development Program, was unexpectedly abolished in 1995. In contrast, in Uganda the unit responsible for participatory poverty assessments is strategically located in the Ministry of Finance—well placed for influencing sectoral ministries and sharing information from ongoing participatory poverty assessments in the districts.
- *Awareness and commitment should be built at different levels in government.* Both the Shinyanga and Uganda participatory poverty assessments have enhanced awareness and commitment at the district level by involving government staff. There are indications that this is affecting district-level priorities and implementation generally.

- *Participatory poverty assessments should be a way of life for government.* The participatory poverty assessment process is long term and includes participatory monitoring and evaluation. The participatory poverty assessment process should become—progressively and at different levels—the way in which governments and donors do business.

Scaling Up Participation in National Development Programs

Perhaps the best-known success story in taking participation to scale in a government bureaucracy is the Philippines National Irrigation Administration's step-by-step approach to help build user associations' capacity to manage local irrigation systems. Of particular relevance to CDF implementation is a learning process approach (D. Korten 1980) and managerial innovations that allow local priorities and processes to guide bureaucracy work—not the other way around (D. Korten 1988).

Benjamin Bagadion and Frances Korten (1991) argue that the Irrigation Administration's institutional learning process began when a working group brought together frontline workers and high-level staff to define a common vision of change. The group then worked through a five-step learning cycle over a number of years: they identified the need for an innovation, conceptualized a new approach, tested it on a small scale, systematized the lessons, and developed institutional capacities to adopt the change on a wider scale.

Supporting ownership of local user associations in defining how and when to build, rebuild, and maintain their irrigation systems was not something that could be achieved by decree or by pumping huge resources into the system early. The key was to take the time to complete each stage of the learning cycle and to resist spending large sums at the start, as often happens in multilateral donor programs (Thompson 1995, 1998). Long-term success also required resisting an attempt by the World Bank to go to scale too fast with an expanded program that would have seriously undermined participation and sustainability.

Procedural Inflexibility Can Quash Participation: The Doon Valley Project

Changing organizational systems and procedures to facilitate participatory development is complex and problematic. But the costs of not doing so can be heavy, as the Doon Valley Project shows (Shepherd 1998).

The government of Uttar Pradesh's Doon Valley Project, funded by the European Union, seeks to promote sustainable management of Himalayan hillsides by farmers. Although a participatory method of village planning has been initiated, village facilitators have been unable to apply a participatory approach further into the program cycle. The constraints derive in part from government and donor unwillingness to challenge a requirement that predetermined quantifiable targets be achieved within set time frames, which clashes with the needs of a participatory approach to program implementation.

The lesson is clear: participation cannot be "bolted on." Sticking participatory rural appraisal onto existing programs as an appendage will not lead to participation. All too often, the priorities revealed by participatory rural appraisals contradict those already fixed by the program, and development organizations—from field units to foreign funders—find themselves unable or unwilling to change. Resistance by those far up in the hierarchy leads to friction. And field staff, often the only people to receive relevant training, can easily become disillusioned. The quality of participatory rural appraisal drops, and staff begin to apply the approach in a mechanical, routine way without the creative enthusiasm needed to make a real difference (Chambers 1997).

The Dangers of Rapid Scaling Up: The Case of Rushing to Scale in Indonesia

Participation cannot be rushed, as the Indonesian government's attempt to facilitate nationwide village development planning in less than a year illustrates. In June 1995 a central government directive informed all twenty-seven provinces that starting with the 1995–96 cycle, bottom-up planning would begin in villages. Budgets were duly allocated to facilitate the prescribed four-day training for provincial trainers and three-day training for village council heads in some 60,000 villages. Cascade training on such a scale and at such speed seriously diminished the quality of the exercise. Field-based methods inevitably became classroom-based, and the short timeframe hampered learning and consultations with NGOs experienced in participatory methods. Attitudes and behaviors, long recognized as more important in participatory rural appraisal than the methods themselves (Kumar 1996), received little attention (Mukherjee 1998). Quality suffered even more from Indonesia's hierarchical bureaucratic culture.

This case confirms what has been reported elsewhere (Thompson 1995, 1998; Pratt, Pimbert, and Bainbridge 1998): using participatory approaches effectively on a wide scale requires a long, gradual approach to developing strategies, gaining experience, and building capacity. The Indonesian government's attempt to facilitate nationwide village development planning quickly shows what happens when participation is forced: little or no ownership by the village.

Another lesson: trainers must model participation in their behavior and approach to training, and they must have enough time to teach. Effective participatory rural appraisal training takes ten to twenty days and requires field experience. In one country a World Bank staff member reportedly asked a local participatory rural appraisal trainer to conduct training in three days. When the trainer said that was impossible, that training required more time and field experience, the staff member simply found another trainer. The consequence of such behavior by donor staff is low-quality participatory rural appraisal and much disillusionment with participation.

Hanging in There Pays: The Rural Support Program in Tanzania

The Rural Integrated Project Support Program in Tanzania illustrates the importance of long-term commitment in a participation strategy (Freling 1998). The fruits of this program are not a result of quick mass action, but of experience and learning from mistakes for twenty-five years.

The Rural Integrated Project Support program is district-level and holistic, embracing water, healthcare, education, agriculture, local government, savings and credit, transport and marketing, and natural resource management. A 1993 evaluation of phase one (launched in 1988) revealed weaknesses in program delivery at the community level. The evaluation prompted adoption of a unique participatory planning process, implemented in phase two in October 1994.

This participatory approach has accelerated learning. Today's program framework supports and facilitates meaningful dialogue between local communities and government authorities to identify priorities, available resources, and opportunities for action. Remarkable results have been achieved in healthcare, agriculture, natural resource management, and education (with links made to the government's education reform). More remarkable is that this has been achieved with little outside money. External funds from donors and the government come to only $3 million a year.

Champions, Continuity, and Alliances

In cases where governments or NGOs have worked to increase beneficiary participation, key individuals, or alliances of individuals, are often responsible. They take the lead, often battling institutional inertia, individual hostility, and political pressures from the relatively wealthy. The Regional Commissioners of Mtwara and Lindi in Tanzania allied with the Rural Integrated Project Support Program to introduce participatory approaches in government (Freling 1998). Benjamin Bagadion of the National Irrigation Administration in the Philippines and Frances Korten of the Ford Foundation were key allies in developing and spreading participatory irrigation management in the Philippines. The critical pioneering development of joint forest management in India took place in West Bengal during five years when there was strong mutual support and commitment of both the minister responsible for forestry and the chief conservator of forests. A former chief executive transformed the irrigation bureaucracy of the Mahaweli Development Authority in Sri Lanka into a model of participation. Further crucial innovations in participatory forestry, irrigation management, watershed management, and training for attitude and behavior change owe much to the continuity and commitment of Anil K. Shah in Gujarat, first as a secretary in the government and then for more than a decade in the NGO sector.

The challenge is to multiply the number and effectiveness of champions. This means we must find and support them and enable them to network, form alliances, learn from each other, and spread their participatory approaches. And we must foster conditions that encourage and enable champions.

The Primacy of Personal Change

Participatory approaches must be reflected in the attitudes and behavior of all actors at all levels, for these are the means and assurance of sustainable change in organizational cultures (Blackburn and Holland 1998). Again and again, a new authoritarian manager has set the clock back, ruining the participatory culture and practices patiently nurtured by a predecessor. Sustained leadership and support from a high level are critical—progress is often made by incentives and example. The bottom line in participatory change is individual and personal.

It is only recently that the implications of attitude and behavior have been recognized. Leadership generally has been celebrated, but participation goes beyond conventional leadership. To empower others demands special qualities and behaviors. In August 1998 the Indian government held a workshop at the National Academy of Administration at which it was resolved to introduce attitude and behavior change modules in training for probationers for the Indian Administrative Service and the Indian Forest Service (Mathur 1998).

While a leader in policy formulation, the World Bank is often a laggard in behavior and attitude change. But since Bank staff are role models for many development professionals, especially in government, they must place attitude and behavior change at the center of their policies and practices or risk turning the CDF into another exercise in domination. Client government staff cannot be expected to be patient and participatory if Bank staff are not. Bank staff must facilitate, listen, and empower more—and teach, talk, and dominate less. And this may require radical personal change.

Field experiences will also help. Those who have facilitated participatory poverty assessments in the field often speak of how they have been changed by the experience. At a recent global synthesis workshop, leaders of national field teams in the Voices of the Poor project undertaken for *World Development Report 2000/2001* said they had been deeply moved and changed by the experience. But although senior World Bank staff have been immersed in villages and slums, other agencies have not followed suit.

Lessons for Donors

In the 1990s a number of large and small donors began to emphasize the importance of mainstreaming participation in their activities. Four donors— Germany's Gesellschaft für Technische Zusammenarbeit (GTZ), the United Kingdom's Department for International Development (DFID), the United States Agency for International Development (USAID), and the World Bank— agree that they need a more flexible approach to project design.[2] GTZ and DFID are working to make the logical framework more participatory, using participatory rural appraisal. But participatory rural appraisal applications are still too mechanical (Forster 1998). The current USAID discourse has assimilated catch phrases such as "listening to the customer," but La Voy's 1998 study of USAID's organizational change experience says little about methodological innovations at the field level.

New participatory methodologies are needed to secure project ownership of primary stakeholders. The principle of ownership makes little sense unless it extends to beneficiaries. Formal and informal networks of practitioners in participatory rural appraisal and their related methodologies now exist in dozens of countries—an important social capital base on which to draw.

Making Management Frameworks More Flexible

A central challenge for DFID, GTZ, USAID, and the World Bank is to adapt their management frameworks to meet the challenge of mainstreaming participation. At DFID, staff see the existing project cycle management framework as time-consuming, rigid, and too consultant-dependent to let local priorities influence program design effectively (INTRAC 1998). GTZ has been testing a more flexible approach, but wants to see more projects with an "open orientation" phase of up to three years for complex projects (Forster 1998). USAID's response has been to pilot a "strategic objective" approach with partners (La Voy 1998). Recent studies of the World Bank's efforts to mainstream participation revealed similar concerns. The Bank's internal reviews and the NGO Working Group on Participation in the Bank (1999) identified the need to improve feedback systems and make consultations with partners more systematic when designing country assistance strategies.

The four organizations agree: donors need longer and more systematic consultations with primary and secondary stakeholders. The challenge will be to identify and contact civil society organizations in each country that represent the weakest in society. It is also vital for the Bank to share process documentation and encourage partners to make their own contributions. Improvements in communications technology should make this easier.

Improving Collaboration among Institutions

DFID, USAID, GTZ, and the World Bank agree that increasing primary stakeholder participation cannot be achieved without improved coordination and collaboration among the players in the development field. Competition or mistrust among NGOs, or between NGOs and government, continues to impede scaling-up strategies (Fowler 1997). Dangers include the "autistic trend of [each donor] building participatory islands" (Forster 1998) and "consultation fatigue" among partners expected to engage different donors on the same subject. DFID's response is to focus on long-term sectoral investment programs involving several partners. USAID's New Partnerships Initiative is similar. GTZ sees the global trend toward decentralization as an opportunity for strengthening partnerships with local government, NGOs, and other actors in civil society.

Donors who work on their own often urge secondary and primary stakeholders to collaborate. This contradiction has tarnished the move to mainstream participation. Today's shifts toward globalization on the one hand and decentralization on the other require organizations to collaborate more effectively than ever before. The CDF can help make this a reality.

Building the Capacity of Different Stakeholders to Own and Share

More emphasis on human resource development, both within agencies and among partner organizations, can help staff work in more participatory ways. The current debate focuses on what training to use. GTZ and DFID point to staff dissatisfaction with formal courses, and call for alternative in-house training, such as temporary duty assignments, job swaps, shadowing, and distance learning.

Participatory rural appraisal training in donor organizations is most effective when seen as part of a broader strategy of organizational learning (Thompson 1995). USAID has had more than fifty participation forums to raise awareness among staff, but difficulties remain in achieving the internal organizational changes—in systems, procedures, and structures—needed to make customer focus a reality (La Voy 1998). Ideas at the World Bank include immersion training (arranging for Bank staff to spend time face to face with the poor) and using communications technologies. All four donors have said that mainstreaming participation requires better staff screening, new incentive systems, and more emphasis on personnel continuity.

Making Donors More Participatory from the Inside

Participants at an Institute for Development Studies workshop on Institutionalizing Participation (proceedings are summarized in Blackburn and Holland 1998, pp. 145–52) argued that innovative organizational changes could increase the flexibility of organizations supporting participatory projects on the ground. The notions of flexible accounting and downward accountability may be useful to the CDF.

The rationale for flexible accounting is to broaden the number of people entrusted to make budget decisions, making it easier to move money from one item to another and to roll unspent balances forward. This is considered necessary because participatory projects are evolutionary by definition: their spending priorities will shift over time. Just as customers increasingly define what firms produce, clients or potential beneficiaries must do the same for development agencies. No literature documenting specific cases of flexible accounting can be traced, but empirical experience is growing as development organizations grapple with the challenges of taking participation to scale. More research in this area could be useful to the CDF.

Finally, there is much talk of the need to move toward models of downward accountability, though there is little knowledge of how to put this into practice. The ever-widening applications of participatory monitoring and evaluation offer some clues.

Participatory Monitoring and Evaluation

Donor organizations are exploring new ways of measuring the impact of their work. How can results be tracked continuously over time? How can we know what works and what doesn't? How can a learning process be established to support strategic choices for improvement?

Conventionally, such questions have been answered through a monitoring and evaluation approach that involved outside experts measuring performance against preset indicators, often after a project or initiative was over. But recently, large organizations have been searching for ways to monitor that are continuous and oriented toward organizational improvement. A number of developments contribute to this shift:

- the increased emphasis on performance measurement, or management by results, in the U.S. Government Performance and Results Act of 1993;
- the shift within organizations, especially in the private sector, toward more flexible, learning-systems approaches;
- the surge of interest in participatory approaches, which involve people in the assessment process; and
- the pressure for greater accountability by donor agencies, especially at a time of scarce resources.

Participatory monitoring and evaluation is attracting interest from many quarters—it offers ways of assessing results and of learning from them that are more inclusive and more in tune with the aspirations of those directly affected and that allow development organizations to better focus on their goal of improving poor people's lives. By broadening involvement in identifying and analyzing results, a clearer picture can be gained of what is happening on the ground.

Participatory monitoring and evaluation builds ownership. It puts local stakeholders in charge, helps them develop skills, and demonstrates that their views count for assessing results and needs. It enables and supports partnership by involving all stakeholders. The principles of participatory monitoring and evaluation are:

- *Participation.* All stakeholders participate in all aspects of participatory monitoring and evaluation, including choosing indicators and analyzing data.
- *Negotiation.* Stakeholders negotiate what will be monitored and evaluated, how and when data will be collected and analyzed, what the data mean, and how findings will be shared and action taken.
- *Learning.* Participation and negotiation lead to collective learning, ownership, and investment in key findings by those most able to use the results for corrective action.
- *Flexibility.* Since the purpose of participatory monitoring and evaluation is improved learning for improved results, leading to ongoing change and adaptation, flexibility is essential. Blueprint approaches to evaluation, in which standard indicators are imposed and held constant to measure change over time, will do little to encourage a flexible, results-oriented learning approach (Estrella and Gaventa 1998).
- *Involvement of All Stakeholders.* When multiple stakeholders work together to develop indicators, they also clarify expectations and priorities, negotiate a more common framework, build ownership of outcomes, and ensure that the assessment reflects principles of partnership.

Examples include the process used by the InterAmerican Foundation to develop its Grassroots Development Framework, which involved consultations with hundreds of stakeholders to create a common framework that reflected the importance of tracking tangible and intangible indicators at micro, meso, and macro levels (Ritchey-Vance 1998; Abbot and Guijt 1998).

Indicators of success must track holistic goals, both tangible and intangible. Developing indicators for intangible concepts like ownership, partnership, inclusion, empowerment, and transparency is a difficult but not impossible task. When dealing with a holistic definition of development, it is important not to reduce goals to those measurable by traditional quantifiable means. Many times, qualitative approaches are based on observations and intuitive judgments based on field experience. At other times they are expressed in stories, anecdotes, or drawings by stakeholders. While these may not be rigorous or precise, they are critical to learning how to create a holistic assessment.

Developing a large-scale assessment involving multiple stakeholders can strengthen ownership, partnership, and a results-based orientation. But large-scale participatory monitoring and evaluation require skills and approaches to monitoring and evaluation that are not traditional:

- *Capacity building in indicator development*, monitoring, and negotiation for all stakeholders;
- *Joint indicator development* and the design of processes for gathering and sharing data openly that are built in from the beginning, not tacked on at the end;
- *Skills in group facilitation, negotiation, conflict resolution,* and participatory methods. Traditional evaluation departments often lack these skills and an understanding of why they are important. Reorienting donor agencies, government staff, and civil society organizations means changing attitudes and behaviors and learning new skills and approaches;
- *Support for high-level champions.* Because most evaluation professionals do not fully understand participatory approaches to monitoring and evaluation, and because involving stakeholders empowers them to demand transparency, insist on accountability, and raise critical questions, use of the approach may be opposed by people resistant to change. High-level champions may be needed who will support the new process and justify the need to address critical questions or uncomfortable findings (Gaventa, Creed, and Morrissey 1999).

Participatory monitoring and evaluation can strengthen accountability and transparency. Partnership and ownership cannot be sustained without clear information accessible to all parties. Take consultations on country assistance strategies. Failing to make results available to consultants has limited new partnerships (Tandon and Cordeiro 1998). In other cases, lack of transparency has led to strong grassroots movements, such as the Right to Information campaign in Rajasthan, India, to demand accountability locally (Jenkins and Goetz 1999). Outside citizen monitoring, like the report cards developed by the Public Affairs Center in Bangalore or by the NGO Working Group on the World Bank Flagship Participation programs, is an important mechanism for insuring greater accountability and transparency.

Creating Enabling Environments

While ownership should be built from the bottom, it can be strengthened from the top through interventions and policies that create enabling environments for participation (Gaventa and Robinson 1998). A growing body of research indicates that primary and secondary stakeholder participation can be maximized with the right enabling framework.

Enabling frameworks may range from protecting the rights to free speech, assembly, and association to legislation that gives legitimacy and power to the voices of poor people. In recent years we have seen the birth of government policies that promote participation of poor people through legislation or administrative decree. The widespread move toward more democratic decentralization has opened new spaces for grassroots participation to merge with state policy (Gaventa and Valderrama 1999).

The implications for the implementation of CDF are clear. Legislative frameworks can enable or disable partnership and ownership. Many rules and regulations weaken and discriminate against poor people. Others require or enable positive change (Box 4.1).

Both the Bolivia and the Andhra Pradesh examples in Box 4.1 show that interventions from the top must be combined with other elements:

- *Vigorous community-based organizations* that can take advantage of the space that is offered by institutional reform. If these do not exist, support must be provided for community organization and capacity building from below for change from above to be effective.
- *Government officials, mayors, and local councilors who are open to new ideas.* This kind of leadership encourages innovation. When leaders are not open to new ideas, training, capacity building, and leadership development programs are important for success.
- *A local political culture built on trust and information-sharing.* Training political and civil society leaders in participatory planning and budgeting methodologies will foster such a culture.

Holism and Coordination

The CDF, PRSP, and other integrative approaches seek to develop an enabling environment through a holistic approach, including greater coordination of actors and programs. But trying to take everything into account, especially in a top-down, center-outwards mode, might cause paralysis. Dangers with coordination became evident in approaches to integrated rural development in the 1970s: centralization, standardization, paralysis from more meetings and more communication, and turf wars over who coordinates at the country level (the World Bank, the United Nations, the government?). The result was more frustration and less effective development. Both holism and coordination need to be optimized, not maximized, and need to originate and operate at appropriate levels.

Holism is most natural at the very local level. The experiences of poor people are diverse, integrated, and not divided into programs and sectors. The "three Ds"—decentralization, democracy, and diversity—can create holism, reducing the need for coordination higher up (Chap. 5). Holism grounded in local realities, with coordination low in the system, can sharpen the relevance of national policy and reduce the needs for centralizing coordination at the national level.

Holistic partnership and coordination can thus be achieved in the district,

Box 4.1
Creating Environments for Partnership

The Andhra Pradesh Farmers' Management of Irrigation Systems Act
The 1970s and 1980s saw a series of initiatives to improve canal irrigation management throughout the world (Chambers 1988). In Andhra Pradesh learning was enhanced by the continuity in leadership of a committed champion, Sayed Hashim Ali, secretary, command area development for close to a decade. Ali supported such innovations as participatory committees of farmers at the lower levels of large irrigation systems (see, for example, Ali 1982). But because they lacked statutory power, these committees were never strong and gradually dissolved. Ali's allies in government, however, learned quite a bit. In the late 1990s populist Chief Minister Chandrababu Naidu provided a new, participation-friendly environment.

This led to the supervised election of over 10,000 water users' committees for more than 4 million hectares of irrigated land. Thus, an enabling environment has been created with the potential to transform the equity and efficiency of canal irrigation. Early information shows that larger areas are already being irrigated, and more water is passing to the deprived tailends of the systems.

The Bolivian Law of Popular Participation
The Bolivian Law of Popular Participation passed in 1994 is another interesting example of how to combine decentralization and participation to promote local ownership of development. The law empowers registered community-based organizations in both rural and urban municipalities to participate in making five-year municipal development plans and implementing local development projects. Municipal participatory planning is now being applied across the country (Booth et al. 1997).

Citizen participation in local governance has been enhanced by vigilance committees of five to eight elected community-based organization leaders who act as watchdogs to ensure that community-level project priorities are reflected in municipal investment decisions. The committees can also request independent audits of municipal governments.

Through these initiatives, Bolivia has created legal and methodological frameworks that allow community-based organizations to directly influence the investment decisions of municipal councils. But this influence does not translate into ownership. Vigilance committee members are unpaid and easily co-opted—and silenced—by the mayor. Despite the participatory rhetoric, key decisions are still made behind closed doors. Creating the climate of trust needed for effective popular ownership will take time.

where initiatives from the top and actions from the bottom intersect. The Uganda Participatory Poverty Assessment Program is feeding directly into the district level and informing national and sectoral policies, showing how the holism of open-ended participatory analysis can feed in higher up. In Tanzania, the government, Danida, the Royal Netherlands Embassy, the SNV–Netherlands Development Organization, Irish Aid, Finland, and the World Bank are supporting district programs. As illustrated by the Rural Integrated Project Support Program, there has been substantial learning and improvement. At the same time, the new donor focus on sectoral programs, and now the CDF, could endanger support for district-level partnerships in what are already substantially holistic programs, and where recent learning and improvements have been accelerating.

Conclusion

The history of mainstreaming and scaling up participation in development offers many lessons and insights for strengthening partnership and ownership through the CDF and the PRSP.

Strengthening ownership requires institutional change at all levels, not only among primary stakeholders. NGOs, governments, donors, and the World Bank—as the champion of this approach—will need to change how they behave and operate. But this won't be easy. The Bank has to lend large sums quickly, and its incentive system remains linked to the scale and speed of disbursement rather than the quality of the recipient country's partnerships or ownership. Also, the Bank is more lender than grantor. Loans, including International Development Association credits, lead to debts that eventually have to be repaid. This limits the capacity and incentives to take the risks that lead to institutional learning and change. And as perhaps the most powerful partner in these projects, the Bank finds it difficult to learn from others. If the Bank demonstrates its willingness to change and share power and ownership, the rest will follow.

Large-scale consultations with the poor are feasible and helpful. The history of participatory poverty assessments show us the importance of:

- taking time in the process, including a wide range of civil society actors, and feeding back the results of consultations to all parties;
- involving government, especially key ministries of finance and planning, to ensure follow-up and use of results;
- linking these consultations to policy formation and change, including the development of the country assistance strategies;
- linking these consultations to capacity building, trust building, and attitude and behavior change among stakeholders that may continue after the formal consultation.

Institutional change enables donor staff and secondary stakeholders to develop more participatory behaviors and approaches. While building partnership and ownership through consultation with primary and other stakeholders is necessary, it is not sufficient to ensure participation over time. This requires attitude and behavior change at all levels, especially for Bank staff. Instituting a learning process approach is also key, and takes flexibility and long-term commitment. Key champions for the process can form alliances with other champions to promote effective change.

Donors must change too. They should be more flexible in designing and managing projects. They should collaborate and coordinate better with other institutions. And they should be more innovative in their internal organization—using flexible accounting, moderating pressures to disburse large sums quickly, and strengthening mechanisms of downward accountability and consultation. Training, recruitment, and incentives can be changed to encourage attitudes and behaviors that foster ownership and partnership.

Participatory monitoring and evaluation can build ownership and partnership—when all stakeholders help develop indicators of success, and when this cooperation in gathering and sharing information is built in from the beginning, not tacked on at the end. Capacity building for participatory monitoring and evaluation is needed for all stakeholders, as is strong support for critical champions who can help articulate the value of this new approach. Since the CDF and PRSP are proposing a holistic framework, indicators also need to be able to track holistic goals, both tangible and intangible.

Participatory monitoring and evaluation may also strengthen accountability and transparency, especially as new methods of downward accountability are linked with traditional methods for upward accountability.

Interventions from above can help create an enabling environment for participation. These interventions work best when there are vigorous community-based organizations to take advantage of the space offered through institutional reform; when government officials, mayors, and local councilors are open to change and innovation; and where there is a local political culture built on trust and information-sharing.

Holism and coordination are the means—not the ends—of poverty reduction. If greater coordination creates more meetings, more power struggles, and more planning, countries will see less participation. The key is to recognize the diverse, yet holistic, realities and priorities of poor people, enable them to analyze and express them, and then reflect them in policy and practice, with local coordination.

None of these lessons offers an instant solution. All entail long-term commitment. And all can be achieved through champions and alliances sustained by continuous support. There is much experience and much to learn—a challenge for all the new frameworks is to recognize this ignorance as an opportunity to learn, change, and improve.

Notes

1. Participatory rural appraisal has been described as a family of approaches, methods, and behaviors that enable poor people to express and analyze the realities of their lives and to plan, monitor, and evaluate their actions (Chambers 1994). It is based on the ideas that local people have the knowledge and ability to conduct their own development and that those who facilitate rural appraisals must pay attention to how they behave when interacting with local people.
2. At a conference at the World Bank on Mainstreaming and Up-Scaling Primary Participation in November 1998, USAID, DFID, GTZ, and the World Bank presented papers reflecting on their institutional experiences in this regard. These unpublished papers form the basis of the findings and discussion in this section.

References

Abbot, J., and I. Guijt. 1998. "Changing Views on Change: Participatory Approaches to Monitoring the Environment." SARL Discussion Paper 2. London: International Institute for Environment and Development.

Ali, Syed Hashim. 1982. *Report of the Commission for Irrigation Utilization.* Hyderabad: Government of Andhra Pradesh.

Aspen Institute. 1996. *Measuring Community Capacity Building: A Workbook-in-Progress for Rural Communities.* Rural Economic Program: The Aspen Institute.

Attwood, H., and J. May. 1998. "Kicking Down Doors and Lighting Fires: The South African Participatory Poverty Assessment." In *Whose Voice? Participatory Research and Policy Change.* London: IT Publications.

Aycrigg, M. 1998. "Participation and the World Bank: Successes, Constraints, and Responses: Draft for Discussion." World Bank Social Development Paper No.29. Washington, D.C.: World Bank.

Bagadion, B., and F. Korten. 1991. "Developing Irrigators' Organizations: A Learning Process Approach." In Cernea, Michael M., ed, *Putting People First: Sociological Variables in Rural Development*, 2nd ed. Oxford, UK: Oxford University Press for the World Bank.

Blackburn, J., and C. De Toma. 1998. "Scaling-down as the Key to Scaling-up? The Role of Participatory Municipal Planning in Bolivia's Law of Popular Participation." In Blackburn, J. and J. Holland, eds. *Who Changes? Institutionalizing Participation in Development.* London: IT Publications.

Blackburn, J., and J. Holland, eds. 1998. *Who Changes? Institutionalizing Participation in Development.* London: IT Publications.

80   Making Development Work

Booth, D., et al. 1997. *Popular Participation: Democratizing the State in Rural Bolivia*. Report to SIDA, commissioned through Development Studies Unit, Depart-
ment of Social Anthropology, Stockholm University. Stockholm: SIDA.
————. 1998. Participation and Combined Methods in African Poverty Assessment:
Renewing the Agenda. London: DFID.
Brocklesby, M.A., and J. Holland. 1998. *Participatory Poverty Assessments and Public Services: Key Messages From the Poor*. London: DFID.
Cernea, Michael M., ed. 1991. *Putting People First: Sociological Variables in Rural
Development*. 2nd ed. Oxford, UK: Oxford University Press for the World Bank
Chambers, Robert. 1974. *Managing Rural Development: Ideas and Experience from
East Africa*. Uppsala, Sweden: Scandinavian Institute of African Studies.
————. 1988. *Managing Canal Irrigation: Practical Analysis from South Asia*. Ox-
ford and IBH, New Delhi, and Cambridge, U.K.: Cambridge University Press.
————. 1997. *Whose Reality Counts? Putting the First Last*. London: IT Publica-
tions.
Dogbe, T. 1998. "The One Who Rides the Donkey Does Not Know the Ground is
Hot: CEDEP's Involvement in the Ghana Participatory Poverty Assessment." In
Whose Voice? Participatory Research and Policy Change. London: IT Publications.
Estrella, M., and J. Gaventa. 1998. "Who Counts Reality? Participatory Monitoring
and Evaluation: A Literature Review." IDS Working Paper No.70. Brighton, U.K.:
Institute for Development Studies.
Forster, R. 1998. GTZ's Experience with Mainstreaming Primary Stakeholder Partici-
pation." International Conference on Mainstreaming and Up-Scaling of Primary
Stakeholder Participation—Lessons Learned and Ways Forward. Washington, Nov.
19–20, 1998.
Fowler, A. 1997. *Striking a Balance*. London: INTRAC-Earthscan.
Freling, D. 1998. *Paths for Change: Experiences in Participation and Democratiza-
tion in Lindi and Mtwara Regions, Tanzania*. RIPS Program Phase II. Helsinki:
Finnagro.
Gaventa, J. 1998. "The Scaling Up and Institutionalization of P.R.A: Lessons and
Challenges." In Blackburn, J. and J. Holland, eds., *Who Changes? Institutionaliz-
ing Participation in Development*. London: IT Publications.
Gaventa, J., V. Creed, and J. Morrissey. 1998. "Scaling Up: Participatory Monitoring
and Evaluation of a Federal Empowerment Program." In E. Whitmore, ed., *Un-
derstanding and Practicing Participatory Evaluation*. San Francisco, CA: Jossey
Bass.
Gaventa, J., and M. Robinson. 1998. "Influence from Below and Space from Above:
Non-elite Action and Pro-poor Policies." Paper presented at Conference on "What
Can be Done About Poverty?" June 1998. Sussex, U.K.: Institute for Develop-
ment Studies.
Gaventa, J., and C. Valderrama. 1999. "Participation, Citizenship, and Local Gover-
nance." Background note prepared for workshop on Strengthening Participation in
Local Governance, IDS, June 21–24, 1999. Sussex, U.K.: Institute for Develop-
ment Studies.
Hanmer L., G. Pyatt, and H. White. 1996. *Poverty in Sub-Saharan Africa: What Can
We Learn from the World Bank's Poverty Assessments?* The Hague: Institute of
Social Studies.
Hart, M. 1995. *Guide to Sustainable Community Indicators*. Ipswich, MA: QLF/
Atlantic Center for the Environment.
Holland, J., and J. Blackburn, eds. 1998. *Whose Voice? Participatory Research and
Policy Change*. London, U.K.: Intermediate Publications Limited.

INTRAC. 1998. The Participatory Approaches Learning Study (PALS): Executive Summary and Recommendations. Report commissioned by the Social Development Division of the UK Department for International Development, November 1998.

Institute for Development Studies. 1998. *Participatory Monitoring and Evaluation: Learning from Change.* IDS Policy Briefing Issue 12. Brighton: Institute for Development Studies.

Jenkins, R., and A.M. Goetz. 1999. "Accounts and Accountability: Theoretical Implications of the Right-to Information Movement in India." Workshop on Strengthening Participation in Local Governance. June 21–24, 1999. Sussex, UK: Institute for Development Studies.

Kane, E., Bruce, L., and M. O'Reilly de Brun. 1998. "Designing the Future Together: P.R.A and Education Policy in The Gambia." In *Whose Voice? Participatory Research and Policy Change.* London, U.K.: IT Publications.

Korten, D. 1980. "Community Organization and Rural Development: A Learning Process Approach." *Public Administration Review* 40, No. 5: pp. 480–511.

———. 1988. "From Bureaucratic to Strategic Organization." In Korten, F.F. and R.Y. Siy, Jr., eds., *Transforming a Bureaucracy: The Experience of the Philippine National Irrigation Administration.* West Hartford, CT: Kumarian Press.

Korten, F.F., and R.Y. Siy, Jr. 1988. *Transforming a Bureaucracy: The Experience of the Philippine National Irrigation Administration.* West Hartford, CT: Kumarian Press.

Kumar, Somesh, ed. 1996. "Attitude and Behaviour Change: ABC of Participatory Rural Appraisal." Report of a South-South Workshop. Bangalore, India: Action Aid and Madurai, India: SPEECH.

La Voy, D. 1998. "Engaging 'Customer' Participation: USAID's Organizational Change Experience. Contribution to the International Conference on Mainstreaming and Up-Scaling of Primary Stakeholder Participation—Lessons Learned and Ways Forward," Washington, Nov. 19–20.

Leonard, David. 1991. *African Successes: Four Public Managers of Kenyan Rural Development.* Berkeley: University of California Press.

Long, C. 1999. *Participation in Development: The Way Forward.* Draft. Boston, MA: Institute for Development Research.

Mathur, Yaduvendra. 1998. Proceedings of the Workshop on Attitude and Behaviour Change in Participatory Processes, August 24–28, 1988, National Society for Promotion of Development Administration, Research and Training, LBSNAA, Mussoorie, India

May, J. 1998. *Experience and Perceptions of Poverty in South Africa.* Durban: Participatory Rural Appraisal Publishing.

Milimo, J., A. Norton, and D. Owen. 1998. "The Impact of P.R.A Approaches and Methods on Policy and Practice: the Zambian Participatory Poverty Assessment." In *Whose Voice? Participatory Research and Policy Change.* London, U.K.: IT Publications.

Mukherjee, N. 1998. "The Rush to Scale: Lessons Being Learnt in Indonesia." In Blackburn, J. and J. Holland, eds. *Who Changes? Institutionalizing Participation in Development.* London: IT Publications.

Narayan, D. 1993. *Participatory Evaluation Tools for Managing Change in Water and Sanitation.* Washington, D.C.: World Bank.

New Economics Foundation. 1998. *Communities Count! A Step by Step Guide to Community Sustainability Indicators.* London, U.K.: New Economics Foundation.

NGO Working Group on the World Bank. 1999. CDF Statement. Draft. Washington, D.C.

Norton, A., and T. Stephens 1995. *Participation in Poverty Assessments*. Environment Department Papers, Participation Series. Social Policy and Resettlement Division, Washington, D.C.: World Bank.

Osuga, B. 1998. "Towards Community-sensitive Policy: Influencing the Uganda National Health Plan." In *Whose Voice? Participatory Research and Policy Change*. London, U.K.: IT Publications.

Owen, D. 1998. "Whose Participatory Poverty Assessment Is This? Lessons Learned from the Mozambique Participatory Poverty Assessment" In *Whose Voice? Participatory Research and Policy Change*. London, U.K.: IT Publications.

Pratt, G., M. Pimbert, and V. Bainbridge. 1998. Transforming Bureaucracies: Institutionalizing Participatory Approaches and Processes for Natural Resource Management—An Annotated Bibliography. Draft. Sussex: Institute for Development Studies and IIED.

Ritchey-Vance, M. 1998. "Widening the Lens on Impact Assessment: the Inter-American Foundation and its Grassroots Development Framework." J. Blauert and S. Zadek, eds., *Mediating Sustainable Development: Growing Policy from the Grassroots*. London, U.K.: Kumarian Press.

Robb, C. 1999. *Can the Poor Influence Policy?* Participatory Poverty Assessments in the Developing World. Washington, D.C.: World Bank.

Shepherd, A. 1998. "Participatory Environmental Management: Contradiction of Process, Project and Bureaucracy in the Himalayan Foothills." In Blackburn J. and J. Holland, eds., *Who Changes? Institutionalizing Participation in Development*. London, U.K.: IT Publications.

Shinyanga Human Development Report Project. 1998. *Participatory Poverty Assessment, Shinyanga Region, Tanzania*. New York: UNDP/SHDRP.

Society for Participatory Research in Asia (PRIA). 1998. "Lessons Learned and Ways Forward." Recommendations Presented at the Concluding Session of the International Conference on Participation of Primary Stakeholders, November 20, 1998.

Stiefel, M., and M. Wolfe. 1994. *A Voice for the Excluded. Popular Participation: Utopia or Necessity?* London, U.K.: Zed Books Ltd. and UNRISD.

Tandon, R. and A. Cordeiro 1998. "Participation of Primary Stakeholders in World Bank's Project and Policy Work: Emerging Lessons." Contribution to the International Conference on "Mainstreaming and Up-Scaling of Primary Stakeholder Participation—Lessons Learned and Ways Forward." Washington, D.C., Nov 19–20.

Thompson, J. 1995. "Participatory Approaches in Government Bureaucracies: Facilitating the Process of Institutional Change." In *World Development*, Vol. 15, No. 4.

———. 1998. "Participatory Approaches in Government Bureaucracies: Facilitating Institutional Change" in Blackburn, J. and J. Holland, eds., *Who Changes? Institutionalizing Participation in Development*. London, U.K.: IT Publications.

UNDP/PromPT. 1996. Report on Human Development in Bangladesh, Part 3: Poor People's Perspectives. Dhaka: United Nations Development Program.

Uphoff, N. 1992. Learning from Gal Oya: Possibilities for Participatory Development and Post-Newtonian Social Science. Ithaca, NY: Cornell University Press.

Uphoff, N., et al. 1998. *Reasons for Success: Learning from Instructive Experiences in Rural Development*. London, U.K.: Kumarian Press.

World Bank. 1994. The World Bank and Participation. Washington, D.C.

5

Democratic Decentralization

Richard Crook and *James Manor*

Since the mid-1980s, more than sixty governments, mainly in developing countries, have experimented with some form of decentralization.[1] Democratic decentralization can be an extremely useful part of the enabling environment, facilitating many of the goals of the Comprehensive Development Framework (CDF) and Poverty Reduction Strategy Papers (PRSPs).

In what follows, we consider the main elements of the CDF, discussing in each case what current research tells us about the utility and limitations of democratic decentralization. We first examine the impact of democratic decentralization on the sense of ownership of development programs by governments and citizens. Then we examine the contributions of decentralization to holistic development and local partnerships. Next, we assess and look briefly at its utility to several structural, social, human, and other development concerns and the conflicting evidence on the contribution of decentralization to financial capacity and growth. Finally, we sum up the potential results from decentralization and make some suggestions for donors to encourage potential decentralizers and to avoid the unintended consequences of grand top-down projects.

For democratic decentralization to work well, elected bodies at lower levels must have substantial powers and resources, and strong accountability mechanisms must be created to hold bureaucrats accountable to elected representatives and elected representatives accountable to citizens. Several other features are helpful but not essential to effective democratic decentralization: a free press, multiparty systems, a lively civil society, experience with democratic politics, and respect for laws and formal rules. It helps if wealth and property are widely and relatively equitably shared and if a middle class exists but does not exercise unyielding hegemony over poorer groups. It also helps if the region is free of severe social conflict and if there is effective government administration.

Our principal conclusion is that democratic decentralization has considerable potential in facilitating many of the goals of the CDF and the PRSPs. Given time, decentralization can enhance ownership by government and citizens of development programs, contribute to local coordination, speed up decisionmaking, enliven civil society, build social capital, encourage partnerships between local government and the private sector, and promote transparency and accountability. Decentralization can also facilitate the adaptation of national programs to local needs, improve citizen's understanding of these programs, and help scale up and replicate successful projects.

But decentralization is also susceptible to elite capture, which means benefits could get diverted from the people who need them most. When prejudices against disadvantaged groups are stronger at lower levels in political systems than at higher, democratic decentralization can make it more difficult to tackle poverty. Recent experiments with decentralization have revealed no evidence that decentralization would encourage long-term development perspectives or enhance the state's financial capacity.

Decentralization and Ownership

A central concern of the CDF is the need to ensure country ownership of reforms and development policies. This implies (at least) two things: ownership by governments and ownership by people. What does democratic decentralization have to offer here?

Ownership by Governments

Can governments that experiment with democratic decentralization acquire a sense of ownership over decentralized systems? The answer is yes— and no.

Nearly all governments that have started to decentralize have done so by choice, not because of pressure from international agencies. In fact, most international agencies lagged behind a number of developing country governments in recognizing the benefits of decentralization. Since those governments initiated their decentralization—mostly using models from other developing countries—they tend to feel they own it.

In almost all decentralizing governments, however, many high-level politicians and bureaucrats resent their loss of powers and resources. Some come around when they see that decentralization enhances government legitimacy;

others do not. Thus, not everyone in the upper levels of a decentralizing government feels a sense of ownership. Some even try to regain their powers and resources—and they sometimes succeed.

Over time, if decentralized systems are allowed to survive with most of their powers intact, a more pervasive sense of ownership may develop. Evidence shows that bureaucrats who have worked at lower levels in such systems often become sympathetic to them after initial hesitancy. They do so because they see that such systems vastly increase the flow of information from below to civil servants (thereby empowering them) because they enhance the responsiveness and effectiveness of government, and because they yield many other benefits. When such bureaucrats move to higher-level posts as the years pass—and when politicians who began their careers in decentralized institutions attain higher-level office—a larger portion of the political elite acquires a sense of ownership over decentralized systems. These people also bring an enthusiasm for the more consensual, transparent, and responsive policy processes and governance modes that tend to develop in decentralized systems. Such systems are breeding grounds for the perspectives the CDF seeks to foster (Kasfir 1993; Mawhood 1993).

Ownership by People

When democratic decentralization works well, people at lower levels of government acquire a sense of ownership of development projects. Elected authorities are able to make decisions that address local needs long overlooked by development programs designed in capital cities. As local residents come to identify with local development projects, they tend to maintain, repair, and renew them more assiduously. Such enhanced maintenance makes development more sustainable.

Decentralization can also foster popular ownership of programs originating higher in the political system. When elected decentralized institutions are given a role in implementing such programs, elected representatives must explain to their constituents why the programs make sense. Explanations by representatives whom ordinary people know, elected, and trust can seem more credible than explanations by bureaucrats. Since those representatives understand the views and experiences of their constituents, they are better able to explain the need for such programs in terms that ordinary citizens can grasp and accept.

In South Asia, elected members of local and intermediate-level councils (especially women members) can explain the benefits of programs for prenatal and postnatal care and the need for mothers to bring their children to health centers for inoculations. The result is a clear increase in the use of such programs, resulting in fewer illnesses and longer lives. That inspires greater trust in, and a sense of popular ownership of, health programs and other government programs more generally.

But elected members of decentralized councils in many countries prefer small-scale building projects (school construction, road repair) to service delivery. To prevent funds from being diverted from service provision to building projects, resources should be earmarked for service delivery. Since small-scale building projects are often popular—because they address needs that have long been ignored by large-scale projects (like dams or big hospitals) favored by higher-level officials—they inspire greater confidence in and ownership of government institutions.

Small local projects can also help convince ordinary citizens that there is some logic in government service delivery programs. Even when decentralized systems are new and underresourced, they can ease popular cynicism toward government. In Mozambique, for example, elected municipal councils achieved more (in construction projects and service delivery) within a few months of their creation than the central government had achieved over the previous two decades. Despite their imperfections and limited funding, the councils were seen by local residents as a major improvement.[1]

Civil Society and Ownership

Civil society comprises organizations of a voluntary character that enjoy some autonomy from the state. In developing countries, civil society includes national associations and large nongovernmental organizations (NGOs) as well as small grassroots associations and everything in between.

In the context of the CDF, several dilemmas arise about civil society. At and just above the local level, civil society is often largely excluded from interactions with government, its voice absent from political and policy processes. This prevents civil society from enhancing the effectiveness of government programs, from checking malfeasance and misjudgments in program implementation, and from evaluating programs. Moreover, it can impede the development, within civil society, of a sense of ownership of government development policies and projects. Making matters worse, civil society is also often somewhat disorganized and conflict-ridden. And civil society organizations are less than fully accountable to their members and to the people whom they claim to serve.

Although democratic decentralization cannot solve these problems, it can diminish them. When significant powers and resources are devolved to lower levels, especially to elected bodies at or near the village level, existing associations become more active and engage more with government agents and institutions. And new associations, sometimes among disadvantaged social groups, are created. So if strengthening civil society at the grassroots level is an important element of the CDF, democratic decentralization can have a substantial impact.

When elected bodies near the grassroots level acquire influence, civil society organizations often find it easier to influence their decisions. Civil society organizations sometimes have members elected to such bodies. Even when that does not occur, they contact and lobby elected representatives and bureaucrats more often and usually more effectively. But if elected bodies are largely controlled by elites, as often happens, associations representing disadvantaged people often fail to gain.[2]

With greater influence comes a greater sense of ownership of development policies and projects. Civil society organizations can make government projects more effective by ensuring that they are appropriate for local conditions and local preferences. As decentralization renders politics more transparent and open, associations can more easily discern and call attention to malpractices and misjudgments.

Decentralization usually does not make civil society less disorganized, but it enables civil society organizations to exercise their newfound influence using the more ordered, focused processes that prevail in elected bodies. Although democratization at lower levels often creates conflict as candidates compete for elective office, it moderates this conflict with democratic processes like elections and council proceedings. Although democratic decentralization does not make civil society organizations more accountable, it creates opportunities for them to exercise influence in elected bodies that are accountable to the electorate. This fosters a sense of ownership of government projects and even of government institutions (Gibson and Hanson 1996).

Another benefit is that democratic decentralization can ease bottlenecks and delays at intermediate and local levels. When an elected council has the authority to make decisions and commit funds in particular policy areas, it need not seek approval from the capital city. This can (often greatly) accelerate the speed of government responses to urgent problems.

Holistic Development

Holistic development requires greater coordination, resonance, and mutual reinforcement among line ministries and their policies and programs. Democratic decentralization best supports holistic development when powers and resources are devolved to elected bodies at intermediate levels—to districts, counties, and the like. Decentralization to the local level seldom fosters holistic development because villages and towns lack elected councils. Such councils can exercise influence over an array of reasonably well-staffed line ministry offices found at the intermediate level. If the work of these offices can be more thoroughly integrated and coordinated, development will be more holistic.

Giving elected councils influence or control over line ministry personnel at intermediate levels leads to greater coordination. Prior to democratic decentralization, individual senior bureaucrats usually supervised these personnel in isolation. Empowering elected councils makes officials in line ministries accountable not only to their superiors in capital cities, but also to council leaders.

Council leaders often understand that improving the design and implementation of development projects requires guidance from officials from a variety of government departments. This understanding, and council leaders' habit of insisting that officials from all line ministries attend council meetings, mean that greater coordination among government departments is another result of democratic decentralization. In Bangladesh in the late 1980s, discussions of work on a minor irrigation canal involved not only the chief engineer and an irrigation department official, but also officials specializing in fisheries, agriculture, and forestry. Bureaucrats found this collaboration both annoying because it intruded on their autonomy, and satisfying, because it allowed them to influence things beyond their narrow specialization and because it led to better development projects (Crook and Manor 1998, chap. 3).

Local Partnerships

The CDF seeks to foster partnerships that link the public sector, the private sector, and civil society. Democratic decentralization holds considerable promise for partnerships and synergy between institutions and agents of government on the one hand, and civil society and grassroots communities on the other. It can also contribute to partnerships between the public and private sectors.

Elected members of decentralized councils are often more open than bureaucrats to partnerships with (usually small-time) contractors. This usually implies partnerships for small-scale building projects, which decentralized authorities favor. But it also implies, to a lesser degree, contracting out service delivery to private firms.

Bureaucrats who have held a monopoly or near monopoly on construction projects and service delivery are naturally reluctant to give up their control. By contrast, elected members of decentralized bodies are often small-scale entrepreneurs or are closely linked to such entrepreneurs, and are therefore unconcerned when monopolies topple. Indeed, they are often eager to give projects to contractors. At the same time, these elected representatives often award contracts for construction projects or service delivery to friends and relatives—or even to themselves, even where this is illegal—and fail to closely monitor how funds are used.

When opposition parties are represented on decentralized councils, they can provide a check on such cronyism by insisting that contracts be awarded only when it saves money and enhances performance. But they are not always successful. Over time, these parties will become better informed and better able to anticipate and combat cronyism. Thus, decentralization should eventually help foster healthy partnerships with the private sector.

The contributions of elected, decentralized bodies to partnerships with the private sector will always be small. This is true because such bodies have small budgets and concern themselves with modest (though locally important) projects. A larger, cumulative effect on private sector partnerships can occur when associations of local bodies take collective action to develop contracts with private firms, or when higher-level ministries foster links among local bodies to develop links to the private sector. The World Bank might consider encouraging both of these tendencies to enhance decentralization's impact.

Structural Concerns

Democratic decentralization can also support several of the social and structural concerns identified in the CDF and the new emerging consensus on development: transparency, openness, accountability, probity, social programs, and social capital (Chap. 1).

Transparency

Democratic decentralization can make government processes more visible and intelligible to ordinary people. When decisions are made at or near the local level, within elected bodies whose proceedings are often publicized and always known to elected representatives, it is far easier for ordinary citizens to find out about them. Elected representatives can also explain these decisions in terms that citizens understand.

Sometimes, however, a paradox emerges when transparency is enhanced in these ways. Ordinary people may consider the newly visible proceedings of government institutions as less healthy than those that existed before— even when that is not true. For example, in Karnataka, India, democratic decentralization in the late 1980s reduced the amount of money diverted by powerful people. But since citizens were now aware of these comparatively modest rake-offs, they concluded that corruption had increased as a result of decentralization. Thus, transparency can be a mixed blessing.

Openness

Democratic decentralization tends to produce systems that are more open— that is, they are more transparent and easier for individuals and groups at local and supralocal levels to access and influence. This is especially the case when the previous system was not democratic. Instead of a single national legislator or governor for a large region, citizens can approach a large number of elected members of local or intermediate-level bodies. They also learn that elected representatives have new leverage over bureaucrats. Citizens thus tend to contact and lobby elected representatives, as well as bureaucrats, more often. This tendency, and that of democratic bodies at lower levels to become more responsive, makes systems more open than before democratic decentralization.

Probity

In most places where democratic decentralization has been tried, corruption has not decreased. But evidence suggests that corruption might decrease if decentralized systems survive. Prior to decentralization in Karnataka, the total amount of development funds available in a given year in a subdistrict was known only to five or six people at that level. These people would meet behind closed doors to rake off and divide among themselves a hefty percentage of the funds, then present the rest to the public as the annual budget.

Once decentralized bodies were established near the local level, hundreds of elected representatives learned the true amount of development funds, making major theft impossible. Although members of decentralized bodies engaged in profiteering from the funds, the new system's transparency meant they could only divert small amounts. Although the number of thefts increased (as it always does in decentralized systems), the amount being stolen declined substantially (Crook and Manor 1998, Chap. 3). If decentralized systems survive and take root, such changes could eventually take place more widely.

Accountability

Democratic decentralization also tends strongly to foster more accountable government. Elected decision-makers are closer to the citizens who elect them, and often live locally. Thus, they face greater pressure than higher-level officials to govern according to their constituents' wishes. They worry about reelection in a few years, and they receive more direct indications of discontent between elections.

Bureaucrats operating in field offices of line ministries also feel greater pressure because elected representatives are now closer and more powerful. Citizens quickly discern this, and apply greater pressure on bureaucrats through elected representatives. Thus, despite difficulties in creating and sustaining accountability mechanisms, systems can become more accountable under democratic decentralization.

The devolution of responsibility for managing public finances can enhance accountability. But it requires a system that can sustain effective mechanisms of institutional and public accountability. Whether decentralized government can provide this depends on the political context. It matters little whether a decentralized system is funded mainly by local revenues or by central transfers if accountability mechanisms are ineffective and local political authorities are simply extensions of centrally run patronage networks.

Because the local revenue base is generally inadequate or inaccessible, most decentralized governments in developing countries receive the majority of their funding through intergovernmental transfers from central government. Transfers have economic and administrative costs, particularly since most central governments doubt (with some justification) the capacity of local authorities to manage finances, and are thus reluctant to entrust them with transferred funds or to give them authority over line ministry budgets (Bahl and Linn 1994). But concerns about spatial equalization and pursuit of social and economic policy goals (as well as political considerations) mean that most governments have adopted one or more of three types of funding: block grants from a guaranteed share of national public revenue, earmarked funds for specific delegated functions or programs, and incentive or matching funds (known as social funds in Latin America) that aim to respond to local proposals. These three kinds of central funding transfers have different implications for the effectiveness and probity of public financial management, and for the effects of decentralization in such areas as transparency, accountability, social equity, and human development.

Earmarked funds and, to a lesser extent, block grants can deliver effective control to local governments (unless there are political arguments about whether the transfer can meet the actual costs of the function). But both types of transfers require a well-resourced and effective deconcentrated administration (as in India or Indonesia).

Although block grants can be costly if they involve complex distribution and equalization formulas and monitoring and auditing mechanisms, they are essential. Central grant funding for many decentralized systems has been so generous and so subject to political patronage that the whole reform has been undermined by corruption, lack of accountability, and often lack of capacity to handle the funds (as in Bangladesh, Egypt, and Nigeria).

The francophone unified tax and payment system, centrally monitored by a prefectoral administration, seems to reduce corruption and maintain administrative efficiency and has recently been adopted in some Latin American countries (notably Chile). The central bureaucracies also provide technical support, but local authorities are not involved in mixed supervision of these agencies. The main drawbacks are heavy administrative costs, bureaucratic delay, and lack of local autonomy.

Demand-driven social funds and matching grant systems increase local autonomy and capacity but tend to create problems of waste and formal fulfillment of accounting requirements that hide inefficient or nontransparent practices. Mexico's PRONASOL fund gave rise to the infamous "basketball court syndrome," in which the need to show that funds had been spent on something before the end of the year, combined with the desire of local politicians to provide something electorally popular, produced thousands of new basketball courts throughout the country (Fox 1995).

Even more difficult to control is funding with increasingly large inputs from external funders—official external aid, NGO grants, and loans—often by default when national government funds have dried up. In some countries (Bangladesh, The Gambia, Mozambique, Nepal, Uganda), external money is virtually the only source of local development funding. Waste, idiosyncratic and isolated projects, regional or local distortions, and lack of ownership are all possible outcomes of this trend unless strong mechanisms of central control and coordination are introduced.

Whatever method or combination of methods is adopted, decentralized government involves considerable extra costs. Larger numbers of smaller authorities require more—and more high-level—staff, and more complex mechanisms of coordination and control. Decentralization requires considerable spending on local administrative infrastructures and more monitoring and assistance unless local systems have full autonomy and accountability for disbursing centrally granted funds.

Social and Human Concerns

Democratic decentralization offers both promise and difficulties for social and human concerns, especially for safety nets for poorer groups (Fabian and Straussman 1994).

Social Programs

Several difficulties stand out for social programs:

- Elites may capture elected decentralized authorities and deal ungenerously with poor people.
- Decentralized bodies charged with selecting beneficiaries of programs aimed at the neediest may choose only people who are well connected politically.
- Decentralized bodies may divert funds from services (including safety net programs) to construction projects. These last two problems exist mainly in rural areas (Dillinger 1994).

And what of the promise? Many systems require elected representatives to consult entire local populations when selecting beneficiaries. Representatives often avoid doing so, even though that is usually illegal. But in time, local people (including poorer groups) will become more organized, assertive, and politically aware and thus able to ensure that benefits reach the right recipients, and that safety net programs do not lose funds to construction projects. Local people can also play a role—as elected decentralized councils already do—in adapting social programs to local conditions.

Democratic decentralization can enhance the creative impact of programs in education, health, and water and natural resource management by making them more responsive to the conditions and needs of people in local areas, and by integrating local knowledge and local arrangements for managing resources into government programs (Narayan 1994). It can also empower local residents to tackle such problems as absenteeism of local school teachers and professionals in local health centers.

Social Capital

If violence and social unrest in an area are severe, it is difficult to make democratic decentralization work. But where unrest is caused by anger over the under-representation of grassroots or regional groups—as in Colombia and central India—democratic decentralization can be a solution.

At the same time, democratic decentralization tends to spark political competition and conflict (Robinson 1988) but also to "civilize" or moderate it within comparatively polite democratic processes. It catalyzes it because competing candidates (and often parties) naturally tend to promote division among electors in order to win seats on decentralized bodies. But in most cases, the moderating influence of the process tends to outweigh the strife that results. Thus democratic decentralization tends to ease violence and social unrest rather than exacerbate them.

Poverty Alleviation

When poverty arises from disparities between regions or localities, democratic decentralization tends to play a creative role. Many decentralized systems have arrangements for providing poorer areas with better-than-average resources. They also give elected officials from poorer areas more equitable representation in the wider political system, and that helps them seek a more equitable distribution of resources.

But democratic decentralization tends not to alleviate poverty that arises from disparities within regions or localities. When prejudices against disadvantaged groups are stronger at lower levels in political systems than at higher, democratic decentralization can make it even more difficult to tackle poverty. In such cases, provisions need to be made to ensure that poverty programs remain the responsibility of higher levels of government. In much of Latin America (unlike most of Asia and Africa), poor groups are comparatively well organized in pursuing their interests (Fox 1994; Nickson 1995). As a result, decentralization has enhanced efforts to address poverty. But this is not the case in most countries.

Other Development Concerns

Democratic decentralization also influences a range of issues raised by the CDF and the PRSPs:

- *Fostering sustainable development.* Because democratic decentralization helps people at the grassroots feel a sense of ownership of projects undertaken by decentralized bodies, it also facilitates efforts to maintain these projects (especially small building projects) once they have been completed. That makes development more sustainable. Projects for managing natural resources often benefit from inputs by elected representatives who are well versed in local knowledge about resource management and local mechanisms for ensuring that resources are managed creatively. This enhances environmental sustainability (Evers 1994; Hessling and Ba 1994; Leach and Mearns 1996; Painter 1991).
- *Contributing to monitoring of government performance.* Local residents served by decentralized bodies are, thanks to greater transparency, far better informed about the workings and decisions of political institutions that affect them. Periodic elections give them opportunities to register their evaluations. And the tendency for public meetings to occur more often after decentralization—whether officially organized for consultative purposes or unofficially organized for protests or shows of appreciation—provides them with further opportunities.
- *Encouraging a long-term perspective on development.* We can expect little of elected bodies at lower levels on this front. Indeed, they may sometimes make this goal more difficult to achieve because elected members tend to take a very short-term view.
- *Sequencing policies, programs, and projects.* It is also unrealistic to expect elected members of decentralized bodies to contribute much here. They tend to have rather rough and ready perceptions in matters such as this. Although efforts by higher-level authorities to explain the importance of sequencing might make some impact, we should not expect major breakthroughs on this front.
- *Contributing to the appropriate pacing of reforms.* For reasons noted above, elected members of decentralized bodies cannot be expected to play much of a role. But evidence from Eastern Europe suggests that democratic decentralization helps citizens better tolerate stresses of economic reform—elections at lower levels give them a sense of ownership of their government, and they react with greater forbearance. Evidence from many countries shows that decentralization enhances government legitimacy. So perhaps decentralization could have this effect more broadly. On the other hand, if economic reform means that decentralized bodies are starved of resources, this could wreck experiments with decentralization. The bodies need abundant funds to break down popular cynicism about government.

Enhancing Financial Capacity

Some people argue that decentralization is desirable because it both should and will in practice maximize the growth of local revenue resources. Others argue that in most developing countries the majority of funding for decentralized bodies will inevitably come from central government. The main argument for maximizing local revenues is that it puts the responsibility for costs, tax levels, and expenditures on the shoulders of local beneficiaries and local decision-makers. It therefore maximizes the accountability of government to taxpayers and underpins genuine local political and managerial autonomy (Bennett 1990; Bird 1994; 1990; Ostrom, Schroeder, and Wynne 1993; UNESCAP 1991).

Given the general inadequacy of local revenue bases and the control of governments over financial transfers, it is unlikely that decentralization will lead to fiscal indiscipline (Prud'homme 1995; Tanzi 1996). The problems facing local revenue mobilization are of a different order:

- The efficiency (cost to yield) of most local taxes is low. They have the most potential in cities, which have a broader commercial revenue base than rural areas.
- Unless local authorities outside the big cities are delimited at a large scale, there is an inherent lack of resources. Davey (1994) argues that, at best, improvements in local revenue mobilization will be important "at the margin." More radical attempts to force local authorities to be more self-reliant (often a major motivation for governments facing a budget crisis) are only acceptable if one is prepared to accept the reduction of local government to minimal functions or to a form of community action with limited capacity.
- Political cynicism and distrust will deepen if local politicians try to increase taxes. The legitimacy of local taxation has long been undermined by poor performance caused by lack of resources coupled with the unwillingness of taxpayers to pay taxes when there are no perceived benefits. Pump priming is therefore essential in many countries where local government has a history of failure and corruption (Latin America and Africa).
- Not only are local resources limited, they are unevenly distributed, so increasing reliance on local revenues can create spatial inequality. What determines the success of a local government, at least in its capacity to provide services, may be the accidents of location and the endowments of the local economy rather than its institutional design or administrative performance (Aziz and Arnold 1996; Therkildsen and Semboja 1992).
- Lack of administrative capacity increases the difficulty of developing new tax bases.

Those who argue for continued and substantial central funding suggest that the source of funds is less important than expenditure and managerial autonomy, which depend on the kinds of central control exercised regardless of source (in other words, revenue autonomy must be distinguished from expenditure autonomy). Effective financial management depends on a balance between expenditure autonomy and mechanisms of central monitoring and auditing that are rigorous but not too administratively cumbersome. Effective decentralized bodies require, above all, stable and assured sources of income that are appropriately matched to their functions.

Those who advocate decentralizing the responsibility for revenue raising to the local level often encourage user charges. This is a way of making the most direct link possible between cost and benefit to the user of a service or facility. But user charges are only suitable for services that can be purchased by individuals, and a full "economic cost" charge may not be feasible. The charges do not solve the problem of endowing local authorities with the capacity to provide the service, and there are still considerable difficulties with their use in poor communities. Transportation services can be run successfully on private lines, but experience shows that sanitary facilities or waste disposal services will simply not be purchased if there are user charges, and will disappear. The charges have been most successful where they relate to common agreed management of an economic facility by the beneficiaries, as in irrigation (Paul 1994).

Over time, as decentralized bodies gain acceptance, as they erode popular cynicism about government institutions, and as citizens become more concerned with the substance of local projects than the extra taxes needed to fund them, modest enhancement in resource mobilization should be expected.

Enhancing Government Legitimacy

The CDF intends governments to be important players in development. Indeed, development is to proceed "under the leadership of government." Governments seen as legitimate by their constituents will be able to operate as more constructive players and leaders. Democratic decentralization tends to enhance the legitimacy of governments in the eyes of citizens. The generous devolution of powers and resources to elected bodies at lower levels tends to make government more transparent, open, accountable, effective, and responsive, and increases participation and associational activity. These things will erode popular cynicism toward government institutions. The only cases where this has not happened are those in which a government delivered too few powers and resources to decentralized bodies. In these circumstances, popular cynicism toward government tends to be reinforced (Crook and Manor 1998; Dukesbury 1991; Manor 1999, pp. 87–93).

Promoting Economic Growth

Despite claims by some theorists, almost no empirical evidence suggests that democratic decentralization can help accelerate economic growth. Its impact is probably neutral.

Improving Governance and Information Flows

Decentralization can benefit substantially from improvements in telecommunications. This was evident at the district level in Karnataka, India, where computer and Internet facilities available to senior district bureaucrats were turned to good use once those bureaucrats became persuaded that elected district and subdistrict councils had great promise. Elected councils used computerized data on land and other available resources in localities all across various districts to make informed decisions.[3]

But the main contribution of democratic decentralization is its tendency to increase the amount of valuable information that moves from the local level to government institutions. Decentralization enhances the overall flow of quality information into the information technology system. Bureaucrats presiding over such systems quickly become adept (with the help of the elected heads of decentralized bodies) at distinguishing garbage from reliable intelligence. So while decentralization cannot improve information technology systems, it can enhance the quantity and quality of inputs.

Adjusting Government Policies to Local Conditions

When local councils are empowered, they acquire the capacity to adjust government policies and programs to local conditions. The conditions are not just topographical or ecological but include local knowledge of such features and how to make the best use of them, plus local processes for resolving disputes, for managing resources, and the like. Government bureaucracies often find these difficult to comprehend and respect, and may ignore them. Democratic decentralization can integrate these local features into the formal political and development processes—so governance tends less toward hegemony over society at the grassroots and more toward synergy between local forces and government institutions.

Scaling up from Successful Local Experiments

How can governments scale up from successful experiments and replicate them elsewhere? Decentralized systems can help in scaling up because they can act as networks through which news of local success may pass to higher levels of government and to other localities. They are less helpful in replication, partly because most decentralized systems have no mechanisms to accomplish this, and partly because local successes rooted in local conditions cannot be easily replicated.

Maintaining Higher-Level Influence When Decentralization
Threatens Public Welfare

Some researchers on decentralization and the World Bank staff worry that democratic decentralization may prove damaging in a few spheres. These analysts therefore ask whether higher-level authorities—at central or intermediate (provincial, district, county) levels—should retain control of certain programs. Two main concerns have been expressed.

The first is that democratic decentralization may damage the environment. A recent World Bank (OED 2000) review of forestry programs shows that decentralization of environmental regulation has enabled local interests to capture and misuse programs and to damage the environment. But most of the evidence on the environmental impact of decentralization points in the opposite direction. It shows that democratic decentralization tends to enable people at the grassroots level to bring valuable local knowledge of environmental microsystems to bear on centrally designed programs. It also enables them to integrate central programs with creative local mechanisms for managing environmental resources.

The main problem is not the perversity of local interests but the difficulty that national or regional bureaucracies have in adapting to more consultative processes. Many such bureaucracies—especially in Commonwealth countries—have long acted as guardians over natural resources such as forests. It is understandably hard for them to now partner with people over whom they once served as game keepers.

The second concern is that democratic decentralization may undermine programs intended to assist the poor or socially excluded groups (such as women and ethnic or religious minorities). In some countries where decentralization has occurred, elites at lower levels are prejudiced against the poor, women, and minorities—more so than elites at higher levels. When that is true, it may make sense to keep programs to assist those groups in the hands of higher-level authorities (either bureaucracies or, often more prominently, elected authorities at intermediate levels in multitier decentralized systems).

But when prejudices at lower levels are no stronger than at higher levels, the impact of democratic decentralization will be neutral. Indeed, it may enhance the impact of programs to address inequality and exclusion because elected representatives on local councils may have a better understanding of the needs of the poor, women, or minorities in their communities than people higher up.

Policymakers must also determine how well organized the poor, women, or minorities are at the grassroots level. Evidence from Latin America indicates that because its poor people tend to be better organized than their counterparts in much of Africa and Asia, democratic decentralization tends not to damage poverty programs—as it sometimes does in Africa and Asia.

Policymakers also need to determine whether political parties that will likely be influential in decentralized systems will be committed to tackling poverty and social exclusion. Where they are, democratic decentralization tends not to damage programs to promote equity and to erode social exclusion.

It is also possible to reserve a certain number of seats on elected councils for members of poor or socially excluded groups. It is crucial, however, that such reserved places on councils be filled by election and not by nomination, since nominees tend to remain under the control of elites who select them. In these systems (and even in systems without such reservations), evidence suggests that within a few years, poor and socially excluded groups recognize the promise of democratic decentralization, and they more actively seek representation on councils. So over time, in countries where democratic decentralization may have undermined programs to tackle poverty and exclusion, it is realistic to expect this effect to diminish.

Potential Results from Democratic Decentralization

Democratic decentralization has considerable potential in many areas, especially in strong political systems with reliable accountability mechanisms and in which decentralized bodies possess adequate funds and powers. Given time, decentralization can:

- give governments a sense of ownership of more consensual approaches to governance, by persuading them that they now have more information and can perform more effectively;
- give ordinary citizens a greater sense of ownership both of locally designed development projects and of programs that originate higher up;
- contribute to greater coordination of policies and personnel from numerous line ministries [although this tends to happen with decentralization at intermediate levels (provinces, districts, counties) rather than local levels];
- break up bottlenecks and reduce delays in decision-making;
- enhance local political participation and quicken local associational activity. It thus enlivens civil society and draws it into structured and moderating political processes, even when it also catalyzes greater competition and conflict among people seeking election. In the process it tends to give civil society organizations a greater sense of ownership over government policies, processes, and projects.;
- encourage partnerships between government agencies and the private sector. (usually small-scale, local partnerships);

- make government processes more transparent to ordinary citizens (although this sometimes leads them to incorrectly conclude that government has become more corrupt);
- make government institutions more open by providing opportunities for elected representatives at lower levels to influence official decisions and the design and implementation of government programs;
- enhance the accountability of bureaucrats to elected representatives and the accountability of elected representatives to citizens;
- reduce overall corruption in the political system through greater transparency and accountability. Although this has only happened in a few cases, as decentralized systems take root and become better understood by citizens, the effect may be more widespread;
- enhance citizens' understanding of government health, education, and sanitation programs. Local elected representatives can explain these details better than government employees;
- help programs be more responsive and appropriate to local conditions. This in turn can increase the uptake on such programs, and modestly reduce absenteeism among local-level government employees in schools, health dispensaries, and the like, thus strengthening service delivery;
- make government appear more legitimate in the eyes of its people, thanks to accountability, transparency, and to the enhanced effectiveness and responsiveness of government more generally (Crook and Manor 1998);
- help scale up successful projects, and occasionally replicate them.

But democratic decentralization has less promise in other areas:

- Although it can help to adapt social programs to local conditions, it is susceptible to elite capture, which means benefits get diverted from people in need to clients of elite politicians. This, and strong prejudices against poor, low-status, and minority groups in local areas often mean that decentralization does not alleviate poverty.
- Decentralization does little to encourage long-term development perspectives, or to help promote sequencing and pacing of reforms. Nor (on present evidence, early in the lifetimes of many experiments with decentralization) does it assist much in enhancing the state's financial capacity by mobilizing local resources, or in promoting economic growth.

Despite these limitations, decentralization has enough virtues to make it worth encouraging as one element in a strategy to achieve the goals of comprehensive development and poverty reduction.

What Can Donors Do?

Although most governments that have experimented with decentralization have done so on their own initiative, some have held back, hampering their development and long-term interests. How can they be encouraged? Since many decentralizing governments have been persuaded to act after learning of creative experiments in other (often neighboring) developing countries, donors may want to call attention to the established benefits of decentralization elsewhere. Potential decentralizers might be put in contact with officials from other developing countries who understand the promise of decentralization. Such officials can be found in Bangladesh, Bolivia, India, the Philippines, and Tanzania.

Donors might also consider making proposals to extend funds directly to decentralized authorities, as some have already done in Bangladesh. But this is a delicate matter, as central government officials in some countries may react jealously.

Donors might indicate that greater support by developing country governments for democratic decentralization would produce more loans. This would work best in countries whose administrative agencies have been deconcentrated or where fiscal decentralization has occurred, but without any democratization at lower levels. It could also be useful where democratic decentralization has begun, but where only limited powers and resources have been devolved. Whether this should take the form of conditions or suggestions is a matter of judgment, but either could encourage creative responses.

Donors can also find out if donor-assisted projects and policy reforms have discouraged democratic decentralization (not an easy question). This discouragement can occur unintentionally when assistance causes national governments to continue focusing on grand, high-tech, top-down projects. Evidence on democratic decentralization from many countries indicates that there is grassroots demand for programs that enable lower-level authorities to allocate public funds, even though their preferred projects may appear puny and hopelessly low-tech to leaders higher up. Grander projects often distract national governments from this demand and other local needs, such as more voice in the development process, and small but (in the eyes of people at the grassroots level) critically important projects.

Notes

1. Defined as the transfer of powers and resources from higher to lower levels in a political system, decentralization can take three forms. These forms can stand alone or work together. Deconcentration, or administrative decentralization, occurs when agents in higher levels of government move to lower levels. Fiscal decentralization occurs when higher levels of government cede influence over budgets and financial decisions to lower levels. Devolution, or democratic decentralization, occurs when resources, power, and often tasks are shifted to lower-level authorities who are somewhat independent of higher authorities, and who are at least somewhat democratic (Manor 1999). This simple typology is derived from a recent World Bank adaptation (Parker 1995) of Dennis Rondinelli's (1981) earlier typology.
2. This is apparent from doctoral research by Fidel P. Kulpipossa at the Institute of Development Studies at Sussex University.

3. This is based on encounters with officials in Mysore District by a contributor to this study and by Joel Barkan of the University of Iowa.

References

Aziz, A., and D.D. Arnold, eds. 1996. *Decentralised Governance in Asian Countries.* Thousand Oaks, CA: Sage Publications.

Bahl, R., and J. Linn. 1994. "Fiscal Decentralization and Intergovernmental Transfers in Less-Developed-Countries." *Publius-The Journal of Federalism* 24 (1): pp. 1–19.

Bennett, R.J., ed. 1990. *Decentralisation, Local Governments and Markets.* Oxford, U.K.: Clarendon Press.

Bird, R. 1990. "Intergovernmental Finance and Local Taxation in Developing Countries: Some Basic Considerations for Reformers." *Public Administration and Development* 10 (3): pp. 277–88.

———. 1994. "Decentralizing Infrastructure: For Good or for Ill." Working Paper and Background Paper for *World Development Report 1994: Infrastructure for Development.* New York: Oxford University Press.

Blair, Harry. 1989. *Can Rural Development Be Financed from Below?* Dhaka: United States Agency for International Development.

———. 1995. *Assessing Democratic Decentralization: A Center for Development Information and Evaluation (CDIE) Concept Paper.* Washington, D.C.: United States Agency for International Development.

Brillantes, Alex B. 1994. "Redemocratization and Decentralization in the Philippines: The Increasing Leadership Roles of Nongovernmental Organizations." *International Review of Administrative Sciences,* December: pp. 575–86.

Crook, Richard, and James Manor. 1998. *Democracy and Decentralization in South Asia and West Africa: Participation, Accountability and Performance.* Cambridge, U.K.: Cambridge University Press.

Davey, K. 1994. "Local Resource Generation: Role and Potential." In D. Rothchild, ed., *Strengthening African Local Initiative.* Hamburg, Germany: Institute für Afrika Kunde.

Dillinger, William. 1994. "Decentralization and Its Implications for Urban Service Delivery." Urban Management Program Discussion Paper 16. Washington, D.C.: World Bank.

Dukesbury, J.M. 1991. *Decentralization and Democratic Pluralism: The Role of Foreign Aid.* Washington, D.C.: United States Agency for International Development/CDIE/POA.

Evers, Yvette. 1994. "Local Institutions and Natural Resource Management in the West African Sahel: Policy and Practice of 'Gestion de Terroir' in the Republic of Mali." Rural Resources, Rural Livelihoods 5. Manchester, U.K.: Institute for Development Policy and Management.

Fabian, Katalin, and Jeffrey Straussman. 1994. "Post-Communist Transition of Local Government in Hungary: Managing Emergency Social Aid." *Public Administration and Development* 14: pp. 271–80.

Fox, J. 1995. "Governance and Rural Development in Mexico: State Intervention and Public Accountability." *Journal of Development Studies* 32 (1): pp. 1–30.

———. 1994. "Latin America's Emerging Local Politics." *Journal of Democracy,* April: pp. 105–15.

Gibson, John, and Philip Hanson. 1996. "Decentralization and Change in Post-Communist Systems." In John Gibson and Philip Hanson, eds. *Transformation from Below: Local Power and the Political Economy of Post-Communist Transitions.* Cheltenham, U.K.: Edward Elgar.

Hessling, G., and B.M. Ba. 1994. "Land Tenure and Resource Management in the Sahel—Regional Synthesis and Summary." Paper presented at the CILSS, Organisation for Economic Co-operation and Development, Club du Sahel Regional Conference on Land Tenure and Decentralisation in the Sahel, January, Praia, Cape Verde.

Kasfir, Nelson. 1993. "Designs and Dilemmas of African Decentralization." In Mawhood, ed., *Local Government in the Third World: Experience of Decentralization in Tropical Africa.* Second edition. Africa Institute of South Africa.

Leach, Melissa, and Robin Mearns. 1996. *The Lie of the Land: Challenging Received Wisdom on the African Environment.* Portsmouth, N.H.: James Currey and Heinemann.

Manor, James. 1999. *The Political Economy of Democratic Decentralization.* Washington, D.C.: World Bank.

Mawhood, Philip, Ed. 1993. *Local Government in the Third World: Experience of Decentralization in Tropical Africa.* Second edition. Africa Institute of South Africa.

Narayan, Deepa. 1994. *The Contribution of People's Participation: Evidence from 121 Rural Water Supplies.* United Nations Development Programme–World Bank Water and Sanitation Program. Washington, D.C.: World Bank.

Nickson, R. Andrew. 1995. *Local Government in Latin America.* Boulder, CO: Lynne Rienner.

OED (Operations Evaluation Department). 2000. "A Review of the World Bank's Forest Strategy and Its Implementation." Washington, D.C.: World Bank.

Ostrom, E., L. Schroeder, and S. Wynne. 1993. *Institutional Incentives and Sustainable Development: Infrastructure Policies in Perspective.* San Francisco, CA: Westview Press.

Painter, Thomas M. 1991. *Approaches to Improving the Use of Natural Resources for Agriculture in Sahelian West Africa.* New York: Agricultural and Natural Resources Unit, CARE International.

Parker, Andrew. 1995. "Decentralization: The Way Forward for Rural Development?" Policy Research Working Paper 1475. Washington, D.C.: World Bank.

Paul, S. 1994. *Does Voice Matter? For Public Accountability, Yes.* Washington, D.C.: World Bank.

Prud'homme, Remy. 1995. "The Dangers of Decentralization." *World Bank Research Observer* 10 (August): pp. 210–26.

Robinson, Marguerite S. 1988. *Local Politics: The Law of the Fishes: Development through Political Change in Medak District, Andhra Pradesh (South India).* New York: Oxford University Press.

Rondinelli, Dennis. 1981. "Government Decentralization in Comparative Perspective: Theory and Practice in Developing Countries." *International Review of Administrative Sciences,* Vol. XLVII, No. 2. Sage Publications, London, U.K.

Shah, Anwar. 1996. "Quality of Governance and Fiscal Decentralization: Fine in Theory But What Is the Practice?" Washington, D.C.: World Bank.

Tanzi, Vito. 1996. "Fiscal Federalism and Decentralization: A Review of Some Efficiency and Macroeconomic Aspects." In Michael Bruno and Boris Pleskovic, eds. *Annual World Bank Conference on Development Economics 1995.* Washington, D.C.: World Bank.

Therkildsen, O., and J. Semboja. 1992. "Short Term Resource Mobilization for Recurrent Financing of Rural Local Governments in Tanzania." *World Development* 20 (8): pp. 1101–13.

Tordoff, William. 1994. "Decentralisation: Comparative Experience in Commonwealth Africa." *Journal of Modern African Studies* 32 (December): pp. 555–80.

UN-ESCAP (United Nations Economic and Social Commission for Asia and the Pacific). 1991. *Fiscal Decentralization and the Mobilization and Use of National Resources for Development: Issues, Experience and Policies in the ESCAP Region.* Bangkok: ESCAP.

6

Helping People Help Themselves: Autonomy-Compatible Assistance

David P. Ellerman

There is a subtle paradox in the very notion of development assistance: how can an outside party (the helper) assist those who are undertaking autonomous activities (the doers) without overriding or undercutting their autonomy?[1] This is the classic problem of helping people help themselves, one of the central themes of the Comprehensive Development Framework (Wolfensohn 1997, 1998, 1999a, 1999b; Stiglitz 1998).

There is a constellation of related themes, such as the presumption in favor of inclusion, popular participation, involvement, and ownership as well as the suspicion that externally applied carrots and sticks do not "buy" sustainable policy changes (World Bank 1998). This chapter addresses the paradox of "assisted autonomy," the problems presented by current practice of conditionality (see Chap. 3), and the need to move away from dogma and blueprints (see Chaps. 1 and 2) to an "open learning" model that places the country in the driver's seat, actively helping itself. Thus, this chapter extends the search for modes of development assistance that enhance ownership, beyond participation (Chap. 4) and democratic decentralization (Chap. 5). Chapter 7 draws further implications from the open learning model for modalities of development planning and analytical and advisory services.[1]

The chapter explores a theory of autonomy-compatible assistance, drawing on a range of fields—John Dewey in pedagogy and social philosophy, Douglas McGregor in management theory, Carl Rogers in psychotherapy, Saul Alinsky in community organizing, Pablo Freire in community education, and Albert Hirschman and E.F. Schumacher in economic development. Though very diverse, these thinkers arrive at very similar conclusions.

Their contributions to an open learning model might be summarized through five themes:

- **Theme 1: Helper Has to Start Where the Doers Are.** A utopian social engineering approach tries to impose a clean model, wiping away the old solution if need be to make room for the new. Using an architectural metaphor, an old building is torn down to create a cleared space, a *tabula rasa*, for constructing the new building. The alternative, nonutopian incremental approach would be to repair part of the building at a time, ending eventually with a completely rebuilt building. Rebuilding the old, rather than destroying it to engineer a new model on the cleaned slate, is one way of introducing the theme of starting where the doers are. To help the doers help themselves, helpers have to design their assistance based on the current starting point of the doers, not an imaginary clean slate.
- **Theme 2: Helper Has to See through the Doers' Eyes.** Since the goal is for doers to help themselves, helpers providing assistance need to see the situation through the doers' eyes. The doers' actions will be guided by their own knowledge, conceptual framework, values, and world view, not those of the helpers.
- **Theme 3: Helper Cannot Impose Change on Doers.** Transformative change comes from the internally motivated activities of doers. Carrots and sticks used by the helpers stifle the self-motivation of the doers and produce only superficially conforming behavior, not transformation.
- **Theme 4: Help as Benevolence Is Ineffective.** Autonomy-compatible assistance is neither an imposition (theme 3) nor a gift (theme 4). Benevolent charity helps people, but it does not help people help themselves. It promotes dependency, putting doers in the humiliating position of being unable to help themselves and leading to resentment and thwarted self-reliance.
- **Theme 5: Doers Must Be in the Driver's Seat.** "Being in the driver's seat" is a metaphor for autonomous self-activity and can be extended to the other four themes: the car must start its journey from where the doer-driver is, the vision of the road ahead is from the driver's vantage point, it would be folly for guides (or "backseat drivers") to grab the steering wheel and try to drive, and being driven by someone else weakens the driver's ability to get there alone.

The following section applies these five themes to development assistance: starting from present institutions, seeing the world through the eyes of the client, inducing but not imposing change to facilitate transformation, avoiding paternalism and oppressive benevolence, and supporting social learning. The current model of transmitting knowledge from agency to client generates problems of ownership, self-efficacy, cognitive dependency, and moral hazard. Different types of development knowledge need to be applied in various contexts. Global knowledge must be adapted and blended with local knowledge, tacit and practical knowledge remains fundamental to success, and social learning is primarily a decentralized bottom-up process. The analysis has implications for development organizations as storehouses or brokers of knowledge that need to avoid the dangers of a dogma-based church model. An open and active learning model is needed where genuine debate, open discussion, and competing views are allowed, indeed encouraged.

Applying the Five Themes to Development Assistance

The standard model of development assistance tends to be nonautonomous, which is the root of its ineffectiveness. One way or another, a country must find the internal motivation necessary for autonomous development. For external development assistance to "do no harm"—not to mention to be effective—it must be autonomy-compatible. To explore this notion, the chapter looks next at the five themes of assisted autonomy in the context of economic development.[2]

Theme 1. Applied: Starting from Present Institutions

To be transformative, a process of change must start from the present endowment of institutions. Otherwise, the process will create only an overlay of new behaviors that is not sustainable (without continual bribes or coercion). Yet this is a common error.

> An unwillingness to start from where you are ranks as a fallacy of historic proportions; [i]t is because the lesson of the past seems to be so clear on this score, because the nature of man so definitely confirms it, that there has been this perhaps tiresome repetition throughout this record: the people must be in on the planning; their existing institutions must be made part of it; self-education of the citizenry is more important than specific projects or physical changes. (Lilienthal 1944, p. 198)

There are a number of reasons why development interventions are often not designed to begin with existing institutions. Revolutionaries and reformers oriented toward utopian social engineering (see Popper 1962) aim to wipe the slate clean in order to install a set of "ideal" institutions. Any attempt to evolve out of the current "flawed," "retrograde," or even "evil" institutions is viewed as polluting the change process. For instance, in the transition economies such as Russia, the "leap over the chasm" imposed by institutional shock therapy fell far short of the other side since people "need a bridge to cross from their own experience to a new way" (Alinsky 1971, p. xxi). It will take a country much longer to climb out of the chasm than it would have taken to incrementally build a bridge over the chasm in the first place.

Despite a rather moralistic outlook, Woodrow Wilson made a case for an incremental approach in his first inaugural address:

> We shall deal with our economic system as it is and as it might be modified, not as it might be if we had a clean sheet of paper to write upon; and step by step we shall

> make it what it should be, in the spirit of those who question their own wisdom
> and seek council and knowledge, not shallow self-satisfaction or the excitement of
> excursion whither they cannot tell. (Quoted in Braybrooke and Lindblom 1963, pp.
> 71–72)

Similar considerations argue for an evolutionary and incremental strategy
in poor countries rather than trying to "jump" to new institutions.

> The primary causes of extreme poverty are immaterial; they lie in certain deficien-
> cies in education, organization, and discipline. . . . Here lies the reason why devel-
> opment cannot be an act of creation, why it cannot be ordered, bought, comprehen-
> sively planned: why it requires a process of evolution. Education does not "jump";
> it is a gradual process of great subtlety. Organization does not "jump"; it must
> gradually evolve to fit changing circumstances. And much the same goes for
> discipline. All three must evolve step by step, and the foremost task of develop-
> ment policy must be to speed this evolution. (Schumacher 1973, pp. 168–69)

Given a choice between the momentum of bottom-up involvement in
"flawed" reforms and top-down imposition of what reformers see as "model"
institutions, the start-from-where-the-doers-are principle would argue in favor of using knowledge and experience to improve flawed reforms through
the bottom-up approach to transformation—rather than throwing it overboard
in favor of utopian social engineering based on the false hope of imposed
first-best models.[3]

Theme 2. Applied: Seeing the World through the Eyes of the Client

If a utopian social engineer could perform an institutional lobotomy to
erase present institutions, development advice would not need to be tailored
to present circumstances. Generic advice would suffice. But failing that, it is
necessary to acquire a deeper knowledge of present institutions. This is done,
in effect, by learning to see the world through the eyes of policymakers and
other people in the country.

An autonomy-compatible interaction between teacher and student requires
that the teacher have an empathetic understanding with the student in order to
effectively use superior knowledge to help the student. This help does not
take the form of telling the student the answer, but of offering guidance. The
teacher, according to Dewey's theory, must be able to see the world through
the eyes of the students and within the limits of their experience and at the
same time apply the adult's viewpoint to offer guidance.[4] In the context of
adult transformation, how does the educator find out about the students'
world? That is the role of Freire's notion of dialogue. Instead of ready-made
best-practice recipes, Freire, like Dewey, saw the educational mission as
posing problems, essentially the problems that were based on the students'

view of the world, where their own generative themes are found (Freire 1970, p. 101).

Yet often to development professionals, "it seems absurd to consider the necessity of respecting the 'view of the world' held by the people" (Freire 1970, pp. 153–54).

> Development experience has shown that when external experts *alone* acquire, analyze, and process information and then present this information in reports, social change usually does not take place; whereas the kind of "social learning" that stakeholders generate and internalize during the participatory planning and/or implementation of a development activity *does* enable social change. (World Bank 1996, p. 5)

Theme 3. Applied: Imposing Change Externally is not Transformation

Carrots and sticks can be applied only to behavior within the scope of deliberate action. We choose according to our preferences and beliefs, but we do not directly choose our preferences or beliefs. Transformation is the indirect by-product of authentic activities, not the direct object of choice. External incentives can buy "loving behavior," "assertions of belief," or "gestures of faith"—but falling in love, believing in a principle, and having faith all come only by the grace of transformation.

> This much seems clear: effective change cannot be imposed from outside. Indeed, the attempt to impose change from the outside is as likely to engender resistance and barriers to change, as it is to facilitate change. At the heart of development is a change in ways of thinking, and individuals cannot be forced to change how they think. They can be forced to take certain actions. They can be even forced to utter certain words. But they cannot be forced to change their hearts or minds. (Stiglitz 1998)

The idea that a person cannot simply change a judgment or preference at the behest of another has an old and venerable tradition. Martin Luther's principle of liberty of conscience was one of the root principles of the Reformation and one of the main sources of the theory of inalienable rights (which placed limits on the reach of the market).

> Furthermore, every man is responsible for his own faith, and he must see it for himself that he believes rightly. As little as another can go to hell or heaven for me, so little can he believe or disbelieve for me; and as little as he can open or shut heaven or hell for me, so little can he drive me to faith or unbelief. (Luther 1942 [1522], p. 316)

Authorities, secular or religious, who try to compel belief, can only secure external conformity.

> Besides, the blind, wretched folk do not see how utterly hopeless and impossible a thing they are attempting. For no matter how much they fret and fume, they cannot do more than make people obey them by word or deed; the heart they cannot constrain, though they wear themselves out trying. For the proverb is true, "Thoughts are free." (Luther 1942 [1522], p. 316)

Thus a person's sentiments and beliefs are not subject to choice on the marketplace. Development agencies that try to "buy" policy changes "cannot do more than make people obey them by word or deed; the heart they cannot constrain, though they wear themselves out trying."

An externally forced intervention, based on the theory that the coerced client will then see the light and continue along the reformed path without further externally applied incentives, might be called the bait and switch theory. External incentives (bait) will lead to a transformation, inducing the client to switch over to something akin to intrinsic incentives that will thereafter suffice. This strategy is not impossible, but it is unlikely to lead to sustainable changes.

> Moreover, the method of awakening and enlisting the activities of all concerned in pursuit of the end seems slow; it seems to postpone accomplishment indefinitely. But in truth a common end which is not made such by common, free voluntary cooperation in process of achievement is common in name only. It has no support and guarantee in the activities which it is supposed to benefit, because it is not the fruit of those activities. Hence, it does not stay put. It has to be continually buttressed by appeal to external, not voluntary, considerations; bribes of pleasure, threats of harm, use of force. It has to be undone and done over. (Dewey and Tufts, 1908, p. 304)

Development agencies often have a short time horizon, so they tend to interpret the purchased outward performance as evidence of sustainable change. Thus, the bait and switch theory is falsely "verified" and reapplied again and again. In fact, however, the attempt to buy or force transformation can provoke resentment and pushback. Dewey (1916, p. 26) noted that extrinsic incentives administered in a controlling manner would arouse the "instincts of cunning and slyness." McGregor (1960, p. 68) saw that such incentives would lead to "passive acceptance" at best but more likely to "indifference or resistance." Eventually, the reliance on carrots and sticks can induce an atrophy effect. Any original intrinsic motivation dries up, and the doer becomes an aid-dependent marionette responding only to external strings.

There is a closely related problem where the incentive of receiving aid corrupts motivation (in the sense of changing originally intrinsic motivation into extrinsic motivation). Aid programs usually start with a mental model in which the beneficiaries are undertaking a development project on their own volition but they have a resource gap. Aid is made available to enable the project to go forward. But then over the course of time, the availability of such aid creates a "supply response" in the sense of inducing projects motivated primarily by the desire to receive aid. The aid transformed a situation in which projects had intrinsic motivation (ends being done for their own reasons) into a situation in which the projects are a means to receive aid. The original model of independently given projects no longer applies, but the aid usually continues (due to success in funding more projects), even though such projects are quite likely to fail.

There is thus always the need to "sterilize the emission" of an aid offer to neutralize the supply response—so that the aid is enabling (autonomy-compatible) but not controlling or motivating. One standard mechanism is the requirement that the beneficiaries themselves put up a certain percentage of the resources (although this requirement is commonly gamed by placing the project within the context of larger already-funded activities or by allowing contributed time to count). A variation is to only jump on board moving trains in the sense of only providing second-stage aid so that the beneficiaries would have to undertake the start-up by themselves. Another strategy is to make aid something that cannot be applied for, so that aid could only come to the recipients out of the blue.

Nor is it only a problem of incentives. Similar problems arise concerning the cognitive elements in the client country's decisionmaking. The imposition of beliefs in the form of best practice recipes can temporarily override local judgment but will probably not lead to any sustainable change in conviction. This carries us back to the activist pedagogy and the reasons why the Socratic guide or Deweyan teacher does not simply give the answers (even assuming that the "answers" are available).

> Learning is *not* finding out what other people already know, but is solving our own problems for our own purposes, by questioning, thinking and testing until the solution is a new part of our lives. (Handy 1989, p. 63)

Through direct observation and structured experiments, the learner is guided to actively rediscover and reappropriate knowledge with ownership and adaptation to local circumstances. This pedagogy assumes an active role for the learner, who can be said to be in the driver's seat.

Theme 4. Applied: Employing Addams-Dewey-Lasch's Critique of Benevolence

Help that is not autonomy-compatible is not always imposed. There is also a soft form of control through gifts, paternalism, and benevolence that may be even more insidious.[5] How can forms of help that are compatible with the autonomy of the beneficiary be differentiated from forms that are paternalistic and controlling? Dewey developed a critique of oppressive benevolence, and Christopher Lasch (1995) contrasted the "ethic of respect" and the "ethic of compassion."

Dewey's thinking about the controlling aspects of paternalistic employers was prompted by the Pullman Strike of 1894 and by the critique of Pullman's paternalism in the Chicago reformer Jane Addams's essay "A Modern Lear" (1965). Addams's essay was an extended analogy of Pullman's relationship with his workers to King Lear's relationship with his daughter Cordelia.

> Like Lear, Addams suggested, Pullman exercised a self-serving benevolence in which he defined the needs of those who were the objects of this benevolence in terms of his own desires and interests. Pullman built a model company town, providing his workers with what he took to be all the necessities of life. Like Lear, however, he ignored one of the most important human needs, the need for autonomy. (Westbrook 1991, p. 89)

Jane Addams's Hull House in Chicago was a leading example of settlement houses at the turn of the century (see Davis 1967). Settlement workers lived and worked with the poor, replacing the ethic of benevolence applied by the charity organizations of the day with an ethic of respect, based on the poor working to improve their own affairs, not being a target for "betterment."

Dewey developed at some length his critique of "oppressive benevolence." According to Westbrook, Dewey held that

> self-realization was a do-it-yourself project; it was not an end that one individual could give to or force on another. The truly moral man was, to be sure, interested in the welfare of others—such an interest was essential to his own self-realization—but a true interest in others lay in a desire to expand their autonomous activity, not in the desire to render them the dependent objects of charitable benevolence. (Westbrook 1991, pp. 46–47)

Aid granted out of benevolence, without carrot or stick, reinforces a lack of self-confidence and may create a moral hazard situation that weakens reform incentives and attenuates efforts for positive change (see Maren 1997). "*It tends to render others dependent*, and thus contradicts its own professed aim: the helping of others" (Dewey and Tufts 1908, p. 387). This is the self-reinforcing cycle of tutelage and dependency.[6] An autonomy-compatible interaction would instead work to establish the conditions that

> permit others freely to exercise their own powers from their initiative, reflection, and choice. . . . The best kind of help to others, whenever possible, is indirect, and consists in such modifications of the conditions of life, of the general level of subsistence, as enables them independently to help themselves. (Dewey and Tufts 1908, pp. 302, 390)

Otherwise the prayer of a freeman would be to be left alone, and to be delivered, above all, from "reformers" and "kind" people. (Dewey 1957, p. 270)

Theme 5. Applied: Employing an Activist Philosophy of Social Learning

The central CDF theme of the country in the driver's seat is the application of the activist philosophy of education to social learning. Because transformation can come only from within, through activities carried out by an
individual, organization, government, or country, any intervention by a development agency should be autonomy-compatible. While compliant behavior
can be elicited externally, only a country in the driver's seat can undergo a
sustainable transformation. Similarly, ownership of an outcome comes only
when it results from self-directed activities, rather than a gift or imposed
activity.[7] Development assistance should focus on changing the institutional
matrix of policymaking (the local intrinsic motivation), which is a more
subtle and longer-term affair, a by-product of other actions.

What does this mean for the way a development agency initiates a project?
One strategy is expressed in Schumacher's favorite slogan, "Find out what
the people are doing and help them to do it better." Development assistance
should look for positive changes that are already beginning in the underlying
institutions ("moving trains") and then apply development incentives to
strengthen those tendencies.

Where no promising beginnings are in evidence, any change induced by
bribes is unlikely to transform the underlying institutions. An education-
based strategy may lay a better foundation for sustainable change than purchased demonstration projects. Policy advice from development professionals
anxious to show their expertise and backed by conditions on lending risks
undermining people's incentives for developing their own capacities and weak-
ening their confidence in finding their own solutions. There is little or no
ownership of such externally imposed reforms. Compliance might be only
perfunctory; the quick transplant might soon wither and die—to be replanted
in an "improved" form by the next generation of development professionals
anxious to show their improved expertise.

Knowledge-Based Development Assistance

When a development agency seeks to provide knowledge-based assistance
(as well as financial or material aid) to the "doers of development"
(policymakers and government officials), the standard theory in use (regardless of the espoused theory) is that the agency has development knowledge in
the form of answers encapsulated in standard core courses that need to be
taught, transmitted, and transferred to the target population of trainees. That
methodology is taken as so obvious that the focus is simply on how to deliver

the knowledge, how to scale up the knowledge transmission in the client country, and how to measure and evaluate the impact of these efforts. A prominent example is the vision of the World Bank as knowledge bank.

To see why the reality falls so far short of the rhetoric, it is important to consider how this view came to dominate practice despite sometimes very different statements of espoused theory.

Ownership Problems

In the standard view of knowledge-based assistance, the helpers are teachers or trainers actively transmitting knowledge for development to passive but grateful doers (clients). Development is seen almost as a technical process like building an airport or dam, with the development agency having technical social engineering knowledge to be transmitted to the clients.

Since this knowledge for development is offered below cost or at no cost as an international public good, developing countries are tempted to accept this sort of assistance. Other positive incentives are also offered to those who undergo training, such as travel abroad, pleasant accommodations, generous per diems, and other vacation-like benefits. On the supply side, management pushes task managers or trainers to show results—particularly results that can be observed and evaluated back at headquarters (such as number of trainees). Thus, the managers need to take ownership of the process of assistance in order to show results, and the clients are agreeably induced to go along.[8] This is tutelage, not active learning; it develops dependency, not autonomy or self-direction.

Self-Efficacy Problems

This standard view of delivering knowledge for development undermines the self-confidence and self-efficacy of the clients. The message behind the messages is that the clients are unable to organize their own learning process to find these things out in their own way. They need to be helped—to be shown the way.

In psychology, *externality* is the condition of attributing what happens to oneself to external causes. Externality leads to a condition of learned helplessness, apathy, and fatalism. In contrast, *internality* is the condition of seeing one's actions as having a real effect—of having an internal locus of control over what happens to oneself.[9]

The conditions of externality and internality tend to be self-reinforcing. Externality leads to resignation and fatalism. Individuals do not make a concerted effort to change their condition, so little changes, and their fatalism is confirmed in a continuing vicious circle. If, however, individuals believe that their efforts will make a difference, they are more likely to make a concerted effort and thus are more likely to succeed, and their internality is confirmed in a virtuous circle.

The poor already have a history of ineffectual action to better their condition, so any kind of assistance that reinforces that perceived inability to help themselves is simply the wrong kind of assistance, no matter how well intentioned.

Cognitive Dependency Problems

Individuals may lack self-confidence in their own cognitive skills in addition to lacking self-confidence in the efficacy of their actions. In an extreme state of dependency, they might be marionette-like not only in their actions but also in their knowledge and opinions. This cognitive aspect of dependence is clearly relevant to understanding the detrimental forms of knowledge-based development assistance.

With the standard methodology of knowledge-based assistance, the "best learners" are often the most marionette-like trainees, who quickly learn to parrot the main messages. Those best learners are then qualified to staff the local missions that are the staging areas and repeater stations for scaling up the transmission of the main messages to others in the target population—all in the name of capacity building. Those local mission organizations are sometimes also the gatekeepers for other aid and resources flowing from the development agency to the client country.

The cognitively dependent recipients of the main messages also help perpetuate the stifling of critical reasoning in favor of bureaucratic reasoning in development agencies. Cognitively dependent clients, accustomed to being told the best practices to follow, might be distressed to hear the authorities arguing among themselves about development knowledge and development strategies. How can a patient who overhears the doctors arguing about the best treatment have faith in them? Thus, the complaints (real or imagined) of the cognitively dependent clients are used to keep any real debate about development strategies well behind the closed doors of the major development organizations. Only when sufficient agreement has been reached in a process of bureaucratic reasoning does an agreed-on policy go public and receive the financial and intellectual backing of the agency.

Moral Hazard Problems

The reinforcing of a perceived lack of cognitive and volitional self-efficacy is closely related to the moral hazard aspects of traditional aid and charity. The possibility of moral hazard arises when people are shielded from the effects of their own actions, as when people who are over-insured act carelessly and fail to take normal precautions.

Benevolent charity softens the incentives for people to help themselves. The conservative and isolationist response to this moral hazard, aspect of conventional aid is disengagement. Then the poor have no alternative except to help themselves. While this form of tough love might be a useful shock therapy to jar a country out of a state of dependency, the real goal ought to be to seek methods of assistance that are compatible with the autonomy of the clients—that help them help themselves.

In the insurance example, the limit case of no insurance (complete self-insurance) certainly "solves" the problem of moral hazard, since the individual then has full incentives to take precautions to prevent accidents. Yet the no-insurance option is not optimal; it amounts to throwing out the baby of risk pooling and diversification to get rid of the bathwater of moral hazard. Nor is there any first-best solution of complete insurance without moral hazard. There are partial solutions in the form of co-payments and deductibles to "sterilize" the effect of the insurance on incentives, so that the insured party retains some risk and thus incentive to take normal precautions.[10]

Similarly, the extreme of no assistance could be seen as the limit case of autonomy-compatible assistance. It certainly "solves" the problem of softened incentives for self-help, but it forgoes forms of positive assistance that might be autonomy-compatible. The idea of co-payments and deductibles carries over to the idea of partially matching funds from clients to show their own commitment to the learning programs.

Types of Development Knowledge

So far, the focus has been on the standard methodology of knowledge-based assistance (transmitting development knowledge from agency to clients) and how that methodology undercuts the ownership, self-direction, and capacity-building efforts of developing countries. The standard methodology is, however, also flawed in its implicit assumptions about the nature of crucial development knowledge.

Universal and Local Knowledge

Can a money bank also function as a knowledge bank? Money travels better than knowledge. General knowledge is knowledge that holds across countries, cultures, and times; local knowledge takes account of the specifics of place, people, and time. A best practice might work well in some countries but fail miserably in others. One size may not fit all. In questions of institutional development, it is very difficult to know ahead of time just how gen-

eral is a best practice. Global best practices usually need to be locally rein-
vented.

> The significance of this point of view is that contrary to the simplistic use of the
> term by many economists, there is, in principle, no such thing as diffusion of best
> practice. At best, there is only the diffusion of best practices, practices that evolve
> in the course of their diffusion. Contrary to popular wisdom, there are times when
> it pays to reinvent the wheel! (Cole 1989, p. 117)

Prudent counsel is to scan globally for best practices but to test locally,
since local adaptation often amounts to reinventing the best practice in the
new context. Many foreign experts have painfully discovered that the devil is
in the (local) details. It is the local component of knowledge that requires
adaptation—which in turn requires the active participation of those who know
and understand the local environment. Local adaptation cannot be done by
cognitively dependent recipients of development knowledge; it must be done
by doers of development in the course of their self-activity.

There are two points here that need to be teased apart: making knowledge
locally applicable and having local doers of development make the adaptations (rather than provide them as a gift or impose them as a condition from
the outside). It is through local selection and adaptation of knowledge that
doers make it their own. Thus it is not a matter of being open or closed to
outside knowledge; it is a matter of being open to outside knowledge in a
way that reaffirms autonomy. For Gandhi, this was intellectual *swaraj* (self-
rule or autonomy). "I do not want my house to be walled in on all sides and
my windows to be stuffed. I want the cultures of all lands to be blown about
my house as freely as possible. But I refuse to be blown off my feet" (quoted
in Datta 1961, p. 120). Only by remaining on one's feet intellectually can
local doers have the self-confidence to select, assimilate, and adapt the external knowledge—instead of being overwhelmed and rendered intellectually
dependent and subservient.

Considerable effort is required to adapt development knowledge to local
conditions and culture. Policy research institutes can help. In developed countries, think tanks have become important agents for introducing and adapting
new policy initiatives. Think tanks or similar research institutions are also
needed to transplant social innovations to new contexts. The Japanese use a
metaphor based on the gardening technique called *nemawashi* of slowly preparing and wrapping each root of a tree before transplanting it (Morita 1986,
p. 158). A successful transplant is much likelier than if the tree is simply
pulled up from one place and planted in another.

When advocating a certain type of organization (such as local policy research institutes), it is also important to indicate what is *not* being advocated.
In the relationship between the center (such as a multilateral development

agency) and the periphery (a developing country), there may be local organizations that are legitimized not by their role in the country but by their role as local gatekeeper for the central authority. The center judges the local organization by its ability to parrot the "universal" messages from the center, not by its ability to adapt the experiences of others to the local situation.

If anyone in the center should doubt the applicability of the central messages, the local accommodating elite will be more than willing to supply positive "local feedback"—which also validates the intermediary role of the local counterpart elite as gatekeepers for the resources and influence emanating from the center. This mutual reinforcement locks in the relationship, so the center ends up having little transformative effect on indigenous local structures, yet all the while receiving positive feedback on the wonderful job it is doing.

Those in the center who are legitimized in their expertise, prestige, and privileges by the "universality" of their messages are disinclined to recognize limitations in the local applicability of their technical expertise. Novel complexity, genuine uncertainty, conflict of values, unique circumstances, and structural instabilities are all downplayed or ignored since they might diminish the perceived potency of the center's expertise and undercut the client's faith in that potency. The client often wants the childlike security and comfort of being in the hands of the professional expert who will solve the perplexing problems.[11] Thus, the center and periphery may well set up a transmission belt for transferring the universal expert messages and best practice recipes between the "wholesale" source and the local "retailers." These are some of the strong institutional forces leading to an under-appreciation of the subtleties of local knowledge, impeding the growth of autonomous client ownership and the development of indigenous local knowledge institutions.

Codified and Tacit Knowledge

Explicit or codified knowledge is knowledge that can be spoken, written, and codified to be saved on a computer disk or transmitted over a telephone line. But we know more than we can say. We know how to ride a bike or recognize a face, but we would be hard put to codify this knowledge and archive it in a database for dissemination over the Internet. Michael Polanyi (1962) pioneered the distinction between tacit (or personal) and explicit knowledge in the philosophy of science, and the distinction has since proven important in understanding problems in the transfer of technologies and institutions.[12]

There is much more to a technological system than can be put in an instruction book. This is all the more so for social technologies or institutions. Some tacit knowledge might be transformed into codified knowledge

(Nonaka and Takeuchi 1995) so that it could be transferred by conventional methods.[13] But the remaining tacit knowledge needs to be transmitted by special methods, such as apprenticeship, imitation, twinning relations, and guided learning by doing. These are horizontal methods of knowledge transfer in contrast to the vertical method of codifying knowledge, transmitting it to a central repository or library, and then retransmitting it to students.

The tacit component in local or general development knowledge is best learned through such horizontal methods as study tours, cross training, and twinning. International development agencies have the perspective to scan globally to identify the success stories and thus to fruitfully play a facilitating and brokering role in horizontal learning—not a training role.

Because of the tacit component in practical development knowledge, many of the real reasons for successes may not be captured in the codified knowledge of a best practice case study that might be written up and taught to the developing country (not to mention *Rashomon* effects, academic predilections, and ideological precepts in the best-practice case studies). For instance, government officials, legislators, and business people from an African country might better learn directly and horizontally from a nearby East Asian country that recently faced similar problems than from codified and stylized case studies from a development agency.

Centralized and Decentralized Experimentation and Social Learning

A central organization often determines policy solutions and then faces the problem of translating the results to the peripheral units of the organization or to clients. The problems of center-periphery relation are described by Donald Schön (1971) in a context close to a development agency's work.

> [The standard approach] treats government as center, the rest of society as periphery. Central has responsibility for the formation of new policy and for its imposition on localities at the periphery. Central attempts to "train" agencies at the periphery. In spite of the language of experimentation, government-initiated learning tends to be confined to efforts to induce localities to behave in conformity with central policy. Localities learn to beat the system. Government tends to bury failure or learn from it only in the sense of veering away from it. Evaluation, then, tends to be limited to the role of establishing and monitoring the extent of peripheral conformity with central policy. (p. 177)

But social learning can take place in a decentralized, bottom-up manner. In large multiplant companies, innovation may take the form of new ways of socially organizing and structuring productive processes (quality circles, self-managed work teams). Separate plants might perform pilot experiments to find out what works and what does not. Headquarters frames the experiments, detects the successes, and plays the knowledge-broker to help other plants cross-learn from the successful ones. Schön (1971) described a similar process between the central government and local units trying to carry out a certain social reform.

> Government cannot play the role of "experimenter for the nation," seeking first to identify the correct solution, then to train society at large in its adaptation. The opportunity for learning is primarily in discovered systems at the periphery, not in the nexus of official policies at the center. Central's role is to detect significant shifts at the periphery, to pay explicit attention to the emergence of ideas in good currency, and to derive themes of policy by induction. The movement of learning is as much from periphery to periphery, or periphery to center, as from center to periphery. Central comes to function as facilitator of society's learning, rather than as society's trainer. (pp. 177–78)

Social learning is often very different from laboratory learning. Novel complexity, genuine uncertainty, conflict of values, unique circumstances, and structural instabilities all argue against laboratory conditions for discovery and learning. Decentralized experimentation with centrally sponsored framing and quality benchmarking followed by cross-learning in the periphery is a more appropriate model than classical normal science research at a central facility followed by the teaching-dissemination of the results.

Knowledge-Based Development Organizations

This chapter has so far considered the methodology of knowledge-based development assistance and the subtleties introduced by different types of development knowledge. Here, it focuses on the organization or agency involved in knowledge-based development assistance (see also Ellerman 1999).

Implications for Knowledge Bank as Storehouse or as Broker

Every consulting firm faces a basic question of strategy. Should the firm operate in a "library mode," providing clients with access to the right codified knowledge, or focus on tacit knowledge, choosing staff members with an eye to scarce practical how-to skills or by specializing in arranging horizontal cross-learning between clients and benchmark companies?[14]

A development agency working as a knowledge bank faces a similar choice. Should it pursue the library-storehouse model or the knowledge-broker model? In the broker model, knowledge still needs to be catalogued, but it is primarily the second-order knowledge of where to find the how-to knowledge. Since the storehouse model focuses on documents, it specializes in codified knowledge available at the agency, while the broker model focuses on codified pointers to sources of knowledge and experience (which could be codified or tacit) throughout the world. In pedagogical terms, the storehouse model sees the agency as the teacher transferring knowledge from its storehouse to the passive client. The broker model sees the client in the more active role of scanning for knowledge and relevant experience and sees the agency in the more intermediary role of assisting in that search by helping to frame the questions and apply experience in locating relevant sources.

The difference between the models should not be overdrawn. The storehouse model would not suppress other knowledge sources or rule out referrals, but there is a very real difference in emphasis. Which model becomes the working model providing the strategic direction for a development agency as knowledge bank makes a big difference. The approach of bureaucratic reason is to use both models and thus to implement poorly the more difficult broker model.

As the information revolution rolls into the twenty-first century, codified knowledge will more and more approximate the theoretical limit of a free nonrivalrous good. Clients will have access to vast storehouses of codified knowledge, and the agency's own storehouse will increasingly pale in comparison. The scarce knowledge will be that of the reflective and experienced practitioners, wherever they are around the world. Following the broker model, the knowledge bank would be a central clearinghouse in that subtle form of professional expertise (which cannot be downloaded over a phone line). It would play a key global role in putting those who have acquired practical development knowledge at the disposal of those who are willing and able to learn.

Church or Learning Organization?

In the modern world it is now commonplace to accent the importance of intellectual capital and knowledge management. Most organizations want to be seen as learning organizations. Yet many old habits persist that are directly opposed to learning and to the advancement of knowledge. There are several roadblocks in the way of organizational learning for an organization or agency involved in knowledge-based development assistance. Often, the new rhetoric of learning is applied as a veneer onto a church-like organization proselytizing its own dogmas.

Roadblock to Learning 1: Branded Knowledge as Dogma. Put simply, the basic problem is that despite an espoused learning organization model, the applied model is often that of a "development church" giving definitive *ex cathedra* views on all substantive questions. As with church dogmas, the brand name of the organization is invested in its views. Once an "Agency (substitute the name of the relevant development institution) View" has been announced, questioning that view is seen as an attack on the agency itself and the value of its franchise, so new learning is discouraged. The church model fits perfectly with the standard default methodology of knowledge-based development assistance. The agency has the best knowledge for development, which is to be transmitted through various forms of aid-sweetened proselytization to the authorities in the developing world.

A university is an open learning organization that does not set itself up as an arbiter of truth, but as an arena in which contrary theories can be examined in open debate. When an agency takes an official view on questions or considers its views as branded knowledge, the genuine collision of opinions and the rule of critical reason tend to give way to the rule of authority and bureaucratic reason within the hierarchy of the organization. The authorities in the organization decide on its official views and tend to shut off any feedback loops that might lead to the questioning of the official views and thus diminish the franchise value of the brand name. Learning from errors, which involves changing official views and modifying branded knowledge, is minimized so the organization tends to function more as a secular church than as an open learning organization—regardless of the espoused theory.

The church model of direct proselytizing by development agencies contradicts autonomous or self-directed learning in client countries. The project manager from the agency wants the clients to learn so long as they "learn" the right thing. Any genuinely self-directed learning process in the client country might veer off in a wrong direction that the project manager could not support. The project manager would return to headquarters as a failure without a project. Therefore the flow of knowledge must be managed. Clients must be kept from being "distracted" by alternative views. The standard model of the relationship between development organization and client country is a corollary of the church model.

Roadblock to Learning 2: Funded Assumptions as Dogma. Why do development agencies have to take an official view on the one best way to solve a development problem? A common answer is that a development agency is not a university. The development agency puts money as loans or grants behind projects based on various assumptions. University professors do not put money on the table and so they are free to debate questions forever. Once an agency has committed significant resources to certain assumptions, it is time to fall in line and support the funded assumption.

There are obvious bureaucratic reasons why individual project managers and their supervisors would like assumptions behind a funded project to be treated as gospel, but these are not reasons for a whole institution to take such a stand. The commitment of funds and prestige even seems to alter perceptions.[15] But theories are corroborated by evidence, not by commitments of funds. Many businesses have come to grief because managers would not revisit strategies after initial costs were sunk. In view of the record of international development aid, there is little support for the similar practice of seeing project assumptions as hardening into gospel because of the commitment of funds.

Roadblock to Learning 3: Social Science as Dogma. Science has long since replaced religious authority as the source of dogmas that can be appealed to without further reason or corroboration. Though completely misrepresenting the scientific method and the role of critical reason, that perception is nonetheless common. The all too human factors that once led to an appeal to church dogma have not suddenly disappeared, so the appeal to science can be expected to be thoroughly abused. This is nowhere more evident than in the social sciences (see Andreski 1972). Economics rules the social sciences roost, so much can be expected to be passed off in the name of economics. Yet many of the "truths" of economics imposed by bureaucratic power would not pass without serious challenge in any open scientific forum. Thus, many of the official views that are presented as truths of economics have some other, less than scientific basis.

It is particularly unfortunate when a Tayloristic one best way mentality creeps into development policymaking in the name of science. Problems of developing and transition economies are much too complex to yield to formulaic best practice. Many different approaches need to be tried on an experimental basis, so when a major development agency stakes its reputation on the one best way, the development effort as a whole is impoverished.

Consider, for example, the problem of fighting corruption. Economists might approach the problem by trying to minimize discretionary regulations that present rent-seeking opportunities to officials who might offer to relax a restriction for appropriate consideration. Accountants might emphasize transparency and uniformity of data and the independence of auditing. Civil servants might emphasize codes of ethics and disclosure requirements. Lawyers might encourage civil discovery procedures and criminal sanctions. Others will promote a free and independent press, a high standard of public ethics, and a vigorous civil society. A multipronged approach is advisable, since there seems to be no one best way. Yet when different groups from an international development agency take different approaches to fighting corruption and air these differences at international conferences, the dogmatic mentality becomes alarmed. How can passive, dependent clients put themselves in the hands of international experts who cannot agree on the one best way to fight corruption?

This has implications for the question of a client-centered rather than paternalistic approach to learning. What is wrong with two different parts of an international development institution expressing two different views on a complex question at an international conference? What is wrong with listeners realizing that affiliation with an elite institution is not the touchstone of truth? This realization might lead them to think the matter over themselves and thus to take responsibility for forming their own opinion. In short, it would foster active learning rather than passive acceptance of the "truth" promulgated by a church-like organization.

The Open Learning Model

Science as a loosely structured international open learning organization is hardly agnostic in any given area. Certain theories are the received or current theories in a field. The difference from a church-like organization lies in the methodology used to sustain or overturn the hypotheses. In mathematics, proof, not authority, is the basis for theorems. In the empirical sciences, hypotheses are developed on the basis of intellectual coherence and factual cues, and are then subjected to experiments that can be verified and reproduced.

This methodology of science shows, at least in general terms, how an open learning model of a knowledge-based development agency might operate. More important than teaching a client country the "truth" is conveying an active learning methodology for finding and corroborating or disproving truths (hypotheses and theorems). If a knowledge-based development organization wants to promote the one best way of reforming or changing certain institutions (say, the best model of fighting corruption or the best form of privatization), it should be willing to share the source of that knowledge, to promote experiments in the country to corroborate the hypothesis or to validate a local adaptation, and to encourage horizontal cross-learning from similar experiments documented in the organization's knowledge management system—all before the reform is accepted as a blueprint for the country as a whole. The message to policymakers would sound like this:

> To the best of our accumulated experience (which we deem to call knowledge), here is what works best in countries like yours. Why don't you study these principles together with their corroboration to date (best practice success stories), take a look at these case studies, contact the people who designed these reforms, set up horizontal learning programs with those best practice cases, and try some experiments to see what works in your own country? After carrying out this learning process on your own, you might call us back if you feel that we could help by providing some (not all) funding for the reform program you have decided on.

Most important is to get away from the model of teaching as the transmission of knowledge from the development agency to the developing country. As George Bernard Shaw put it, "If you teach a man anything he will never learn it" (1962, p. 174). Or Ortega y Gasset: "He who wants to teach a truth should place us in the position to discover it ourselves" (1961, p. 67). To impose a model without this local learning would be to bypass the active learning capability of the local policymakers, to substitute authority in its place, and perpetuate the passivity of tutelage.

Competition and Devil's Advocacy in the Open Learning Model

How can a large bureaucratic agency advance from the church model to the open learning model? One way is for the agency to take some of its own medicine by fostering competition in a marketplace for ideas within the agency. The judge in a U.S. courtroom does not go to the jury before both sides of the argument have been heard, and a patient should not go to surgery before getting a second opinion. Even the Roman Catholic Church, when considering someone for sainthood, has a devil's advocate to present the case against sainthood. A development agency should not pretend to greater authority or infallibility in canonizing a good practice success story as the one best way.

Thus, devil's advocacy might not only be tolerated but also fostered in a development agency functioning as an open learning organization.[16] The political scientist Alfred De Grazia (1975) recommends such a countervailance system as a part of any large bureaucracy. Devil's advocacy might yield a constructive alternative to the proposed policy. Economics uses the concept of opportunity cost to evaluate an option, comparing its value to that of the best alternative. If plan B is the best alternative to plan A (and the plans are mutually exclusive), then the opportunity cost of choosing plan A is the value forgone by not choosing plan B. Plan A is preferable if its value exceeds its opportunity cost (assuming both can be quantitatively measured).

Application of the opportunity cost doctrine requires the analysis and evaluation of the best alternative—and that is the more general role of devil's advocacy, even when quantitative values are unavailable. By eliciting plan B, devil's advocacy generalizes the opportunity cost doctrine from cost-benefit analysis to general policy analysis. In a rivalrous market, competition provides the B plans, so organizational devil's advocacy could be seen as an attempt to provide benchmark competition within an organization.

The general case for a more systematic devil's advocate or countervailance role in an organization is much the same as the case for genuine debate and open discussion. The classic presentation of that argument is John Stuart Mill's 1859 essay "On Liberty." If little is known on a question or if only partial truths are known, then the clash of adverse opinion is one of the best engines of discovery. Mill (1972, p. 105) argued that even in cases of settled opinions, debate and discussion serve to disturb the "deep slumber of a decided opinion" so that it might be held more as a rational conviction than as an article of faith:

> So essential is this discipline to a real understanding of moral and human subjects that if opponents of all important truths do not exist, it is indispensable to imagine them, and supply them with the strongest arguments which the most skillful devil's advocate can conjure up.

Toward an Open Learning Agency

The idea that a development agency must always have an "official view" (rather than house competing views) is about as scientific as the "scientific" socialism of the Communist parties of the past. John Dewey (1939, p. 96) quotes the English Communist John Strachey's statement that the

> refusal to tolerate the existence of incompatible opinions . . . [is] simply asserting the claim that Socialism is scientific. . . . [It] would be difficult, probably impossible, to find a more direct and elegantly finished denial of all the qualities that make ideas and theories either scientific or democratic than is contained in this statement.

In contrast, critical reason and scientific methodology go in quite the opposite direction, fostering a

> willingness to hold belief in suspense, ability to doubt until evidence is obtained; willingness to go where evidence points instead of putting first a personally preferred conclusion; [and] ability to hold ideas in solution and use them as hypotheses to be tested instead of as dogmas to be asserted. (Dewey 1939, p. 145)

This part of the scientific attitude is translated into the policy domain as multiple advocacy (Haas 1990, 210) and double visioning (see Schön 1983, 281), among other suggestions. It is not wanton perversity that prevents this scientific attitude from being implemented in major development agencies and other large organizations. There are quite human impulses that push for conformity and rigidity.

> To hold theories and principles in solution, awaiting confirmation, goes contrary to the grain. Even today questioning a statement made by a person is often taken by him as a reflection upon his integrity, and is resented. For many millennia opposition to views widely held in a community was intolerable. It called down the wrath of the deities who are in charge of the group Baconian idols of the tribe, the cave, the theater, and den have caused men to rush to conclusions, and then to use all their powers to defend from criticism and change the conclusions arrived at (Dewey 1939, p. 146)

If development agencies are to promote knowledge-based development as education writ large, they should learn organizational lessons from universities and other educational institutions about the need to foster open debate and competing theories within the organization. The scientific method demands no less. If the development agency can move beyond the church (or science-as-dogma) model to an open learning model, it can also move from the standard knowledge transmission methodology toward autonomy-compatible knowledge-based development assistance.

The aim of teaching is not only to transmit information, but also to transform students from passive recipients of other people's knowledge into active constructors of their own and other's knowledge. The teacher cannot transform without the student's active participation, of course. Teaching is fundamentally about creating the pedagogical, social, and ethical conditions under which students agree to take charge of their own learning, individually and collectively. (Elmore 1991, p. xvi)

That activist pedagogy adapted to developing countries as the learners would constitute autonomy-compatible knowledge-based development assistance.

Notes

1. The essentially Kantian notion of autonomy is emphasized, but there is considerable overlap with Amartya Sen's (1999, 1982, 1984) emphasis on capabilities and agency.
2. Previous work in this direction includes Goulet (1971), Korten and Klauss (1984), Verhagen (1987), Rahman (1993), and a good overview in Carmen (1996).
3. For recent literature on institutional reforms in a world of "second bests," see Komesar (1994) and Rubin (1996).
4. Similarly, in Carl Rogers' notion of client-centered therapy, the counselor needs to enter the "internal frame of reference of the client" in order that assistance can be given that respects and relies upon the actual capacity of the person. Maurice Friedman (1960) emphasizes the importance of seeing through the eyes of the other in Buber's notion of dialogue. "The essential element of genuine dialogue . . . is 'seeing the other' or 'experiencing the other side.'" (p. 87) "This 'inclusiveness' is of the essence of the dialogical relation, for the teacher sees the position of the other in his concrete actuality yet does not lose sight of his own." (p. 177) "Particularly important in this relationship is what Buber has variously called 'seeing the other,' 'experiencing the other side,' 'inclusion,' and 'making the other present.' This 'seeing the other' is not . . . a matter of 'identification' or 'empathy,' but of a concrete imagining of the other side which does not at the same time lose sight of one's own." (pp. 188–89)
5. In addition to being wary of Greeks bearing gifts, Thoreau noted: "If I knew for a certainty that a man was coming to my house with the conscious design of doing me good, I should run for fear that I should have some of his good done to me" (quoted in Carmen 1996, p. 47).
6. In 1784, Immanual Kant wrote a short but influential pamphlet *What is Enlightenment?* "Enlightenment is man's release from his self-incurred tutelage. Tutelage is man's inability to make use of his understanding without direction from another. Self-incurred is this tutelage when its cause lies not in lack of reason but in lack of resolution and courage to use it without direction from another. *Sapere aude!* 'Have the courage to use your own reason!'—that is the motto of enlightenment." (quoted in Schmidt 1996)
7. Success for a leader or, in general, a helper, may be paradoxical in the sense that the helper creates the situation in which the doers take success as *their* own accomplishment (see Edmunson 1999 for a practical overview of such paradoxes). Charles Handy notes these results after the doers internalize the activity as their own. "Internalization . . . means that the individual recipient of influence adopts the idea, the change in attitude or the new behavior, as his own. Fine. He will act

on it without pressure. The change will be self-maintaining to a high degree. . . . The successful psychotherapist is the one whose patients all believe they cured themselves—they internalized the therapy and it thereby became truly an integral part of them. Consultants suffer much the same dilemma of the psychotherapist—the problem of internalization. If they wish the client to use the right solution with full and lasting commitment then they must let him believe it is *his* solution." (1993, p. 145) This echoes the notion of the Taoist ruler who governs in such a way that when the task is accomplished, the people will say "We have done it ourselves." (Lao-Tzu, *Te-Tao Ching*, chap. 17)

8. See Deci and Ryan (1985) for development and extensive use of this distinction.
9. McClintock (1982) tells the story in a broader historical context that "as passionate causes wracked human affairs, . . . people found it hard to maintain restraint, they ceased to be willing merely to help in the self development of their fellows; they discovered themselves burdened, alas, with paternal responsibility for ensuring that their wards would not falter and miss the mark. . . . Pressures—religious, political, social, economic, humanitarian pressures—began to mount upon the schools, and it soon became a mere matter of time before schools would be held accountable for the people they produced." (quoted in Candy 1991, p. 32)
10. There is an enormous literature on the economics of information from the work of the pioneers such as Arrow and Stiglitz (see Eatwell and others 1989 for introductory articles) to a number of recent textbooks such as Campbell (1995).
11. See Schön's treatment (1983) of the technical expert in contrast with reflective practitioner.
12. See Ryle (1945–46) for the earlier distinction between knowing how and knowing that, Oakeshott (1991) for a treatment of practical knowledge versus technical knowledge, Schön (1983) for a related treatment of professional and instrumental knowledge, Marglin (1990) on *techne* and *episteme*, and Scott (1998) on *metis* and *episteme/techne* (see p. 425 on the terminological differences with Marglin's usage).
13. Even the codified part may suffer from the "*Rashomon* effect" described in Schön (1971).
14. See Hansen, Nohria, and Tierney (1999) on the contrasting strategies.
15. When predictions fail, then skewed perceptions and rationalizations are a likely outcome. See Festinger and others (1956), Festinger (1957), Lane (1991, part II), and Elster (1983). See Akerlof and Dickens (1982) for an economic treatment of cognitive dissonance.
16. Devil's advocacy (see Schwenk 1984) is interpreted broadly to include a number of related techniques to better elicit the main policy alternatives. A *Cassandra's advocate* (Janis 1972, p. 217) is a person who emphasizes alternative interpretations of data and focuses on all the things that can go wrong ("Murphy's Law"). The *Rashomon* effect (see Schön 1971, 210) illustrates that the same set of circumstances and events can be interpreted very differently by different people. Discussion organized as a debate between the proposed policy and the best alternative has been called the *dialectical method* (see Schwenk 1989; or Tung and Heminger 1993). *Multiple advocacy* (Haas 1990, p. 210) and *double visioning* (see Schön 1983, p. 281) refer to the practice of not only allowing but also fostering the presentation of two or more policy options.

References

Addams, Jane. 1965. "A Modern Lear." In Christopher Lasch, ed., *The Social Thought of Jane Addams*. Indianapolis, IN: Bobbs-Merrill.

Adler, Paul S., and Bryan Borys. 1996. "Two Types of Bureaucracy: Enabling and Coercive." *Administrative Science Quarterly* 41: pp. 61–89.

Adler, Paul S., and Terry Winograd. 1992. "The Usability Challenge." In Paul S. Adler and Terry Winograd, eds., *Usability: Turning Technology into Tools*. New York: Oxford University Press.

Akerlof, George. 1984. *An Economic Theorist's Book of Tales*. New York: Cambridge University Press.

Akerlof, George, and William Dickens. 1982. "The Economic Consequences of Cognitive Dissonance." *American Economic Review* 72 (June): pp. 307–19.

Alinsky, Saul. 1969. *Reveille for Radicals*. New York: Vintage.

———.1971. *Rules for Radicals*. New York: Vintage.

Andreski, Stanislav. 1972. *Social Sciences as Sorcery*. New York: St. Martins.

Arrow, Kenneth. 1963. "Uncertainty and the Welfare Economics of Medical Care." *American Economic Review*. 53: pp. 941–73.

———. 1972. "Gifts and Exchanges." *Philosophy and Public Affairs* 1: pp. 343–62.

Bandura, Albert, ed. 1995. *Self-Efficacy in Changing Societies*. Cambridge, U.K.: Cambridge University Press.

Black, H. 1968. *Black's Law Dictionary*. St. Paul: West Publishing.

Braybrooke, David, and C. Lindblom. 1963. *The Strategy of Decision*. New York: Free Press.

Brehm, Jack. 1972. *Responses to the Loss of Freedom: A Theory of Psychological Reactance*. Morristown, N.J.: General Learning Press.

Buber, Martin. 1965. *Between Man and Man*. New York: Macmillan.

Campbell, Donald. 1995. *Incentives: Motivation and the Economics of Information*. New York: Cambridge University Press.

Candy, Philip. 1991. *Self-Direction for Lifelong Learning*. San Francisco, CA: Jossey-Bass.

Carmen, Raff. 1996. *Autonomous Development*. London, U.K.: Zed Books.

Cole, Robert E. 1989. *Strategies for Learning*. Berkeley, CA: University of California Press.

Datta, Dhirendra Mohan. 1961. *The Philosophy of Mahatma Gandhi*. Madison, WI: University of Wisconsin Press.

De Grazia, Alfred. 1975. *Eight Bads-Eight Goods: The American Contradictions*. Garden City, NY: Anchor Books.

Davis, Allen F. 1967. *Spearheads for Reform: The Social Settlements and the Progressive Movement 1890–1914*. New York: Oxford University Press.

Deci, Edward, and Richard Ryan. 1985. *Intrinsic Motivation and Self-Determination in Human Behavior*. New York: Plenum Press.

Deming, W. Edwards. 1994. *The New Economics for Industry, Government, Education*. Cambridge, MA: MIT Center for Advanced Engineering.

Dewey, John. 1916. *Democracy and Education*. New York: Free Press.

———. 1927. *The Public and Its Problems*. Chicago, IL: Swallow Press.

———. 1939. *Freedom and Culture*. New York: Capricorn.

———. 1957. *Human Nature and Conduct: An Introduction to Social Psychology*. New York: Modern Library.

Dewey, John, and James Tufts. 1908. *Ethics*. New York: Henry Holt.

Eatwell, John, et al., 1989. *The New Palgrave: Allocation, Information, and Markets.* New York: W. W. Norton

Edmunson, Charles. 1999. *Paradoxes of Leadership.* Cambridge, MA: Charles R. Edmunson.

Ellerman, David. 1999. Global Institutions: Transforming International Development Agencies into Learning Organizations. *Academy of Management Executive,* 13 (1): pp. 25–35.

Elmore, R. 1991. "Foreword." In C.R. Christensen, D.A. Garvin, and A. Sweet, eds., *Education for Judgment.* Boston, MA: Harvard Business School Press.

Elster, Jon. 1983. *Sour Grapes: Studies in the Subversion of Rationality.* Cambridge, U.K.: Cambridge University Press.

Elster, J., et al. 1998. *Institutional Design in Post-communist Societies: Rebuilding the Ship at Sea.* Cambridge, U.K.: Cambridge University Press.

Festinger, L. 1957. *A Theory of Cognitive Dissonance.* Stanford, CA: Stanford University Press.

Festinger, L., et al. 1956. *When Prophecy Fails.* New York: Harper Torchbooks.

Freire, Paulo. 1970. *Pedagogy of the Oppressed.* New York: Continuum.

Frey, Bruno. 1997. *Not Just for the Money: An Economic Theory of Personal Motivation.* Cheltenham: Elgar.

Friedman, Maurice. 1960. *Martin Buber: The Life of Dialogue.* New York: Harper Torchbooks.

Goulet, Denis. 1971. *The Cruel Choice.* New York: Atheneum.

Haas, E. B. 1990. *When Knowledge Is Power: Three Models of Change in International Organizations.* Berkeley, CA: University of California.

Handy, Charles. 1989. *The Age of Unreason.* Boston, MA: Harvard Business School Press.

——. 1993. *Understanding Organizations.* 4th ed. London: Penguin.

Hansen, M., N. Nohria, and T. Tierney. 1999. "What's Your Strategy for Managing Knowledge?" *Harvard Business Review* March–April: pp. 106–16.

Hayek, Friedrich. 1979. *The Counter-Revolution of Science: Studies on the Abuse of Reason.* Indianapolis, IN: Liberty Fund.

Hirsch, Fred. 1976. *Social Limits to Growth.* Cambridge, MA: Harvard University Press.

Hirschman, Albert O. 1958. *The Strategy of Economic Development.* New Haven, CT: Yale University Press.

——. 1973. *Journeys Toward Progress.* New York: Norton.

——. 1991. *The Rhetoric of Reaction: Perversity, Futility, Jeopardy.* Cambridge, MA: The Belknap Press.

——. 1992. *Rival Views of Market Society.* Cambridge, MA: Harvard University Press.

——. 1995. *A Propensity to Self-Subversion.* Cambridge, MA: Harvard University Press.

Janis, I. L. 1972. *Victims of Groupthink.* Boston, MA: Houghton Mifflin.

Killick, Tony, with R. Gunatilaka, and A. Marr. 1998. *Aid and the Political Economy of Policy Change.* London, U.K.: Routledge.

Kohn, Alfie. 1993. *Punished by Rewards: The Trouble with Gold Stars, Incentive Plans, A's, Praise, and Other Bribes.* Boston, MA: Houghton Mifflin.

Komesar, Neil. 1994. *Imperfect Alternatives: Choosing Institutions in Law, Economics and Public Policy.* Chicago, IL: University of Chicago Press.

Korten, David C., and Rudi Klauss, eds. 1984. *People-Centered Development.* Hartford, CT: Kumarian Press.

Kreps, David. 1997. "Intrinsic Motivation and Extrinsic Incentives." *American Economic Review* 87: pp. 359–65.

Lane, Robert E. 1991. *The Market Experience*. New York: Cambridge University Press.

Lasch, Christopher. 1995. *The Revolt of the Elites and the Betrayal of Democracy*. New York: Norton.

Lawrence, Elizabeth. 1970. *The Origins and Growth of Modern Education*. Baltimore, MD: Pelican.

Lefcourt, Herbert. 1976. *Locus of Control*. Hillsdale, N.J.: Erlbaum/Wiley.

Lepper, Mark R., and David Greene, eds. 1978. *The Hidden Costs of Rewards: New Perspectives on the Psychology of Human Motivation*. Hillsdale, N.J.: Erlbaum.

Lilienthal, David. 1944. *TVA—Democracy on the March*. New York: Harper.

Lindblom, Charles. 1990. *Inquiry and Change*. New Haven, CT: Yale University Press.

Luther, Martin. 1942 (1522). "Concerning Secular Authority." In F. W. Coker, ed. *Readings in Political Philosophy*. New York: Macmillan.

Lutz, Mark. 1999. *Economics for the Common Good*. London, U.K.: Routledge.

Maren, Michael. 1997. *The Road to Hell: The Ravaging Effects of Foreign Aid and International Charity*. New York: Free Press.

Marglin, Stephen. 1990. "Losing Touch: The Cultural Conditions of Worker Accommodation and Resistance." In Prederique Marglin and Stephen Marglin, eds., *Dominating Knowledge: Development, Culture, and Resistance*. Oxford, U.K.: Clarendon.

McClintock, Robert. 1982. "Reaffirming a Great Tradition. In R. Gross, ed., *Invitation to Lifelong Learning*. Chicago, IL: Follett. [http://www.ilt.columbia.edu/Publications/papers/studyplace/title.html].

McGregor, Douglas. 1960. *The Human Side of Enterprise*. New York: McGraw-Hill.

———.1966. *Leadership and Motivation*. Cambridge, MA: MIT Press.

Mill, John Stuart. 1972 (1859). *On Liberty*. In H. B. Acton, ed, *J.S. Mill: Utilitarianism, On Liberty* and *Considerations on Representative Government*. London, U.K.: J.M. Dent & Sons.

Morita, A. 1986. *Made in Japan*. New York: E.P. Dutton.

Nonaka, I., and H. Takeuchi. 1995. *The Knowledge-Creating Company*. New York: Oxford.

Oakeshott, Michael. 1991. *Rationalism in Politics and Other Essays*. Indianapolis, IN: Liberty Fund.

Ortega y Gasset, Jose. 1961. *Meditations on Quixote*. New York: Norton.

———. 1966. *Mission of the University*. New York: Norton.

Pauly, Mark. 1980. *Doctors and Their Workshops: Economic Models of Physician Behavior*. Chicago, IL: University of Chicago Press.

Polanyi, Michael. 1962. *Personal Knowledge: Towards a Post-Critical Philosophy*. Chicago, IL: University of Chicago Press.

Popper, Karl R. 1962. *The Open Society and its Enemies: The High Tide of Prophecy: Hegel, Marx, and the Aftermath*. New York: Harper and Row.

Prendergast, Candice. 1999. "The Provision of Incentives in Firms." *Journal of Economic Literature* 37 March: pp. 7–63.

Putnam, Robert. 1993. *Making Democracy Work*. Princeton, NJ: Princeton University Press.

Rahman, Md. Anisur. 1993. *People's Self-Development*. London, U.K.: Zed Books.

Rheinfrank, John, William Hartman, and Arnold Wasserman. 1992. "Design for Usability: Crafting a Strategy for the Design of a New Generation of Xerox Copiers."

In Paul S. Adler and Terry Winograd, eds., *Usability: Turning Technology into Tools*. New York: Oxford University Press.

Robertson, D.H. 1921. "Economic Incentives." *Economica,* October.

Rogers, Carl R. 1951. *Client-Centered Therapy*. Boston, MA: Houghton Mifflin.

———. 1961. *On Becoming a Person*. Boston, MA: Houghton Mifflin.

———. 1969. *Freedom to Learn*. Columbus, OH: Charles Merrill.

Ross, Stephen. 1973. "The Economic Theory of Agency: The Principal's Problem." *American Economic Review* 63 (May): pp. 134–39.

Rousseau, Jean-Jacques. 1979 (1762). *Emile, or on Education*. Translated by Allan Bloom. New York: Basic Books.

Rubin, Edward L. 1996. "The New Legal Process, the Synthesis of Discourse, and the Microanalysis of Institutions." *Harvard Law Review* 109: pp. 1393–411.

Ruskin, John. 1985 (1862). *Unto this Last*. London, U.K.: Penguin.

Ryle, Gilbert. 1945–46. "Knowing How and Knowing That." *Proceedings of the Aristotelian Society* 46: pp. 1–16.

Schön, Donald A. 1971. *Beyond the Stable State*. New York: Norton.

———. 1983. *The Reflective Practitioner: How Professionals Think in Action*. New York: Basic Books.

Schelling, Thomas C. 1984. *Choice and Consequences: Perspectives of an Errant Economist*. Cambridge, MA: Harvard University Press.

Schmidt, J., ed. 1996. *What is Enlightenment? Eighteenth-Century Answers and Twentieth-Century Questions*. Berkeley, CA: University of California Press.

Schumacher, E. F. 1964. "A Humanistic Guide to Foreign Aid." In David Novack and Robert Lekachman, eds., *Development and Society*. New York: St. Martins.

———. 1973. *Small Is Beautiful: Economics As If People Mattered*. New York: Harper and Row.

Schwenk, C. R. 1984. "Devil's Advocacy in Managerial Decision Making." *Journal of Management Studies* April: pp. 153–68.

———.1989. "A Meta-Analysis of the Comparative Effectiveness of Devil's Advocacy and Dialectical Inquiry." *Strategic Management Journal* 10 (3): pp. 303–06.

Scitovsky, Tibor. 1976. *The Joyless Economy: An Inquiry into Human Satisfaction and Consumer Dissatisfaction*. Oxford, U.K.: Oxford University Press.

Scott, James C. 1998. *Seeing Like a State: How Certain Schemes to Improve the Human Condition Have Failed*. New Haven, CT: Yale University Press.

Sen, Amartya. 1982. *Choice, Welfare and Measurement*. Oxford, U.K.: Blackwell.

———. 1984. *Resources, Values and Development*. Cambridge, MA: Harvard.

———. 1995. "Rationality and Social Choice." *American Economic Review* 85.

———. 1999. *Development as Freedom*. New York: Knopf.

Senge, Peter 1990. *The Fifth Discipline: The Art and Practice of the Learning Organization*. New York: Currency Doubleday.

Shaw, George Bernard. 1962. *The Wit and Wisdom of Bernard Shaw*. New York: Collier.

Simmons, John, and William Mares. 1983. *Working Together*. New York: Knopf.

Stiglitz, Joseph.1998. "Towards a New Paradigm for Development: Strategies, Policies, and Processes." Raul Prebisch Lecture, October 19. United Nations Conference on Trade and Development, Geneva.

Titmuss, Richard. 1970. *The Gift Relationship*. London, U.K.: Allen and Unwin.

Tung, L. L., and A. R. Heminger. 1993. "The Effects of Dialectical Inquiry, Devil's Advocacy, and Consensus Inquiry Methods in a GSS Environment." *Information and Management* 25: pp. 33–41.

Verhagen, Koenraad. 1987. *Self-Help Promotion: a Challenge to the NGO Community*. Netherlands: CEBEMO/KIT.

von Humboldt, Wilhelm. 1969. *The Limits of State Action*. Cambridge, U.K.: Cambridge University Press.

Westbrook, Robert. 1991. *John Dewey and American Democracy*. Ithaca, NY: Cornell University Press.

Whyte, William Foote. 1955. *Money and Motivation: An Analysis of Incentives in Industry*. New York: Harper and Row.

Wolfensohn. James D. 1997. "Annual Meetings Address: The Challenge of Inclusion." Address given in Hong Kong [www.worldbank.org/html/extdr/am97/jdw_sp/jwsp97e.htm.].

———. 1998. "Annual Meetings Address: The Other Crisis." Washington, D.C.: World Bank [http://www.worldbank.org/html/extdr/am98/jdw-sp/index.htm].

———. 1999a. "Annual Meetings Address: Coalitions for Change." Washington, D.C.: World Bank.

———. 1999b. "A Proposal for a Comprehensive Development Framework." Washington, D.C.: World Bank.

World Bank. 1996. *The World Bank Participation Sourcebook*. Washington, D.C.

———. 1998. *Assessing Aid*. Policy Research Series. Washington, D.C.

Zuboff, Shoshana. 1988. *In the Age of the Smart Machine: The Future of Work and Power*. New York: Basic Books.

7

Development Advisory Services: From Blueprints to Learning

Nagy Hanna

Demand for analytical and advisory assistance is likely to increase under the Comprehensive Development Framework (CDF) and the closely related Poverty Reduction Strategy Papers (PRSPs), to empower clients and support local processes and institutions. Facilitating client learning is vital for client ownership and sustainable policy change (Chaps. 4, 5, and 6). Donor-led economic analysis and policy prescriptions and supply-driven technical assistance programs must give way to country-led approaches that build on local processes and experiences, nurture commitment for policy reforms, and emphasize local learning and capacity building. New staff skills and attitudes will be required, along with changes in the incentive systems of development assistance agencies. A Copernican revolution is needed in development activities, moving from a perspective revolving around development agencies (and their influential donors) to a perspective revolving around developing countries and their realities and institutions.

This chapter focuses on experience with comprehensive assessments and planning exercises in the public and private sectors and their implications for implementation of the CDF and PRSP. Examples are drawn mainly from evaluations of the World Bank's economic and sector work and analytical and advisory tools. The Bank has devoted significant resources to its tools and frameworks, and has imposed them on clients and partners. With its emphasis on its role as a knowledge bank, the World Bank in particular will need to adopt a learning mode for its role in knowledge services for development. Economic and sector analyses should go beyond a preoccupation with "due diligence" and unilateral diagnosis of problems toward collaborative definition of the challenges and search for solutions. Analytical tools and frameworks should advance knowledge transfer and capacity building, and support domestic generation and discussion of options.

This chapter draws lessons from two very different development regions and experiences to explore approaches to vision and strategy development. It highlights the experience of the Long-Term Perspective Studies in Africa, which were similar in spirit to the CDF, and the country-driven development strategies of East Asia, shaken but still sound. It also draws lessons from multisectoral development planning and business corporate planning. It also considers lessons from World Bank evaluations of its comprehensive diagnostic tools (public expenditure reviews, poverty assessments, and social and structural policy reviews). It asks why it has been so difficult to move away from blueprints. The chapter concludes with implications for aid agencies and their practices in carrying out economic analyses and advisory services, as well as research, knowledge management, technical assistance, and capacity building.

Lessons from the African Long-Term Perspective Studies

In February 1992, the United Nations Development Programme (UNDP) launched "African Futures," a proposal to engage in national long-term perspective studies with African governments. The approach focuses on strategic thinking, shared vision, stakeholder participation, long-term planning scenarios, and strategic management of national development.

After seven years, evaluators noted a clear enhancement of social dialogue in all countries that implemented a national long-term perspective study (Ohiorheunan 1998). They found increased awareness that development management is a process that views short- and medium-term programs within a long-tem perspective. Focusing on developing long-term visions has contributed to national consensus building on the broad goals and directions of development, bringing together national administrations, universities, researchers, the private sector, and civil society. The media, too, contributed to a public discussion on the results of the studies.

Putting the long-term vision studies into practice proved difficult. The exercise provoked many questions and doubts about the utility of long-term reflections when there are pressing problems and external shocks in the short term.

Some studies were too general and failed to address real-life tradeoffs and choices. Others were not analytically sound enough to draw meaningful conclusions on programs and policies. While the participatory approach was useful in strategy formulation, when it came to resource allocation the realities of government processes and donor disagreements over elements of the long-term vision intervened.

Mauritius was the lone implementation success story, something evaluators (Ohiorheunan 1998) attributed to the relative simplicity of the institutional framework for implementing this national long-term perspective study. The country's policymakers initiated the study and remained committed to it. Working groups were free to choose subject areas and issues to study. A small core group provided guidance and monitored the study, acting from a secretariat set up under the Ministry of Economic Planning and Development. The objectives of the national long-term perspective studies were clarified from the beginning. The biggest challenges were developing an approach based on the principles of participation and developing arrangements for national consultations.

Several lessons for long-term, holistic planning can be drawn from this experience with national long-term perspective studies:

- The country has to be author as well as owner of development programs from the very beginning.
- The process of developing broadly shared, long-term visions and translating them into specific policies and investment programs is likely to be long and demanding.
- Long-term strategies must address the changing global environment, uncertainties and vulnerabilities to external shocks, and creation of dynamic comparative advantage.
- Tools should be developed to engage stakeholders, to scan systematically for opportunities and threats, to assess the country's strengths and weaknesses, to explore fundamentally different future scenarios, and in general to enhance the rigor and realism of long-term visions.
- PRSPs should be anchored in poverty diagnosis and a framework for constant monitoring and evaluation of results to ensure timely adaptation and learning from experience.
- Implementation processes, capability constraints, and institutional change dynamics must be integral to, not an afterthought of, strategy design.

Lessons from the East Asian Development Strategies

In contrast with these visions and futures exercises, the East Asian governments, working closely with businesses and think tanks, formulated and successfully implemented development policies and strategies that anticipated (rehearsed and explored, not predicted) the challenges and opportunities generated by changes in global and local environments. Their strategies focused on creating comparative advantage in successively more sophisticated branches of production. They acquired these advantages sequentially, through coordinated investments, incentives, and institutions. The thrust of their policies and investments changed with changes in domestic and international conditions, technological and demographic trends, institutional infrastructure, and cumulative learning.

In choosing which new competencies and economic activities to stress, these countries took account of the linkages of these activities in factor and input markets, their optimal scale, externalities, backward linkages, and local initial conditions. Investment in human resources was coordinated with trade and industrial policies to generate comparative advantage in labor-intensive, then skill-intensive, and more recently, knowledge-intensive exports. In contrast, the experience of Latin America up to the 1980s suggests that countries that have used static rather than dynamic comparative advantage to guide their development strategy have stagnated.

Another source of the strength and dynamism of the East Asian strategies has been the partnership between the public and private sectors. In the first three to four decades after the establishment of the Bretton Woods institutions, orthodox development economics viewed government as a necessary prime mover. Then, during the Washington Consensus (turned into orthodoxy) period, the pendulum swung against government-led and toward market-led development.

The East Asian countries followed their own paths. They adopted a dynamic mix of government and market, adapting it as development proceeded (Adelman 2000). Governments worked closely with the private sector to orchestrate public investments in human resources and infrastructure, to link incentives to export performance, to target new activities for infant industry protection, and to replace protection with export orientation once the infants had become adolescents. Coordinated actions and selective promotion were informed by extensive consultations with the private sector. For example, in Japan and the Republic of Korea, technocrats used deliberation councils to supplement the market's information transmission function and establish contests among firms (World Bank 1993). The role of the councils changed over time, from industry-specific promotion to a more indicative and consensus-building role. Public-private partnerships in designing and implementing development strategies also allowed for dynamic adaptation of the roles over time.

While relying on markets to promote efficiency and competitiveness, East Asian countries used a variety of instruments to anticipate the future and adjust to changes, taking account of potential synergies and externalities. National economic plans indicated broad development directions and the contribution expected from various sectors. The process of preparing the guiding visions provided a national forum for identifying and discussing future policy needs (World Bank 1993), engaging different segments of society, and helping politicians mobilize public support for development programs.

To combine flexibility with broad consultation, governments had to be selective in the goals they emphasized and their national strategies concentrated on selected themes or thrusts at a time. Governments also used an immense variety of policies to achieve three critical determinants of growth: accumulation, efficient allocation, and rapid productivity growth. They did this with combinations of policies and institutional instruments, ranging from market-oriented to state-led, that varied across economies and over time (World Bank 1993; Wade 1990; Rodrik 2000; Adelman 2000). Willingness to learn and experiment and to adapt policies and institutions to changing circumstances was a key element of success.

An important lesson from this development experience is the premium derived from agility, flexibility, pragmatism, and innovation in pursuing long-term visions. No blueprint plan or policy orthodoxy could anticipate all the nonlinear and dynamic changes involved in development or the external shocks and uncertainties. There is a growing recognition that the development process is path-dependent, which implies a need to understand the country's history and current initial conditions. Development is often uneven and unpredictable. It involves many choices and institutional innovations, even among countries at similar levels of development (Adelman 2000). Recent research also indicates that external shocks were an important determinant of country growth and poverty reduction over the last two decades, in many cases more than offsetting the positive impact of policy improvement during this period (Easterly 2000). All these findings suggest that *long-term visions should not be turned into detailed and rigid long-term plans. Rather, the focus should be on building strategic flexibility and developing local capabilities to capture opportunities, manage uncertainties, and learn quickly.*

Lessons from Multisectoral Planning

Multisectoral planning approaches share many features with the CDF approach—and present many of the same challenges. Experience suggests key and common pitfalls: overambitious goals and rigid targets, overemphasis on data collection and comprehensive analysis at the expense of implementation, imposition of new administrative and hierarchical structures, excessive focus on forms and documentation, political naivete about the scope for genuine national consensus, and poor linkage between planning and implementation (Chap. 2).

A recent review of national strategies for sustainable development illustrates these lessons and suggests new directions (OECD 1999). The Development Assistance Committee set 2005 as the target date for countries to have begun to implement national sustainable development strategies. The goal is to integrate sustainability with socioeconomic development strategies. Many national sustainable development strategies have had little impact because they focus mainly on the production of a document as an end product, a reflection of a tendency by donors to ignore local processes. The review notes that the integration of sustainability issues is often impeded by sectoral turf battles. Similarly, government capacity to involve the private sector in policymaking and planning is often inadequate, even though the private sector is a major agent of environmental degradation. Finally, there is the risk of a proliferation of strategy and action plan processes, notably in response to international conventions, which can result in overburdening governments and reducing their capacity for action.

Another example of multisectoral planning is the United Nations Development Programme's (UNDP's) program approach, which has received close attention since 1993. Embodying principles similar to those of the CDF, it emphasizes country ownership, development partnerships, participation of all of society, and a focus on results. Specific forms vary from multisectoral programs focusing on specific objectives, geographic areas, or beneficiaries to sectoral approaches, to projects managed independently but placed under a single umbrella program.

A recent assessment of this approach offers pointers for bringing the CDF principles into country assistance programs (UNDP 1999). Preliminary findings suggest both significant startup costs and gains from improved ownership and partnership. Multisectoral programs demand coordination across sectors, while national administrations and aid agencies are most often organized sectorally. Though conducive to aid coordination and partnerships, the approach has made only modest progress. UNDP resources have been limited, and donors vied for visibility and autonomy for their own programs. Progress on results-based monitoring and evaluation of programs was limited because of local capacity deficiencies, donor tendencies to set up parallel systems, neglect of the information needs of many stakeholders, and the inadequacy of local information systems for monitoring multidonor programs. The program approach also fell into the trap of excessive preoccupation with formats, procedures, and documentation.

Donors and central governments have too often adopted a hegemonic planning mentality that enhances the power of international agencies and external technical assistance to the neglect of local institutions, indigenous knowledge, and practical experience (Scott 1998). Large-scale programs are typically products of top-down and centrally driven planning. The subjects of development are abstracted and standardized, and one-size-fits-all solutions are used to facilitate central design and top-down implementation. Such planning ignores that poverty is diverse and context-specific, and that the poor are vulnerable yet possess few means of managing risk. It also routinely ignores uncertainty about the future and the learning and adaptation that must be mobilized during implementation. It takes a social engineering approach that reflects little confidence in the skills, initiative, intelligence, and experience of intended beneficiaries. This posture may enhance the authority and apparent precision of the donors and central planners. But it diminishes the morale, learning, and human capital of other stakeholders, particularly the poor and voiceless.

These experiences, and many others from diverse aid agencies and developing countries, point to a need to shift from blueprint to process approaches for comprehensive development assistance. Process approaches start small, with a built-in bias to action and learning. The learning process approach emphasizes flexible, evolutionary, and participatory methods that are results-oriented and client-centered. Top-down approaches to planning are combined with bottom-up approaches to link together local initiatives, facilitate exchange of information and experience, capture tacit knowledge, and promote stakeholder commitment and active learning (Hanna et al. 2001).

Lessons from Corporate Planning

Corporate planning in the private sector has been relatively more advanced than national or public sector planning in learning to adapt, remaining outward looking and client-oriented, and working through strategic partnerships. Business organizations have faced challenges in adapting and positioning themselves in response to fast-changing environments in an increasingly turbulent, competitive, and knowledge-intensive global economy. Corporate strategy development and strategic planning practices have undergone fundamental transformations. Recent understanding of strategic decisionmaking in organizations suggests that it is a social and political process, involving communication and negotiation. Strategic problems are not always amenable to forecasting and blueprint solutions, and strategy formulation is an adaptive learning process (Hanna 1985; Mintzberg 1998).

While businesses have different objectives than public institutions and aid agencies, their experience in strategic planning and management processes provides valuable lessons in building strategic planning capabilities, managing strategy formulation, creating strategic alliances, and monitoring for sustainable performance:

Ownership of strategy by line managers and other stakeholders is essential for successful implementation. Corporate planning during the 1960s and 1970s was centrally driven, with elaborate form-bound planning processes, complex planning documents and technocratic tools, large-scale data collection, elaborate controls, and large central planning departments. Rather than facilitating creative thinking and dialogue across functions and management layers, planning processes often degenerated into mechanistic thinking that stifled creativity, ownership, and commitment. Most such plans were never implemented: planners became the primary producers and users of plans, and planning tools and documents became ends in themselves.

Reforms to strategic planning aimed to revitalize the process by promoting participation and dialogue with all levels of management, suppliers and partners, and clients. Ownership and commitment were built incrementally through action learning and broad involvement. From being preoccupied with data and forms, planning processes shifted to establishing conditions for effective participation, capturing the tacit knowledge of participants, and mobilizing grassroots learning.

Results-focused feedback mechanisms are essential to strategy making and adaptive learning. No amount of forecasting or blueprint planning can substitute for flexibility, timely response, and systematic learning from experience. Traditional planning assumed predictable trends, a controllable internal environment, and no fundamental changes to the external environment. Blueprints typically led to inflexibility and obsolete plans, and degenerated into inward-looking processes. Formal feedback was often too little and too late. Management consulting firms often perpetuated the myth that such blueprint strategies could be created on behalf of their clients.

Strategy evolves when internal decisions and external events flow together to create a new, widely shared consensus for action. Strategies often emerge where people have the capacity and resources to learn. Once recognized as promising, pilots and emergent strategies can be selectively propagated and scaled up. Thus, organizations discover their strengths and weaknesses and hone their competitive advantage by testing the market and learning with clients. Recent advances in strategic management emphasize an agile, selective, results-focused, and continuous strategy process. Such processes rely on cross-functional teams for quick and integrative response and on a rich variety of feedback and learning mechanisms, drawing on qualitative and quantitative information throughout the process. Best practice in management consulting aims at enhancing clients' capabilities and processes to generate their own strategies and adaptive responses.

Strategies must be congruent with current capabilities and structures for the short term, while building competencies and transforming capabilities for the long term. Centrally driven planning either overestimated implementation capabilities or ignored implementation and change management challenges. Central planners discovered that they have no power to impose blueprints and that incentives, capabilities, and managerial systems must match strategy. Strategy management thus focuses on implementation dynamics through nurturing, adjustment, venturing, and change management. It integrates strategic planning with resource allocation, information and communication systems, skills, values, and incentive and organizational structures. Such change requires strong leadership to build coalitions and facilitate learning at all levels.

The essence of strategy is a dynamic strategic fit. Strategy is about choosing a position in a competitive market, a process requiring a decade or more (Ghemawat 1991). There is a need to build core competencies and transform capabilities. An organization achieves a strategic fit through the selective and effective use and accumulation of its invisible assets, such as technological and market know-how.

Strategies should not be captive to static comparative advantage and inherited systems. In diversified corporations, competitive advantage is rooted in core competencies, which bind together existing activities and drive new business development. Vision and strategic intent embody the aspirations and commitment of the organization and set the direction for long-term resource commitment, core competency development, and organizational learning (Hamel and Prahalad 1994). Strategic vision thus complements and guides bottom-up learning. Building strategic positions or competitive advantage for nations follows similar processes but takes much longer to establish (Porter 1990).

Corporations are increasingly entering into alliances to improve responsiveness to clients, gain new knowledge, focus on core businesses and competencies, lower overhead costs, enhance flexibility, mobilize resources, and increase reach. They are becoming increasingly networked and multi-organizational. The Internet is multiplying collaborative planning, global reach, and learning and action across teams and organizations. Managing partnerships and strategic alliances has become a core competency.

The processes underlying strategic partnership development are evolutionary. They require continuous maintenance and evaluation. Partnerships have to be founded on good understanding of an organization's core competencies and the type of relationship each partner wants. Successful partnerships require clear strategic fit and mutual agendas, incremental processes of increasing involvement and sharing information, cultural fit and partnership orientation, mutual respect, collaborative planning and learning, dedicated interorganizational communication, investment in mutually beneficial goals, and a sense of "co-destiny" (Johnston and Lawrence 1988; Kantor 1994; Buono 1997; Doz and Hamel 1998).

Lessons from World Bank Evaluation of Its Knowledge Services

Two key analytical tools underpin much of the World Bank's business strategy in a country: poverty assessments and public expenditure reviews (see Boxes 7.1 and 7.2). Reviews of these and other analytical work have highlighted inadequacies associated with policy prescriptions and limited country participation and ownership.

The impact of poverty assessments at the country level was found to be strongly correlated with their quality, the time available for preparation, the timeliness of the results, and the degree of partnership, consultation, information sharing, and knowledge transfer (World Bank 1999). An evaluation study of the effectiveness of the Bank's poverty reduction strategy finds that diagnostic treatment of poverty in the country assistance strategy has improved substantially, but that the links between diagnosis and policies and assistance strategies remain weak or implicit (Evans 2000). Progress has been slow in moving from the policy generalities of the Bank's poverty strategy to dealing with the specifics of poverty and structural inequality and producing context-specific recommendations. Few country assistance strategies explicitly identify the links between recommended policies and investments and expected changes in the asset or employment status of the poor. And few deal with institutions and regulatory systems—such as financial services, gender discrimination, and justice systems—that are distinctly anti-poor in many countries. A review of the country assistance strategies of the U.K. Department for International Development (Shepherd 2000) reaches similar conclusions: there is a "missing middle" between documenting the poverty profile of a country and formulating generic recommendations and assistance programs, a consequence of relatively standardized and top-down processes of country strategy formulation.

An evaluation study of *public expenditure reviews* found that they too remain primarily Bank documents that evoke only lukewarm interest from the concerned government (World Bank 1998; Evans 2000). Public expenditure reviews typically present a narrow and short-term focus on spending and input controls, while giving short shrift to poverty issues and the distributional implications of public expenditure reform. The study suggests that public expenditure reviews need greater:

- breadth, with better coverage of institutions and constraints, roles of subnational governments, and public-private-civil society partnerships in public service provision;
- depth, with adequate specificity and concern for outputs;
- timeliness, especially for reviews related to government planning, budgeting, and policy reform cycles.

A comprehensive framework and long-term vision are meaningful only when linked to budget constraints and translated into choices on priorities and sequencing. There are some promising examples of how the process can be assisted through a medium-term expenditure framework. Ghana has established a clear policy framework based on its "Vision 2020" exercise and has tried to operationalize it through a rolling three-year framework (DFID 1998). Government departments set out their goals and budget plans for achieving them and then formalize them through performance contracts. The medium-term expenditure framework attempts to bring donor funding within budget

Box 7. 1
How Well Do Poverty Assessments Incorporate the Principles of the Comprehensive Development Framework?

Poverty assessment is a key instrument in the World Bank's poverty reduction strategy. How well has this tool been applied in ways that incorporate the CDF goals?

Holistic, long-term approach. Poverty assessments are intended to combine analysis of macroeconomic and sectoral policy with the poverty profile, taking into account the impact of policy on the poor and the need to design programs for the poor within a consistent macroeconomic framework. A 1999 review found that nearly half of poverty assessments do not address individual elements of the poverty reduction strategy well (OED 1999).[1]

A common shortcoming is the failure to address macroeconomic linkages to poverty (such as trade and exchange rate policy) and the contribution of sectoral issues (food policy, agriculture, rural development) to poverty reduction. Regional dimensions of a poverty reduction strategy also receive limited attention. The review found progress in combining quantitative and qualitative analysis in poverty assessments and in using interdisciplinary approaches to poverty reduction. It also found progress in incorporating social, political, and institutional perspectives in poverty assessments, though these findings tended to be used illustratively only, rather than to sharpen analytical focus and integration.

Participation, partnership, and ownership. Poverty assessments are intended to provide the basis for a collaborative approach to poverty reduction by country officials and the Bank. The fact that the Bank usually initiates a poverty assessment has implications for ownership of the poverty assessment by the government. Actively seeking government support and involvement is crucial. In Côte d'Ivoire, starting an early dialogue with a reluctant government paid off by building mutual trust and fostering greater government ownership.

The bulk of partnership and consultation with governments during preparation of poverty assessments has been with cross-sectoral central ministries (finance, planning) and specialized policy and analytic units. Operating ministries (line agencies) and local governments have been much less involved. In a stakeholder survey conducted as part of the 1999 OED review, only a small number of countries and Bank staff thought that local government officials had strong or moderate influence on the final assessment report. Since operating agencies and local governments are responsible for implementing government policies, their lack of involvement hampers subsequent implementation. A majority of assessments involved NGOs and civil society in some capacity, though roughly half the country clients thought that these groups had exerted only a slight influence, if any. Furthermore, the NGOs involved in the assessments were international rather than national.

Dissemination and follow-up are important instruments for cementing ownership. Only about half the assessments were translated into the local language, a relatively low-cost way of improving readership and buy-in. The stakeholder survey shows that about a third of country clients and Bank staff are dissatisfied with the overall dissemination effort for assessments, and more than half the NGOs are dissatisfied.

Results focus. The first precondition of a results orientation is clarity about goals and expected results. In the stakeholder survey, large majorities of country clients and Bank staff listed multiple goals for the assessment: establishing a cooperative effort between Bank and government in reducing poverty, allowing the Bank to influence the government's poverty reduction policies, building country-level capacity to analyze and monitor poverty, and helping the Bank refine the poverty focus of its own operations. Few assessments were designed to respond to all of these goals. The failure to identify and prioritize goals is a serious omission. Specific goals help to focus the assessment on the particular circumstances of the country and to specify the technical design of assessments. Bangladesh and Thailand are good examples in tailoring the scope and content of poverty assessments to a country's priorities.

[1] Based on an OED review covering nineteen poverty assessments and updates (all those done in fiscal years 1997 and 1998, plus a sample from fiscal year 1996). The 1999 OED review is a follow-up to OED's first review of poverty assessments conducted in 1996, which examined poverty assessments completed through December 1994.

processes, so that donor financial flows are taken into account when resources are allocated (see Chap. 8).

Recently, the World Bank introduced the *social and structural policy review* to its toolkit to broaden the scope of its analysis. Introduced too quickly, without deploying the multidisciplinary skills required for a comprehensive view of development, the social and structural policy reviews tended to concentrate on economic dimensions. Staff competencies required for in-depth analysis of social and structural dimensions were often lacking. That limited the tool to the worldviews of the aid agency's macroeconomists.

Box 7.2
**How Well Do Public Expenditure Reviews Incorporate
the Principles of the Comprehensive Development Framework?**

The Bank has traditionally used public expenditure reviews to examine overall public sector performance. Public expenditure reviews typically analyze public spending and public expenditure management at the central government level. A recent impact evaluation of public expenditure reviews includes some findings that are relevant to the CDF principles (World Bank 1998).

Holistic, long-term approach. Public expenditure reviews typically take a narrow, short to intermediate term look at spending and input controls. Many lack breadth (coverage of institutions and constraints, roles of subnational governments, public-private-civil society partnerships in service provision), depth (adequate specificity and concern for outputs), and timeliness (relative to government and donor planning and budgeting and policy reform cycles).

Often, technical public expenditure reviews draw extensively on well-known normative frameworks in economics, finance, and public management. Institutional realities—such as the budgeting process in Cameroon or the legal and regulatory framework in Honduras—that may affect the selection and implementation of proposed reforms are often dealt with only selectively. Important political constraints are rarely dealt with. Yet institutional and political factors determine the pace and likely success of reforms.

Partnership, participation, and ownership. Public expenditure reviews have failed to forge a partnership approach to external assistance. They have also failed to build a public-private-civil society partnership for social service delivery within client countries. Public expenditure reviews play an insignificant role in Bank dialogue with other donors (except the IMF) or in overall aid coordination. Views of external partners are not solicited or they have no impact on the form of the public expenditure review. In only a few cases has there been significant interaction with other donors. As a result, the broad objectives of many public expenditure reviews have had little relevance to the specific projects in which external partners were involved.

With a few partial exceptions (Ghana, Zimbabwe), public expenditure reviews remain primarily Bank documents. In some cases, such as Pakistan, client governments are aware of the problems addressed by the public expenditure review and are already addressing them. In others, governments perceive the public expenditure review to be simply a prerequisite for donor funding. In still other cases, the governments views the recommendations as unrealistic or too politically contentious to implement. Governments may also believe that they cannot influence the public expenditure review process and perceive it as an attempt by the Bank to micro-manage their expenditure policies.

Results focus. The quality of analyses in public expenditure reviews is improving slowly, with a new focus on results and attention to the institutional and macroeconomic context of public expenditure reform, budgetary decisionmaking, and the discrepancies between authorized and actual expenditures. Often, however, objectives and intended audiences are not identified. In most cases, expected impacts are not mentioned explicitly, and monitoring and evaluation indicators are lacking.

Most public expenditure reviews focus on monitoring and controlling inputs while neglecting outputs and outcomes, such as public sector performance in the delivery of services. Nor do they provide convincing analyses of efficiency, equity, budgetary, or political economy considerations associated with policy changes. Implementation and transition issues, such as building a consensus for reform or sequencing reforms, get little coverage. Most formal public expenditure reviews take too long to emerge and end up "out of sync" with the client's budgetary cycle. Informal reviews are better synchronized with clients' decisionmaking processes and are therefore better positioned strategically to achieve results.

More recently, the Bank and the Fund have introduced a new tool, the country-led Poverty Reduction Strategy Paper (PRSP). The PRSP is expected to be country-driven, prepared and developed transparently with broad local participation, and linked clearly with agreed international development goals—principles embedded in the CDF. It aims to sharpen the focus on poverty by using participatory country-led approaches and by building partnerships among donors. To deliver on its promises, the poverty reduction strategy process should be guided by the lessons of experience from the social and structural policy reviews and other comprehensive planning approaches.

The pace of progress in preparing these poverty reduction strategies must be consistent with the time needed to build ownership and capacity among key stakeholders—civil society, government, and local private sector (IMF and IDA 1999). Early experience suggests that this requires a change in both institutional and staff mindset as well as new skills. The preparation of PRSPs is tied to debt relief, and the World Bank and International Monetary Fund play mediating roles in the process. Hence the risks are real that home-grown development agendas and broad ownership could be sacrificed in favor of orthodoxy and the Washington Consensus. The need for long-term commitment and realistic expectations for development assistance cannot be overstated.

In sum, World Bank experience suggests the following lessons:

- The PRSP should be viewed as an evolving strategy. The emphasis should be on the quality of the process within the country, not the quality of the written document provided to the Fund and the World Bank or the adherence of the PRSP to a universal blueprint.
- Analytical and advisory services and technical cooperation programs should be used to build broad participation and commitment to strategy development and policy reforms—and to build the capacity of local think tanks, consulting firms, and implementing institutions. Technical assistance programs should assist countries to build their capabilities for managing their own development.
- Analytical and advisory services should support country-led processes. They should facilitate the generation of options and the promotion of local debate and national consensus. This requires a shift in aid agency attitudes—more humility, problem-solving, and teamwork are crucial. Incentives to staff should encourage client understanding, and support to local decisionmaking. Incentives should be aligned with development results and sustainability, not volumes of lending and reporting.
- Development assistance agencies should mobilize multidisciplinary teams to assist countries in leading the production of comprehensive assessments and strategies that build on lessons of the past. This requires a change in skills, as well as integrative and multidisciplinary frameworks.

Implications for Analytical and Advisory Services

Why has it been so difficult to promote intellectual partnerships, jointly owned frameworks, local capacity building, and bottom-up processes? A key reason is that the World Bank and other aid agencies tend to reify their own instruments, models, and blueprints. These are often justified as embodying the greater wisdom of the agencies and as responsive to their agendas and experiences. This conceptual hubris overlooks the great complexity and variability of local conditions. It ignores the impact of the centrally and externally imposed templates on local initiative and adaptive capacity. It misses the opportunities for developing countries to learn from each other directly, and for local think tanks to invent institutional solutions and adapt international best practices to local conditions and culture. The "authorizing environment" of the Bank and other aid agencies (consisting of the western NGOs and donor governments) also tends to set universal standards that are not always consistent with local realities. And because of the intellectual dominance of economics as the scientific paradigm for the human sciences in most aid agencies, it overlooks the contributions of other social sciences that are more context-based or sensitive to institutional conditions (see Chap. 6).

In developing new-style analytical and advisory instruments, the Bank and other development assistance agencies should be concerned with:

- motivation and empowerment, to ensure that development assistance is compatible with client autonomy (see Chap. 6);
- learning, capacity building, and sustainability, to avoid cognitive dependency and build on local knowledge;
- quality—as defined by all stakeholders, not just by internal peer groups and bureaucratic norms—to enhance relevance and ownership; and
- partnership with other donors, to harmonize donors' frameworks, draw on diverse experiences, reduce transaction costs, and improve selectivity.

The Department for International Development's (DFID 1998) sustainable livelihood approach illustrates the new-style analytical tools and their implications for local knowledge management and capacity building. An analytical framework guides understanding of the factors that influence poverty and identifies where interventions might best be made, based on a holistic view of poverty and poor people's livelihood. The approach thus facilitates cross-sectoral and multidisciplinary thinking. Recent applications of the tool raise new challenges, particularly in finding an institutional locus for the tool and in engaging sectoral institutions. Used to empower clients and enhance learning, such tools will also require better understanding of the knowledge systems surrounding various stakeholders (Nicol 2000). Information on changes taking place in a given setting, essential for avoiding blueprint approaches, requires informed stakeholders and continuous feedback from participants.

Common approaches to national development strategy typically ignore the gap between the "grand design" and implementation capacity, create enclave project units, and engage in drawn-out analysis as a substitute for action and practical learning. To overcome these tendencies, new approaches should be sought to blend bottom-up with top-down strategies. For example one approach is to engage clients in a series of small-scale, results-producing, and momentum-building initiatives (Matta, Ashkenes, and Rischard 2000). These rapid-results projects can be linked with each other and with longer-term, more traditional project activities into an implementation strategy grounded in the capacity limitations and potential of the client country. Each project is aimed at achieving a small-scale strategic result, building capacity for change, generating learning, and reducing the execution risk of long-term and large-scale project activities. The rapid-results approach would move quickly from an overall view of the comprehensive changes needed to small-scale experiments, to learning about what it takes to achieve broader results and build confidence and capacity in the client. This learning is fed back into an evolving comprehensive strategy. Strategy formulation and implementation, analysis, and action are thus blended, shortening the feedback loop.

Blueprints versus Local Knowledge and Experimentation

As the Bank and other aid agencies move toward support of comprehensive development strategies such as the PRSPs, they are likely to use more broad forms of conditionality (Chap. 3) and programmatic lending (Chaps. 8 and 9). These practices will require, in turn, more integrated assessments and comprehensive diagnostic tools that attempt to capture the institutional underpinnings of market economies and address the structural dimensions of development. These trends are on the whole positive and consistent with the holistic principle of the CDF. But they also pose significant challenges and risks, as blueprints (standard designs or formulas, detailed plans rigidly implemented) could be imposed on whole national strategies, not just projects or a single assistance activity.

There are two basic modes of acquiring institutions and development strategies: importing a blueprint from the more advanced economies such as the "Washington Consensus," or developing them locally, relying on local knowledge, experimentation, and hands-on experience (Rodrik 2000). Wholesale importation or imposition of blueprints (called best practices) is often inappropriate, since institutions are highly specific to local conditions, and the institutional repertoire available in advanced economies may be limiting or inappropriate to the diverse needs of developing countries. Much of the know-how of institutional development is tacit knowledge, leaving the blueprints highly incomplete. The East Asian development strategies involved much experimentation and new models of public-private partnerships that were not available in—or even inconsistent with—the blueprints of the World Bank and donors. Similarly, home-grown Chinese gradualism proved more effective than the shock therapy that was considered the best practice of the leading aid agencies in the 1990s.

Are the two modes mutually exclusive? Is one mode always superior to the other? Even with the best fit, an imported blueprint requires local expertise for successful implementation. Alternatively, when initial local conditions differ greatly, it would be unwise to deny the possible relevance of innovations or home-grown solutions. Of course, the institutional arrangements and strategies adopted elsewhere provide lessons even if they cannot be transplanted. Blueprints and international standards may meet the need for some narrowly technical issues. But large-scale institutional reforms and development strategies essentially require a process of discovery about local needs and capabilities (Rodrick 1999).

Given the dominance of international agencies such as the World Bank and the International Monetary Fund (IMF), and their proclivity toward blueprints on best practices, a development assistance mode that relies more on local knowledge and experimentation seems preferable on balance. The blueprint approach is largely top-down, relying on technocrats and foreign advisors. It is most convenient for large and centralized aid bureaucracies. It empowers external experts and knowledge codifiers. But blueprints tend to perpetuate dependency, overwhelm local capacity, and distort reform priorities. Meantime, local skills knowledge and learning remain highly underutilized resources that could otherwise enrich the repertoire of development practitioners. All successful development strategies are fundamentally built on local innovations and adaptations. This mode of assistance is also more legitimate and sustainable, as it is consistent with ownership and participatory democracy (Chaps. 5 and 6). Participatory political institutions could be used to elicit and aggregate local knowledge and thereby help build better institutions (Rodrick 1999).

Implications of the Information Revolution

The opportunities presented by the information revolution and the central role of knowledge and learning for development have major implications for implementing the CDF principles.

First, knowledge strategies should be integral to development strategies. Building on the findings of *World Development Report 1998/99: Knowledge for Development,* aid agencies should understand the ongoing transformation in knowledge production and dissemination in society and systematically assist clients to develop appropriate institutions, including local think tanks and research and extension agencies. Global and local knowledge need to be blended and adapted to local conditions. Development assistance should address the growing gap between the information haves and have nots. Participation, ownership, and partnership require fair access to information and to opportunities for learning. Since the poor suffer most from information market failures, particular attention should go to the information and learning needs of the poor and rural populations. Information and knowledge relevant to the poor would not have to come from aid agencies, but could come from other providers of such knowledge, including local and international NGOs.

Second, aid agencies such as the UNDP and World Bank should accelerate their development of competencies to assist clients in positioning themselves for the information age and exploiting the revolution in information and communication technologies. Aid agencies should assist developing countries to design and implement strategies for a knowledge-based economy. They should help countries build local capacity to effectively apply and adapt the new technologies and enable them to become full partners in a globally networked economy. Information systems and infrastructure components are already present in all sectors in a majority of aid-supported projects. But quality is uneven and impact uncertain. These activities should be evaluated, scaled up, and integrated into overall sectoral and country strategies.

Third, technical cooperation should be rethought in order to promote knowledge sharing and exploit the power of the new technologies for collaborative and just-in-time learning. Emphasis should shift from providing expert and technical assistance staff to collaborating with and empowering local institutions and expertise. Modern information and communication technologies could be central to this shift.

Finally, large development agencies such as the World Bank should see themselves not as information monopolists or sole keepers of development know-how, but as hubs, knowledge brokers, and participants in a growing global network of communities of practice. This implies a shift in self-perception from an agency that has all the answers to one that is looking for answers, from one full of doers and teachers to one full of listeners, learners, and connectors. Adopting this perspective may call for a new business model that puts knowledge and learning at the center of these agency's services and strategies.

Implications for Aid Agencies

Lessons from strategy development in the public and private sectors point to a common pitfall in comprehensive and top-down planning approaches: tools, models, and frameworks often become ends in themselves.[1] The modalities by which the new and more comprehensive analytical tools are applied need to support ownership and learning. The tools must be considered not in isolation from client processes, but in relation to local tools for policymaking and in the context of local processes for strategy formulation and implementation.

As development strategies must be formulated and implemented at all levels of society, it is important to use both top-down and bottom-up approaches and to promote interaction and dialogue among all levels. Top-down approaches may be used to generate national consensus, provide strategic direction, facilitate coordination, provide frameworks and tools for local initiatives, mobilize national resources, and build capabilities for scaling up. Bottom-up approaches may be used to tackle the specificity of poverty, engender ownership and commitment, mobilize local assets and knowledge, promote innovation, and generate new models and ingredients for future strategies. This should be viewed as an interactive and continuous process.

All this calls for new skills within development agencies in promoting participatory processes, building partnerships, developing institutions, and sharing knowledge and learning services. In that sense the CDF can be a tool for changing the way aid agencies work. Changes in behavior and culture do not come quickly or easily, but they are key to meeting the challenges of CDF implementation and the development of new-style knowledge services and technical assistance.

With development conceived of as a social transformation process, aid agency staff need to be equipped to understand the dynamics of such change and to work with local change agents. Incentives have to be revamped to reward new competencies and behaviors, such as learning, information sharing, and concentration on sustainable results. Leadership development should emphasize motivation and change management, and the building of ownership within the client system. Staff need to become adept at empowering and facilitating the development of local counterparts. To become selective and make room for genuine partnerships, aid agencies should be honest and modest about their comparative advantage, acknowledging weaknesses as well as strengths.

Key to practicing comprehensive and country-led development will be building client capacity to access knowledge and nurture local learning processes. Knowledge management initiatives at the World Bank have focused on its own knowledge content and systems to improve its knowledge and share its best practices. These are important steps toward exploiting the information revolution for development. But they have so far neglected helping clients build their own capacity to access and manage global and local knowledge and to develop the policies and institutions, information and communication infrastructures, and human resources necessary for knowledge-based economies. A shift to client-focused knowledge development is due.

As learning has become more important now than at any other time in history, a central objective of aid agencies should be to help clients build learning economies and learning societies. Investment projects, technical cooperation, and advisory services should all become means and opportunities for building local learning systems and capabilities. In the increasingly integrated and competitive world economy, individuals, firms, and countries will be able to create wealth in proportion to their capacity to learn (Drucker 1993). Such learning occurs on an economy-wide basis, within and across communities and organizational boundaries. Active learning and tacit knowledge, rooted inside firms and communities, have a central impact on growth, poverty reduction, and global competition (Mansell and When 1998, Lundvall 1996, Hanna et al. 2001).

From Retooling Aid Agencies to Retooling Countries

The CDF calls for a critical shift in perspective: from one revolving around the aid agency and its concerns to one revolving around the country and its institutions—with the aid agency acting as the intellectual partner and enabler, not the planner or doer of development. With this must come an enabling shift in the design and use of analytical tools and the delivery of knowledge and advisory services. It is time to move beyond a preoccupation with developing tools and frameworks for unilateral definitions of problems and solutions in the name of due diligence, and on to applying instruments and approaches that support participatory diagnosis and improve local processes for development planning, decision-making, and learning.

The World Bank is reexamining its economic and sector work, a process likely to lead to a fundamental choice: either to further invest in its diagnostic tools to reinforce due diligence and independent assessment of country policies and institutions, or to invest in new tools and modalities that allow for joint and participatory diagnosis and assessment with its clients.[2]

The first choice would assume the existence of a country development vision, articulated in a poverty reduction strategy paper, and developed and led by the country. The World Bank's economic and sector analyses and diagnostic tools would then be used to carry out due diligence and independent "professional' assessments of the policies and institutions to implement the vision. While the country would own its vision and programs, the Bank would own and be accountable for its diagnosis and the programs its supports. This choice calls for more resources to build the Bank's knowledge about each country, fill the due diligence gaps, and keep this knowledge current and comprehensive. This choice also implies little facilitation or analytic support to the country's own diagnosis and formulation of its development strategy. There is a clear division of labor between the Bank (and other donors) and the client, each using its own tools, and with external assistance strategies starting from where the country's strategy formulation ends. The promise of this approach is that it would allow "space" for clients to develop their own tools and "own" their development visions and strategies.

The alternative is to shift to a new style of advisory services and technical cooperation in which economic and sector analyses are carried out with other aid agencies and with client countries. Accordingly, the Bank would play empowering, facilitating, and advisory roles. Due diligence work and independent assessment would be kept to a minimum, to avoid crowding out customized and collaborative economic and sector work or imposing outside frameworks. Tools and assessments would become transparent, would draw on and help build local knowledge, and would be adapted to local skills and processes. On request from clients, aid agencies would move upstream and support—not supplant—the analytical and diagnostic activities required for designing long-term visions and strategies. Countries would be encouraged to experiment and build on local knowledge. Clients would be engaged downstream in both due diligence and other diagnostic and customized economic and sector work and in the shaping and monitoring and evaluation of assistance strategies and services.[3]

The World Bank, UNDP, IMF, and most key donors and aid agencies are introducing strategic and diagnostic frameworks to focus on poverty reduction, to capture the holistic nature of development, or to coordinate assistance among an increasing number of partners in each country. This proliferation of tools and concepts puts an enormous administrative burden on developing countries as they strive to "negotiate" multiple frameworks, priorities, processes, and performance indicators with multiple donors and aid agencies. It may also divert local resources and managerial talents away from improving local processes and building new ones for strategy formulation and implementation.

Developing countries should have a stronger voice in shaping and harmonizing these new tools and standards. Attention should shift from imposing externally driven tools and frameworks to enriching and strengthening local tools, processes, and information systems. Aid agencies would then devise their business strategies and operational standards to take account of local contexts and client-centered processes.

Acknowledgments

Special thanks to David Ellerman and John Eriksson for their helpful comments on this paper, to Ramgopal Agarwala for his contribution to the lessons learned from the African Long-term Perspective Studies, and to Sonya Cavalho for her contribution to the section on poverty assessments.

Notes

1. This tendency to view planning models and frameworks as ends in themselves has been long recognized in the development planning literature. Yet the tendency prevails. See, for example, Hanna (1976).
2. "Due diligence" economic and sector work at the World Bank currently covers such areas of work as poverty assessments, public expenditure reviews, social and structural policy reviews (or country economic memoranda), and fiduciary (financial management) assessments.
3. This implies a paradigm shift in the role of professionals in development assistance agencies away from a focus on techniques and unilateral control of problem definition and prescription and toward collaborative diagnosis, mutual control over the analysis, and the search for solutions.

References

Adelman, Irma. 2000. "Fifty Years of Economic Development: What Have We Learned?" Paper presented at a World Bank economic conference, June, Washington, D.C.

Buono, A. F. 1997. "Managing Strategic Alliances: Organizational and Human Resource Considerations." *Business and the Contemporary World* 3 (4): pp. 90–101.

DFID (Department for International Development). 1998. *Sustainable Rural Livelihoods: What Contribution Can We Make?* London.

Drucker, P. 1993. *The Post-Capitalist Society,* Oxford, U.K.: Butterworth Heinemann.

Easterly, Bill. 2000. "The Lost Decade . . . and the Coming Boom?" Washington, D.C.: World Bank.

Evans, Allison. 2000. "The Effectiveness of the World Bank's Poverty Reduction Strategy: An Evaluation." Washington, D.C.: World Bank.

Ghemawat, Pankaj. 1991. *Commitment: The Dynamics of Strategy.* New York: Free Press.

Hamel, Gary, and C.K. Prahalad. 1994. *Competing for the Future.* Cambridge, MA: Harvard Business School Press.

Hanna, Nagy. 1976. *Towards a Methodology of Planning for Developing Countries.* Philadelphia, PA: University of Pennsylvania.

—— —. 1985. *Strategic Planning and Management.* World Bank Staff Working paper 751. Washington, D.C.: World Bank.

Hanna, N., S., Boyson, and S. Gunaratne. 1996. "The East Asia Miracle and Information Technology: Strategic Management of Technological Learning," *World Bank Discussion Papers No. 326,* Washington, DC: The World Bank.

Hanna, Nagy, with David Ellerman, and Stephen Denning. 2001. "Active Learning and Development Assistance." *Journal of Knowledge Management.* Vol. 5, No. 2: 171–179. MCB University Press, U.K.

IMF (International Monetary Fund) and IDA (International Development Association). 1999. *Poverty Reduction Strategy Papers: Status and Next Steps.* Washington, D.C.

Johnston, R., and P. R. Lawrence. 1988. "Beyond Vertical Integration—The Rise of the Value-Adding Partnership." *Harvard Business Review* 66 (4): pp. 94–101.

Kantor, R. M. 1994. *When Giants Learn to Dance: Mastering the Challenge of Strategy, Management and Careers in the 1990s.* New York: Simon and Schuster.

Lundvall, B.-A. 1996. "Information Technology in the Learning Economy—Challenges for Development Strategies." Background paper for the UNCSTD Working Group of IT and Development.

Mansell, R., and U. When. 1998. *Knowledge Societies: Information Technology for Sustainable Development.* Oxford, U.K.: Oxford University Press.

Matta, Nadim, Ron Ashkenes, and Jean-Francois Rischard. 2000. "Building Client Capacity through Results." Washington, D.C.: World Bank.

Nicol, Alan. 2000. *Adopting a Sustainable Livelihood Approach to Water Projects.* ODI Working Paper 133. Overseas Development Institute, London.

OECD (Organisation for Economic Co-operation and Development). 1999. "Developing Country Scoping Workshop on National Strategies for Sustainable Development." November 18–19, Sunningdale.

Ohiorheunan, Lily. September 1998. "National Long-Term Perspective Studies—Lessons from Experience." Paper prepared for a United Nations Development Programme workshop in Entebbe, Uganda.

Porter, Michael. 1990. *The Competitive Advantage of Nations.* New York: Free Press.

Rodrik, Dani. 1999. "Institutions for Higher-Quality Growth: What They Are and How to Acquire Them." Paper prepared for the IMF Conference on Second-Generation Reforms. Washington, D.C.

—— —. 2000. "Development Strategies for the Next Century." Paper prepared for Annual Conference on Development Economics. Washington, D.C.: World Bank.

Scott, J.C. 1998. *Seeing Like a State: How Certain Schemes to Improve the Human Condition Have Failed.* New Haven, CT: Yale University Press.

Shepherd, Andrew. 2000. "Lessons Learned from Evaluation DFID's Aid Program in Evaluation and Poverty Reduction." Washington, D.C.: World Bank.

UNDP (United Nations Development Programme). 1999. *Evaluation of the Programme Approach*. New York.

Wade, Robert. 1990. *Governing the Market: Economic Theory and the Role of Government in East Asian Industrialization*. Princeton, NJ: Princeton University Press.

World Bank. 1983. *World Development Report 1983*. New York: Oxford University Press.

———. 1993. *The East Asian Miracle: Economic Growth and Public Policy*. A World Bank Policy Research Report. Washington, D.C.

———. 1997. "Review of Technical Assistance Loans in the World Bank." Washington, D.C.

———. 1998. "The Impact of Public Expenditure Reviews: An Evaluation." Washington, D.C.

———. 1999. "Poverty Assessments: A Follow-up Review." CODE99–50. Washington, D.C.

———.2000. "Fixing ESW: Where Are We?" Operations Policy and Strategy, Washington, D.C.

Part 3

Focus on Results

8

Government-Donor Partnerships in Support of Public Expenditure

Mick Foster and *Felix Naschold*

The medium-term expenditure framework and sectorwide approaches are two new instruments in development cooperation that focus on donor-government partnership in the budget process. The budget is a crucial instrument for operationalizing the objectives of the Comprehensive Development Framework (CDF) at the country level. This chapter focuses on the key concerns of achieving a holistic approach to a budget process owned by government, supported in a spirit of partnership, with a strong emphasis on achieving results.

In the past, instruments of cooperation, such as the policy framework paper, tended to be standardized documents, reflecting mainly the concerns of the World Bank or the International Monetary Fund (IMF). Today, a new approach focuses on an overall development vision, with a strong emphasis on poverty reduction. The most obvious manifestation of the approach is the Poverty Reduction Strategy Papers that low-income countries are now required to prepare, through a broadly participatory national process. Though not mandatory, a key element in giving substance to the poverty reduction strategy of a number of countries, notably Uganda, has been the development of a medium-term expenditure framework as the key instrument for shifting resources in favor of expenditures important for reducing poverty. This chapter reviews attempts to develop the budget process at macroeconomic and sector levels as a framework for coordinating government and donor efforts more closely in support of agreed objectives. Most of the examples of recent policy innovations are drawn from Africa, though many of the lessons should be relevant in other aid-dependent countries.

The chapter looks at several countries that have sought to inform resource allocation decisions with a clear view of the role of the state and to introduce a medium-term expenditure framework that integrates donors within the budget framework. The chapter also examines experience with sectorwide approaches to coordinating government and donor efforts under the leadership of government. These approaches are not equally feasible or relevant in all countries. The chapter concludes with a framework for adapting program aid to country circumstances and for making public expenditure more responsive to poverty reduction.

A Wider Context for Integrating Government and Donor Efforts

A key insight motivating the search for a CDF is that "there is much too little coordination of effort, much too much suspicion between participants and in many cases a simple absence of a framework to coordinate and bring together under government guidance an agreed set of objectives and effective and accountable programs" (Wolfensohn 1999, p. 21). The budget process provides one key focus for better integration of government and donor efforts (Foster and Merotto 1997).

Country Experience

Both government and donor efforts need to be set in the context of a clear vision of the roles of the state, the private sector, nongovernmental organizations (NGOs), and civil society. In the 1970s this context would have been provided by national development plans. In the 1980s and much of the 1990s, the policy framework paper, negotiated with the government through a process of dialogue with the World Bank and IMF on behalf of donors, has often set out the agreed program of policy reform in many of the poorest counties. But in the view of many ministers and senior officials "it has become a rather routine process whereby the Fund brings uniform drafts (with spaces to be filled) from Washington, in which even matters of language and form are cast in colorless stone . . . the [policy framework paper] document has become so uniform—it is difficult to distinguish one from the other" (Botchwey et al. 1998, p. 40). Furthermore, the process is dominated by the World Bank and IMF, with no representation of development partners such as civil society, the private sector, and NGOs

These criticisms have evoked a constructive response from the IMF and the Bank. In poor IDA-only countries, the policy framework paper has been replaced by the poverty reduction strategy paper. This strategy paper is drafted by the government itself, with the Bank and IMF providing their assessments separately. There is a strong emphasis on evidence of ownership and commitment, with specific monitorable objectives specified. There is also a strong emphasis on the strategy paper being the culmination of a broad participatory process to define where the country is going and what the government's role should be in helping it get there (World Bank and IMF 2000; ODI 1998).

Ghana. Ghana (1995) has established a clear policy framework for the country, based on its Vision 2020 policy statement. Vision 2020 was approved by Parliament and is widely known and quoted throughout the country. Though the statement itself is ambitious and is not linked to resources, it has provided the policy framework for civil service and budgetary reform, which are both linked to resource allocation through the medium-term expenditure framework.

The Civil Service Performance Improvement Program involved a careful review of the role of each ministry and department, informed by a series of beneficiary assessments to determine what the public wants and what it currently gets from government. This exercise is also linked to the medium-term expenditure framework, which presents a rolling three-year framework for the budget. The medium-term framework asks departments to set out what they want to achieve and how they will achieve it, formalized in performance contracts, with the promise—and threat—that resources will be linked to performance. This cost center approach works its way down to individual cost center managers within each line ministry or agency.[1]

The medium-term expenditure framework is also bringing all donor funding within the budget process, ensuring that donor flows are taken into account when resources are allocated. The process establishes the overall resource envelope within which sector-wide approaches are developed and implemented with government and donor resources (Booth 1999; Muggeridge 1999; Robson et al. 1999). This resource allocation process is supported by one of the most developed poverty monitoring systems in Africa, featuring both household expenditure surveys and large core welfare indicator questionnaire (CWIQ) surveys that give feedback on critical welfare indicators and views of the population on government services (Booth 1999; Strode 1999).

Ghana's experience, though encouraging, should not be oversold. The run-up to elections has been associated with inflationary increases in public spending, which can undermine the credibility of medium-term budget planning. There have been disagreements between the government and donors on spending priorities, notably over regional hospitals. Poverty monitoring data have not so far been central to policy decisions, though actions are in hand to improve the relevance and timeliness of evidence-based policy analysis. The medium-term expenditure framework and the sector programs are still struggling with how to link resources to meaningful indicators of achievement. The focus on service delivery needs to be strengthened.[2] Yet there is much to be learned from bringing together various levels of policy from the macro level to delivery at the sector level and using the medium-term expenditure framework and sector programs to ensure that all actors are pulling in the same direction.

Uganda. Uganda also has a clear vision of the public sector's role in poverty eradication, linked to a well-developed process of consultation. The Poverty Eradication Action Plan involved wide consultation inside and outside government. Consultation has been extended directly to the poor through the Participatory Poverty Assessment Program of the Ministry of Finance, Planning, and Economic Development, which aims to institutionalize participatory planning and monitoring down to the district level (Goetz and Jenkins 1998). Uganda was also one of the first countries to attempt to implement the public finance management guidance of the Special Program of Assistance for Africa (SPA).[3] This involved the introduction of a medium-term expenditure framework incorporating government and donor flows, as in Ghana. The main innovation since 1998 has been to include a process of annual consultation on the medium-term budget framework with the donor community and with civil society (Tumusiime-Mutebile 1998).

One positive consequence of this open process was a dialogue with the IMF on the extent to which donor flows could be incorporated into higher government spending.[4] At the 1998 meeting the government set out a high scenario, showing how additional donor commitments would be used to fund higher spending on poverty programs. Donors responded with increased commitments of on-budget support—multiyear support in some cases.[5] Though no direct causal link can be proved, the IMF did agree to a more accommodating fiscal stance that allowed larger donor flows to be spent on the poverty programs.[6] The poverty programs have been largely protected, despite pressures for higher defense spending. Resources freed through the Heavily Indebted Poor Countries (HIPC) Debt Reduction Initiative have been used to create a Poverty Action Fund, which will direct additional resources to the poverty-focused budgets of line ministries (Goetz and Jenkins 1998).

Uganda has also developed information systems for feeding policy relevant information back to decision-makers. Its record in taking action on them is good. When a tracking study revealed that resources for primary health and primary education were not being used as intended (Economic Policy Research Centre and Management Systems and Economic Consultants Ltd. 1996), the government acted vigorously to increase transparency. Fund transfers to the district level are publicized in the press. Schools have to display the financial and other resources received, together with a list of staff employed there. The increased access to information should empower intended beneficiaries to work to see that funds are not diverted. Placing the poverty unit within the Ministry of Finance and giving it responsibility for conducting the participatory poverty assessment have reinforced ownership and helped to ensure that the unit is consulted on policy issues.

The success of Uganda in defining a clear strategy for poverty reduction has been reflected in moves by the World Bank, DFID, and a number of other donors to provide the bulk of their assistance in the form of multiyear commitments to support the medium-term budget framework.

While problems remain—the quality of public expenditures is weak, and corruption is widespread, reflecting in part the legacy of low salaries—the structure for identifying and addressing problems is now in place and can yield lessons for others.

Rwanda. The difficult political, social, and economic conditions following the genocide required that the new government deliver quick improvements to hasten reconciliation. A traditional IMF approach would not have permitted the growth of spending required to achieve rapid change, especially in recurrent spending, given fears about sustainability. The U.K. Department for International Development (DFID), led by Secretary of State Claire Short, made a long-term commitment to support Rwanda with flexible finance over a ten-year planning horizon. The U.K. committed to providing £30 million in flexible assistance over three years and "to remain engaged at least at the same financial level" for at least ten years; Rwanda agreed to continue its commitment to national reconciliation, good governance, macroeconomic stability, and actions on poverty reduction and human resource development (Government of the United Kingdom and Government of the Republic of Rwanda 1999). Several indicators are identified for joint review of progress and commitment. This holistic approach jointly considered political and development factors.

Though not an unconditional commitment, the U.K.'s willingness to make this unprecedented long-term pledge helped persuade the IMF to relax fiscal targets, with donor funds sustaining higher levels of recurrent spending than would otherwise be feasible. Other donors, including the European Union, have also responded. The process has been high-risk on all sides, in a situation where low-risk alternatives were not available. The key point has been the need for transparent dialogue to sustain long-term commitment and for donors to provide support in ways that assist the rebuilding of state capacity while delivering early poverty reduction.

The problems of accountability for donor funds loom large in Rwanda, where state capacity is weak. They are being addressed by developing capacity within government, rather than by setting up parallel structures. Accountability for the use of funds is secured by supporting government accounting and audit capacity. The importance of results orientation is also recognized by supporting poverty surveys, studies of expenditures, and customer surveys on access to services and evidence of their quality (DFID 1998b).

Problems and Lessons of Country Experience. Moving toward a more strategic and medium-term approach to policy and resource allocation is not

Box 8.1
Donor Discipline and the Budget Process in Uganda and Tanzania

Uganda and Tanzania have both worked to bring donor funding into the budget process. Sector working groups coordinate between center and line agencies and will prepare draft sector frameworks for the medium-term expenditure framework. Government will lead the groups, with donors providing technical advice where needed. The public expenditure review, a donor-driven process before 1998 unlinked to government decisionmaking, now involves coordinated budget workshops on preparing medium-term budget submissions, a process that also helps raise awareness of intersectoral allocation issues. Donors and consultants were encouraged to act as facilitators of a process fully integrated with the budget cycle, rather than as lobbyists for particular sectors or projects (Moon 1998, p. 15). The intention is to involve both partners in a process that leads to expenditure programs that have strong government and donor support. The government cedes some influence to donors, but gains greater influence on its own budget by avoiding the fragmentation of numerous donor-driven projects inconsistent with the framework. (See Joekes 1999 for a discussion of Benin, where high aid dependency and the absence of donor coordination undermines the budget process.) The jury is still out on whether governments can succeed in disciplining donors in this way: Uganda's experience is encouraging, Tanzania's less so.

without difficulty. In some countries, expenditure does not follow even the annual budget closely, much less a medium-term expenditure framework. Tanzania's attempt to introduce a medium-term framework has yet to gain credibility (Moon 1998), and even in Uganda development of the first year of the budget framework has tended to dominate the discussion. Sector program managers have not always respected the medium-term expenditure framework discipline. While the 1998 Uganda education sector investment plan was linked explicitly to the medium-term framework (Government of Uganda 1998; Ratcliffe 1999), Tanzania, as of the March 1999 appraisal, had not yet submitted a funding proposal for its education sectorwide approach consistent with the medium-term expenditure framework. This is despite having been four years in gestation and having had four consultant-supported financial projection consultancies (Chijoriga and others 1999).

One of the key lessons from this experience is that a comprehensive framework only becomes meaningful when it is linked to the budget constraint and forces choices about priorities and sequencing.

The Medium-Term Expenditure Framework and the Role of Donors

By bringing donor resources within a clear framework of priorities, the medium-term expenditure framework puts the government in control. Successful government-donor coordination to implement a medium-term expenditure framework thus requires strong domestic backing for the policy, as well as active donor support for government ownership.

Since responsibility for the overall budget usually rests with the ministry of finance, donors should support the ministry's role in establishing national priorities. Line ministries may try to circumvent fiscal discipline by seeking donor support outside the medium-term expenditure framework. Donors can avoid undermining national priorities by keeping the finance ministry fully informed and by ensuring that program design and approval is integrated with the budget. Donors need to provide accurate and timely information on their financing intentions and disbursements, something they have almost uniformly failed to do well.[7]

Greater respect for the budget process is critical if public spending goals are to be met and sustained. Donor support is more likely if national expenditure priorities can be shown to be the outcome of an accountable and participatory process for reaching agreement on objectives, linked to the resources needed to achieve them (Box 8.1).

Sectorwide Approaches

Sectorwide approaches have been concerned primarily with establishing a single policy and expenditure program for public sector action within the sector, though it is important to emphasize that actors outside government are important in every sector, and the first requirement is for government to define the broader policy environment and the roles it will play within it. The emphasis is on government leadership, moving eventually to a system in which government procedures account for all funds and their disbursement. The approach emphasizes a holistic (sectorwide) approach and government ownership, partnership, and outcomes, rather than inputs. Experience with sectorwide approaches should therefore yield lessons for the still more ambitious CDF approach.

A good example is the Ethiopian Education Sector Development Program. The government decided to implement an education sector program without pressure from the donor community. The government asked for donor support only after the decision was made. Most of the relevant documents were written by Ethiopians. Technical specialists from donors contributed advice but did not impose their views on the program design.[8] There were no predetermined policy prescriptions; in the words of the Ethiopian Head of the

Regional Education Bureau: "Nothing was imposed. Advice and ideas were provided by the mission members, but the Regional Education Bureau took the decisions. The only thing that limited our freedom was our own capacity. . . . We had the right to say 'No' at any point" (Martin, Oksanen, and Takala 1999, p. 32). The program also illustrates the tradeoffs between local ownership and openness to dialogue with funding partners. The government has been reluctant to allow donors to influence the policy and resource allocation process, especially on the current budget, and some key issues on the quality of education have yet to be adequately addressed.

Building a broad base for program ownership is crucial for the sustainability of reforms, as the contrasting experience of Ghana and Zambia with health sector reform shows (Box 8.2). Communication alone will not lead to action unless the message is clear and credible and accompanied by positive incentives, as in Ghana (which also had a fortunate combination of rising budgets and increased delegation of authority, which empowered and motivated district staff).

The Bangladesh Health and Population Sector Program has also devoted considerable effort to explaining the objectives and new procedures to staff. However, the messages were more mixed, and delays in resolving concerns about staff retention may have undermined confidence in other measures. Powers have been redistributed within the line ministry, but without significant delegation down the line. Procedures have been changed but remain subject to interdepartmental dispute, and the new structures and procedures are quite complex. The lesson from the reported lack of staff understanding of the program, despite the efforts to communicate it, may be that staff resisted absorbing a message they perceived as provisional, complex, and offering few immediate benefits to them or their work.[9]

Ghana's health sector program is another good example of partnership between government and donors. In taking a sectorwide approach, the Ministry of Health became more assertive in controlling and coordinating donors. It urged donors to work within existing government structures, rather than creating parallel systems. At the same time, key donors such as the World Bank, DFID, Danida, the European Union, and the U.S. Agency for International Development were becoming more flexible in their funding, more aware of sector concerns beyond narrow project interests, and more willing to give time for government commitment to develop.[10] A sectorwide approach has to be built on the foundations of previous work. Before the sector program in health was started, Ghana had already gone through "10 years of institutional development, 4 years of major policy/strategy work, 3 years of strengthening of core management functions, 2 years of negotiations, planning and design, and 1 year of slippage and delays" (NORAD 1999, p. 14, presentation by Smithson).

Box 8.2
Health Sector Reforms in Ghana and Zambia
Demonstrate the Need for Ownership

Reforms in Ghana's health sector benefited greatly from broad local participation and ownership. There were regular consultations with stakeholders from all levels of the central ministry and the district level, and with key representatives of central government agencies. These extensive two-way communications with staff at all levels have been sustained and constitute a major strength of the program. The May 1999 annual review involved a wide cross-section of staff, and field visits confirmed strong understanding and commitment down to district level and below. To keep the process manageable, large twice-a-year meetings with strong involvement by local stakeholders had to be supplemented with smaller business meetings at which concerns of government and donor partners could be raised openly and addressed in greater detail.

Zambia's new health sector program had strong high-level political and administrative backing; it even survived a change of minister. The Ministry of Health was involved with donors in determining conditionality and used the conditions to protect key reforms and health expenditures against domestic opposition. However, participation in the preparation of the program was weak. Other ministries and even some Ministry of Health staff, nongovernmental oganizations, private health providers, and local communities were left out of the consultations (Jones 1997b). As a consequence, local ownership was not broad enough to prevent reversals in policies. When the sectorwide approach then appeared to fail to deliver, government expenditures switched back from primary health to hospital funding.

Source: Observations on Ghana based on author's participation in 1999 health sector investment program review.

A sectorwide approach should not be conceived of as a blueprint, with all activities defined in advance and all starting from day one. Premature implementation of complex components can be self-defeating. The sectorwide approach should be thought of as a process. The definition of the policy framework and the commencement of institution building need to start early. So does the definition of expenditure priorities. Progress toward common procedures should be sequenced to take place as capacity and confidence allow. Expenditure planning should occur within the medium-term framework, with only first-year spending firm and the planning horizon rolled forward each year. The sectorwide approach should be viewed as a new way of doing business, with neither start nor end date, though it will have time-bound objectives and indicators for measuring progress.

A consensus between government and donor partners on the policy framework is the one critical precondition. Capacity to implement can be built, but there is no substitute for agreement on aims and instruments. Where agreement on policies is absent, skepticism about the sectorwide approach is inevitable. A lesson for the CDF is the need to allow time for local consensus on policy to develop, without too strong a push toward closure. The process often takes longer than anticipated, and the initial agreement requires constant maintenance through further discussion and promotion as participants and events change. This can be a problem if donors become tied too early to an inflexible approval schedule. Stakeholder participation can be formulaic. True partnership fails to develop, which often results in an ill-defined role for the state, a failure to win the backing of senior officials, and little or no representation of the poor (Jones 2000).

Zambia's agriculture sector program is a case in point (Jones 1997c). The absence of genuine partnership was evident from the beginning. Technical assistance consultants funded by USAID drafted the original Ministry of Agriculture policy document. At the same time, the government was announcing contradictory policies implying a substantially larger role for the Ministry of Agriculture. Later, during the appraisal stage, there was a sense within government that the World Bank was dominating the proceedings, with an enormous number of staff participating in appraisal missions and Bank and other donor staff writing all the aide-memoires for supervision missions.

Partnership can also suffer because the government fails to take charge, as in the Education Sector Development Program in Tanzania. During 1996 and 1997 a strong government-donor partnership seemed to be developing, but after a common sector development work program was endorsed and many donors had signed on to a sector development partnership paper in early 1998, the partnership began to unravel. No steps have been taken on implementation. Government failed to lead government-donor meetings, which were often chaired by mid-level technical staff. Turnover in policymaking staff was rapid, potential reformers in the ministry became marginalized as vested interests recognized the impact of reform, and hard decisions on education expenditure and policy were delayed (Ratcliffe 1999, p. 41). The lesson from this example may be that a sectorwide approach that is attempting major reforms faces a high risk of policy reversal if time is not spent in developing broad political support for the program.

The experience shows that, provided there is a consensus on goals, there are significant benefits from donors providing their assistance in support of a single development policy and expenditure program under government leadership. However, the circumstances are not always so favorable. The next section discusses which aid instruments are appropriate in different circumstances, depending on the policy environment, the capacity of the public sector, and the degree of aid dependence.

Country Circumstances and the Choice of Program or Project Aid

The 4-by-4 matrix in Table 8.1 classifies country situations according to the quality of macroeconomic and budget management, degree of aid dependence, quality of sector-level policies (including whether they are realistic given available resources), and quality of sector-level management.

An aid-dependent country with good policies and good sector management (cell 1), for example, should be supported with general program aid, which enables higher spending on priority programs and allows governments to prioritize their use of all available resources. This situation is also suitable for the World Bank's proposed public expenditure reform credit, which simplifies the aid relationship to a single annual transaction to support the overall budget. It is also the direction in which the Swedish International Development Cooperation Agency is moving. Under program aid, donor earmarking does not distort government budget priorities, and the transactions costs of dealing with donors are minimized. The problem? Though few if any countries meet the criteria in full, the closest example may be Uganda, where a number of donor agencies are providing general budget support, though with conditions related to overall and sectoral budget priorities and management.

More common in aid-dependent countries is to have reasonably good macroeconomic management and sector policy but weak civil service management capacity (cell 2). Most sector programs in Africa operate in this kind of environment. The case for a program approach does not, at the macroeconomic or sector level, rest on a need for policy dialogue and conditionality. Rather, it rests on the need to improve planning and management by minimizing the problems caused by uncertain donor support and multiple donor projects with different approaches and procedures. But where administrative capacity is weak, donors may be concerned about the loss of direct control without project-based support. The country needs financial transfers, but it also needs capacity building support so that it can deliver effective services and account for resources.

Here, the suggested approach is to provide program support at the sector level with extra support for capacity building, additional safeguards on accountability, and close monitoring and evaluation. The transition to government procedures for disbursing aid may be gradual, as capacity and confidence are built, though there are advantages to early commitment to disburse some funds this way. Gaining access to donor funds can provide an incentive to improve financial management; in Ghana's health sector program, districts had to meet specific criteria before they could manage donor funding. Most sector programs are still hybrids, following common procedures for the use of some donor flows, especially support to local services (often with additional financial checks), and following donor procedures for the use of other flows, especially technical assistance and off-shore procurement.

Where sector policies are weak but macroeconomic and sector management is stronger (cell 3), there is a case for donor technical support and policy dialogue, working with ministry of finance and sector officials to facilitate sector policy development. A medium-term budget framework approach can clarify the need to bring aspirations in line with resources. Project support could be used to develop pilot projects demonstrating the potential of new approaches to service delivery. Program support could follow the development of a supportable policy package but would depend on whether pro-reform forces in the sector are strong enough to implement improved policies. The Pakistan social action program, supported by a consortium of donors including the World Bank and DFID, was in part an attempt to encourage better government policies, with donor funds conditional on additional government spending to avoid the risk of fungibility. Deciding whether to support a sector program can be difficult in situations where poor past policies reflected political pressures or corruption.

If both sector policy and sector management capacity are weak (cell 4), significant sector finance of any kind, whether program or project, is unlikely to yield sustainable benefits, even where the macro framework is sound. Limited development assistance, mainly technical assistance, might facilitate policy and capacity development.

Where policy and management are good but aid dependency is low (cell 5), government may nevertheless welcome general program aid linked to an agreed policy program because, in addition to the direct value of the finance provided, World Bank and IMF endorsement may help to restore investor confidence following a financial crisis—as in the case of program lending to countries affected by the Asian financial crisis.

Except when in crisis, countries with low aid dependence are likely to prefer project aid to policy-conditioned program aid. Arguments for program aid based on the distorting effect of project support are less likely to be made where aid is low relative to the size of the budget, while government is more able to resist unwelcome donor influence on policy. China has used project aid to pilot new activities that are later taken up through local finance. If aid dependence is low, and sector policy or management is weak (cells 6–8), project support and technical assistance are still likely to be the most appropriate instruments to facilitate policy development and pilot new approaches, possibly in tandem with civil service and budget reform.

Where the overall macroeconomic and budget management framework is weak, the most useful donor intervention may well be to support the overall macroeconomic reform process with general program aid, possibly including reaching agreement with the ministry of finance on the share of budget resources to be spent on specific sectors. In practice, good sector performance (cell 9) is unlikely to be sustained in a weak macroeconomic environment (cells 10 and 11). Policy is unlikely to be effective where fund releases are unpredictable, while capacity will be eroded by falling real salaries and personnel policies that fail to reward effort. The sustainability of sector programs depends on the budget resources the government is able to commit. If the macroeconomic policy environment is weak, sector programs need a conservative view of the future growth of budget resources. Overoptimism about the government's contribution affected sector programs in Zambia, an early leader in developing the approach. If support is to be provided to the sector despite the weak macroeconomic context, the sector program will need to make optimal use of limited resources, which argues for the flexibility of program support, preferably as longer-term commitments. It may also argue for support for increasing the budget autonomy of the sector, by supporting greater clarity for the public sector's role and increased cost recovery as long as the poor are not thereby excluded from services.

If both macroeconomic and sector policies and management are weak (cells 12 and 16), support is unlikely to yield sustainable benefits, no matter what its form, so the donor role should be limited to policy dialogue and analysis.

Lessons for the Comprehensive Development Framework

Interaction between government and donors occurs at the level of the policy framework, the overall budget, sector programs, and project interventions.

Making the CDF effective will require government to articulate a clear vision of the role of the state, linked to resources through a medium-term budget process, as in Ghana and Uganda. Donor support can facilitate and provide technical support, but government must lead and own the process.

With the vision for state action established, the medium-term expenditure framework can be used by government and donors to prioritize expenditures. In return for a transparent dialogue that provides scope for donor concerns and influence, donors should ensure that interventions are fully in accord with the budget process. To enable governments to make optimal use of resources, donor funding should be longer-term and in flexible form.

Prioritizing expenditures within a medium-term expenditure framework is a political process, but donors will want to assess success by the effectiveness of government actions to reduce poverty. There is no general guidance on how best to allocate resources between sectors, such as between roads and health. Even the reallocation of resources to poor regions can be problematic: it may be more effective to invest in regions of higher potential and to help people relocate there. It may be easier to shift the budget than to shift well-motivated staff able to make effective use of it. Studies often fail to find any clear relationship between funding levels and the quality or quantity of services provided.[11]

For making the budget process more pro-poor:

- *Leadership commitment is essential.* This could be encouraged by actions to bring poverty to the attention of the political leadership in ways difficult to ignore. One way is by making good information and analysis widely available and allied to a political process in which power is contested and the poor have a voice. The election process, for example, clearly had an impact on the commitment to universal primary education in Malawi and Uganda.
- *Transparency is important.* Alone, however, it may not help the poor, since better-off groups can organize more readily. Trade unions may represent the well-off formal sector workers, while local Rotary or other charities may prioritize secondary education over primary education. There may be good returns to training groups representing the poor to enable them to make more effective demands on government resources at national and local levels.
- *Poverty spending is most likely to be effective when those who spend are directly accountable to those who are supposed to benefit.* This works best at the community level—for example, with power over resources vested in parent committees for schools or in local water committees. It can also be made to work for health services, though market failure due to asymmetric information and less regular contact causes problems. The formal local government structure may be less responsive than the national government to poverty concerns, with fewer protections against financial malpractice—one reason Uganda opted for conditional grants and wide publicity about how they were to be spent. Even without the transfer of financial power, transparency along with clear information on entitlements and on actual financial transfers, as in Uganda, can enable the general public to enforce accountability.

The national budget process needs to strike a balance between prioritizing resources and remaining responsive to local needs. Centralized, detailed allocation should be avoided. Local managers need a clear strategy on what they are expected to deliver and a hard budget constraint to force choices, with flexibility on how best to use the resources. In more sophisticated systems, it may be feasible to hold budget managers accountable for achieving specific outcomes or outputs, perhaps linked to a service standard defined in affordable terms. Essential services packages defined in health sector programs, for example, have too often been beyond the scope of the budget.

Donors too may need to adapt their procedures to enable them to support a process in which detailed budget allocation is delegated. Donors should:

- support the ministry of finance in its efforts to secure a single framework;
- exercise restraint, avoiding the temptation to work independently with line ministries (which may try to circumvent the budget process);
- adopt sectorwide approaches, based on plans prepared by government officials;
- encourage participation and a broad base of ownership. Decentralization and delegation within ministries may play an important role;
- allow time for these processes to occur and to generate results and for trust and respect to be built on both sides;
- be flexible in the implementation of sectoral programs (a recommendation in keeping with the advocacy of process planning);
- invest in capacity building.

For complex development processes to be sustained, ownership needs to be broad as well as committed. Some sectorwide approaches have run into problems by underestimating the time required to build and sustain the broad consensus needed to implement programs successfully. The ambitious CDF approach will require herculean efforts in consensus building if it is to be more than a top-level exercise unconnected to the realities of implementation.

A meaningful CDF will need to be informed by good evidence and analysis, especially on poverty and what is needed to reduce it. A more effective response to poverty concerns may be encouraged by centrally locating poverty analysis in the finance ministry, with a stress on linking analysis to budget decisions and on encouraging transparency to empower people to hold government to account. There may be too much of a lag for outcomes to directly inform policy performance reviews, but there are good examples of the use of core welfare indicator questionnaire surveys, participatory poverty assessments, service delivery surveys, and tracking studies designed to generate proxy indicators likely to be correlated with ultimate outcomes.

Finally, while similar principles can be applied to other aspects of development policy, like the regulatory framework, the sectorwide approach on its own is not enough. Not all aspects of development cooperation are amenable to the structured approach of the medium-term expenditure framework and sectorwide approach tools. There are areas that will not be reached by these new procedures and where codes of good practice may be required. They will still require systematic thought in order to define basic partnership principles and guides to good practice.

TABLE 8.1
Quality of Macroeconomic and Budget Management, Aid Dependence, and Sector-Level Policies and Management

		Good Sector Policies, Linked to Resource		Weak Sector Policies, Not Linked to Resources	
		High Sector Management Capacity	Low Sector Management Capacity	High Sector Management Capacity	Low Sector Management Capacity
Good Overall Macroeconomic and Budget Management	High Aid Dependence	**1.** Government-owned sectorwide approach, using government procedures; aid role mainly finance. No examples.	**2.** Sectorwide approach with extra safeguards on accountability, support for capacity building, close attention to monitoring and evaluation, transition to using government procedures. Examples: Ghana and Uganda	**3.** Work with ministry of finance and sector officials to facilitate policy development, possibly linked to medium-term expenditure framework, to force policy choices. Finance sectorwide approach if enough change agents are present for realistic prospect of success.	**4.** Sectorwide thinking-- support ministry of finance, medium-term expenditure framework, explore interests in debate on direction, support donor coordination around the budget, use aid to facilitate policy and capacity development. Defer major sector finance, whether sectorwide approach or project.
	Low Aid Dependence	**5.** General program aid to restore private sector confidence by endorsing policies, as in the East Asia crisis. In noncrisis situations, aid provides project support, managed by government using its own procedures, possible aid role in underwriting innovation, promoting stronger poverty focus. Example: China.	**6.** Potential aid role for technical assistance support to build capacity, within a framework set by ministry policymakers.	**7.** No case for sectorwide approach but possibly technical assistance to facilitate national consultation on policy, project support to demonstrate new approaches and support drivers of change within the sector. Support reform processes led by ministry of finance.	**8.** Absence of sector leadership or capacity suggest support for central economic ministry reform processes is the best option: build sector policy and capacity through technical assistance support to medium-term expenditure framework and civil service reform processes.

TABLE 8.1 *continued*

		9. Sustainability of sectorwide	**10. Capacity constraints not likely to**	**11. Weak sector policies despite high**	**12. No sector support is likely to yield**
Weak overall macroeconomic and budget management	**High aid dependence**	approach requires policy dialogue on macro framework and budget shares; conservative view of resources available; general program aid a likely instrument. Long term donor commitments, possible support to cost-recovery from non-poor to preserve good sector performance despite weak macro framework.	be solved without macro level reform to ensure predictable budgets, staff incentives. sectorwide approach requires both macro and sector reform process to be in place. Cost recovery from nonpoor is an option if quality of services is high enough.	sector capacity may be caused by a macro framework which does not provide secure budgets or impose priorities. No sectorwide approach unless commitment to a credible program can be built, including ministry of finance ability and willingness to finance it. Support macro reform process, facilitate policy development at macro and sector level, possibly support increased sector autonomy through cost recovery.	sustainable benefits, in whatever form it is given; technical assistance, project. or sectorwide approach; donor role limited to policy dialogue and analysis.
	Low aid dependence	**13. Most useful donor role will be** for technical assistance support to overall reform process, not sector level. Possible technical assistance role to support cost-recovery . reduce dependence on macro policies.	**14. Weak capacity at sector level is** probably a symptom of overall budget and macro policies, not possible to achieve much with sector level technical assistance unless linked to increased autonomy including financial resources and personal policies. Macro-level technical assistance the priority.	**15. Possible case for modest technical** assistance to facilitate policy development at macro and sector level. Support increased autonomy at sector level.	**16. No case for aid at any level, other** than policy dialogue.

Notes

1. Earlier experience of performance contracts in the context of public enterprise reform in low-income countries is not especially encouraging, however (see World Bank 1997, p. 90).
2. For a health sector example, see Asamoah-Baah and Smithson (1999).
3. Now called the Strategic Partnership with Africa. The SPA 5 (1999) document places considerable emphasis on implementing the SPA public finance management guidance and discusses the Uganda, Tanzania, and Ghana cases. For discussion of the evolution and application of the guidance, see GTZ (1996); SPA (1997); Moon (1998).
4. On the issues surrounding the treatment of future aid flows in the budget projections for the IMF programs, see Foster and Thomas (1998). For the specific Uganda case, see Bevan (1998).
5. For example, DFID shifted general budget support to a two-year time frame and made a five-year commitment of budget support to the education sector.
6. Tumusiime-Mutebile (1998) explains that the inclusion of future donor funding was vital in the IMF agreement to increase the sustainable budget deficit ceiling. It is probable that Bevan's (1998) macroeconomic analysis of the Uganda IMF program was also influential. This suggested macro stability was consistent with using future aid flows to finance an increase of the budget deficit by 2 percent of GDP over the previous IMF ceiling.
7. This is reflected, for example, in donors' unwillingness to disclose information on their funding intentions on recent consultancy work in Tanzania carried out by Kessy.
8. For more details on the Ethiopian Education Sector Development Program see Martin, Oksanen, and Takala (1999) and NORAD (1999). The Ghana health sector provides another example where government leadership in the reform process was vital. In managing the transition to a sector program, it was essential that the Ministry of Health maintain leadership; otherwise, as Asamoa-Baah and Smithson (1999, p. 20) argue, "the strategic direction would have been quickly obscured by competing [donor] agency interests."
9. Observations based on participation in the April 1999 Health and Population Sector Program Annual Review.
10. For more details on partnership in the Ghanaian health sector, see Asamoa-Baah and Smithson (1999).
11. For example, there is evidence from South Africa that some districts receiving increased funding did not deliver more or better services, while those losing funds often maintained or in some cases improved services discussions at DFID-financed seminar on "Good Practice in public expenditure management" (Oxford, July 1999).
12. The U.N. Development Assistance Framework is defined by four criteria: it is a strategic document sensitive to the needs of the partner country; it is jointly owned by the U.N. and the partner government (explicitly identified as the dominant partner); it should help the U.N. to identify areas in which it can contribute the most in any given country and program cycle; and it should provide the means of operationalizing at the country level resolutions and initiatives passed at the global level (Adedeji et al. 1998).
13. Other U.N. Development Assistance Framework pilots include (as of November 1998) Guatemala, India, Kenya, Malawi, Morocco, Mozambique, and Romania.

References

Adedeji, Adebayo, Devaki Jain, and Mary McCowan. 1998. "External Inputs for the Development of the United Nations Development Assistance Framework (UNDAF)." Report of the High-Level Team of Experts, New York.

Asamoa-Baah, Anarfi, and Paul Smithson. 1999. "Donors and the Ministry of Health: New Partnerships in Ghana." WHO Discussion Paper 8. Geneva: World Health Organization.

Barrow, Christopher J. 1998. "River Basin Planning and Management. A Critical Review." *World Development* 26 (1): pp. 171–86.

Baulch, Bob. 1996a. "Poverty, Policy and Aid." Editor's introduction to special issue of *IDS Bulletin* 27 (1).

————. 1996b. "Neglected Trade-offs in Poverty Measurement." Special issue of *IDS Bulletin* 27 (1).

Bekker, Simon, and Peter Robinson. 1996. "Development Planning in the Provinces: A Methodology during the Transition." *Development Southern Africa* 13 (4): pp. 539–54.

Belshaw, D. 1990. "Food Strategy Formulation and Development Planning Ethiopia." *IDS Bulletin* 21.

Berg, Elliot, and Associates. 1990. *Adjustment Postponed: Economic Policy Reform in Senegal in the 1980s.* Bethesda, MD: Development Alternatives Inc.

Bernander, Bernt, Joel Charny, Marita Eastmond, Claes Lindahl, and Joakim Öjendal. 1995. "Facing a Complex Emergency: An Evaluation of Swedish Support to Emergency Aid in Cambodia." SIDA Evaluation Report 1995/4. Stockholm, Sweden.

Bevan, David L. 1998. "Uganda Public Expenditure Review—Macroeconomic Options in the Medium Term." Working paper prepared for the government of Uganda and the World Bank. U.K., St John's College.

Birgegard, L-E. 1987. "A Review of Experiences with Integrated Rural Development." Issue Paper 3, International Rural Development Centre, Swedish University of Agricultural Sciences, Uppsala.

Booth, David. 1999. "Creating a Framework for Reducing Poverty: Institutional and Process Issues in National Poverty Policy–Ghana Country Report." Overseas Development Institute, London.

Bossuyt, Jean, and Geert Laporte. 1994. "Partnership in the 1990s: How to Make it Work Better." ECDPM Policy Management Brief 3. Maastricht.

Bossuyt, Jean, et al. 1999. "Comparing the ACP and EU Negotiating Mandates." ECDPM Lome Negotiating Brief 3. Maastricht.

Botchwey, Kwesi, et al. 1998. "Report of the Group of Independent Persons Appointed to Conduct an Evaluation of Certain Aspects of the Enhanced Structural Adjustment Facility," IMF, Washington, D.C.

Bradford, D.L., and A.R. Cohen. 1997. *Managing for Excellence: The Leadership Guide to Developing High Performance in Contemporary Organisations.* New York: John Wiley and Sons Ltd.

Buchanan-Smith, M., and S. Davies. 1995. *Famine Early Warning and Response—the Missing Link.* London: IT Publications.

Burke, Michael. 1998. "Partnership–Policy, Principles, and Practices." CARE USA paper on partnership [available http://www.linkingpartners.org/docs/policy.html].

Burnside, C., and D. Dollar. 1997. "Aid, Policies and Growth." Policy Research Working Paper 1777. Washington, D.C.: World Bank.

Butler, Richard, and Jas Gill. 1999. "The Dynamics of Trust in Partnership Formation and Operation: Project Summary." University of Bradford Management Centre.

Chambers, Robert. 1983. *Rural Development: Putting the Last First*. Harlow: Longman Scientific and Technical.

———. 1993. *Challenging the Professions: Frontiers for Rural Development*. London: IT Publications.

———. 1997. *Whose Reality Counts? Putting the Last First*. London: IT Publications.

Chang, Ha-Joong. 1995. "Explaining 'Flexible Rigidities' in East Asia." In Killick, ed. *The Flexible Economy: Causes and Consequences of the Adaptability of National Economies*. London: Routledge.

Charles, Chanya L., Stephanie McNulty, and John A. Pennell. 1998. "Partnering for Results: A User's Guide to Intersectoral Partnering." Paper prepared for the U.S. Agency for International Development's Mission Director's Conference.

Chenery, Hollis, and T.N. Srinivasan, eds. 1989. *Handbook of Development Economics* Vol. 2. Amsterdam: North Holland.

Chijoriga, Marcelina, et al. 1999. "Appraisal of the Education Sector Development Program: Report of the Financial Planning and Management Sub-Group."

Collier, Paul. 1995. "The Marginalization of Africa." *International Labour Review* 134 (4–5) : pp. 541–57.

Crane, Randall. 1995. "The Practice of Regional Planning in Indonesia: Resolving Central-local Coordination Issues in Planning and Finance." *Public Administration and Development* 15: pp. 139–49.

Crawford, Gordon. 1996. "Wither Lomé? The Midterm Review and the Decline of Partnership." *Modern African Studies* 34 (3): pp. 503–18.

Crener, M.A. 1984. "Integrated Rural Development: State of the Art Review, 1983/4." Organisation for Economic Development and Development Assistance Committee. Ottawa, Canada: CIDA.

DAC (Development Assistance Committee). 1996. *Shaping the 21ˢᵗ Century: the Contribution of Development Cooperation*. Paris, France: Organisation for Economic Development and Development Assistance Committee.

Davies, S. 1994. "Public Institutions, People, and Famine Mitigation." *IDS Bulletin* 25: pp. 46–54.

De Soto, H. 1989. *The Other Path: The Invisible Revolution in the Third World*. New York: Harper and Row.

DFID (Department for International Development). 1997 *Eliminating World Poverty: A Challenge for the 21st Century*. ("1997 White Paper.") Cm 3789. London.

———. 1998a. *Action Research for Community Forestry: Sharing Experiences from Nepal*. London: The Stationery Office.

———. 1998b. "Submission to the Projects Evaluation Committee, Rwanda Program Aid 1998–2001." London.

Dhungel, Yadav N., and Walter E.J. Tips. 1987. "Rural Development in Nepal, Part I: Coordination in the Rasuwa-Nuwakot Integrated Rural Development Programs." *Public Administration and Finance* 7: pp. 43–58.

Dollar, David, and Lant Pritchett. 1998. *Assessing Aid: What Works, What Doesn't, and Why*. New York: Oxford University Press.

ECDPM. 1999. "Comparing the ACP and EU Negotiating Mandates." ECDPM Lomé Negotiating Brief 3.

Economic Policy Research Centre and Management Systems and Economic Consultants, Ltd. 1996. "Tracking of Public Expenditure on Primary Education and Primary Health Care: Report." Kampala, Uganda.

The Economist. "The 1999 UN Development Program: Staying On." July 10, 1999: p. 66.

Escobar, Arturo. 1992. "Planning." In Wolfgang Sachs, ed. *The Development Dictionary: A Guide to Knowledge as Power.* London and NJ: Zed Books.

EU (European Union). 1998. "Negotiating Directives for the Negotiation of a Development Partnership Agreement with the ACP Countries." Information Note, Brussels, Belgium.

FAO (Food and Agriculture Organization) and WHO (World Health Organization). 1992. "International Conference on Nutrition: World Declaration and Plan of Action for Nutrition." Rome: FAO.

Field, J.O. 1987. "Multi-sectoral Nutrition Policy: A Post-mortem." *Food Policy* February.

Foster, Mick, and Dino Merotto. 1997. "Partnership for Development in Africa: A Framework for Flexible Funding." London: Department for International Development.

Foster, Mick, and Theo Thomas. 1998. "Design of IMF Programs in Aid-dependent Countries." Department for International Development, London.

Ghana, Government of. 1995. *Ghana-Vision 2020 (The First Step: 1996–2000).* Accra, Ghana.

Goetz, Anne-Marie, and Rob Jenkins. 1998. "Creating a Framework for Reducing Poverty: Institutional and Process Issues in National Poverty Policy—Uganda Country Report." Institute of Development Studies and Birkbeck College, London.

Goudie, Andrew. 1998. "Is a Good Government Approach to Development Practical? An Approach to Governance." Paper presented at ODI, March 25.

GTZ (German Agency for Technical Cooperation). 1996. "Report on a Seminar on Improving Budget Management and Public Expenditure Reviews: Vision for Future Co-operation." Fiscal Policy Series, No. 1. Department for Economic and Social Policy, Law and Administration. Lilongwe, Malawi.

Gwyer, D.G., and J.C.H. Morriss. 1984. "Some Findings from Key ODA Evaluations in Selected Sectors: Natural Resources." In B.E. Cracknell, ed. *The Evaluation of Aid Projects and Programs.* London: ODA.

Handy, C.B. 1985. *Understanding Organisations.* Harmondsworth, U.K.: Penguin.

Hanmer, Lucia, G. Pyatt, and H. White. 1997. *Poverty in sub-Saharan Africa.* The Hague: Institute of Social Studies.

Hindle, R. 1990. "The World Bank Approach to Food Security Analysis." *IDS Bulletin* 21: p. 62–66.

Huddlestone, B. 1990. "FAO's Overall Approach and Methodology for Formulating National Food Security Programs in Developing Countries." *IDS Bulletin* 21: pp. 72–80.

IDS (Institute of Development Studies) and IVED. 1994. "Poverty Assessments and Public Expenditure: A Study for the SPA Working Group on Poverty and Social Policy." Sussex: IDS .

Joekes, Susan. 1999. "Creating a Framework for Reducing Poverty: Institutional and Process Issues in National Poverty Policy—Benin Country Report." Brighton, U.K.: Institute of Development Studies.

Johnson, John H., and Sulaiman S. Wasty. 1993. *Borrower Ownership of Adjustment Programs and the Political Economy of Reform.* World Bank Discussion Paper 199. Washington, D.C.: World Bank.

Jones, Stephen. 1999a. "Increasing Aid Effectiveness in Africa? The World Bank and Sector Investment Programs." Oxford, U.K.: Oxford Policy Management.

182 **Making Development Work**

————. 1997b. "Sector Investment Programs in Africa—Issues and Experiences." Oxford, U.K.: Oxford Policy Management.

————. 1997c. "Sector Investment Programs in Africa–Issues and Experiences: Evidence from Case Studies." Oxford, U.K.: Oxford Policy Management.

Kahler, Miles. 1992. "External Influence, Conditionality, and the Politics of Adjustment." In Stephan Haggard and Robert R. Kaufman, eds. *The Politics of Economic Adjustment*. Princeton, NJ: Princeton University Press.

Kayizzi-Mugerwa, Steve. 1998. "Africa and the Donor Community: From Conditionality to Partnership." *Journal of International Development* 10 (2): pp. 219–25.

Kennes, W. 1990. "The European Community and Food Security." *IDS Bulletin* 26: pp. 67–71.

Kifle, Henock, Adebayo O. Olukoshi, and Lennart Wohlgemuth, eds. 1997. *A New Partnership for African Development: Issues and Parameters*. Upsalla, Sweden: Nordiska Afrikainstitutet.

Killick, Tony. 1998. *Aid and the Political Economy of Policy Change*. London, U.K.: Routledge.

Kleemeier, L. 1988. "Integrated Rural Development in Tanzania." *Public Administration and Development* 8: pp. 61–73.

Koppel, B. "Does Integrated Area Development Work? Insights from the Bicol River Basin Development Program." *World Development* 15 (2): pp. 205–20.

Korten, D. 1980. "Community Organisation and Rural Development: A Learning Process Approach." *Public Administration Review* September/October.

Korten, D., and R. Klauss, eds. 1984. *People-Centred Development*. West Hartford, CT: Kumarion Press.

Kotter, John P. 1996. *Leading Change*. Boston, MA: Harvard Business School Press.

Leigh, A., and M. Maynard. 1995. *Leading Your Team: How to Involve and Inspire Teams*. London, U.K.: Nicholas Brealey.

Levinson, F. James. 1995. "Multi-sectoral Nutrition Planning: A Synthesis of Experience." In P. Pinstrup-Anderson et al., eds. *Child Growth and Nutrition in Developing Countries: Priorities for Action*. Ithaca, NY: Cornell University Press.

Lister, R. 1988. *The European Community and the Developing World*. Avebury, U.K.: Aldershot.

Lowe, D. 1996. "The Development Policy of the European Union and the Mid-term Review of the Lomé Partnership." *Journal of Common Market Studies* 34: pp. 15–28.

Malik, Khalid, et al. "1998 UNDF Assessment Report." New York, United Nations Development Programme.

Martin, John, Riitta Oksanen, and Tuomas Takala. 1999. "Preparation of the Education Sector Development Program in Ethiopia: Reflections by Participants." Final Report. Cambridge: Cambridge Education Consultants.

Mathbor, Golan M. 1997. "The Importance of Community Participation in Coastal Zone Management: A Bangladesh Perspective." *Community Development Journal* 32 (2): pp. 124–32.

Maxwell, Simon. 1991. "National Food Security Planing: First Thoughts from Sudan." *To Cure All Hunger: Food Policy and Food Security in Sudan*. London, U.K.: IT Publications.

————. 1996a. "The Use of Matrix Scoring to Identify Systemic Issues in Country Program Evaluation." *Development in Practice* 7 (4): pp. 408–15.

————. 1996b. "Food Security: A Post-modern Approach." *Food Policy* 21 (2): pp. 155–70.

————. 1996c. "A Food Charter for the Millennium." *Appropriate Technology* 23 (2).

————. 1997. "Implementing the World Food Summit Plan of Action: Organisational Issues in Multi-sectoral Planning." *Food Policy* 22 (6): pp. 515–31.

————. 1998. "International Targets for Poverty Reduction and Food Security: A Mildly Sceptical but Resolutely Pragmatic View with a Call for Greater Subsidiarity." *Canadian Journal of Development Studies* 19: pp. 77–96.

Maxwell, Simon, and Roger Riddell. 1998. "Conditionality or Contract: Perspectives on Partnership for Development." *Journal of International Development* 10 (2): pp. 257–68.

Mohiddin, Ahmed. 1998. "Towards a New Partnership: Assessment of Government Performance." ECDPM Working Paper 55. Maastricht.

Moon, Allister. 1998. "Aid, MTEFs and Budget Process." ECSPE. Washington, D.C.: World Bank.

Moore, M. 1993. "Competition and Pluralism in Public Bureaucracies." *IDS Bulletin* 23.

Mosley, Paul, Jane Harrigan, and John Toye. 1991. *Aid and Power: The World Bank and Policy-based Lending*. Vol. 1. London, U.K.: Routledge.

Moseley-Williams, R. 1994. "Partners and Beneficiaries: Questioning Donors." *Development in Practice* 4 (1): pp. 50–57.

Mosse, David. 1998. "Process-oriented Approaches to Development Practice and Social Research." In Mosse, Farrington, and Rew, *Development as Process: Concepts and Methods for Working with Complexity*. London, U.K.: Routledge/ODI.

Muggeridge, Elizabeth. 1999. "The MTEF, Donor Coordination and Flexible Funding." Consulting Africa Ltd., Woodstock.

Murray, R. 1992. "Towards a Flexible State." *IDS Bulletin* 23: pp. 78–89.

Nelson, Joan M., ed. 1990. *Economic Crisis and Policy Choice: The Politics of Adjustment in the Third World*. Princeton, NJ: Princeton University Press.

Norwegian Agency for Development Cooperation. 1999. "Report from Seminar on Sector-Wide Approaches–Linking Macroeconomic Concerns with Sector Strategies: A Review of Donor Experiences." NORAD, Oslo, Norway.

ODI Partnership for Development. 1998. "Report of a Meeting Held at the Overseas Development Institute." London.

Oppenheim, Carey. 1998. "Changing the Storyline." *Manchester Guardian* April: 6–7.

Oppenheim, C., and L. Harker. 1996. *Poverty: The Facts*. London, U.K.: Child Poverty Action Group.

Peters, T.J. 1987. *Thriving on Chaos*. London, U.K.: Pan Books.

Peters, T.J., and R.H. Waterman. 1982. *In Search of Excellence*. New York: Harper and Row.

Plant, Roger. 1987. *Managing Change and Making It Stick*. New York: Harper Collins.

Ratcliffe, M., and M. Macrae. 1999. *Sector Wide Approaches to Education: A Strategic Analysis*. Ratcliffe Macrae Associates.

Riddell, Roger. 1993. "Discerning the Way Together: Report on the Work of Brot für die Welt, Christian Aid, EZE and ICCO." Executive summary Brot für die Welt, Christian Aid, EZE, and ICCO.

Rischard, Jean-François. 1998. "Putting Partnership into Practice." Remarks by Jean-François Rischard, Vice-President for Europe, World Bank, at the senior-level meeting of the Organisation for Economic Co-operation and Development—Development Assistance Committee, December 2–3, Paris.

Robson, Ken, Malcolm Holmes, Grace Adzroe, Sam Kabo, Oscar Bognone, and George Dakpallah. 1999. "Public Financial Management Reform Program—Medium Term Expenditure Framework." March.

Rondinelli, D. 1983. *Development Projects as Policy Experiments*. London, U.K.: Methuen.

Rugumamu, Severine M., and Robert Mhamba. 1997. "Merit Criteria for Aid Allocation: Tanzanian Perspectives in EU-ACP Partnership Proposals." ECDPM Working Paper 50. Maastricht.

Sanyal, B. 1991. "Antagonistic Co-operation: A Case Study of Nongovernmental Organisations, Government and Donors' Relationships in Income-generating Projects in Bangladesh." *World Development* 19 (10): pp. 1367–79.

Schaffer, P. 1996. "Beneath the Poverty Debate: Some Issues." Special issue of *IDS Bulletin* 27 (1).

Scott, James C. 1998. *Seeing Like a State: How Certain Schemes to Improve the Human Condition Have Failed*. New Haven, CT: Yale University Press.

SPA (Special Program of Assistance for Africa). 1997. "Guidelines for Strengthening Public Finance Management in Sub-Saharan Africa." SPAAR Working Paper 16. Washington, D.C.: World Bank.

———. 1999. "Outlook and Agenda for SPA 5: The Challenge of Poverty Reduction."

Tendler, Judith. 1997. *Good Government in the Tropics*. Baltimore, MD: The John Hopkins University Press.

Toye, J., and C. Jackson. 1996. "Public Expenditure Policy and Poverty Reduction: Has the World Bank Got It Right?" *IDS Bulletin* 27 (1).

Tumusiime-Mutebile, E. 1998. "Uganda/Tanzanian PER Exercise: Rationale and Design." Paper presented to a video conference as part of a World Bank workshop on budget processes and foreign aid, November 2–3, Washington, D.C.

Uganda, Government of. 1998. "ESIP Work Plan." Education Planning Department, Ministry of Education and Sports. Kampala, Uganda.

UNDP (United Nations Development Programme). 1997. *Human Development Report 1997*. New York: Oxford University Press.

UNICEF (United Nations Children's Fund). 1990. *The State of the World's Children*. New York: Oxford University Press.

United Kingdom, Government of, and Government of the Republic of Rwanda. 1999. "Understanding on the Development Partnership between the Government of the United Kingdom of Great Britain and Northern Ireland and the Government of the Republic of Rwanda."

Vohra, Rajiv. 1987. "Planning." In John Eatwell, Murray Milgate, and Peter Newman, eds., *The New Palgrave: A Dictionary of Economics*. London, Basingstoke, New York, Tokyo: Macmillan/Stockton/Maruzen.

Wade, Robert. 1997. "Development and Environment: Marital Difficulties at the World Bank." Global Economic Institutions Working Paper 29. Centre for Economic Policy Research, London.

World Food Summit. 1996. *Rome Declaration on World Food Security and World Food Summit Plan of Action*. Rome, Italy: World Food Summit.

Whiteman, K. 1998. "Africa, the ACP and Europe: the Lessons of 25 Years." *Development Policy Review* 16 (1).

Williamson, John, ed. 1994. *The Political Economy of Policy Reform*. Washington, D.C.: Institute for International Economics.

Wolfensohn, James D. 1999. "A Proposal for a Comprehensive Development Framework (a discussion draft)." Memo to the Board, Management, and Staff of the World Bank Group, January 21, Washington, D.C.

World Bank. 1990. *World Development Report 1990: Poverty*. New York: Oxford University Press.

————. 1991. "Effectiveness of SAL Supervision and Monitoring." Operations Evaluation Department Report 9711. Washington, D.C.

————. 1992. "Effective Implementation: Key to Development Impact" (Wapenhans Report) Portfolio Management Task Force, Washington, D.C.

————. 1994. *Adjustment in Africa: Reforms, Results and the Road Ahead.* New York: Oxford University Press.

————. 1995. *Annual Report on Portfolio Performance, FY 1994*, Volume 3. Washington, D.C.

————. 1996. *World Development Report 1996—From Plan to Market.* New York: Oxford University Press.

————. 1997. *World Development Report 1997—The State in a Changing World.* New York: Oxford University Press.

————. 1998a. "Partnership for Development: Proposed Actions for the World Bank." Paper presented at an informal meeting of the Partnerships Group, World Bank, May 20, Washington, D.C.

————. 1998b. "Partnership for Development: From Vision to Action." Briefing to the World Bank Board of Directors, September 24, Washington, D.C.

————. 1999. "Country Assessments and IDA Allocations (discussion draft)." Joint World Bank/DFID Technical Workshop on Enhancing the Country Performance Assessments, Washington, D.C.

9

Moving from Projects
to Programmatic Aid

Stephen Jones and *Andrew Lawson*

Donor agencies and multilateral lending institutions are looking increasingly for ways to turn traditional project-based approaches into aid for broader public expenditure programs (programmatic aid). Aid resources would be more fully incorporated into country budgets, using the government's systems instead of special project systems and multiple donor accountability instruments. The recent introduction of the Poverty Reduction Strategy Papers (PRSPs) is likely to accelerate this movement. But such a change requires capacity-building, donor cooperation, and strong leadership from the aid-receiving government. And it implies moving along a continuum of approaches—from individual projects to sector approaches with common financing mechanisms, and then to multisector budget support or programmatic lending.

This chapter reviews experience with sectorwide approaches, attempts to improve fiscal management through medium-term expenditure frameworks, and the potential role of World Bank lending instruments in those efforts. It complements the views expressed in Chap. 8 on prioritizing expenditures within a medium-term framework and sums up emerging best practice in applying sectorwide approaches and other specific programmatic lending instruments. Although there is no necessary connection between a sectorwide approach and a particular financing instrument, some instruments are more useful than others. Sector investment and maintenance loans have been used to support sectorwide approaches, but their relative inflexibility makes them impractical for a lender-of-last-resort role in support of a sector program.

More flexible adaptable program loans may be used to support processes where there is agreement on long-term results but a need for short-term flexibility in how to achieve them.

Experience with Sectorwide Approaches

Lack of agreement on definitions of sector programs and approaches has caused confusion. Here, a sectorwide approach is defined as an effort to bring donor support to a sector within a common management and planning framework. It brings the sector budget back to the center of policymaking and unifies expenditure management in pursuit of agreed sector objectives. This definition highlights several key elements:

- A sectorwide approach is a *process*, not a particular instrument or program.
- At its core are the sector strategy and the public expenditure program that supports it.
- A common management and planning framework may be involved, but does not necessarily imply a common pool funding mechanism.

This definition is broader than that of Harrold (1995), which defines six essential features of a sector investment program:

- Sectorwide in scope and covering both current and capital expenditures.
- Based on a clear sector strategy and policy framework.
- With local stakeholders fully in charge.
- Signed on by all main donors in a process led by government.
- With common implementation arrangements.
- Using local capacity rather than long-term technical assistance for design, management, and implementation.

Using definitions based on this set of features has created problems, since it encompasses both the broader sectorwide approach (based on integrated budget support) and a more controversial view about particular problems and proposed solutions. Specific stakeholder consultation mechanisms and roles for technical assistance were argued to be central to ownership—an approach not endorsed by all donors. At the same time, the Harrold definition set out guidance for a specific type of World Bank operation. Narrow donor concerns—the definition of a sector, how many features a program needs to be classified as a sector investment program—dwarfed more fundamental issues in discussions. There has been a tendency to focus on specific financing mechanisms rather than other process markers that might be implied by the broader definition of sectorwide approach given above. There is no necessary tie between the sectorwide approach as defined here and specific loan instruments: a range of instruments could support such a process. By the same token, using a sector investment and maintenance loan as a lending instrument, for example, does not imply a sectorwide approach.

Donor organizations have also used the sector terminology to refer to the coordination of their project activities with government activities while not necessarily implying a broader coordination with other donor programs or with the government. This confusion has created difficulties for discussion of the concept with governments, contributing to the frequently long and unsatisfactory preparation processes for sector investment programs.

The Underlying Problem

Why do we need sectorwide approaches? Because there is inadequate planning for the recurrent costs of investments, too many project management systems, too much or too little technical assistance, and too little coordination among donors. Underlying this is the breakdown of the budget process for managing activities in a sector. Where sectorwide approaches are most relevant (where aid dependence is high), the budget process has failed to deliver a single integrated planning and management system for public funds, including resources supplied by donors.

Donors contributed to this failure by attempting to bypass macroeconomic and administrative constraints to maintain funding for particular activities. These constraints intensified during pre-adjustment macroeconomic and political crises, and were exacerbated by the pressures on government expenditure and central bank lending (not matched by improved civil service efficiency) accompanying structural adjustment programs. This made it more difficult to meet counterpart funding obligations. The increasing emphasis given by donors to social sectors under adjustment also contributed to high sector-level aid dependence.[1] Aid increased just when government management capacity was severely eroded.

Governments have accommodated this movement of donor funds beyond the budget for a variety of reasons. Since the budget process cannot guarantee a reliable and timely supply of funds (especially for nonstaff costs), managers have an incentive to bypass the budget to secure resources directly from donors and to resist integrating management of donor funds into the budget. The expansion of the project and donor bureaucracy increases demand for management and policy analysis skills, often in posts far better paid and with better equipment and conditions than the civil service can provide. And donor willingness to fund particular sectors (such as health, education, and agriculture) may have allowed governments—in a time of fiscal stringency—to sustain funding to politically sensitive sectors unattractive to donors. The price: increased donor dependence and higher transactions costs.

The result has been a comprehensive breakdown of accountability and management of public expenditure. The sectorwide approach tries to bring the sector budget back to the center of policymaking to unify expenditure management. This can increase the effectiveness of aid and government expenditures in achieving agreed development objectives.

Progress with Sectorwide Approaches

No initiative by aid-dependent countries has realized all elements of the sectorwide approach:

- A common management and planning framework encompassing all major donor and government activities.
- A strategy-led public expenditure program that integrates recurrent and development expenditure and is embedded in a broader medium-term budget framework.
- A common pool funding arrangement that includes most of the sector budget.

Though experience is incomplete, we can look at why some processes have progressed more slowly or encountered more problems than expected. And we can look at promising approaches that have yet to bear fruit.

One starting point is an exercise under the Special Program of Assistance for Sub-Saharan Africa (Jones 1999) that used survey responses from donors to classify sectorwide approaches based on five criteria (Table 9.1).

- Existence of a comprehensive sector policy and strategy framework.
- Existence of a medium-term sectoral expenditure framework and an annual sectoral expenditure program.
- Consistency between the sectoral expenditure program and the overall macroeconomic framework.
- Satisfactory macroeconomic management (compliance with International Monetary Fund macroeconomic program).
- Donor coordination organized by the government, with all major donors providing support within the agreed sector framework.

Of the sectoral issues reviewed, roads made the most progress, followed by health and education. Despite strong initiatives by the World Bank, agriculture has achieved little (Jones 1999).[2] Why the disparity? The roads sector boasts simple institutions and clearly (and narrowly defined) policy problems. Problems usually come from unpredictable funding or corruption in contracting institutions.[3] Health and education receive a large share of budget expenditure (as does roads) and are a central focus of poverty-oriented development strategies. Broad consensus around at least some key sectoral policy issues (including the role of the state in primary healthcare and education) has emerged in several countries.[4] Agriculture, however, has complex institutions and downward budget pressure as the state withdraws from a direct role in production, marketing, and service provision. There are also disagreements between governments and donors (and among donor agencies) about the role of the state.

Only Ethiopia and Uganda have programs that meet all five criteria in more than one sector.[5] Both have strong and effective finance ministries and high-level political commitment to fiscal discipline, and thus predictable budgets. Although other countries (such as Ghana and Zambia) have achieved progress at the sector level, macroeconomic and fiscal instability have undermined the gains.

Regarded as particularly advanced and significant initiatives, the processes reviewed in 1996 (Jones 1997b)—agriculture and health in Zambia, health in Mozambique, and roads in Tanzania—did not meet the five criteria three years later, for several reasons. As pioneering programs, they were treading untested ground, and both the Zambia Agricultural Sector Investment Program and the Tanzania Integrated Roads Program had design defects. And macroeconomic instability and increasing tension between government and donors over governance undermined programs in Zambia.

More generally, promising processes took more time. For example, Asamoa-Boah and Smithson (1999) argue that there were four stages in developing the Ghana health program. The first began in the late 1980s as dissatisfaction developed with donor-inspired projects. The second, in the early 1990s, experimented with new forms of donor support and broad consultation on options. The third, 1993–95, developed a medium-term strategic framework. And the last, from 1996 to the present, elaborated common management arrangements, and a sector program began to replace projects. In 1999, the process survived its strongest test when concerted donor action prevented hospital spending that was outside the agreed expenditure framework. A new medium-term expenditure framework process may provide greater budget predictability.

Asamoa-Boah and Smithson (1999) identified the following as factors in Ghana's success:[6]

- A history of intensive capacity-building created a critical mass of potential supporters of reform with a common vision. It also helped the Ministry of Health reorganize along functional lines, and it strengthened management systems and budgetary reform, making resource allocation more transparent.
- The Ministry of Health became more assertive as donors became more flexible. Official development assistance from the World Bank, Danida, and the United Kingdom linked preparation of new tranches of support to the broader process, while long-term technical assistance helped bridge donors and the ministry.
- The Ministry of Health argued that government management systems, not special units like a health reform secretariat, should undergird program implementation.
- Modest in its commitments and timetables, the Ministry of Health concentrated

on building support from a broad constituency in the health system (particularly senior managers at the regional level).

Problems in Applying the Sectorwide Approach

Key preconditions for moving toward a sectorwide approach are:

- Strong and effectiveness leadership at the sector ministry level.
- Commitment to the process elsewhere in government, particularly in the ministry of finance and at a senior political level.
- Broad consensus between government and donors on key policy and management issues for the sector.
- A reasonable degree of macroeconomic and political stability, leading to a relatively high level of budget predictability.

If these conditions fail to hold, problems arise.

Weak leadership from the sector ministry. If the sector ministry is not the leader the donor will be, and its concerns (policy, ideology, project cycle and timetable, desire to maintain the flow of funds) will drive the process. When this happens, planning and consultation processes (donor-funded) run parallel to normal government systems. In agriculture, for example, long and costly processes of "program preparation"—in Kenya, Lesotho, and Malawi—center on "secretariats" and "task forces" with only loose ties to government. At best, donor initiative will spark discussions of key sector problems and help achieve some rationalization of donor activities. At worst, the ministry will see the sector program as another set of donor requirements for project preparation, and other donors can become alienated. Weak (or poorly embedded) ownership at the wider political and stakeholder level can leave the process vulnerable to shifts of personnel or political power.

Lack of commitment from the ministry of finance and senior politicians. Lack of involvement and commitment from the ministry of finance means that the process is not integrated into the budget cycle and there can be no assurance that plans will be funded. In this situation, there are few incentives for the sector ministry to seek more transparency in the use of donor resources (by bringing them within the budget envelope) and no prospect of implementing a coherent medium-term expenditure program for the sector.

No consensus between government and donors on policy and management. Ideally, disagreement will lead to consultation, discussion, and research from which consensus may develop. But if the desire of both donors and government to maintain funding flows and to keep the process formally on track causes them to fudge key issues, these will re-emerge as points of contention. What was perceived by donors as persistent backtracking by the Zambian government on commitments not to intervene in maize and fertilizer markets undermined credibility. Divergent expectations are another problem, as seen in the early stages of the Ethiopian Health and Education Sector Development Programs (Jones 1997a). Typically, a ministry exercising strong leadership has a clear agenda aimed at moving quickly to common pool financing and reducing transaction costs in aid management. Some donors may see this as unrealistic and may be more interested in having policy discussions.

Macroeconomic and political instability. A weak macroeconomic environment and disagreements about governance can easily derail sectorwide approaches. Failure to embed the program in a broader macroeconomic and expenditure framework increases its vulnerability to budget shocks.

If these problems are not resolved, donors and aid-receiving governments will face several management problems.

Financing arrangements, particularly the scale and form of pooled funding arrangements. Even relatively advanced arrangements (like the common pool funding of district health services in Ghana and Zambia) account for only a small fraction of donor expenditure and a minority of donors, and require heavy prior investment in system development. For some donors (the United States and Japan), such funding arrangements are infeasible for fiduciary reasons.

Measuring performance and setting conditions for tranche release. Limited experience with time-slice financing through common pool arrangements means there has been little opportunity to address this problem. Donors need to decide what form of conditionality can ensure accountability. The most straightforward arrangement would link disbursements to government performance in providing counterpart resources (to achieve incentive compatibility). More ambitious would be to link them to sector performance targets and key policies. This may require an unrealistic degree of donor flexibility. While common financial systems are not necessary to ensure coordinated sector financing, some agreement on appropriate performance criteria is necessary. In the Zambia Agriculture Sector Investment Program, slow data collection and processing delayed implementation of a highly sophisticated sector performance measurement system, and ultimately no attempt was made to tie disbursements to these performance criteria.

Decentralization. In many countries, sectorwide approaches coexist with decentralization. Although compatible in principle, the two may conflict in practice (Akroyd and Duncan 1998). The amount of tension depends on the level of government at which intersectoral resource allocation decisions are made. Under a system of tied or conditional grants, central budget planning and service standard setting can be the basis for a sectoral program. If a local government can freely use its revenue or block grants, the scope for national sectorwide approaches will be limited. In Ghana, there are national services for education, health, and forestry. This preserves unified sector management but limits decentralized decisionmaking. Field staff from the Ministry of Food and Agriculture are moving to local government, and it is unclear how budget mechanisms will maintain an integrated sector approach.

Weak capacity. One reaction to weak government capacity (and sometimes to disagreements between donors and government on the role of the state) has been to increase direct donor funding to NGOs that provide services that complement or substitute for government services. Improved government capacity makes it easier for donors to channel funds through government to NGOs, or to switch funding to government services.

Emerging Best Practice in Applying Sectorwide Approaches

Several basic principles have emerged from experience:

- Let the government lead—with donor support. Resist the urge to substitute donor initiatives for local ownership, and do not mistake one for the other. Donors with a strong history of involvement in the sector, but without a strong commitment to particular projects, are the best sources of information and guidance.
- Avoid parallel systems. Instead, strengthen and reform government budgeting and planning.
- Involve the ministry of finance—there are strict limits to what a sector ministry can achieve alone. Where the ministry of finance has not been closely involved from the start (and has not provided guidance on the resource envelope for planning), the process may be derailed or delayed by budget disagreements.[7] But it is also important that line ministries have the authority to set priorities to match agreed strategies (in the event of unforeseen budget cuts, for example).
- Build and economize on management, planning, and policy skills within government. This will reduce the transaction costs of aid management.
- Be realistic about decentralization. Are plans feasible, given current institutional capacity? Do they clearly define roles of different levels of government?
- Learn from similar experiences in other sectors and countries. The ministry of finance should take the lead to make this happen.
- Move slowly and realistically when developing pooled funding arrangements. This requires careful preparation and capacity-building. Unified planning and resource management may not be necessary. Rather, the priority should be on establishing common review processes and timetables.
- Educate stakeholders. What is the rationale behind a sectorwide approach? What problems does pooled funding create, and what solutions are realized? How should safeguard policies be addressed? Must all government activities in the sector be compatible with donor safeguards, or just those for the project?

What should donors do when a precondition is not met? They must decide whether engagement or disengagement will best foster change and consensus building, and whether to focus more on the central or sectoral level. Dropping all conditions for a sector program initiative is not the answer. Donors should simplify and coordinate their activities while engaging in strategic discussion and building common vision (through sector and public expenditure reviews, for example). The ministry of finance and senior political leaders should be encouraged to provide strategic guidance.

Experience with Medium-Term Expenditure Framework Initiatives

Failing to link policy, planning, and budgeting may be the single biggest contributor to poor budget outcomes at the macro, strategic, and operational levels in developing countries. A rigorous medium-term expenditure (or budget) framework is now generally accepted as an effective institutional and technical solution. The World Bank's "Public Expenditure Management Handbook" describes the medium-term approach as the "linking framework" that "facilitates the management of the tension between policy and budget realities to reduce pressure throughout the whole budget cycle." The International Monetary Fund's (1999) "Manual on Fiscal Transparency" also emphasizes the need for a "clear statement about the broader fiscal policy objectives of the government, the implications of current fiscal policies in future years, and the sustainability of the fiscal position over the medium term." These must be stated in a fiscal and economic outlook paper. In public expenditure reviews, inadequate medium-term frameworks are given more attention than any other budgetary issue.

In many respects then, the medium-term framework has become the new panacea of public expenditure management and a logical mechanism around which to structure public expenditure reform loans or other governmentwide instruments of budget support.

If the medium-term expenditure framework (or medium-term budget framework) is to be a useful operational tool for aid agencies, three questions must first be answered:

- How is a medium-term expenditure framework defined, and how does it differ from a medium-term budget framework?
- What are the essential institutional and technical features that distinguish a successful framework?
- Is the medium-term expenditure framework agenda too ambitious? How have developing countries handled these new frameworks, and what does that tell us about the preconditions for success?

The answers to these questions will yield some preliminary conclusions about what the medium-term framework can do as an integrating macro perspective for sector programs and as a mechanism around which to structure scaled-up lending instruments.

Distinguishing Medium-Term Budget Frameworks and
Medium-Term Expenditure Frameworks

The medium-term framework can evolve through three developmental stages. It begins as a medium-term fiscal framework—a statement of fiscal policy goals and a set of integrated medium-term macroeconomic and fiscal targets and projections. (The International Monetary Fund's "Manual on Fiscal Transparency" includes this as part of the minimum requirements.)

The next step is a medium-term budget framework, comprising both the medium-term fiscal aggregates and a set of integrated, consistent, medium-term estimates broken down by spending agency. The idea is to express strategic priorities in terms of medium-term resources, thereby providing a measure of budget predictability to spending agencies while respecting the constraints of fiscal discipline. Thus, the medium-term budget framework might be considered the most basic type of medium-term expenditure framework. Taken in this sense, medium-term expenditure frameworks and medium-term budget frameworks are synonymous. A basic framework of this kind focuses on the level one and level two objectives of public expenditure management: maintaining aggregate fiscal discipline and strategic prioritization of resource allocations. Insofar as it succeeds in making policies and budgets more predictable, it may also achieve the level three objective of operational efficiency.

In practice, medium-term expenditure framework initiatives have often involved additional budgetary innovations aimed at moving towards activity-, output-, or outcome-based budgeting. Reforms that seek to improve operational efficiency in addition to reinforcing fiscal discipline and improving strategic prioritization are called extended medium-term expenditure frameworks.

There are advantages and disadvantages to integrating medium-term budget frameworks and more detailed, performance-focused reforms within extended medium-term expenditure framework initiatives. On the one hand, integration promotes consistency in budgetary reform and gives an overall performance focus to budgetary initiatives. And if output-focused budgeting approaches can reveal the true cost of policies, they will facilitate a more informed debate on strategic priorities and thus a more robust set of decisions on intersectoral resource allocations. There is significant evidence that inefficiencies in government expenditure may mean that boosting sectoral expenditure levels will do little to improve outcomes (for examples, see Gupta, Honjo, and Verhoeven 1997, and Ablo and Reinikka 1998 for Uganda).

On the other hand, establishing and maintaining a rigorous and effective medium-term budget framework requires addressing many technical, political, and human resource issues. Simultaneously introducing radical changes to the structure of budgeting may overload fragile management and implementation capacity. Any resources directed elsewhere may prejudice effective introduction.

Lessons from Experience

Several lessons have emerged from basic medium-term budget frameworks in South Africa and Uganda to more advanced medium-term budget frameworks in the OECD countries, and from extended medium-term expenditure frameworks in Ghana and Malawi:

- Stringent conditions must be met to achieve the full benefits of a medium-term budget framework (IMF 1999).
- Developing countries probably cannot meet these conditions. But the gap between the expenditure implications of policies and the resources available to finance budget operations is typically so large that even basic acceptance of the principles of a medium-term budget framework will make sector policies and plans more realistic.
- Government commitment to fiscal policy objectives must override all other policy commitments. Governments facing overriding political pressure to increase spending (as in Ghana pre-1996) can undermine this commitment; senior political leaders and the ministry of finance can reinforce it (Uganda, South Africa). The weakness of the Malawi medium-term expenditure framework is largely attributable to the lack of such commitment.
- Opportunities for obtaining extrabudgetary resources should be controlled. This is difficult in highly aid-dependent economies, especially in highly aid-dependent sectors (typically, agriculture). Sectorwide arrangements can help, as they did in Uganda and Ghana's education sectors.
- Budget-driven policy change is sustainable only if resource allocations (and ideally the actual level of funding) become more predictable as a result of the establishment of medium-term expenditure frameworks. South Africa achieved this (South Africa Department of Finance 1997; Abedian 1999); and Uganda has made significant progress too. Uganda has been able to sustain this reform by bringing in more aid for programs and sectorwide approach arrangements (Stasavage and Moyo 1999). Ghana and Malawi still have unpredictable budgets, and indications show that this is impeding budget coverage and reforms for policies to improve sustainability (Kitabire 1999). There is a severe danger of undermining the credibility of the process if governments are unable to stick to their commitments. For example, budget outcomes in Ghana appear to have been significantly out of line with the medium-term expenditure framework even during the first year of implementation (Foster 1999).
- Technical improvements to revenue and debt forecasting and measures to smooth the flow of budget support grants will quickly make the budget more predictable. And technical improvements highlight situations where government is inflating revenue estimates to avoid hard decisions on the budget.
- Making policy and program costing more accurate will take a while—it requires a full base of information and a sector ministry interested in improving policymaking and budgeting. Incentives for this need to be introduced and sustained.

The Role of Programmatic Instruments

Although there is no necessary connection between a sectorwide approach and a particular financing instrument, some instruments are more useful than others. Gavras (1998) identifies four types that can help a sectorwide approach create common funding arrangements:

- traditional investment financing for specific components, with or without special accounts;
- tranches that may be linked to progress indicators;
- reimbursement of certain expenditures over a certain period in line with agreed priorities (time-slice financing);
- some combination of these.

Gavras argues that time-slice financing is the most flexible and therefore is particularly suitable for financing sectorwide approaches because it can provide targeted reimbursable support. Time-slice mechanisms are applied to specific policies or outcomes, and can be easily adapted to different preparation and implementation cycles. And using them can eliminate special accounts (which bypass and complicate normal government procedures and can lead to severe disbursement delays, as with the Zambia Agricultural Sector Investment Program (ASIP). In principle, donor coordination around simple time-slice financing could be achieved. In practice, several factors are likely to complicate the financial arrangements supporting the sectorwide approach: differing terms of financing, desire for a geographic or specific subsector or functional expenditure category focus, and differential financing rates or conditions on the recurrent-development budget split.

The World Bank has used two main types of programmatic instruments to support sectorwide approaches: sector investment and maintenance loans, or credits and adaptable program loans.

Sector Investment and Maintenance Loans

Sector investment and maintenance loans are a traditional lending product of the World Bank. Their objective is to bring investments, policies, and performance in a specific sector or subsector in line with economic priorities and to ensure efficient operation and maintenance of investments. The focus is on public sector expenditures and institutional capacity to plan, implement, and monitor investments. The approach requires agreement on policy reforms, institutional strengthening, and the composition of the public investment program in the sector.

Such loans have supported several candidate sector programs in the 1990s in Zambia (health, $56 million; agriculture, $60 million), Ghana (basic education, $50 million), and Ethiopia (education, $100 million). But the sector investment and maintenance loan's inflexibility—in relation to the lender of last resort role that the World Bank sought to fulfil—created problems in both Zambia programs (Jones 1997b).

The Morocco Agricultural Sector Investment Loan I (1992–94) was conceived to provide time-slice financing for the government's agriculture investments, improve how this money was invested, strengthen the Ministry of Agriculture's institutional capacity, and continue key sector policy reforms. But there was no attempt to agree on performance benchmarks or on the expenditure program for the sector, or to coordinate with other donors. Another key problem was the ministry's lack of interest—it did not believe that the operation was increasing budget resources. And problems implementing complex procurement and disbursement procedures dominated supervision.

The Performance Audit Report for the Morocco Agricultural Sector Investment Loan (World Bank 1999b) found that the operation did not achieve its objectives of extending the policy dialogue or contributing to substantial institutional capacity-building (with the exception of its contribution to privatizing veterinary services). Specifically, it found that time-slice financing for sector investment program should be deferred until all key policy reforms have been implemented; requires prior implementation of government restructuring based on comprehensive expenditure reviews, which must be coordinated with other donors; and requires clear progress benchmarks.

Adaptable Lending Instruments

Adaptable lending instruments are programmatic across time and project components rather than across spending categories. The adaptable program loan "provides funding for long-term development programs where there is clear agreement on long-term objectives but where the path to achieve them requires much learning from results. A sequence of adaptable program lending starts with a first loan to fund the initial set of activities: subsequent funding is provided when agreed milestones are met" (World Bank 1998b, box 4.1). The expected outcomes are:

- greater flexibility in adapting project design as borrower conditions and partnerships evolve;
- more structured support for projects entailing behavioral change;
- less money and time committed to preparing operations that need flexible planning;
- encouragement of a results culture;
- reduced risk to both parties, since both can exit easily from operations.

Adaptable program loans have also supported some sector programs: Turkey Basic Education (1999, $300 million), Mozambique Agriculture (1999,

$30 million), Guinea Population and Reproductive Health (1999, $11.3 million), Zambia Basic Education (1999, $40 million), and Uganda Roads (1999, $40 million).

A review of initial experience (World Bank 1998b) with the two adaptable lending instruments was positive. The instruments are responding to borrowers' needs while providing greater flexibility and opportunities to improve partnerships. The main problems relate to the difficulty of reaching internal agreement on how to meet fiduciary and safeguards policies, and how to set and use sector performance targets as a basis for joint donor fund-release decisions. Three main types of adaptable program loans were identified:

- *Horizontal expansion.* An approach is tested in one area and then scaled up geographically.
- *Vertical deepening.* The program develops through successive, logically sequenced stages of reform or investment.
- *Maturation process.* Complementary activities are carried out from the beginning, becoming more sophisticated and effective through learning.

In each case, the key test is whether the program can meet the performance conditions that will trigger second and subsequent phases and funding, and whether these performance conditions are fair. The "Quality at Entry" report (World Bank 1999d) reviewing eight adaptable program loans noted the need to focus more closely on setting appropriate triggers linked to key issues. Otherwise, there would be a risk of being locked into financing longer-term programs without sufficient progress on substantive issues. For example, the quality at entry review of the Turkey Basic Education Project (World Bank 1999a) criticized the triggers for second tranche release as too conservative and relating to the Bank's investment, rather than to the government program. The review also found that the operation ignored the risks of recurrent cost increases implicit in expanding basic education.

Adaptable program lending may prove to be the most appropriate instrument for supporting sectorwide approaches, at least in sectors that require lots of flexibility in financing (where a lender of last resort role is envisaged, for example). The review found that "most operations support broad sectoral development agendas at the level of full sectors and nations, or subnational regions. Again, it is likely that several operations would not have been brought to approval stage without the new instrument, owing to the difficulty in specifying adequately a priori activities, costs, implementation arrangements, and results beyond a three-to-four-year time horizon" (World Bank 1998b).

TABLE 9.1
Results from the Special Program of Assistance
for Sub-Saharan Africa Survey

Threshold Level Passed[a]	Sector	Country[b]
1 and 2	Roads	Benin
		Cameroon
		Côte d'Ivoire
	Health	Ethiopia
		Senegal
		Uganda
		Zambia
	Education	Ethiopia
	Agriculture	Guinea?
	Energy	Madagascar
		Mali
		Senegal
		Ethiopia
		Uganda
		Mozambique
		Kenya
1	Roads	Ghana
	Health	*Burkina*
		Ghana
	Education	Mauritania
	Agriculture	Mozambique
		Zambia
		Ghana
		Mozambique
		Kenya
None	Roads	Tanzania
	Health	Côte d'Ivoire
	Education	Niger
	Agriculture	Tanzania
	Urban Sector	Zambia
	Water	Tanzania
		Mozambique

[a] Threshold 1: existence of a comprehensive sector policy and strategy framework, and existence of a medium-term sectoral expenditure framework and an annual sectoral expenditure program. Threshold 2: consistency between the sectoral expenditure program and the overall macroeconomic framework, satisfactory macroeconomic management (compliance with International Monetary Fund macroeconomic program), and donor coordination organized by the government with all major donors providing support within the agreed sector framework.
[b] Italics designate answers on a single donor response. A question mark indicates incomplete consensus.
Source: SPA Working Group on Economic Management 1999.

Conclusions

The key requirement for moving from project-based planning and implementation to sector approaches with common financing mechanisms is the overall strengthening of the budget process. When the amount of aid is large, the key is to bring it all within the budget envelope. When the amount of aid is small (and is used for pilot programs or capacity building, and the like), lower level solutions may be better.

Sectorwide approaches can succeed in the proper environment: strong leadership and commitment to improving public expenditure management at the sector, ministry of finance, and most senior political levels, donor cooperation and some consensus among donors and government on sector objectives and strategies, and a coherent process of capacity development that will make all this possible.

Notes

1. For example, aid to the health sector in Ghana increased from $1 million in 1984 to $12 million in 1990, and $25 million by 1995. By 1992 there were fifteen major external agencies supporting the health sector (Asamoa-Baah and Smithson 1999, p. 3).
2. This may reflect a general problem with the quality of agricultural operations. The "Quality at Entry" report (World Bank 1999d) found that one in three new projects in the agricultural sector in 1998 should be rated less than satisfactory, with the main weaknesses being in sector analysis, financial risk assessment, and inappropriate conditionality and monitoring and evaluation arrangements (World Bank 1999d).
3. Both these problems were encountered in the Tanzania roads sector, previously seen as a pioneering sectoral initiative.
4. Hay (1999a) argues, though, that there has been a tendency in several health sector programs to avoid confronting fundamental issues about the role of the state in the sector. This has caused subsequent delays or problems.
5. Hay (1999b), however, argues that in the Uganda health sector there are major unresolved issues about the fiscal sustainability of the extensive role envisaged for government in service provision that are likely to limit further progress.
6. Problems in macroeconomic management probably account for the classification of the Ghanaian programs in this exercise.
7. This happened in the case of both the Kenyan and Mozambican agricultural programs, where the costed programs developed at the sector level far exceeded budget ceilings subsequently indicated by the Ministry of Finance.

References

Abedian, I., 1999. "Early Lessons from the South African Medium-term Expenditure Framework." *International Workshop: Good Practice in Public Expenditure Management*. Oxford, U.K.: Office of Policy Management.

Ablo, E., and R. Reinikka. 1998. "Do Budgets Really Matter? Evidence from Public

Spending on Education and Health in Uganda." *Policy Research Working Paper 1926*. Washington D.C.: World Bank.

Akroyd, S., and A. Duncan. 1998. "The Sector Approach and Sustainable Rural Livelihoods." In Carney, ed. 1998. *Sustainable Rural Livelihood: What Contribution Can We Make?* London, U.K.: DFID.

Anipa, S., F. Kaluma, and E. Muggeridge. 1999. "Medium-term Expenditure Framework Case Study from Malawi and Ghana." *Background Papers for OPM Conference on Good Practice in Public Expenditure Management*. Oxford, U.K. Office of Policy Management.

Asamoa-Boah, A., and P. Smithson. 1999. "Donors and the Ministry of Health: New Partnerships in Ghana." *Forum on Health Sector Reform Discussion Paper No. 8*. Geneva: World Health Organization.

Carney, D., ed. 1998. "Sustainable Rural Livelihoods: What Contribution Can We Make?" London: Department for International Development.

Craig, R., A. Lawson, and N. Smithers. 1999. "Implementing Medium-term Expenditure Framework in the Malawi Education Sector." Report for DANIDA. Oxford Policy Management.

Foster, M. 1999. "Lesson of Experience from Health Sector Sectorwide Approaches." Draft. Center for Aid and Public Expenditure. London: Overseas Development Institute.

Gavras, P. 1998 "Disbursement Strategies under Sector-Wide Approaches and Time-Slice Financing." Draft. Washington D.C.: The World Bank

Gupta, S., K. Honjo, and M. Verhoeven. 1997. "The Efficiency of Government Expenditure—Experiences from Africa." *IMF Working Paper 97/153*. Washington, D.C.: International Monetary Fund.

Hansen, H., and F. Tarp. 1999, "Aid Effectiveness Disputed." Copenhagen: University of Copenhagen.

Harrold, P., and associates. 1995. "The Broad Sector Approach to Investment Lending." *Discussion Paper 302*. Washington, D.C.: World Bank.

Hay, R. 1999a, "Strategic Issues in Health Sectorwide Approaches." Paper prepared for seminar on DANIDA Health Sector Program Support in Africa. Harare, February.

———. 1999b. "Uganda Health Sector Support Program Review." Oxford Policy Management.

International Monetary Fund. 1999. "Manual on Fiscal Transparency." Available http://imf.org/fiscal/manual.

Jones, S. 1997a. "Ethiopia Social Sector Development Programs." Report to ODA. Oxford Policy Management.

———. 1997b. "Sector Investment Programs in Africa: Issues and Experience." *World Bank Technical Paper* No. 374. Washington D.C.: World Bank.

———. 1999. "Increasing Aid Effectiveness in Africa? The World Bank and Sector Investment Programs." Oxford Policy Management.

Kitabire, D. 1999. "The Cash Budgeting System in Uganda." *Background Papers for OPM Conference on Good Practice in Public Expenditure Management*. Oxford, U.K.

Kostopoulos, C. 1999. "Progress in Public Expenditure Management in Africa: Evidence from World Bank Surveys." *Africa Region Working Paper Series No. 1.*, Washington, D.C.: World Bank.

McGillivray, M., and O. Morrissey. 1999. "Aid Fungibility in *Assessing Aid*: Red Herring or True Concern?" Paper for session on "Assessing Aid." ESRC-DESG Annual Conference, Reading, U.K.: University of Reading.

— — —. 1999. "Linking Macro-Economic Concerns with Sector Strategies: A Review of Donor Experiences." *Report from Seminar on Sector-Wide Approaches*. Oslo, Norway: NORAD.

OPM. 1999. "International Experience in Aid Effectiveness." Background paper prepared for Workshop on Partnership and ODA Effectiveness. Hanoi, Vietnam.

South Africa Department of Finance. 1997. "Three Year Budget Policy Statement Published." Press Release, Pretoria, 2 December.

SPA Working Group on Economic Management. 1999. "Tracking of Support Provided under Sector Programs." Special Program of Assistance for Sub-Saharan Africa Plenary Meeting, Washington, D.C.

Stasavage, D., and D. Moyo. 1999. "Are Cash Budgets a Cure for Excess Fiscal Deficits (and at What Cost)?" *Working Paper Series 99–11*. Oxford, U.K.: Center for the Study of African Economies.

World Bank. 1997. "Ethiopia—Education Sector Development Program." Project Identification Document. Washington, D.C.: World Bank.

— — —. 1998a. "Adaptable Lending: Review of the First Year's Experience." Operational Core Services Network. Washington, D.C.: World Bank.

— — —. 1998b. "Annual Report 1998." Washington, D.C.: World Bank.

— — —. 1998c. "Assessing Aid: What Works, What Doesn't and Why." New York: Oxford University Press for the World Bank.

— — —. 1998d. "Public Expenditure Management Handbook." Washington, D.C.: World Bank.

— — —. 1999a. "Final Report: Quality at Entry (QAE) In-Depth Assessment Turkey Basic Education Project." Washington, D.C.: World Bank.

— — —. 1999b. "Kingdom of Morocco: Agricultural Sector Investment Loan (ASIL I) (Loan 3403-MOR)—Performance Audit Report." *Report No. 19529*. Operations Evaluation Department. Washington, D.C.: World Bank.

— — —. 1999c. "Lending Retrospective: Volumes and Instruments—Issues Paper." Discussion draft. Washington, D.C.: World Bank

— — —. 1999d. "Quality at Entry in CY98—A QAG Assessment." Quality Assurance Group. Washington, D.C.: World Bank.

— — —. 1999e. "A Proposal for a Comprehensive Development Framework." Discussion Draft. Washington, D.C.: World Bank.

10

Applying the Comprehensive Development Framework to USAID Experiences

James Fox

Using the four main principles of the World Bank's Comprehensive Development Framework (CDF)—a long-term development plan, host country ownership, donor partnership, and results orientation—to analyze development activities yields useful insights into successes and failures. Here, it is applied to six U.S. Agency for International Development (USAID) activities. Five were chosen because they are broadly regarded within USAID as conspicuous successes—assistance to the Republic of Korea, family planning, agricultural research, university training, and smallpox eradication. The sixth case—assistance to Egypt—is included because it is typically regarded within the institution as one of the least effective in development terms. The analysis sheds light on how the main elements of the CDF contributed to USAID's performance and offers suggestions on additional dimensions to be considered in applying the CDF.

Two of the case studies—Korea and smallpox eradication—involve programs completed in the late 1970s for which the outcome is clear and a wealth of evaluative material exists. The other four cases represent ongoing activities, for which achievement of neither the ultimate outcome nor the specific goal is yet evident. The evidence in these cases is necessarily more tentative.

This chapter draws lesson from USAID's experience to guide the practice of CDF principles:

- Decentralization of authority to country offices can enhance adaptation and ownership of assistance programs.
- "Success" is not always easy to assess in the short term.
- New knowledge and technological advances are critical to success in most cases.
- The search for long-term strategies should not detract from investing in targets of opportunity, focusing on the most strategic, and paying attention to implementation.
- Government ownership should not be equated with country ownership—in some successful cases, ownership for reforms had to be nurtured outside the government.
- There is a risk when efforts to partner lead to least common denominator approaches.
- Results-orientation is perhaps the most important factor in program effectiveness, yet difficult to achieve in practice. Results are better monitored and evaluated through decentralized management—not global indicators and remote controls.

Republic of Korea: The Making of a Miracle

Korea was one of the largest recipients of U.S. aid during the 1950s and early 1960s. Many U.S. officials feared that this was encouraging a permanent dependence on high levels of aid to maintain economic stability. In 1962–63, however, changes in government policy produced rapid export-led economic growth, and dependence on U.S. aid soon came to an end.

The Nature of U.S. Assistance

The basic facts are straightforward. Korea had been under Japanese domination for thirty-five years prior to its occupation by U.S. and Russian forces at the end of World War II. Korea was among the poorest countries in the world in 1945. Partition after the war placed the more industrial north in the Soviet zone and the poorer and more agricultural south in the U.S. zone. In the south, lands owned by the Japanese were redistributed by the U.S. military government after the war; the Korean government also redistributed large Korean-held landholdings. The result was a substantial reduction in rural inequality. In 1950–53 the country was devastated by the war with the People's Republic of Korea.

The Republic of Korea received massive amounts of U.S. foreign aid—$12.7 billion between 1945 and 1975 (more than $50 billion in 1998 dollars)—which constituted the bulk of foreign aid to the country from all sources. Virtually all aid was in grants, roughly equally divided between economic and military aid. Aid was extremely large relative to the size of the Korean economy, averaging 8.1 percent of GDP during 1953–62 and financing 69 percent of imports. Exports were insignificant (2 percent of GDP) during this period, and in 1961 ($39 million) were even below the 1953 level.

The economy grew modestly during the 1950s. Then, beginning in 1963, growth rates rose dramatically, averaging nearly 10 percent a year during 1963–66, a pace maintained for most of the next three decades. Exports took off in 1962, more than quadrupling between 1961 and 1965. The explosive growth in exports moderated only slightly over the next decade. By 1975 exports had reached $5.1 billion, or about 30 percent of GDP.

The change in economic fortunes followed changes in political leadership. The Park Chung He regime, which took power in a coup in 1961, made exports its economic centerpiece. The country's economic dynamism did not falter with Park's assassination in 1972. Rapid growth continued into the 1990s, leading to the World Bank's description of Korea's development as an "economic miracle." In four decades, Korea had transformed itself from one of the poorest countries in the world to a major economic power—the world's ninth largest exporter.

Korea's success continued to surprise external observers. In the mid–1960s, the World Bank thought planned growth rates were too high. In 1971, Cole and Lyman argued that Korea's rapid growth was unlikely to continue, due to structural distortions in the economy and increasing resistance to taking corrective action. Similar assessments followed the 1997 Asian financial crisis, yet despite the structural distortions (the failure to deal with insolvent banks and bankrupt *chaebol*), the Korean economy in mid–1999 appeared to be back on the road to rapid economic growth.

While Korea's growth record is widely recognized, the influence of U.S. economic assistance has long been debated. Eight studies by the Harvard Institute of International Development, summarized in Mason and others (1970) and Steinberg's analyses (1982, 1985, 1989) for USAID are the key explorations of USAID's experience in Korea.

Overall, both Mason et al. and Steinberg suggest that foreign aid contributed only slightly to the Korean miracle, and that rapid growth was due primarily to a combination of domestic factors and a favorable international environment. They agree that foreign aid before and after the Korean war was "essential" to Korea's survival as an independent country and that it added perhaps 1.5 percent a year to GDP during 1953–63 (Mason et al. 1970, p. 203). Nevertheless, because President Syngman Rhee's policies maximized the need for aid, U.S. aid during that period—only 15 percent of which went for investment goods—provided support for unsustainable policies and so had no permanent value.

Mason and others (1970) argue that aid did little to bring about significant social and political change. The aid also was an impediment to the mobilization of domestic savings and government revenues. In their view, attempts by donors—principally the United States in the 1950s and early 1960s—to force the Korean government to give greater emphasis to stability (instead of or along with growth) were ineffectual and probably misguided in that they diverted attention from the real impediments to growth. Finally, they argue that even once the country began to grow rapidly after 1962, the notion that rapid economic growth would lead to a more open and democratic society "proved unrealistic."

Aid to Korea in a Holistic, Long-Term Development Framework

With U.S. encouragement, the Korean government instituted long-run economic planning beginning in 1953. Korea initially relied on foreign advisors but gradually took over leadership of the planning process. After several earlier attempts, the government was able in 1966 to put forward a five-year plan that was generally regarded as economically coherent and supported by government policymakers. Even so, the plan, which called for GDP growth of 7 percent a year, was criticized by the World Bank, which offered "continuing admonitions" that the target growth rate should be held to 6 percent (Cole and Lyman 1971, p. 219).

Yet the central feature of Korean development planning during its high-growth period was not its comprehensiveness, but its focus. The government believed that rapid growth in exports was critical, so this became the focus of economic policies. Krueger (1979, p. 85) writes that "the details of policies that were adopted appear to have resulted in large part in pragmatic response to the fortunes of exports: when export performance was deemed satisfactory, policies were left unaltered; when, however, it appeared that export growth was faltering, changes were instituted until satisfactory performance was again observed."

A telling statistic comes from the Jones and SaKong (1980) survey of Korean entrepreneurs that compared administrative decisionmaking under Rhee and Park. Entrepreneurs indicated that under Rhee, decisions were "always implemented" 3.2 percent of the time and "almost always implemented" 17.2 percent of the time, whereas under Park they were always implemented 78.2 percent and almost always implemented 16.6 percent of the time. This comparison suggests that the seriousness of purpose of the government in implementing its development planning may be more important than the quality or comprehensiveness of the plan itself.

Ownership

Ownership of the country's policy framework was unambiguously Korean for most of the period of U.S. assistance. The Korean position ultimately prevailed whenever there was a disagreement with the United States, which was frequently the case. Neither side was able to walk away from the other.

At least until 1965, Korea's economic stability depended on continued U.S. aid of $200 million or so a year. The U.S. political commitment, particularly after the Korean war, precluded any unilateral withdrawal from Korea or the taking of any large risks on Korea's political stability.

This mutual dependence did not bring harmony. The U.S. and the Rhee administration were usually at odds, with the United States pressing for devaluation of the currency and other orthodox policy measures, with "the Rhee Administration staunchly opposed [to] the U.S. policy package" (Amsden 1989, p. 41). Because the Rhee Administration had the final say on policy and, in the characterization of one economist, sought to maximize aid flows, it perpetuated policies that made high levels of aid necessary. Foremost among them was the maintenance of an overvalued exchange rate.

Tensions did not lessen with the arrival of the Park Administration. "By the early 1960s U.S. officials had become extremely gloomy about the prospects for Korean development" (Mason et al. 1970, p. 195). The United States also saw the country as stable enough that high levels of aid were no longer thought to be required to prevent collapse and began to discuss the phase-out of U.S. economic assistance. This effectively increased U.S. leverage.

The years 1963–64 witnessed some of the harshest bargaining over aid between the United States and Korean officials in the whole postwar period. Faced with severe food shortages, rising prices, and dwindling foreign-exchange reserves, the Koreans were very vulnerable. The United States insisted on a resumption of the stabilization program in 1963, calling for curtailing the budget deficit and limiting growth of the money supply to 5 percent. The following year, similar restrictions plus a 50 percent devaluation were imposed as conditions for aid. While acquiescing to these demands in order to assure an adequate grain supply for the coming months, the Korean government also began a realignment of policies and international relationships that would save it from ever being trapped in such a compromising position again (Mason et al. 1970, pp. 196–97).

Thus, the ability of the U.S. government to force policy change had increased by the early 1960s, and withdrawal of aid was a credible possibility. Steinberg (1985, pp. 88–89) ignores this issue when he states that "Korea demonstrates that policy dialogue is useful and important over time, even if its influence cannot normally be quantified, but that it will not produce results unless it somehow furthers the overall direction that the state is taking and is regarded as being in the interest of those in power." It is possible that aid can be a more powerful vehicle for self-reliant growth in cases where the donor demonstrates the capacity to force decisions on the government. A committed government in this case will undertake the actions necessary to reduce its vulnerability to control by foreigners. For Korea, this would come through higher exports.

Partnership

At least until the early 1960s, USAID was the only significant donor in Korea, so issues of donor coordination did not arise. The aid relationship was directly between the U.S. government and the Korean government, apparently with some participation by nongovernmental organizations (NGOs).

Results Orientation

Korea's export strategy is one of the clearest cases of successful results orientation in the developing world. In addition to providing the means for measuring trends in exports, Korea's approach also focused on steadily and systematically improving the policy and institutional climate for exports.

Korea established ambitious export goals, including firm-by-firm export targets. Monthly meetings of the president with major exporters and representatives of government agencies provided a regular forum for monitoring progress and identifying problems. Collection of current data on exports was given considerable attention. Independent checks on exports to the United States were provided by Korean consulates on the West Coast, which sent weekly cables reporting on arrivals.

In the early days, companies that failed to meet their monthly export target could point to obstacles, such as failure by customs to clear a needed input, or delays in obtaining credit, or some shipping problem. The systematic review of such impediments and the elimination of many of them made exporting steadily easier, thus allowing the rapid growth of exports to continue unabated. The feedback loops thus established probably created external economies for exporters from Korea (Fox 1990).

Smallpox Eradication: Foreign Aid's Unequivocal Accomplishment

Smallpox has been one of the deadliest diseases to plague humanity. Smallpox fatalities have numbered in the billions, including an estimated 300 million in the twentieth century (Hopkins 1989). Most deaths from smallpox in the second half of the twentieth century were of poor people, since the well-to-do have long had the means to protect themselves. As recently as the late 1960s there were 12 to 15 million cases of smallpox a year and more than 2 million deaths (Barquet and Domingo 1997, p. 637). A decade later, not a single person anywhere in the world was in danger from the disease. The source of this achievement is clear and unquestionable. Donors did it. A program funded by USAID in West Africa and carried out primarily by the U.S. Centers for Disease Control (CDC) developed the techniques that made rapid elimination possible. They were subsequently used by the World Health Organization (WHO) to eliminate smallpox in Asia and the rest of Africa.

Conquest of smallpox was not a result of major breakthroughs in technology or vastly greater health spending. Rather, it resulted from a commitment to action and to learning by donors. This led to smarter spending, beginning with a new approach developed during the West Africa eradication campaign that began in 1967.

Routine vaccination managed by national health authorities had virtually eliminated smallpox in more advanced countries by about 1950. Mass vaccination campaigns were also standard practice in poor countries, but the inability to reach remote rural populations and spoiled or ineffective vaccine meant that the disease continued to persist in parts of these countries, leading to large, periodic outbreaks. Thus, in 1967 the disease was still endemic in more than thirty developing countries, containing more than half of the world's population.

Prompted by the continuing threat to developed countries posed by smallpox's persistence elsewhere, health researchers in WHO and CDC began to explore the feasibility of global elimination.[1] In 1958, WHO issued a statement endorsing elimination. Although vague, the statement did stimulate a search for ways this might be done. In 1961 the CDC established a smallpox unit for this purpose. The unit identified a vaccine that would remain stable and potent under tropical conditions, determined the dosage level, and searched for an appropriate injection device. Starting with the jet injector, a mass injection device developed by the U.S. military, the researchers first adapted it to the smallpox vaccine (testing it in 1963) and then eliminated the need for electricity to power the device (testing a foot-powered injector in 1965).

The CDC then pressed for U.S. government endorsement of smallpox eradication, which the U.S. president approved in 1965. The United States and the Soviet Union jointly sponsored a resolution at the 1966 WHO assembly calling for a multilateral campaign to begin in 1967 and to eradicate the disease within ten years. Though the goal was established, one participant noted that "It is clear, in retrospect, that we didn't know how to eradicate smallpox when the eradication effort began" (Foege 1998, p. 412).

The CDC had also been providing technical assistance to USAID on a West Africa measles campaign. When USAID asked the CDC to lead a major expansion of the program in 1965, the CDC proposed including smallpox eradication as well. CDC and USAID spent the next year generating support among the eighteen West and Central African countries that were prospective hosts for the program and working out collaboration with WHO. WHO agreed to meet some of the local costs of the campaign and to manage the program in countries where USAID was not active. USAID provided foreign advisers and vehicles and met other foreign exchange costs. The hope was that the mass vaccination program could interrupt transmission by vaccinating enough people in remote areas. WHO, once guided by the rule' of thumb that the disease would die out after 80 percent of the population had been vaccinated, was moving toward advocacy of a 100 percent vaccination rate. The early results of the West Africa campaign seemed to confirm this. The campaign ultimately vaccinated more than 150 million people—a number larger than the total population of the region—yet almost total vaccination did not seem to be preventing continued transmission.

The conceptual breakthrough that ultimately led to rapid eradication came from a logistics failure in eastern Nigeria. Facing a shortage of vaccine and a civil war that complicated re-supply, the teams suspended mass vaccination and used the limited supply to vaccinate individuals living near people suffering from smallpox. Radio reports from missionaries were used to identify outbreaks. Over the next year, this approach, along with the knowledge that outbreaks were strongly seasonal, became the basis for a major revision in technique. First tested in Sierra Leone, where complete eradication was achieved in nine months, the technique was then used elsewhere in West Africa with similar results. The last case in the program area came in May 1970—less than three and a half years after the effort began.

The new approach depended on quick identification of new smallpox cases and rapid deployment of a vaccination team. Good communication about outbreaks was important, and vaccination teams had to be restructured to move quickly. WHO began to offer rewards for identification of cases— relatively easy for smallpox. The intensive approach worked, and the last naturally occurring case of smallpox in the world was diagnosed in Somalia in May 1977—ten years and four months after the eradication effort began.

Successful eradication has not yet been repeated for other diseases. Why was the smallpox campaign so successful, while the malaria campaign was not? USAID and WHO expended far more resources and effort on malaria than on smallpox. WHO (1980), in its assessment of smallpox eradication, concluded that the malaria effort included too little research into the scientific aspects of the disease and its transmission. The smallpox effort included research into various aspects of the disease, leading to changes in approach over time. The malaria effort concentrated entirely on a single approach— spraying with DDT—to achieve the goal. Indeed, the leaders of the malaria effort had a long history of hostility to other approaches (WHO 1980, p. 382).

When mosquitoes immune to DDT became dominant, there was a resurgence of the disease. In many countries the malaria eradication group developed a strong esprit d'corps and strong local ownership of the technology provided by the donor community. The problem was in the failure to seek more knowledge about the nature of the disease while the eradication campaign was under way.

Smallpox in a Holistic, Long-Term Development Plan

Coverage of smallpox in a country's long-term development strategy involved two key problems. First, a comprehensive development framework in any of the thirty or so countries where smallpox was still endemic in the mid–1960s would have included it as only one among many diseases needing attention. It would have been mainly a poverty issue. Middle- and upper-income children are typically inoculated, so the disease is one that affects primarily the poor. The health problem posed by smallpox would not stand out among the numerous other severe health problems facing poor countries. Thus, it was not the magnitude of the problem that warranted a concerted attack on the disease but the belief that such an effort could eliminate it, promising a high payoff from donor funds.

Second, smallpox was more a global than a national concern. Without global eradication, each country would have to continue to spend considerable resources on inoculation and surveillance. Thus, the disease warranted a global approach, and a lack of interest at the national level would need to be addressed by multilateral efforts.

Ownership

The original concept for eradication of smallpox was developed primarily by donor countries and marketed to developing countries. Because the disease crosses national boundaries, its elimination could not be achieved by working only with governments that were supportive of the program. The WHO mandate provided a basis for claiming that all countries participated in the decision to eradicate the disease, but surely much of this participation was formalistic. Nevertheless, little opposition to elimination would be expected for a disease like smallpox.

As for West Africa's involvement, the governments had initially sought a measles vaccination program from USAID, which USAID then asked the CDC to implement. The CDC's proposal to include smallpox eradication reflected its priorities, rather than those of the West African countries.

Even where there was strong local commitment by health officials, that did not necessarily translate into government willingness to act in a timely fashion. In Nigeria the quick visit by the CDC representative to formalize Nigerian participation turned into a six-week stay as the health minister, the WHO representative, and the U.S. ambassador tried to obtain the signature of the head of state. Finally, it was an introduction to the head of state's fiancée, arranged through the wife of a friend, that made a meeting possible, and the signature was obtained (Ogden 1987, p. 35).

Partnership

The smallpox initiative is one of the most successful cases of partnership among donors. The West Africa initiative was primarily a USAID creation, but WHO provided the political impetus and collaborated closely with the CDC on implementation. The smallpox initiative was not one of equality among participants, of donor coordination in which each party makes some adjustments to programs so as to conform to a common approach. Rather, it was a case of a convinced group of intellectual and technological leaders— mostly veterans of the West Africa campaign—promoting their plans to other donors and the health leadership in affected countries.

Results Orientation

Measuring results proved more difficult than expected. Still, a focus on results was crucial to the success of the smallpox effort, particularly in four areas.

What Data? The first problem was that implementation of the surveillance and containment approach nearly always led to sharp increases in the number of reported cases. The final WHO report (1980, p. 476) estimates that the actual number of smallpox cases in 1967 was probably 12–15 million rather than the officially reported 15,000 or less. More careful monitoring of the disease had resulted in large increases in the number of reported cases.

Which Results? Until the late 1960s, most vaccination campaigns did little to ensure that the vaccine was potent or that inoculations were done correctly. Results were measured by number of vaccinations. Through follow-up surveys and laboratory tests, the CDC was able to establish that large numbers of people were missed in villages where coverage was thought to be complete and that vaccinations sometimes did not "take" because of bad vaccine or poor technique. Through consistent attention to quality control, the campaign became steadily more effective over time.

Maintaining Focus. Even after the surveillance and containment approach had proved effective in eliminating smallpox in several countries, the results were not always evident to local health officials. The WHO effort in eastern India faced a crisis in May 1974, after 11,000 new cases of smallpox were detected in the state of Bihar. The Bihar government and health officials pressed WHO to abandon surveillance and containment in favor of mass immunization. WHO was able to maintain its focus only through strenuous debate and by seeking a delay before changing approach (Ogden 1987, p. 103; Shurkin 1979, pp. 330–31). Just one year later, India recorded its last case of smallpox.

Using Economic Rates of Return. The final evaluation of the West Africa smallpox and measles program concluded that the project was a success: it had eliminated smallpox from the region and sharply reduced the incidence of measles. Using a crude methodology, the evaluators estimated the internal rate of return at 10 percent for the smallpox component and 26 percent for the measles component. The evaluators compared these estimates to much higher estimates of the rate of return to education in Nigeria and suggested that the project may not have been wise compared with alternative uses of the resources. Taken at face value, the evaluation would suggest that further support for smallpox eradication would be undesirable.

Viewed in retrospect, the finding of a low rate of return was erroneous. The evaluators did not identify the new surveillance and containment approach as a significant result of the project. Only later was this new approach seen to be a key to rapid elimination of smallpox worldwide. In addition, the evaluators assumed that mass inoculation against smallpox would continue in West Africa, so that no benefits were assumed to flow from cost reductions in this area. Only total elimination of smallpox from the world could eliminate this cost. Ultimately, the successful 10-year eradication program cost an estimated $300 million—$98 million from donors and $200 million from developing countries. The annual cost of smallpox to the world was estimated in 1967 as $1.35 billion a year—including the cost of inoculations in nonendemic areas, surveillance at border crossings, and deaths from inoculations (WHO 1980, p. 1364). Using these data yields an internal rate of return of 40 percent.

In sum, the smallpox case strongly underlines the importance of a results orientation. It also illustrates the difficulty of measuring progress. The true indicators of the underlying phenomena would show that real progress was being made and that eradication would be a high payoff activity for donors. Yet if USAID leadership had maintained a results orientation based on the data available to them—the increase in reported numbers of smallpox cases and the low internal rate of return for the West Africa project—they would have made wrong decisions. The quantitative indicators and the monitoring of results were essential tools for the practitioners in this activity. In the hands of the overseers, however, they might have led to mistaken decisions.

Family Planning: From Donor Unilateralism to Local Ownership

USAID has been the largest bilateral provider of international assistance for family planning, through grants of more than $6 billion since 1965. USAID activities initially focused almost exclusively on the distribution of contraceptives, but programs gradually became more varied and diverse. By the mid–1990s USAID was operating family planning programs in seventy-seven countries and was providing indirect funding through nongovernmental organizations (NGOs) or the United Nations Fund for Population Activities (UNFPA) to still others.

These activities have been associated with dramatically increased international discussion of population issues and heightened concern about the consequences of continued population growth. Fertility has declined substantially in developing countries, from more than six children per woman in the early 1960s to 3.6 children in the late 1990s.

The early USAID approach identified lack of access to contraceptives as the major reason for high fertility, so delivery of contraceptives was emphasized. Over time, program approaches became much more nuanced and country focused. Various research, policy discussion, and data gathering approaches were used, and various public and private organizations participated as collaborators. The data gathering, including demographic and health surveys, has been an important source of country-specific information on fertility practices and other health and social issues.

Two controversies about family planning programs have never been settled definitively. One concerns the impact of high rates of population growth on development and average living standards. Though the negative impact of faster population growth on per capita income seems self-evident to many, statistical analyses—whether cross-sectional or time-series—have generally yielded ambiguous results. A major review of the evidence (National Research Council 1986) failed to find any significant relationship.

A second controversy relates to the impact of family planning programs themselves. Increased use of contraception to reduce fertility is characteristic of modernizing societies. Some of the most striking cases of sharp fertility decline occurred before organized family planning efforts existed (Gomez 1995 shows this for Costa Rica), and some analysts have used cross-sectional regressions to question whether official family planning programs provide any significant additional increment to fertility reduction (Schultz 1993). Family planning supporters counter with analyses that support a positive role. Bongaarts, Mauldin, and Phillips (1990) estimate that family planning programs reduced world population in 1992 by more than 400 million people from what it would otherwise have been—roughly equal to the reduction in world population in 1995 between the 1968 medium-variant projection by the United Nations and its 1996 estimate of the actual population.[2]

USAID's most extensive evaluation offers a generally positive assessment of the program, suggesting that program effectiveness has improved over time as better and more country-focused techniques have been developed (USAID 1997). It identifies both the measuring of results for internal management and a focus on broad measures of effectiveness as important to effective implementation.

Family Planning in a Holistic, Long-Term Development Framework

In recent years, many developing countries have explicitly established population growth goals as part of their long-term development framework. USAID has long used a quantitative model (called RAPID) incorporating visual images to dramatize the consequences of alternative population growth rates for such national concerns as school construction, food production, and job creation. The model has frequently been used to encourage governments to adopt new population policies by demonstrating the severe negative consequences of continued rapid population growth. Still, other models could be used to produce different results, and the ultimate consequences of different rates of growth of population for long-term national welfare have never been settled.

Some governments—notably China and India during the 1970s—have used coercive measures to affect long-term national population levels. Many others have chosen indirect means, such as lowering the costs or raising the benefits to families of reducing the number of children. The developmental case for using public resources to ensure that all families have access to modern means of contraception is much stronger than the case for any specific national fertility target.

Ownership

USAID involvement in family planning was initially driven more by U.S. concerns about world population growth than by developing country demand for aid in this area. Partly for this reason, U.S. assistance for population has always taken the form of grants, while most other development activities have been partly loan-financed. The expectation was that grants would be subject to less public scrutiny, preventing opponents from mobilizing to oppose the assistance.

When USAID program activity began in 1965, only nine developing countries had policies favoring slower population growth and many were officially opposed to such programs. USAID efforts probably helped change the climate of opinion, so that by the mid-1990s some 70 countries had adopted such policies (USAID 1997, p. 3).

USAID would identify like-minded people in the government or the private sector and encourage them to mobilize public opinion in favor of the delivery of family planning services. Sometimes USAID would invite health officials to international conferences on population growth. As a result, most USAID family planning activities have created a strong domestic constituency capable of continuing programs in the absence of USAID funding.

Partnership

Family planning is perhaps the most successful case of partnership among bilateral, multilateral, and NGO providers. NGOs such as the International Planned Parenthood Federation (IPPF) and the Pathfinder Foundation were the first to provide family planning assistance. USAID and UNFPA were the first bilateral and multilateral providers of such assistance, and they remain the largest official sources. Over the decades, they and NGOs have continued to work closely, sharing information and research and frequently conducting joint activities.

Their shared outlook is particularly striking and helps to explain their easy working relationship. They agree that population growth is a threat to human welfare, that empowerment of women is especially important, and that control over fertility is a key factor in women's empowerment. This shared vision means that USAID family planning professionals may share closer ties with like-minded organizations outside of USAID than with other parts of USAID.

Results Orientation

A results orientation appears to distinguish successful from unsuccessful USAID family planning projects (USAID 1997, p. 31). At the operational level, managerial systems are needed to ensure that commodities and training are used efficiently to achieve the desired results. The availability of contraceptives to end users at all times is critical to program success. This requires good controls on the flow of products.

Demographic and health surveys and censuses have also been crucial for steering programs in the right direction. Information about a program's failure to increase contraceptive prevalence or to reduce fertility or the discovery that large numbers of families are receiving their contraceptives outside of official programs has helped guide experimentation with new approaches and brought to an end programs that failed to achieve the desired results.

Agriculture: Technology Matters Enormously

Agricultural research is a recent phenomenon in the developing world. It has paid huge dividends, increasing agricultural yields more in the past fifty years than in the previous 1,000 years. As a consequence, humanity is gradually being liberated from scratching a meager living from backbreaking work on the land. Throughout most of history, growing enough food meant that some 80 to 90 percent of the population worked in agriculture. Today, in the United States, each farmer feeds seventy-seven people.

In the early years, USAID professionals believed that improving agriculture was largely a matter of transferring existing knowledge to farmers in poor countries. Agricultural extension services were created along the U.S. model, staffed by local agronomists with the support of U.S. advisers with experience in the U.S. extension service. Only gradually did it become clear that agricultural technology is crop- and region-specific, and that improving agricultural technology in developing countries was far harder than imagined (Box 1.11).

USAID has done much to promote agricultural research at the national level. It has also worked with other donors in an international agricultural research effort under the Consultative Group on International Agricultural Research (CGIAR), which coordinates the work of fourteen international centers for particular crops or climates. The first two of these centers, in the Philippines for rice and in Mexico for corn, produced varieties that allowed dramatic increases in productivity.

Regarding the value of agricultural research, USAID's most recent program evaluation concludes:

A single finding from the literature overwhelms all others: investments in agricultural research have generated high economic rates of return, indicating that the social benefits of the investments justify the costs in virtually all countries, for a wide variety of commodities, and under diverse agronomic and climatic conditions. (USAID 1996, p. 15)

Studies of the impact of agricultural research of this type have consistently shown very high rates of return. For ninety-seven studies of the effects of agricultural research in developing countries, the median rate of return was 52 percent. Fifteen of the studies (most often of irrigated rice) found rates of return above 100 percent. The reason that private firms do not do much of this research is that many of the benefits of the research are scientific and cannot be patented or captured by the inventor. Consequently, agricultural research in such cases is inherently a government-financed activity.

The 1996 assessment offers an important caveat to the generalization that research always works: it notes that a favorable policy climate for agriculture is a precondition for effective agricultural research or infrastructure development. "If a threshold level of proper policies is not in place, it is seldom worthwhile for donors to make other investments in agriculture; nor is it worthwhile for farmers to take risks and use new technologies to increase production beyond subsistence levels" (USAID 1996, p. vii).

India in the 1960s illustrates the close links between policy and effective use of new technology.[3] In 1966–67, India was suffering from its second consecutive bad monsoon season. A death toll from famine of as high as 50 million Indians was considered possible in the absence of international help.

Box 11.1
Effective Agricultural Technology Development

One of the first efforts of the USAID evaluation office was to analyze USAID agricultural programs in Latin America. The study showed that the core of the program, agricultural extension, was a failure because the extension agents had little to offer the farmers.

Agricultural research was also of little use because researchers, lacking means to learn what problems farmers faced, worked on problems of little interest. The role of extension agent as intermediary between researchers and farmers, a key feature in the United States, was absent in Latin America.

This finding could have been used to stop funding of agricultural research or extension, for such evaluations are better at finding problems than identifying solutions. The same year, Hayami and Ruttan (1971) were able to demonstrate how critical agricultural extension had been to the development of U.S. and Japanese agriculture—and by extension to any country that desired technical progress in agriculture. In this case, as in many others, program evaluation and economic research can closely complement each other. Dissemination of evaluation results is essential to convincing practitioners that their approach is producing poor results. Successful experience in other places or at other times can provide ideas for more promising approaches. Following these findings, USAID and Latin American governments experimented with alternative approaches to bring farmers and researchers closer together.

To prevent mass starvation, the United States and other donors mobilized enormous amounts of aid, enabling India to import 21 million tons of food.

The United States provided most of the food, with President Lyndon Johnson playing a large personal role. Johnson believed that India's policies were harming its agriculture, and he suspended all U.S. aid to India at the height of the crisis. Only after the Indian secretary of agriculture signed a secret agreement with the U.S. secretary of agriculture was Johnson willing to renew shipments. Even then, they were provided on a month-by-month basis, linked to progress on the agreed agricultural policy changes. These included an immediate 40 percent increase in agricultural investment by the Indian government, increased agricultural prices, new credit policies, and increased availability of fertilizer and new rice and corn varieties.

With the reforms, the green revolution came quickly to India. India required no massive emergency food aid program in 1978–79, when a drought similar to that of 1965–66 occurred. Subsequent droughts have been managed without international notice as a normal fluctuation in weather to be met by drawing down food stocks (India's grain stocks are the largest in the world). Wheat production has quintupled; rice production has more than doubled. These increases occurred with little expansion of the total area planted to these crops. India is now a net exporter of cereals, and the people of India are able to eat better than ever before.

Agricultural Research in a Holistic, Long-Term Development Framework

The place of agricultural technology development in a holistic development framework is not obvious. Such a framework is unlikely to be very useful in determining the level of resources that society should spend on agricultural research or even the areas in which the research should be concentrated. Rather, the magnitude and direction of such effort are likely to be determined incrementally, responding to experience over time. Continuity of effort and emphasis on quality and relevance are probably the elements most likely to produce the greatest results. Yet, as with research in other areas, there is no necessary relationship between input and output. Some activities will yield no useful results, while others will pay huge dividends.

USAID's 1982 assessment of its support for agricultural research mentions a trend toward "use of multidisciplinary teams and a more holistic approach to research" (USAID 1982, p. 1). The study does not characterize the results of the more holistic approach. The next major assessment of USAID agricultural research experience (USAID 1996) does not mention such approaches and suggests that farmers are willing to adopt new technologies that are accessible as long as they offer better risk-adjusted profit prospects.

Ownership

Given the close linkage between farming systems and the usefulness of agricultural research in particular countries or regions, the need for close interaction between farmers and researchers is clear. This cannot happen without extensive local participation.

Partnership

The CGIAR is surely a case of successful donor partnership. The financial cost of the system of international research centers is too large for any single donor to bear, while the alternative of individual international centers run by different donors is unpromising. Research might come to reflect the latest priorities in the donor country's research establishment more than those of developing countries.

The partnership needed in this case is quite different from the coordinated work under a common vision described in the smallpox and family planning cases. The international centers, rather than the donors, should be deciding the research agendas and approaches. The critical issues for the partners are to ensure appropriate burden-sharing among donors and a high quality of leadership for the individual centers.

Results Orientation

Because agricultural research is unlikely to result in gains for agriculture in policy environments that are biased against agriculture and where farmers are unable to profit from the use of better technology, donors should avoid investments in agricultural research in countries with unfavorable policies.

Evaluations have been less clear about the conditions for achieving results from research itself. Two elements would seem to be especially relevant. First, research needs to be of high quality and the research institution needs to monitor performance. Second, since research only pays off when linked to production, communication between researchers and users is essential.

Foreign Academic Training: Producing New Leaders

Donors have long used advanced academic training (usually in the universities of the donor country) as a means of promoting development in poor countries. Such programs, called "participant training" by USAID, have always been a significant feature of U.S. development assistance. Most USAID professionals regard these programs as one of the most successful areas of USAID activity, an assessment generally based on the observation that earlier participants have moved into key positions in government. Former participants are often the most effective interlocutors between the foreign aid agency and the host government.

Since U.S. foreign aid began in 1949, it has funded participant training to perhaps 350,000 people from developing countries.[4] A review of USAID experience conducted in 1986 found more than 200 evaluations of such projects. Nearly all were concerned primarily with operational issues relating to training, and none of them provided a basis for assessing the ultimate benefit of the training to the developing country (USAID 1986a, p. xi).

Most USAID evaluations assess the success of overseas training by looking at whether the participant successfully completed the planned study program, returned home to work, and was satisfied with the training experience.

By these criteria, most USAID training projects were successful—in some cases, strikingly so. Muscat (1990, p. 56) looked at the educational backgrounds of 411 senior officials of the Thai government and found that 162 of them, or nearly 40 percent, had been trained under the USAID program.

There are obvious reasons for the popularity of such training among donor governments, their universities, and participants. The donor country benefits from the participants' presumed favorable attitude toward the country, universities prefer students whose costs are fully paid by others, and participants enjoy a huge educational subsidy. Nevertheless, this enthusiasm conceals a certain anxiety about the program's real effectiveness. Did a particular individual become minister because of his U.S. education or his natural talent? Although participants are prominent among government elites, they are still a minority. Did USAID choose the right people? From an economist's perspective, were participants selected because their education would yield the greatest "social value-added" or because they had already absorbed the cultural and educational values that would make them good students and future leaders?

Answering these questions requires an experimental design for participant training that would compare promising students selected for training with a similar group of students who were not trained and with unpromising groups of students, both trained and untrained. After perhaps forty years of observation, the careers of members of the four groups could be compared in terms of social usefulness, and the real effect of participant training could be scientifically determined. Clearly, it is unlikely that any donor would undertake the experiment.

At the country level, Valdes (1995) describes the case of the Chilean economists (later referred to as the "Chicago boys") trained at the University of Chicago under a USAID project in the late 1950s and early 1960s. They later helped forge the "Chilean model" of development, important aspects of which were adopted by other Latin American governments in the 1990s. The project had several unusual features. Participants' academic mentors were of unusual stature; three (Milton Friedman, George Stigler, and Theodore Schultz) later won Nobel prizes. The program's goal was not to train economic policymakers but to develop a strong academic economics department at the Catholic University of Chile. Like their U.S. mentors, the Chilean participants expected their influence to come through the quality of their research and teaching. An accident of politics thrust them into a policymaking role in the mid–1970s. It would be interesting to calculate the social value added for the welfare of Latin Americans of the influence of this group of economists on policies in the region and to compare it with the value added that would have resulted had they remained in academia as expected. (Valdes does not address this issue.)

Foreign Academic Training in a Holistic, Long-Term
Development Framework

Foreign academic training seems to belong more to an earlier era, when some believed that satisfactory long-term development would require predictable numbers of people with particular academic specializations. Given the long lags between education and full professional competence, planners would program training funding to ensure that the country would have, say, the right number of mechanical engineers twenty years later.

Such ideas no longer hold sway, as experience has suggested that neither the demand nor the supply side can be projected with any confidence. Both exhibit remarkable flexibility in the presence of free labor markets. Consequently, there is no easy answer to the question of how much foreign academic training a country should have. Rather, a future-oriented country might want to provide some general subsidy for foreign (and domestic) academic training in the expectation that it would pay dividends in the long term for society.

Ownership

Peculiar features of training projects give them some self-enforcing mechanisms for encouraging ownership and effectiveness. Training is typically very demanding for the individual concerned, usually requiring learning of a new language and academic performance at a high level. Failure would be harmful to the program and the individual. And the substantial subsidy provided by such programs, and the obvious private benefits to people who complete them successfully, make it easy to find promising candidates.

Country ownership is also apparent in the lives of returned trainees, since the donor no longer has control over how participants use their skills (beyond the typical requirement that participants return to their native country or pay for the training). Trainees have been empowered by the donor to use their skills as they see fit.

Partnership

USAID's participant training programs have been unilateral and have involved no coordination with other donors. Activities of other donors appear to be similar, since programs specialize in training in the donor country.

Results Orientation

Training programs appear to have the main features of a results-oriented approach at the output level, as reflected in the three features mentioned above: selection of suitable candidates, monitoring of their return to the country following training, and interviews with returned trainees following completion of training.

U.S. Assistance to Egypt: Eventual Progress?

USAID professionals have long viewed the aid programs in Egypt and Israel as among the least effective in development terms. Israel is a special case, since there has been little pretense of expected development impact from U.S. assistance. In Egypt, however, USAID has always maintained a large presence, including several hundred U.S. employees and contractors. The program combines project and sector program and balance of payments assistance, either through concessional sales of agricultural commodities or through a general commodity import program. Altogether, the United States has provided Egypt with more than $25 billion in economic assistance since U.S. aid resumed in 1975 (more than double that in 1999 dollars).

Despite all the assistance, Egypt has not performed particularly well. After rapid economic growth during 1976–82, fueled by high oil prices and the reopening of the Suez Canal, Egypt went through a long period of economic stagnation. In the early 1990s the government undertook significant economic reforms, including liberalization of the exchange rate and control of the fiscal deficit, resulting in relatively rapid growth since 1995.

While there has been no USAID long-term assessment of the impact of its aid to Egypt, other studies have concluded that it had little impact. Sullivan (1996) attributes the ineffectiveness to lack of a cohesive growth-oriented approach on the Egyptian side and to the inability of USAID—because it was overruled by the State Department—to demand performance. USAID evaluations of particular projects show the usual mix of success and failure, but those dealing with policy issues are almost uniformly negative until the early 1990s. A 1981 General Accounting Office (GAO 1981) report concluded that USAID's agricultural project in Egypt had produced little. A 1983 USAID assessment of the large program to provide agricultural commodities on concessional terms concluded that the program had had a significant disincentive effect on Egyptian agricultural production and had reinforced already heavy government control over food distribution. And a 1994 evaluation of USAID funding of investment projects concluded that the investments had yielded a low rate of return because of the distortions in the Egyptian policy environment.

Overall, the project evaluations for Egypt (Montrie and Diamond 1999 contains summaries of more than 200 USAID projects) conclude that social sector projects have been relatively successful while economic projects have generally fared poorly, because of a lack of scope for market forces to operate or for the Egyptian government to follow through on promised liberalization or privatization. Some improvement in performance has been evident in recent years, beginning with the agricultural sector in the late 1980s and followed by macroeconomic policies, which improved after a successful IMF–World Bank stabilization and adjustment program. These changes are reflected in more successful USAID projects.

Despite the slow growth of GDP and the negative assessments of the country's economic performance, broad measures of material well-being show a more favorable picture. Life expectancy has increased by about twelve years since 1975, and the share of the population with access to water and electricity has increased dramatically. The evidence that ordinary Egyptians live much better than they did in 1975 is quite compelling (Fox 1999). This dichotomy suggests that the link between per capita economic growth rates and the well-being of the mass of the population is less direct than assumed by economists.

U.S. Assistance to Egypt in a Holistic, Long-Term Development Framework

The Egyptian government has long used planning as a development tool and has sought to promote the country's development by organizing all sectors of society under government direction and ensuring that everyone participates in the benefits of modernization.

This mobilization of society takes place through government-controlled institutions. Reports of various human rights groups, such as Freedom House, paint a picture of an all-pervasive government that leaves very little space for civil society.

Ownership

The Egyptian government had clear ownership of the programs carried out with U.S. funds. Indeed, this was the major source of frustration with the program for USAID professionals. USAID would seek to condition assistance to progress on economic policy goals by the Egyptian government. When the government failed to perform, USAID would be forced to renegotiate performance targets or simply to accept the shortfall.[5]

This case differed from the early Korean situation. There, the high levels of aid were critical to Korean stability and to U.S. foreign policy goals. In Egypt the government could have forgone U.S. assistance without a threat to the country's economic stability.

Partnership

For most of the period, USAID has been the dominant donor in Egypt, and its programs typically did not involve much collaboration with other donors.

Rather, it was the other donors who felt the need to take USAID programs into account in the design of their activities.

Results Orientation

From USAID's perspective, the Egypt program has never been results-oriented. Senior USAID officials have periodically sought to reallocate the Egyptian funds to other, more promising, development programs.[6] In a few projects, some capacity to withhold or to reallocate funds probably influenced some attention to a results orientation. This may explain why social sector activities (in which USAID was largely autonomous) were more successful than activities relating to economic policy, in which State Department involvement was more likely.

The most extreme evidence of the absence of a results orientation is the approval of a project proposal containing an economic analysis showing a negative expected rate of return (USAID 1989a). Surely this is unique in the annals of donor project proposals. (The proposal was for an electric power plant, an investment deemed necessary because of the underpricing of electricity in Egypt.)

Conclusions

Several general conclusions flow from the case studies. First, USAID's decentralization of authority to the country level played a role in most of the cases. Mission management had the flexibility and authority to adapt programs to country conditions and to speak authoritatively about the conditions under which funds would flow. The typical USAID mission includes a large staff of U.S. employees and contractors, who can develop and approve smaller projects (within an overall country program) without seeking approval from Washington on the design or implementation characteristics of the project. This flexibility was absent in the Egypt case. Important policy differences between USAID and the host government were invariably referred to Washington, which frequently overrode country mission positions.

Second, successful programs are not always easy to identify, particularly in the short term. In all of the successful cases, there were uncertainties about whether real progress was being made, yet in retrospect, success was evident. Still, even in the longer term, the contribution of aid to the ultimate outcome is completely unambiguous only in the case of the smallpox eradication program. In all the other cases the inability to be sure about what would have happened in the absence of aid (the counterfactual) meant that skeptics could always raise questions about the impact of the assistance. On the other hand, even in the two cases regarded as failures—aid to the Republic of Korea before 1963 and aid to Egypt, some important positive trends or results were evident. The complexity of the processes that foreign aid is meant to address means that there will always be some ambiguity about results.[7]

Third, new knowledge was critical to the success of most of the cases. This suggests that the issue of technology should be recognized more explicitly in the CDF and in each of its elements:

- Greater effectiveness can be expected from a holistic, long-term framework that incorporates the most current knowledge about development. Korea's focus on exports succeeded because it rejected the export pessimism that had characterized most development plans in that era and incorporated newer empirical evidence on international trade, emulating recent Japanese experience. Egypt's development plans largely ignored this evidence, and the results were far less favorable.
- Host country ownership that also focuses on adapting the best technology to country circumstances will get better results. In the family planning case, programs that continued to experiment with newer birth control technologies often gained more new users than programs applying older approaches.
- Partnerships in which donors share research and discuss new findings collegially are likely to improve the methods used by each partner. Family planning is a good example.
- Activities with a results focus that continually scrutinizes the adequacy of the measurement techniques and the variables being measured will be more effective. The success of the smallpox program was due in no small part to changes in how results were monitored and success was measured, and to a continuing search for better approaches. The failure of the much larger malaria effort was due partly to the failure to question the effectiveness of an approach that appeared to be successful and had produced great early results, even as the real situation deteriorated.

Holistic, Long-Term Development Framework

The need for a long-term focus is evident from all of the cases; how to achieve it is less clear. In the Korean case, development success was related to the government's long-term vision. But while the 1965 development plan offered a holistic vision, its strategy was narrowly focused. Achievement of rapid economic growth and economic independence was the top priority. Once export growth was achieved, the other elements of development success—social sector expenditures, increases in wages for workers, and broadening of the political system—would fall into place. Over the longer term, this belief has held true.

The danger evident in an approach that advertises itself as holistic—particularly when wide public participation is invited into the planning process—is that it can become a "Christmas tree" that includes too much. If the effort to broaden the constituency for the approach means that difficult choices are not made, the program will fail for lack of coherence and focus.

The development strategy also should not distract from investing in promising activities or targets of opportunity that seem likely to have high payoffs. In some of the successful cases, the impact came not because the activity rose to the top in some comprehensive framework, but because it was an excellent investment. Smallpox eradication was desirable because it was possible at a reasonable cost. Foreign training pays off because trainees contribute, in ways that cannot be foreseen clearly, to the development of their country. Agricultural research is desirable because it reduces the real cost of agricultural production, freeing people to work on other things.

A final concern relates to implementation. The difference in implementation between the Rhee and Park regimes in Korea is so striking as to suggest that this may have been as important as differences in the quality of their vision of the country's future.[8]

Ownership

Host country ownership is an important factor, but the cases argue against too narrow an interpretation of ownership. Donors often equate government ownership with country ownership. There is a need to recognize the diversity of perspectives within a country or its government, and to ensure a sense of ownership among those involved in a project. In many cases, governments embraced family planning as a national strategy only after private groups had changed the climate of opinion in the country. Had USAID waited until the government endorsed the concept, millions of people would have been denied access to modern family planning techniques for years or decades.

Country ownership should not mean that donors accept country programs that are inadequate. Hard conditionality proved developmentally productive on two occasions in the case studies—Indian agriculture in the mid–1960s and Korean economic policy in 1962–63. The U.S. government pressed for reforms, and the government ultimately took decisive action that substantially improved the country's long-term situation.

Partnership

Partnership was important in three of the six cases considered: family planning, smallpox eradication, and agricultural research. In the first two it was a shared vision that was critical to success. When donors share a common view of the problem, partnership is easy. The danger in partnership approaches comes when donors have different perspectives on the problem or the solution. Then there is a risk that efforts to coordinate will mean that the most effective approaches are shunned in the search for common denominators. In the case of agricultural research, partnership took the form of mutual encouragement of appropriate burden-sharing.

Results Orientation

A results orientation was the most important factor in project effectiveness in the cases studied. But the cases also suggest that a results orientation is more difficult to achieve in practice than in theory, for several reasons.

First, the results that are most important for monitoring and evaluation may not be readily available, while those that are available may be misleading. The smallpox case shows that regularly reported data by WHO were wrong by a large margin. Implementers may need to develop new data sets for tracking actual performance.

Second, people far from the scene of activity may not be able to monitor progress effectively. This suggests that decentralized management may produce better results. The complexity of the problems being addressed should also be a warning to avoid oversimplification when measuring results. It may be that the development business shares the characteristics of what James Q. Wilson (1989, p. 158) calls a craft organization, in which the top layer of the organization has to rely heavily on the judgments of the professionals on specific issues.

Notes

1. This narrative is drawn mainly from Shurkin (1979), WHO (1980), and Ogden (1987).
2. This comes from comparing the 1968 and 1996 editions of the UN's *World Population Prospects,* adjusting the earlier baseline data for consistency with the later estimate.
3. This case draws on Lele and Bumb (1995) for general data and on Pillsbury's luridly titled (1999) study for the specifics of the negotiations.
4. USAID (1986a) reports that USAID had trained 240,000 participants until that time and was currently training about 8,000 people a year. Assuming that this annual level continued through 1999, this would bring the total to around 350,000.
5. Another explanation derives from Nasser's standing as the leading figure in Egyptian economic and political independence. Although Nasserite socialism never lived up to the promise originally held for it, subsequent political leaders derived their legitimacy in part from their link to Nasser, so repudiation of his policies was difficult. Consequently, Nasser's followers could move only incrementally away from previous policies, even when they were considered inefficient.
6. Development was not the primary purpose of the Egyptian aid program. The State Department's view has been that the Egypt program was aimed at promoting stability in the Middle East. Within this constraint, economic development is a desirable, though not necessary, feature.
7. Even in the case of the Republic of Korea, the country's overall development success into the middle 1990s has been questioned by some. Only slightly before the recent famine in the People's Republic of Korea, one reputed Cambridge scholar maintained that development in the Republic of Korea had not clearly outpaced that in the People's Republic of Korea (Sanderson 1995).

8. A recent paper blames the donor community's most conspicuous failure—Tanzania—on that country's capacity to design programs that donors found very attractive, combined with an inability to implement programs that had looked so good on paper (Bigsten 1999).

References

Amsden, Alice. 1989. *Asia's Next Giant: South Korea and Late Industrialization*. New York: Oxford University Press.

Barquet, Nicolau, and Pere Domingo. 1997. "Smallpox." *Annals of Internal Medicine* *127* (October): pp. 635–42.

Bigsten, Arne. 1999. "Aid and Reform in Tanzania." Economic and Social Research Foundation, Dar es Salaam.

Bongaarts, John, W. Parker Mauldin, and James F. Phillips. 1990. "The Demographic Impact of Family Planning Programs." *Studies in Family Planning* 21(6): pp. 299–310.

Cho, Lee-Jay, and Yoon Hyung Kim. 1991. *Economic Development in the Republic of Korea: A Policy Perspective*. Honolulu: University of Hawaii Press.

Cole, David C., and Princeton Lyman. 1971. *Korean Development: The Interplay between Politics and Economics*. Cambridge, MA: Harvard University Press.

Das Gupta, Monica. 1999. "Liberte, Egalite, Fraternite: Exploring the Role of Governance in Fertility Decline." *Journal of Development Studies* 35(5): 1–25.

Fletcher, Lehman B., ed. 1996. *Egypt's Agriculture in a Reform Era*. Ames: Iowa State University Press.

Foege, William H. 1998. "Confronting Emerging Infections: Lessons from the Smallpox Eradication Campaign." *Emerging Infectious Diseases* 4(3): pp. 412–13.

Fox, James W. 1990. "Feedback Loops and Economies of Scale: A Strategy for Export-Led Growth in the Caribbean Basin." USAID/LAC Staff Paper 2. USAID, Washington, D.C.

———. 1999. "Trends in the Quality of Life in Egypt, 1975–99." Paper prepared for USAID, Egypt, Cairo.

GAO (General Accounting Office). 1981. "U.S. Assistance to Egyptian Agriculture: Slow Progress after Five Years." Report ID–81–19. Washington, D.C.

Gomez, Victor. 1995. "Population and Family Planning in Costa Rica." USAID Costa Rica Evaluation Background Paper, USAID/CDIE, Washington, D.C.

Hasan, Parvez. 1976. *Korea: Problems and Issues in a Rapidly Growing Economy*. Baltimore, MD: Johns Hopkins Press.

Hayami, Yujiro, and Vernon Ruttan. 1971. *Agricultural Development: An International Perspective*. Baltimore, MD: Johns Hopkins Press.

Hopkins, Donald R. 1983. *Princes and Peasants: Smallpox in History*. Chicago, IL: University of Chicago Press.

Hopkins, Jack W. 1989. *The Eradication of Smallpox*. Boulder, CO: Westview Press.

Jones, Leroy, and Il SaKong. 1980. *Government, Business and Entrepreneurship in Economic Development: The Korean Case*. Cambridge, MA: Harvard University Press.

Kim, Ching-yum. 1994. *Policymaking on the Front Lines: Memoirs of a Korean Practitioner, 1945–79*. Washington, D.C.: World Bank.

Krueger, Anne O. 1979. *The Developmental Role of the Foreign Sector and Aid*. Cambridge, MA: Harvard University Press.

Lele, Uma, and Balu Bumb. 1995. "The Food Crisis in South Asia: The Case of India." *The Evolving Role of the World Bank*. Washington, D.C.: World Bank.

Mason, Edward S., Mahn Je Kim, Dwight H. Perkins, Kwang Suk Kim, and David C. Cole. 1970. *The Economic and Social Modernization of the Republic of Korea*. Cambridge, MA: Harvard University Press.

Mazarr, Michael J. 1991. "Investing in Security: U.S. Economic Assistance and Non-economic Goals in Korea." Center for Strategic and International Studies, Washington, D.C.

Montrie, Charles, and Charles Diamond. 1999. "Program Evaluation Study Plan for the USAID Program and Its Impact on Egypt Policy Reform Programs." TAPR/ USAID, Cairo.

Muscat, Robert. 1990. *Thailand and the United States: Development, Security and Foreign Aid*. New York: Columbia University Press.

National Research Council. 1986. *Population Growth and Economic Development: Policy Questions*. Washington, D.C.: National Academy of Sciences Press.

Oehmke, James F. 1997. "Agricultural Technology Development and Diffusion: A Synthesis of the Literature." In Luther G. Tweeten and Donald G. McClelland, *Promoting Third-World Development and Food Security*. Westport, CT: Praeger.

Ogden, Horace, G. 1987. *CDC and the Smallpox Crusade*. U.S. Department of Health and Human Services, Publication (CDC) 87–8400.

Oldstone, Michael B.A. 1998. *Viruses, Plagues, and History*. New York: Oxford University Press.

Pillsbury, Michael. 1999. *Secret Successes of USAID*. Washington, D.C.: National Defense University Press.

Rock, Michael T. 1993. "Can Export Services Assistance Make a Difference? The Korean Experience." AID Technical Paper 7. USAID, Washington, D.C.

Sachs, Jeffrey. 1996. "Achieving Rapid Growth: The Road Ahead for Egypt." Egyptian Center for Economic Studies, Cairo.

Sanderson, Stephen. 1995. *A General Theory of Historical Development*. London, U.K.: Rowman & Littlefield.

Schultz, T. Paul. 1993. "Mortality Decline in the Low-Income World: Causes and Consequences." *American Economic Review 83*(2): pp. 337–41.

Shurkin, Joel N. 1979. *The Invisible Fire: The Story of Mankind's Victory over the Ancient Scourge of Smallpox*. New York: G.P. Putnam's Sons.

Steinberg, David I. 1982. "The Economic Development of Korea: Sui Generis or Generic?" USAID Evaluation Special Study 6. Washington, D.C.

———. 1985. "Foreign Aid and the Development of the Republic of Korea: The Effectiveness of Concessional Assistance." AID Special Study 42. Washington, D.C.

———. 1989. *The Republic of Korea: Economic Transformation and Social Change*. Boulder, CO: Westview Press.

Sullivan, Denis J. 1996. "American Aid to Egypt 1975–96: Peace without Development." *Middle East Policy* (October): pp. 36–49.

USAID (U.S. Agency for International Development). 1966. "West Africa Smallpox/ Measles." Technical Assistance Paper. Washington, D.C.

———. 1969. "Audit Report on Examination of the Field Operations of the West Africa Smallpox Eradication/Measles Control Project 625–11–510–16." Audit Report 70–68. Washington, D.C.

———. 1971. "Evaluation: Smallpox Eradication and Measles Control Program." Bureau for Africa, Washington, D.C.

———. 1979a. "Study of Family Planning Program Effectiveness." AID Program

Evaluation Discussion Paper 5. Office of Evaluation, Washington, D.C.
— — —. 1979b. "Family Planning Effectiveness: Report of A Workshop." AID Program Evaluation Report 1, Office of Evaluation, Washington, D.C.
— — —. 1982. "AID Experience in Agricultural Research: A Review of Project Evaluations." AID Program Evaluation Discussion Paper 13, Washington, D.C.
— — —. 1983. "PL–480 Title I: the Egyptian Case." AID Project Impact Evaluation Report 45, Washington, D.C.
— — —. 1986a. "Review of Participant Training Evaluation Studies." AID Evaluation Occasional Paper 11. Washington, D.C.
— — —. 1986b. "An Analysis of AID Participant Training Projects." AID Evaluation Occasional Paper 12, Washington, D.C.
— — —. 1989. "Egypt Shoubrah El Kheima Thermal Power Plant." Project Paper, Amendment 3 (Project 263–0030), Washington, D.C.
— — —. 1989. "The Role of Participant Training in Building Social Science Capabilities in Asia." AID Evaluation Occasional Paper 32, Washington, D.C.
— — —. 1994. "Capital Projects: Egypt Case Study." AID Evaluation Technical Report 20, USAID/CDIE, Washington, D.C.
— — —. 1996. "Investments in Agriculture: A Synthesis of the Evaluation Literature." Program and Operations Assessment Report 15, USAID/CDIE, Washington, D.C.
— — —. 1997. "USAID's Population and Family Planning Program: A Synthesis of Six Country Case Studies." Program and Operations Assessment Report 16, USAID/CDIE, Washington, D.C.
Valdes, Juan Gabriel. 1995. *Pinochet's Economists: The Chicago School in Chile*. Cambridge, U.K.: Cambridge University Press.
Wilson, James Q. 1989. *Bureaucracy: What Government Agencies Do and Why They Do It*. New York: Basic Books.
WHO (World Health Organization). 1980. "The Global Eradication of Smallpox." Final Report of the Global Commission for the Certification of Smallpox Eradication, Geneva.

Part 4

Partnerships:
Local and Global

11

Perspectives on Partnership

Simon Maxwell and *Tim Conway*

This chapter examines various perspectives on partnership, one of the principles of the Comprehensive Development Framework (CDF). Many donors already have substantial experience with development partnerships, and there are models of partnership from other fields, such as business and law, and in the literature on participation. The question this chapter addresses is how far donor experience and contemporary research can illuminate and extend this vision and identify implementation issues. It concludes with a discussion of possible links between partnership and selectivity in choosing countries, sectors, institutions, and instruments for development assistance.

Several common themes emerge from the diverse experience reviewed:

- There is no blueprint.
- Partnerships will vary by country and stage of political development.
- Partnership depends on trust and nurturing the right values and a genuine commitment to sharing, openness, and accountability on both sides.
- Development partnership is based on empowerment of the weaker party.
- Partnership should include continuous assessment of performance and subsequent reflection and feedback. It should adopt a long-term perspective and an adaptive, sustainable approach.
- Donor selectivity of country partnerships may be guided by different criteria: country ownership and performance, client need, and the long-term comparative advantages of donor and partner institutions.

Experience with Partnership

Partnership is far from straightforward, requiring clarification of the terms on which it is undertaken, its scope, and the mechanisms that underpin it. At one extreme, partnership can be a tool for power held by the donor, agenda setting by the donor, and accountability running from the recipient to the donor but not the other way. At the other extreme, there can be genuine dialogue and decision making based on trust, covering a wide agenda, and backed by reciprocal accountability, often based on a form of contract. Donors and development agencies must make strategic choices about what types of partnerships they are seeking.

World Bank and UN Perspectives

In May 1998 the Partnerships Group at the World Bank published the Discussion Paper *Partnership for Development: Proposed Actions for the World Bank* (World Bank 1998a). The report provided an operational definition of partnership, identified the requirements for successful partnership, and laid out a strategy, short-term actions for the Bank, and a proposal for a partnership code of practice. (Appendix 11.1 contains the report's executive summary.) The report was discussed in the summer of 1998 at a series of roundtables and other consultations around the world. A summary of points made, presented to the Board in September 1998 (World Bank 1998b), noted that there was "overwhelming support" for a partnership approach. It also identified five key challenges for implementation:

- Partner acceptance, including on the part of the Bank, of country-led development strategies, perhaps even when they do not fully agree;
- Broader dialogue, not just on aid, but also on debt relief, market access, and trade policies linked to the idea of a fair deal;
- More open information, especially for civil society;
- Greater involvement, together with recognition of the diversity and pluralism of civil society;
- Greater cohesiveness in delivering development assistance, particularly between the Bretton Woods institutions and other donors.

Subsumed within this list are some key challenges to the implementation of partnership. Will donors really allow partner countries to pursue strategies with which they disagree? Will donors be held accountable for their actions to the same degree that they expect recipient countries to be accountable? Is a national consensus either a realistic option or a necessary condition for change? And are the institutional structures in place internationally to guarantee a coherent and democratically accountable response across aid, trade, and international finance?

The theme of partnership and the need for donor coordination emphasized in the CDF is also central to the evolution of the United Nations Development Assistance Framework approach. The United Nations Development Assistance Framework responds to a slightly different set of institutional problems (the need to coordinate the generally disparate work of a range of United Nations organizations, particularly through the harmonization of program cycles). Nonetheless, there is a great deal of common ground between the two initiatives, particularly with regard to the concept of partnership, and much potential for cooperation and mutual learning.

In two of the eighteen Development Assistance Framework pilot countries (Mali and Vietnam), the Bank and United Nations have already cooperated closely on the development of country-level coordination mechanisms. This experience suggests the following elements as contributions to the effectiveness of the United Nations–World Bank partnership at the country level (Malik et al. 1998, 10):

- close ongoing working relationship and mutual respect (consultative groups, roundtables, sector and thematic coordination groups, statistics and analysis);
- shared recognition of added value brought by each party and of the added value that a stronger partnership brings to government;
- joint and reciprocal contribution to situation analysis (bringing the mandate and comparative advantage of each partner to bear);
- flexibility and commitment to a transparent working relationship by all parties.

A Compact for Effective Partnerships

The starting point for any current discussion of partnership ought to be the work of the Development Assistance Committee, which has put the idea of development partnerships at the heart of *Shaping the 21st Century* (DAC 1996), its development strategy for the twenty-first century. It has also produced a "Working Checklist" for development partnerships.

Shaping the 21st Century describes a "compact" for effective partnerships and identifies the responsibilities of developing countries and external partners, as well as joint responsibilities (summarized in Box 11.1 and detailed in Appendix 11.2.) A preamble lays down the "basic principle" that "locally-owned country development strategies and targets should emerge from an open and collaborative dialogue . . . in ways that respect and encourage strong local commitment, participation, capacity development, and ownership" (DAC 1996, p. 14).

Much of this is entirely consistent with the formulation in the CDF paper (Wolfensohn 1999), especially the emphasis on ownership and participation. There are some important additional points, however, especially a first cut at what might constitute acceptable policies by the developing country, a com-

---

Box 11.1
DAC Compact for Effective Partnership

Jointly
  1. Adequate resources
  2. Policies that minimize conflict
  3. Stronger protections against corruption
  4. Encouragement of civil society
  5. Work with rapidly developing countries and regional develop-
     ment mechanisms
Developing Countries
  6. Appropriate macroeconomic policies
  7. Commitment to social development
  8. Accountable government
  9. Support for stronger human and institutional capacity
  10. Climate favorable to enterprise and savings
  11. Sound financial management
  12. Stable relations with neighbors
External Partners
  13. Stable relations with neighbors
  14. Better international trade and investment system
  15. Adherence to aid guidelines
  16. Support for capacity building
  17. Access to information and technology
  18. Support for coherent policies, including human rights
  19. Better coordination of aid

Source: DAC 1996 (p. 14).

---

mitment to the reliability of external assistance, a recognition of the importance of trade and investment issues, and a shared commitment to good
governance internationally.

In 1998 the DAC compact was further developed as a "Working Checklist
for Strengthening Development Partnerships" (see Appendix 11.3). The checklist called specifically for the untying of aid, more program aid and budget
support, closer links with the private sector, and more joint monitoring and
evaluation of aid. On critical process issues, it is largely consistent with the
CDF paper (Wolfensohn 1999), but on some points more concrete. For example, it called for standing subgroups of partners on themes and sectors,
preferably led by the host government.

The Lomé and Cotonou Conventions

Turning to donor experience, the history of the Lomé (now Cotonou) Convention provides an object lesson in the potential and pitfalls of partnership (Bossuyt and Laporte 1994; Maxwell and Riddell 1998). The conventions (the first was signed in 1975) are legal treaties between the European Union and a group of developing countries in Africa, the Caribbean, and the Pacific—the ACP countries (see Lister 1988 and Whiteman 1998). The treaties define principles of cooperation in aid and trade, establish legal instruments for the transfer of aid, and introduce an element of "contractuality" to the aid relationship. From the start, the Lomé Conventions provided for agreement by donor and recipient on a formal "national indicative program," signed by both parties and fixing, in global terms at least, the level of aid to be provided. It was also clear that the recipient would take the lead in defining how the money would be spent. There were repeated references in the conventions to "objectives that the ACP States set themselves" (Article 47, for example), and a procedure was established for drawing up the European Union's indicative aid program based on proposals made by each state (Article 51).

The history of the Lomé Conventions since the early days is one of gradual retreat from these high principles of partnership (Crawford 1996). Initially, this was because the economic model chosen by some developing countries was clearly at variance with what the European Union believed to be best for the country concerned. In a later phase it was because the European Union could not accept that aid should be provided irrespective of human rights violations. Thus the terms of the treaty were gradually tightened. Specifically, greater importance was attached to policy dialogue in the preparation of the national indicative programs, tighter conditionality was written into the programs, and human rights clauses were introduced (after 1986). The last Lomé Convention, approved in 1990 for a ten-year period, retained an aura of contractuality, but the distance between the European Union and other, more traditional donors had narrowed significantly.

There were, nevertheless, elements of contractuality that left the European Union ahead of some other donors. The formal negotiation over the Lomé Convention and over individual national indicative programs was one; the role of the ACP secretariat was another. In comparing the aid performance of different donors during an evaluation of EU aid, focus groups in Ethiopia expressed particular appreciation of a negotiated (and therefore jointly owned) EU aid framework (Maxwell 1996a).

The remaining tension over partnership could be seen in the negotiating mandates produced by the two sides for the last renegotiation, completed in January 2000. Different views on the political basis of the partnership lay beneath the shared desire for a strengthened partnership that should facilitate poverty reduction, sustainable development, and the further integration of ACP countries into the world economy—and cloaked in diplomatic language. The ACP countries believed that "a true partnership cannot be characterized [or even "tinged"] by conditionalities." The European Union stated that it wished to develop a partnership based on "dialogue, contract rather than conditionality, and the fulfillment of mutual obligations," but was much more specific on the obligations of the ACP countries than on its own.[1]

Finally signed in Cotonou in June 2000 (EU 2000), and valid for twenty years, the convention contained innovations that reflected both positions. Poverty eradication and sustainable development were accorded pride of place (Article 1); equality between the partners was identified as the first principle of a "legally-binding" cooperation (Article 2); and a much-strengthened political relationship was defined, involving a "comprehensive, balanced, and deep political dialogue leading to commitments on both sides" (Article 8). Perhaps most important, the joint institutions of the EU-ACP partnership, particularly the joint Council of Ministers, were given enhanced powers to monitor the relationship and to adjudicate disputes, at least as regards human rights, democratic principles, the rule of law, and corruption (Articles 96 and 97). This may make it more difficult for the donor countries to suspend aid unilaterally. There is still some way to go before the institutions have the mandate and the robustness to monitor the partnership in its entirety, but the initial scaffolding is certainly in place.

Sweden

The Swedish International Development Cooperation Agency (SIDA) has defined seven criteria for partnership (Karlsson 1997, p. 7):

- a subject-to-subject attitude;
- clear values;
- transparency in interests;
- clear standards;
- adherence to the agreements;
- equality of capacity; and
- a code of conduct.

Two notable features of this list are the emphasis on transparency of values and the idea of contractuality (explicitly referred to as "a new contractual relationship") supported by a code of conduct.

The United Kingdom

The United Kingdom introduced the concept of partnership in its 1997 white paper on international development.[2] What the concept means on the recipient side is summarized in Box 11.2. What it means on the donor side is set out in the text: Where low-income countries are committed to the elimination of poverty and pursuing sensible policies to bring that about, the government will be ready to enter into a deeper, long-term partnership and to provide:

- a longer-term commitment;
- an enhanced level of resources; and
- greater flexibility in the use of resources (DFID, 1997, p. 2.21)

This formulation of partnership is set in the wider context of a white paper that deals explicitly with nonaid matters, including trade, finance, and investment. It stresses the commitment required of developing country partners, including commitment to the international development targets and to good government.

The Department for International Development (DFID) formulation raises a number of issues. Are all the criteria for partnership equally important, and if not, how will they be weighted? Is partnership to be based on needs or results? And what will happen to countries that do not qualify for partnership?

Some of these questions were addressed in later thinking by DFID. Thus, in depicting "issues of governance as lying at the heart of our approach to partnership," Goudie (1998, p. 8) listed specific areas of concern with regard to DFID's implementation of a partnership approach:

> Inevitably there are a range of key qualifications that are undoubtedly relevant here and that need to be at the fore of our minds in formulating our approach to particular countries. I might mention, for example, the dangers of attempting to generalise across partner countries whose own circumstances show such immense diversity; secondly, we should avoid drawing up mechanistic rules for decision-making that overlook the subtlety and complexity of each of these context; thirdly, we should shy away from formal rankings or league tables that simplistically seek to capture the manner in which we differentiate between the commitment of different partner countries; fourthly, we should not be formulating messages and approaches in isolation from the rest of the external community, but seeking a collaborative and constructive multilateral approach; fifthly, we should take care not to fall back into conditionality, with only a revamped vocabulary, that many see as having dogged past efforts at partnership.

The United States

Since the 1995 World Summit for Sustainable Development, the U.S. Agency for International Development (USAID) has worked to create partnerships among business, civil society, and government. USAID adopted a strategic approach to development partnering, designed to increase the capacity of local actors to work together and create purposeful coalitions (USAID

Box 11.2
A U.K. Perspective on Development Partnerships

Countries with which we are prepared in principle to embark on a deeper, long-term partnership, involving all forms of assistance, will be low income, containing a large proportion of poor people.

They will also be countries where the United Kingdom is wanted as a partner, has the influence to play a positive role, and has a comparative advantage in being able to make a strategic contribution to poverty reduction.

We would expect partner governments to:
- have a commitment to the principles of the agreed international development targets and be pursuing policies designed to achieve these and other UN targets to which they have agreed;
- be committed to pro-poor economic growth and conservation of the environment and be pursuing appropriate policies;
- wish to engage with us and with the donor community to this end;
- pursue policies which promote responsive and accountable government, recognizing that governments have obligations to all their people;
- promote the enjoyment of civil, cultural, economic, political, and social rights; and which encourage transparency and bear down on corruption in the conduct of both the public services and the business sector.

Source: Excerpted from DFID 1997 (Panel 14).

1997). A number of lessons have been drawn from this experience (Box 11.3). Three stand out:

> First, good partnerships are constructed incrementally. Second, where significant resource transfers are the sole focus of assistance, incentives for local participation are hard to sustain beyond the initial resource transfer. Third, both donors and their partners share a common interest in a clear results framework. (Chanya, McNulty, and Pennell 1998, pp. 11ff.)

Nongovernmental Organizations

A number of researchers have examined the partnership relationship between nongovernmental organizations (NGOs) in developing and developed countries. Fowler (1992), arguing that not all relationships are partnerships,

---

Box 11.3
Lessons from USAID's Intersectoral Partnerships

- Intersectoral partnerships can address large-scale issues that no individual sector can manage alone.
- Partnering requires a long-term commitment, but one undertaken in small steps.
- Partnership does not require a merging of roles by the partners—each retains its own distinctiveness.
- Partnership must be based on a commitment to respect differences and on mutual accountability.
- Partners must keep people focused on the unique win-win situations that partnership produces.
- All key interests should be represented.
- Partners need to disseminate best practice about partnership, to promote future partnerships.
- Successful partnerships encourage creativity and innovation.
- Partnerships are between organizations, not individuals, and should be inclusive.
- Partnerships need to be adapted to local contexts.
- Successful local ownership requires that partners have a stake in resolving the issue and be empowered by the process.

Source: Chanya, McNulty, and Pennell 1998 (pp. 15ff.)

---

suggests that partnerships are characterized by sharing, with a sense of mutuality and equality of the parties involved. Mutuality could not be achieved without agreement on basic development processes, trust, and legitimacy (tied up with accountability) on both sides. A particular risk was to see partnership as "projection," with NGOs in developing countries treated as a vehicle for the delivery of ideas, resources, management styles, and leadership from developed countries.

In reviewing partnerships between developed and developing country NGOs, Riddell (1993, p. 4) identified a series of conditions for establishing and maintaining partnerships:

- recognition of the autonomy of the other partner;
- specification of agency objectives, approaches, and methods;
- listing of the terms and conditions of a partnership agreement, including the responsibilities of the developed country NGO;
- commitment to flexibility, openness, and mutuality;
- acknowledgment that agencies have different interests;

- recognition that developed country NGO partners need in-depth relationships with partners in the developing countries but that practical constraints mean that some relationships will be more limited in scope;
- understanding that partnerships have to include an assessment of performance and subsequent reflection and feedback.

Particular NGOs have adopted similar principles. For example, CARE USA identifies the following characteristics of partnership (Burke 1998, pp. 4–5):

- weave a fabric of sustainability;
- acknowledge interdependence;
- build trust;
- find shared vision, goals, values, and interests;
- honor the range of resources;
- generate a culture of mutual support and respect for differences;
- find opportunities for creative synergy;
- address relationship differences as they occur;
- see partnering as a continuous learning process.

Business and Law

In commerce, of course, the principle of partnership has been developed in legal terms (through contract law). The contractual format, with precise stipulations of the rights and responsibilities of each partner, may provide a source of ideas for drafting development cooperation partnerships. In contractual partnerships, performance criteria are explicit and measurable, reporting requirements are specified, timeframes and the limits on independent (nonconsultative) action are laid out, and required and prescribed actions are delineated.

There are also noncontractual aspects to commercial partnerships that may offer pointers to those crafting and operating within an intergovernmental partnership for development cooperation. Studies of cooperative business partnerships, especially across national boundaries, have found that intangible factors like trust are crucial in establishing cooperative relationships based on mutual obligation. A study of seventeen joint ventures in the United Kingdom and Malaysia found that trust covered both personal and institutional relationships, but that personal relationships were at the core of trust between organizations. Promissory-based trust is the degree of confidence that a party can be relied on to carry out a verbal or written promise. Goodwill-based trust refers to actions and behavior that will benefit the other party. Competence-based trust relates to the knowledge, skills, and expertise of the parties (Butler and Gill 1999).

Connections to Participation

A final set of connections is to the literature on participation, which in many ways mirrors that on partnerships. In particular, analysts have identified different levels of participation (Box 11.4). They range from "manipulative participation," in which participation is "simply pretense," to "interactive participation," in which participation is a right and its implementation is characterized by joint analysis, systematic learning, and local control.

Common Themes

Several common themes emerge from the diverse experiences reviewed here:

- the need for the right values, including a genuine commitment to sharing, on both sides;
- the importance of trust and of taking measures to build trust;
- partnership based on empowerment of the weaker party;
- the scope (or need) for contracts to back up partnership agreements;
- the need for a long-term perspective and for an incremental, sustainable approach to partnership;
- the need to be pragmatic in applying partnership blueprints.

Practical Lessons on Partnerships

It is easy to conclude from this review that the intentions of the CDF initiative toward partnership are honorable: the Bank's heart, so to speak, is in the right place. The key words identified in President Wolfensohn's paper (ownership, coordination, transparency, accountability) are the right words, and they reflect much current thinking on the subject.

At the same time, the experience reviewed shows three things. First, even within contemporary discourse, there are shades of difference that may imply different approaches to partnership: the Bank will have choices to make, analogous to those set out in the participation ladder. Is the intention to have the partnership equivalent of "interactive participation" or something less ambitious? Will different countries be accorded partnerships of different quality? And if so, on what basis? These questions are particularly important in deciding what form Bank partnerships will take in countries with which there is serious disagreement on the aims or instruments of development policy. Goudie's (1998) warnings against mechanistic approaches and formalistic league tables have particular resonance.

The second lesson is that the development of partnership is an organic process, which grows as trust develops. The key idea here is that active steps

---

Box 11.4
The Spectrum of Participation

Interactive participation

People participate in joint analysis, development of action plans, and formation or strengthening of local institutions. Participation is seen as a right, not just the means to achieve project goals. The process involves interdisciplinary methodologies that seek multiple perspectives and make use of systematic and structured learning processes. As groups take control over local decisions and determine how local resources are used, they gain a stake in maintaining structures or practices.

Self-mobilization

People participate by taking initiatives independently of external institutions to change systems. They develop contacts with external institutions for resources and technical advice they need, but retain control over how resources are used. Self-mobilization can spread if governments and NGOs provide an enabling framework of support. Such self-initiated mobilization may or may not challenge existing distributions of wealth and power.

Functional participation

Participation is seen by external agencies as a means of achieving project goals, especially reduced costs. People may participate by forming groups to meet predetermined objectives related to the project. Such involvement may be interactive and involves shared decision-making, but tends to arise only after external agents have al-

ready made major decisions. At worst, local people may still only be coopted to serve external goals.

Participation for material incentives

People participate by contributing resources, for example labor, in return for material incentives. Farmers are involved in neither experimentation nor the process of learning. People have no stake in prolonging technologies or practices when the incentives end.

Participation by consultation

People participate when consulted or when answering questions. External agents define problems and information gathering processes, and so control analysis. Such a consultative process does not concede any share in decision-making, and professionals are under no obligation to take account of people's views.

Passive participation

People participate by complying with what they are told, what has been decided, or what has already happened. Project management makes announcements without listening to people's responses. Any shared information belongs only to external professionals.

Manipulative participation

Participation is simply pretence. The people's "representatives" on official boards are not elected and have no power.

Source: Adapted from Pretty 1995, as presented in DFID 1998 (p. 26).

need to be taken to build trust and to help partnership develop—what CARE describes as "weaving a fabric of sustainability."

A third lesson is that mutual accountability appears to lie at the heart of successful partnership relations and that accountability is often backed up by formal procedures and even a legal framework. This is a big jump for donors to make, as experience with the Lomé Convention has demonstrated. Accountability requires monitoring, but in contractual form it also requires mechanisms to deal with breaches of contract, and a form of redress open to both parties if the contract is broken. Reflecting on this issue, Maxwell and Riddell (1998, p. 265) comment that "perhaps what we need is a kind of WTO agreement for aid administration."

The Bank will want to address all three of these issues and the links between partnerships and strategic selectivity. One way is to take up the idea of a partnership code of conduct, originally proposed in its own paper of 1998 (World Bank 1998a). In conformity with the principles reviewed here, however, the code should probably be prepared jointly by the Bank and its various partners.

Partnership and Selectivity

The concept of partnership must be dealt with in tandem with the concept of donor selectivity. Selectivity is used in different ways, depending on actor and context. Country-level selectivity (or positive conditionality) is sometimes presented as an alternative to conventional conditionality. Donors are advised to reward governments that have already demonstrated commitment to implementing positive reforms (by adopting performance-based aid), rather than demand promises of change before funds are disbursed. In terms of a donor's global operations, then, selectivity implies a bounded application of the partnership principle: recipients must first qualify for partnership by meeting a certain minimum level of performance—or, in a two-tier approach, governments adopting good policies would receive advice and financial assistance, while those without good policies receive advice alone, in the hope that this will move them toward a better policy environment. It is not immediately clear how the concepts of partnership and selectivity can be reconciled without compromise to one or the other.

Bilateral donors, with whom the Bank must work in the evolution of the CDF, often interpret selectivity in global operations differently. Whereas the Bank approaches selectivity in terms of which countries not to work with or lend to (because of unconducive policy environments), bilateral agencies tend to approach it in terms of which countries to work with (because of limited budget and scale). With smaller budgets and less universalistic obligations, bilateral agencies have potentially much to gain from concentrating operations on a smaller number of sectors and partners (often described as concentration or priority countries). Such selectivity helps bilateral agencies achieve more with limited funds. Yet progress has been slow, reflecting the institutional inertia of country operations. Many bilateral agencies still operate on a "watering can" basis, spreading aid thinly between a multitude of countries and achieving significant impact in few.

Selectivity also applies to decisions about development partnerships at other than national levels. The principle of strategic selectivity—choosing sectors, partner institutions, instruments, and the like on the basis of an objective and long-term analysis—can be conceptualized in different ways:

- *On the basis of need.* Need would seem to be the most obvious basis for choosing among different forms of assistance. The difficulty is obviously in obtaining agreement on what is needed, and how urgently, and it is here that the definitions of partnership and ownership are critical. Donors may disagree with the government, or with each other, about which problems, sectors, regions, or groups to select as priorities. Different elements within the partner government may disagree about the relative importance of different interventions and the suitable role for donors. It is also possible to identify different long- and short-term strategies. Taking a long-term perspective, a donor might decide that second-best programs are a necessary price to pay for local ownership, on the grounds that local ownership establishes the conditions for capacity building and more effective actions in the future. This approach, however, runs counter to the ethic of professionalism (and accountability) rightfully stressed within donor management.
- *On the basis of long-term comparative advantage of the donor institution.* Adopting this approach, activities or partners are selected on the basis of what the donor can do best, or can do better than other donors operating in the country. This interpretation has intuitive appeal, but agencies' claims of comparative advantage need to be viewed cautiously. For large, specialized agencies (like UNICEF, the World Food Program, or the World Health Organization) the lines are relatively clear, although even here there is room for overlap (for example, between UNICEF and WHO, which both have an interest in child health). Amongst bilateral donors, especially the smaller ones, claims of comparative advantage are harder to confirm in objective terms.
- *On the basis of the comparative advantage of partner institutions.* Performance-based lending is concerned primarily with the decision on which countries to lend to, but it also provides the basis for more nuanced aid allocation by disaggregating partner performance into different categories. It would seem sensible for donors to work with partner institutions with the will and capacity (analytical, financial, political, and institutional) to make the most of this assistance. However, institutional capacity can be defined or measured in different ways, and different institutions may possess different comparative advantages (Box 11.5).

Strategic selectivity needs to be understood in dynamic terms. There are significant gains from continuity, but donors must also be responsive to changes in the national situation, which may lead to a change in objectively defined

Box 11.5
Comparative Advantage of Partner Institutions in Cambodia

In Cambodia, donors have often preferred to work with the Ministry for Rural Development rather than the Ministry of Agriculture. Comparative advantage here was perceived in terms of openness to ideas, greater level of commitment and willingness to work outside the capital, more holistic conceptualization of rural development problems and solutions, and (arguably) a less patronage-based internal organization. But the Ministry of Agriculture had a larger budget and, being aligned with the most powerful party in the post-election coalition, faced fewer obstacles in implementing decisions through provincial and subprovincial administrations, which were still overwhelmingly loyal to this party. In this case, the ministry with ideas and pro-poor orientation and the ministry with real power did not align.

needs or in the constellation of potential partner institutions, with some improving and some declining in terms of "comparative advantage" (see Box 11.5). It must also be recognized that strategic selectivity is a multiplayer rather than just two-player game: failure to do so may result in suboptimal aid effectiveness.

Strategic selectivity may thus be taken as an argument for or against greater partner ownership of the national development process, depending on the basis for selection. The World Bank sees the gain of strategic selectivity as enhancing the coherence and impact of country programs by concentrating efforts on a narrow rather than broad range of sectors. These sectors are to be chosen on the basis of three criteria:

- potential magnitude of impact;
- likelihood of country action;
- comparative advantage of the Bank relative to other donors operating in the country.

It is clear that in any given case there is a reasonable possibility that these criteria will pull in different directions. In a given country the action most likely to enlist government support and to result in impact may be one in which the Bank has no comparative advantage relative to other donors. Impact—and government-led selectivity—may lead to the Bank contributing to a crowded field, straining existing partner capacities and the ability to achieve donor coherence. And selecting interventions on the basis that they are most likely to demonstrate significant impact may bias action away from the most

---

Box 11.6
The 20:20 Initiative and Primary Education

In some cases, international commitments to global targets have led to distorted aid allocation at the national level. As part of the 20:20 compact, for example, many donors have pledged to allocate 20 percent of official development assistance to basic social services in any country in which the partner government committed a similar proportion. Were this a contract between the partner government and just one donor, it would be unambiguously useful. However, in some countries with low rates of economic growth, a long record of high social spending (often to good effect, as in Tanzania), and a high ratio of dependency on aid, this contract may distort aid allocation. Some African governments, having met the criterion by spending more than 20 percent of the budget on the target sectors, have been deluged with donor funds for primary services (particularly primary education), when some of these funds might have been better directed to alternative activities (such as infrastructure or agricultural production). Here, a global approach to selectivity (a decision that primary social services are key to reducing poverty) contradicts a country-level approach to selectivity.

---

important challenges, which are usually (and unsurprisingly) those where the obstacles to success are greatest (working in countries where the government lacks will or capacity, working with pockets of persistent poverty that do not respond to general processes of growth-led poverty reduction, and so on). While thinking strategically rather than reactively about where, how, and with whom to work is clearly a positive step, it must be recognized that the concept of strategic selectivity does not in itself provide a specific guide to improving development cooperation. There are many—potentially contradictory—criteria on which to base strategic selection.

APPENDIX 11.1
Executive Summary from "Partnership for Development: From Vision to Action"—Proposed Actions for the World Bank

The starting point for the Bank's partnership agenda is its relationship with developing countries and the impact of its services on their development.[3] The single most important theme running through the dialogue on development effectiveness is the need to put committed developing country governments and their people at the center of their development process. Experience shows that developing country ownership of its development strategy is a necessary condition for development effectiveness and poverty reduction.

This paper proposes that the Bank's partnership agenda should be addressed toward attaining this goal. The strategy is to design, with developing country governments and official development institutions, a new approach to development assistance that convenes all major stakeholders around the country's development strategy, programs, and projects.

There is now considerable international support and consensus for these positions, and wide agreement that partnership is needed to improve the efficiency of development assistance and deliver more effective results on the ground. Our vision is that the developing country defines its national development strategy. Official development institutions determine their assistance strategies in support of this national strategy, and in consultation with each other.

The implementation of this partnership approach to development will depend on country-specific circumstances and the result of consultations with key stakeholders. Elements of this approach have already been tested in selected countries in several continents, with promising results. The broad elements of this partnership approach include:

- Promoting and encouraging national capacity and consensus building through joint economic and sector work and through consultative mechanisms led by the government, with participation of civil society, the private sector, and external partners.
- Aiming for a core national development strategy broadly owned by the country, with assistance from official development institutions, pledging their support at a meeting convened by the government—the "Development Partners Coalition."
- Arranging partnership frameworks between key development actors based on shared objectives and comparative advantages in support of the country's national development strategy.

The paper also proposes short-term concrete actions. These actions include supporting national and subnational conferences on development strategy, revamping the consultative group process, developing partnership frameworks and opening a dialogue with partners on joint actions, and transforming the Bank's partnership culture.

APPENDIX 11.2
A Stronger Compact for Effective Partnerships

We have stressed throughout this chapter that each developing country and its people are ultimately responsible for their own development.[4] Thus the developing country is the necessary starting point for organizing cooperation efforts through relationships and mechanisms that reflect the particular local circumstances. Some developing countries will need special help in building the necessary capacities. Development cooperation at the regional level, and on sectoral lines, is also important. However, these approaches should complement and enrich efforts to strength national capacities for sustainable development.

As a basic principle, locally owned country development strategies and targets should emerge from an open and collaborative dialogue by local authorities with civil society and with external partners, about their shared objectives and their respective contributions to the common enterprise. Each donor's programs and activities should then operate with the framework of that locally owned strategy in ways that respect and encourage strong local commitment, participation, capacity development, and ownership.

While the particular elements of partnerships will vary considerably, it is possible to suggest areas in which undertakings might be considered by the partners as their commitments to shared objectives.

Joint Responsibilities

- create the conditions conducive to generating adequate resources for development;
- pursue policies that minimize the risks of violent conflict;
- strengthen protections at the domestic and international levels against corruption and illicit practices;
- open up wide scope for effective development contributions throughout civil society;
- enlist the support of rapidly developing countries and regional development mechanisms.

Developing Country Responsibilities

- adhere to appropriate macroeconomic policies;
- commit to basic objectives of social development and increased participation, including gender equality;
- foster accountable government and the rule of law;
- strengthen human and institutional capacity;
- create a climate favorable to enterprise and the mobilization of local savings for investment;
- carry out sound financial management, including efficient tax systems and productive public expenditure;
- maintain stable and cooperative relations with neighbours.

External Partner Responsibilities

- provide reliable and appropriate assistance both to meet priority needs and to facilitate the mobilization of additional resources to help achieve agreed performance targets;

- contribute to international trade and investment systems in ways that permit full opportunities to developing countries;
- adhere to agreed international guidelines for effective aid and to monitoring for continuous improvement;
- support strengthened capacities and increased participation in the developing country, avoiding the creation of aid dependency;
- support access to information, technology, and know-how;
- support coherent policies in other aspects of relations, including consistency in policies affecting human rights and the risks of violent conflict;
- work for better coordination of the international aid system among external partners, in support of developing countries' own strategies.

APPENDIX 11.3
A Working Checklist for Strengthening
Development Partnerships

As part of the continuing work of the OECD's Development Assistance Committee (DAC) aimed at effective implementation of the Development Partnerships Strategy, a forum of development partners was convened on 19 January 1998 in conjunction with the committee's Senior Level Meeting.[5] The forum presentations "focused on five partner countries, together with much other experience by DAC members . . . [and] led the senior level participants to the following points as a working checklist to guide efforts toward improving partnerships and simplifying and harmonising donor procedures."

Donors should encourage recipient partners to formulate their own development strategies, setting out the local priorities, plans, and instruments for implementing such strategies. This process should systematically involve civil society, as well as consultation with external partners. Where such locally owned strategies are compatible with internationally agreed goals, donors should work to implement their aid programs in a coordinated manner on the basis of such locally owned strategies and accept their discipline.

Donors should stimulate and help strengthen recipient partner-led coordination of development cooperation. The capacity for local coordination (which can and should also strengthen the international process) may be improved by donors' own delegation of decision-making authority from headquarters to field missions. At the international level, the possible advantages and disadvantages of organizing Consultative Group (and Round Table) meetings in the capitals of the recipient partners concerned should be further tested in practice.

Transparency of donor and recipient partner interests and mutual trust should be increased through continuous dialogue, both informal and through systematic work on themes and sectors through standing subgroups, preferably led by the host government.

External partners should agree in principle to adjust more to local procedures, where necessary helping recipient countries to bring their procedures and management capacities up to international standards. There may be useful DAC roles in identifying best practices and helping organize pilot exercises to move toward the simplification and harmonization of procedures.

Practices involving tied aid are prominently identified among procedures that can impair local ownership and capacity building, with substantial economic and credibility costs. The proposal for a DAC recommendation to start with untying aid to least developed countries could be a step toward improved partnerships in this area, yielding additional tangible benefits for partners from competitive bidding and from local procurement.

Donors share the objective of ending the proliferation of projects and providing their aid increasingly in forms of program and budget assistance to support the country's strategic priorities for development. To this end, they need to help strengthen partner countries' capacities to manage such aid, and further test the various approaches and conditions under which they can pool their contributions in country funds for major sectors or key goals, such as poverty eradication. The integration of aid spending into the overall budget context may require donors to manage their own significant inputs differently to help strengthen local revenue pools.

There is a widely felt need to support local capacity building by changing the existing modalities for providing technical cooperation, which often appears expensive and excessive, hampering true ownership and the use and development of local capacities.

The practices of joint monitoring and evaluation of development programs by donor and recipient partners should be further developed and applied, with a view to learning together the lessons of achievements and failures.

Improving the coherence between external partners' development cooperation policies and their other policies affecting recipient partners (such as those affecting trade and investment) is clearly seen as increasingly important to help the developing countries concerned move toward reduced dependence on aid.

Innovative ways of financing should be constructed so as to have ODA play catalytic and leverage roles in generating and attracting other forms of domestic and foreign investment; the roles of grants, loans, forms of support for the local private sector, and "matching" contributions by beneficiaries merit further careful assessment and coherent policies.

External partners should continue to help lessen the debt burden of recipient partners; in this context, among others, the modality of various types of "debt swaps" should be considered.

Notes

1. Specifically, the EU negotiating mandate identified four "fundamental principles" of partnership: ownership; participation and shared responsibility; dialogue contract rather than conditionality; and a differentiated approach, in which cooperation was tailored to a partner's level of development (EU 1998, p. 3).
2. This section draws on Maxwell and Riddell 1998 (pp. 260–61).
3. This appendix is excerpted from World Bank (1998b).
4. This appendix is excerpted from DAC (1996).
5. Taken from the DAC Web site page, "Strengthening Development Partnerships: A Working Checklist"—http://www.oecd.org:80/dac/htm/strength.htm-mmmm.

References

Bossuyt, Jean, and Geert Laporte. 1994. "Partnership in the 1990s: How to Make It Work Better." ECDPM Policy Management Brief 3. Maastricht, December.

Bossuyt, Jean, Andrea Koulaïmh-Gabriel, Geert Laporte, and Henri-Bernard Solignac Lecomte. 1999. "Comparing the ACP and EU Negotiating Mandates." ECDPM Lomé Negotiating Brief 3.

Burke, Michael. 1998. "Partnership—Policy, Principles and Practices." [http://www.linkingpartners.org/docs/policy.html].

Butler, Richard, and Jas Gill. 1999. *The Dynamics of Trust in Partnership Formation and Operation: Project Summary*. University of Bradford, Management Center.

Chanya, L. Charles, Stephanie McNulty, and John A. Pennell. 1998. "Partnership for Results—A User's Guide to Intersectoral Partnering." Paper prepared for the U.S. Agency for International Development Mission Directors' Conference, November.

Crawford, Gordon. 1996. "Wither Lomé? The Mid-term Review and the Decline of Partnership." *Modern African Studies* 34 (3): pp. 503–18.

DAC (Development Assistance Committee). 1996. *Shaping the 21st Century: The Contribution of Development Cooperation*. Paris, France: Organisation for Economic Cooperation and Development.

DFID (Department for International Development). 1997. "Eliminating World Poverty: A Challenge for the 21st Century" (the 1997 White Paper). Cm 3789. London, U.K.: Stationery Office.

———. 1998. "Action Research for Community Forestry: Sharing Experiences from Nepal." London.

EU (European Union). 1998. "Negotiating Directives for the Negotiation of a Development Partnership Agreement with the ACP Countries." Information Note, June 30, Brussels.

———. 2000. "Partnership Agreement between the Members of the African, Caribbean and Pacific Group of States, of the One Part, and the European Community and its Member States, of the Other Part." (Cotonou Agreement), June 30, Cotonou.

Goudie, Andrew. 1998. "Is a Good Government Approach to Development Practical? An Approach to Governance." Paper presented to ODI, March 25.

Karlsson, Mats. 1997. "Foreword." In H. Kifle, A. Olukoshi, and Wohlgemuth, eds. "A New Partnership for African Development: Issues and Parameters." Nordiska Afrikainstitutet, Uppsala, Norway.

Lister, R. 1988. *The European Community and the Developing World*. Aldershot, Avebury.

Maxwell, Simon. 1996. "The Use of Matrix Scoring to Identify Systemic Issues in Country Programme Evaluation." *Development in Practice* 7 (4): pp. 408–15.

Maxwell, Simon, and Roger Riddell. 1998. "Conditionality or Contract: Perspectives on Partnership for Development." *Journal of International Development* 10 (2): pp. 257–68.

Riddell, Roger. 1993. "Discerning the Way Together: Report on the Work of Brot für die Welt." (Executive summary) Brot für die Welt, Christian Aid, EZE and ICCO.

USAID (U.S. Agency for International Development). 1997. "New Partnerships Initiative: A Strategic Approach to Development Partnering." Report of the NPI Learning Team.

Whiteman, K. 1998. "Africa, the ACP and Europe: The Lessons of 25 Years." *Development Policy Review* 16 (1).

Wolfensohn, James D. 1999. "A Proposal for a Comprehensive Development Framework" (a discussion draft). Memo to the Board, Management, and Staff of the World Bank Group, January 21, Washington, D.C.: World Bank.

World Bank. 1998a. "Partnership for Development: Proposed Actions for the World Bank." Paper presented at an informal meeting of the Partnerships Group, May 20.

———. 1998b. "Partnership for Development: From Vision to Action." Briefing to the Board of Directors, September 24.

12

The Role of International
Public Goods

Marco Ferroni

The debate on how to reform the system of development cooperation that has evolved over the past fifty years is alive and well. As implied in many of the chapters in this volume, the debate is motivated by widespread dissatisfaction with the results of conventional country strategies. A further motivating factor emerges in the form of questions about the system's readiness to respond to the transnational development challenges of the global era. Reform of foreign aid must focus on better approaches to both national and transnational partnerships.[1] The last chapter focused on country-level coalitions for development. This chapter addresses the transnational dimension.

As global integration deepens, the number of development problems that call for supranational policy responses grows. These cross-border challenges arise from combinations of market failure, government failure, and systemic failure. Thus, a new development frontier is emerging and with it a new role, and perhaps a new rationale, for foreign aid. In the past, foreign aid has tended to be almost exclusively country-based. While the country focus will remain at the heart of development cooperation, official development finance will likely be called on more frequently to support the supply of international public goods as well.

Investments in international public goods can make national development efforts more productive. This is because they create synergies in the form of desirable crossborder externalities that cannot be produced by country-focused strategies on their own. It is also because of the quality of partnerships that necessarily underlie successful international joint action. In contrast to traditional patterns of development cooperation, now seen to have fostered aid dependency, the new agenda (both nationally and globally) must be embedded in inclusive—and thus legitimizing and mutually empowering—partnerships. This is key to a more productive aid relationship and, in time, to a qualitative shift from aid to accelerated integration and true international cooperation.

International public goods vary considerably in nature and reach. The motivation to contribute to the supply of a particular international public good depends on the degree to which potential contributors are affected by the transboundary problem (or externality) that the public good is designed to correct. The capacity to contribute depends on the ability to pay and institutional considerations. Multilateral agencies are important as catalysts of collective action to produce international public goods.

Why a Transboundary Approach—And Why Now?

The end of the Cold War and the emergence of a newly intensified globalization have altered the development challenge and the motivation for foreign aid. The security rationale for aid, grounded in Cold War geopolitics, has lost meaning. A measure of indifference and aid fatigue has spread in some quarters, while a heightened concern for aid effectiveness has taken hold in others.

Aid effectiveness and the novel facets of the development challenge are linked, and both are beginning to be better understood. Development analysts and practitioners have generated a wealth of insight into the merits and shortcomings of the mainstream aid delivery system. A consensus on how to address fundamental grievances is emerging.

The new thinking stresses the visualization of development as a holistic process for the transformation of society—in contrast with the narrower and somewhat reductionist approaches of the past. It stresses the futility of imposing change from outside, the need to attend to the institutional infrastructure required to make markets and public services work, and the need for meaningful development alliances among donors, recipient governments, civil society, and the private sector (Stiglitz 1998).

The new thinking involves both strategy and process and focuses implicitly on country-based development assistance. In the realm of the strategic, this chapter shows why country-based assistance needs to be complemented by a transnational cooperation agenda—with the aim of developing instruments to deal with an emerging class of issues at that level.

The basic case is simple. "In contrast to conventional foreign aid that focuses on individual countries, transnational problems demand a multi-country, problem-oriented approach to development cooperation" (Gwin 1999).

Take the scourge of tropical disease. Its control requires transboundary action, since disease vectors do not recognize national borders. There normally is a case for action at the national level too. But it may be hypothesized that sector-specific national action works best when embodied in a multicountry effort.

Three arguments based in aid effectiveness support a transnational approach to development cooperation when the problem at hand demands it. The first is tautological and has just been identified—you cannot hope to resolve a transnational problem with an uncoordinated set of national overtures.

The second is prudential. Systemic crises (by definition, transnational in nature in our context) can destroy development achievements financed by foreign aid. In extreme forms, the global phenomenon of financial volatility can quickly spoil the fruits of past economic growth in emerging markets and (indirectly) in commodity-exporting, least-developed economies. Some of this growth may have been financed by foreign aid. Even if not, the setback means that any future official flows to the affected countries will have to engage less favorable initial conditions.

The third reason is procedural. The aid effectiveness literature (developed with reference to country-based experience) calls attention to a flawed process. Its major shortcomings are an asymmetry of objectives between donors and recipients, inadequate attention to institutional development and capacity building, and coordination difficulties with multiple, independent sources of external assistance. A number of these deficiencies, examined in some detail in this chapter, become potentially immaterial under a transboundary approach to cooperation because of fundamental differences in the terms of engagement.

Thus, there are at least two counts for advocating a transboundary way of looking at development and foreign aid: global trends and aid effectiveness. But advocacy alone is unlikely to lead to much testing and gradual adoption of this approach as a complement to nationally focused patterns of cooperation. Two sets of issues are therefore raised in the concluding section of this chapter—the matter of what is sometimes called the "supply technology" for transboundary development solutions and the role of multilateral agencies in bringing to the attention of the international community the potential merits of a transnational approach to cooperation.

On the first, recent literature suggests that the overall supply is not necessarily equal to the sum of individual contributions—a conclusion with implications for the role of the donor community. On the second, a new and demanding role for multilateral institutions can be deduced from the special collective action problems that are inherent in a multicountry, multiactor approach to cooperation.

A New Frontier in Development Cooperation

People's lives are increasingly shaped by global forces. The key to this phenomenon is technology that—in Sandler's (1998) words—continues to draw the planet's nations and citizens closer together. In the process, novel forms of international public goods and bads are created, and the power of the nation-state to influence domestic affairs is called into question.

A Brave New World

Global economic integration brings many transnational public bads into sharper focus. They generate spillover (or negative externalities) that impose costs on other countries. Everyone suffers the loss of biodiversity when rain forests are destroyed, not only the countries where the forests are located. Key cross-border challenges include:

- financial contagion;
- spread of disease;
- loss of biodiversity and cultural heritage;
- cross-border environmental pollution ;
- global environmental problems such as the ozone hole;
- war and conflict (including international spillovers of national civil strife);
- flow of migrants and refugees to foreign destinations where they are not wanted;
- protectionist backlash in advanced industrialized countries in response to rising domestic inequality, labor insecurity, and disagreements on appropriate environmental standards;
- effects of illicit behavior, such as corruption, money laundering, and international crime.

Many of these cross-border challenges are not generically new. War and disease have spread internationally for thousands of years. What is new is the potential velocity of contagion—and the interaction effects arising from the differences in degree and kind that characterize today's interdependent and deeply integrated international system. This system can generate previously unknown hazards of potentially vast geographic reach. It can lead to novel permutations of old problems and new patterns of transition between order, disorder, and renewed equilibrium. In the eyes of many, the global financial crisis of 1997/98—the first crisis of the twenty-first century, as it has been called—fits this bill.

But systemic risk is not confined to finance. Globalization may spawn new diseases and accelerate the spread of old ones (communicable or not) through intensified trade, travel and migration, and associated changes in lifestyles (Chen, Evans, and Cash 1999). Witness the resurgence of tuberculosis. The environment, deepening social inequity, and the digital divide are other conceivable sources of systemic risk. A recent study by the United Nations Development Programme (UNDP) gives examples from several different sectors (Kaul, Grunberg, and Stern 1999).

International public bads can be the product of negative cross-border spillover of action or inaction by a country or a group of countries. They can also be generated by global or regional systemic effects. These effects are the downside that accompanies the material advantages potentially afforded by globalization. For the world—including poor countries—to participate in these benefits on a sustainable basis, it is necessary to manage the sources of systemic risk and, at a minimum, to counteract international public bads. And it is desirable to expand the transnational policy frontier. The task is to preempt future sources of risk and create the best possible basis for widely shared and sustainable world growth. This is where international public goods come in.

Defining International Public Goods

As a first cut, public goods may be defined as development resources capable of generating positive externalities and mitigating undesirable ones. The economics of public goods is reviewed in Box 12.1. The tenets outlined there apply to both national and international public goods, except that the externalities associated with international public goods have a transnational reach. That reach can be global, regional (affecting a subcontinent, continent, or hemisphere), or subregional (touching a small number of neighboring countries). The reach may encompass industrial countries, sets of developing countries (some tropical diseases), or poor and rich countries alike—an increasingly probable prospect. Characteristics of the spillover of positive or negative externalities affect the motivation of different members of the international community to contribute to the creation of particular international public goods (Jayaraman and Kanbur 1999).

In discussing international public goods, it is useful to distinguish between goals and means. The goal definition is comparable to motherhood and apple pie—too general to be useful. Examples include financial stability, peace and prosperity, a rich pool of biodiversity and cultural heritage, preindustrial levels of greenhouse gas emissions, and good international public health. The means definition is the one to focus on for practical purposes. It considers public goods as resources, processes, policies, and institutions for achieving specified goals. Generic deliverables include:

- data, information, knowledge, and technology—for example, drugs and vaccines, and yield-enhancing agricultural technology;
- harmonization of norms and standards and global rule setting;
- consensus on courses of action to be taken and best practice in given fields;

- policies that widen the range of choices open to people (for many developing countries, agricultural liberalization in high-income countries is one example; peace-keeping by the international community is another).

International public goods developed through these means aim to set the stage for (and in the end become synonymous with) better functioning markets, better institutions and governance, greater equity, and enhanced welfare outcomes.

This can be illustrated in many ways, and the public good character of the respective outcomes can be certified by the criteria in Box 12.1. Take the matter of international financial architecture. The central element is financial and banking sector surveillance, including appropriate institutional arrangements to deliver the surveillance, submit data to a process of shared learning and interpretation, and act on the conclusions. Internationally recognized standards are needed on the capital adequacy of banks, auditing and accounting practices, creditor rights, and corporate bankruptcy procedures, among other aspects. These desiderata meet the test for a public good. The benefits of financial surveillance are nonexcludable and nonrival—once produced in a participatory and transparent fashion, data and insights cannot be withheld. Their use by one party does not diminish their value to another—in fact, it most likely increases it. The same is true for epidemiological surveillance, to mention just one example from a different sector.

Public goods tend to be undersupplied. Take the case of worldwide investment in drug and vaccine development for tropical diseases. Investment is far below the needs dictated by the epidemiological and economic importance of these afflictions. Another example is the neglect of regional cooperation (Box 12.2). Many more could be given. The UNDP study mentioned above postulates that many of the crises on today's global agenda can be traced to an underprovisioning of international public goods (Kaul, Grunberg, and Stern 1999). Seen in this light, correction of the undersupply is the central challenge of transnational governance. It is what international collective action is about.

Collective Action

Inertia explains much of the underprovisioning of public goods. Often-encountered sources of inertia in collective action include uncertainty about the problem at hand and the feasibility of potential solutions, suspicion regarding the motivation of others, and doubts about the distribution of costs and benefits. The interests of individual participants may diverge, and the multiplicity of actors may initially give rise to conditions approaching anarchy. Box 12.3 illustrates how this inertia in collective action was overcome in the establishment of the pilot phase of the Global Environment Facility (GEF).

Box 12.1
Public Goods Primer

A *public good* is a commodity, service, or resource whose consumption by one user does not reduce its availability to the next—in jargon, public goods are nonrival in consumption. Public goods are also "nonexcludable," that is, if the good is provided, the provider is unable to prevent anyone from consuming it, whether that user pays for the privilege or not. Users are able to free-ride. Because of this characteristic, public goods tend to be undersupplied. Classic examples of public goods are clean air, national defense, and street lighting.

An *externality,* a close relative of the notion of public goods, occurs when the welfare of an agent depends directly not only on what that agent does but also on what others do or fail to do. The motivation to invest in public goods arises from the desire to bring out positive externalities or to correct or compensate for negative ones. Collective (or government) action is necessary to produce public goods because private solutions often fail. In particular, markets are unable to supply nonexcludable goods.

Public goods are critical to development. Rules and standards, infrastructure, institutions in the public service, property rights, law and order, and, more generally, functional social and political cohesion are development resources with a public good character. Societies at different levels of development distinguish themselves among other aspects by differences in their accumulated wealth of public goods (the nonphysical components of which are called *social capital* by some authors).

Public goods differ according to the publicness of their benefits on a continuum between pure public goods and pure private goods. *Private commodities* and services are said to be rival and excludable. Between these polar opposites are *club goods* (for example, toll roads), which are excludable but nonrival, and *common pool goods* or common property (for example, groundwater or mineral deposits), which are nonexcludable but rival. Common property tends to be overused in the absence of rules. As in the case of "pure" public goods, the prudent or sustainable use of common property is a matter of collective choice. Government action (for example, in the form of regulation) may also be needed to ensure equitable and competitive access to club goods.

> **Box 12.2**
> **Regional Public Policy**
>
> The regional dimension of development has often been overlooked as policymakers and international agencies have tended to focus on national problems. The lack of regional policy instruments—and, in some cases, nationalism—appear to have contributed to the neglect of the regional dimension.
>
> This is beginning to change. Southern Africa is an example. Once divided, the countries of the Southern Africa Development Conference are now seeking cooperation on many levels and through various groups and institutions, both public and private.
>
> The regional harmonization of policy (with or without the goal of eventual formal integration) can help small economies overcome their size disadvantage, which often discourages investment. Regional policies make sense in many sectors, including transport, power grids, telecommunications, law enforcement, public health, riparian issues, trade policy, the regulation of financial markets, and the harmonization of bank clearance and payments systems. Regionally integrated, liberalized financial markets would be expected to be attractive to foreign investors and would be helpful to support cross-border business activity; they would also offer ways of mitigating the risks to financial institutions from operating within a single small economy.
>
> Thus, significant benefits could be derived from regional public policy. That existing regional institutions in many parts of the world may currently not be very strong does not detract from the basic case. They would automatically become stronger under more active regionalism.

The process of engaging the international community in response to a given transnational development challenge is the concern of global public policy (Reinicke 1998), or transnational public policy, since not all international problems are global. Transnational public policy seeks to remedy collective action inertia by crafting issue-focused partnerships and processes for reaching agreement on priorities, procedures, and reciprocal obligations toward specified outcomes.

This is easier said than done. The organization and "technology" of international governance have not evolved as rapidly as the global economic scene. The debate about the new architecture of global governance is unresolved and symptomatic of the range of issues needing attention and the uncertainties about how participants should engage one other. The following aspects seem important:

Box 12.3
The Genesis of the Global Environment Facility

When seventeen donor countries, along with the United Nations Environment Program and the United Nations Development Programme, met in Paris in March 1990 under the World Bank's chairmanship to discuss the proposal for the pilot phase of the Global Environment Facility (GEF) for the first time, international readiness to fund the initiative was lacking. Many fundamental issues were raised. Delegates did not question the need for the international community to address global environmental problems. But the mere recognition of a need and the recognition that no one bilateral or international agency was equipped to deal with the problems were insufficient to overcome barriers to collective action. Suspicion and even cynicism regarding the motivations of key players abounded, and there were major questions regarding burden sharing, the nature of partnerships to be established, and whether additionality was possible.

The pilot phase—and thus the GEF—was nurtured into existence in four major rounds of negotiation during 1990. Key elements that made this possible included an initial, if vague, proposal, backed by an offer of money from a major donor country (this challenged others to follow suit), the choice to place the proposal in the hands of an agency capable of providing leadership (the Bank), the focus on global problems that allowed GEF funds to be distinguished from regular development assistance and thus appeared to satisfy the additionality requirement, the closure on a credible tripartite arrangement for implementation, and the choice to start off with a pilot phase (this made it possible for parties to sign on without necessarily resolving every detail at the outset).

Source: Sjoberg 1994.

- Problems involving multicountry externalities cannot be solved by conventional government-to-government agreements. The net has to be cast more widely to allow for a multicountry and multiactor approach.
- The concept of national sovereignty needs redefinition. As a first cut, it may be said that sovereignty is constructively asserted through contributions to mutually beneficial interdependence.
- In this situation, public sector actors representing a broader range of policy domains than foreign policy are likely to intensify their contacts abroad. All partners with a stake in a problem will tend to be drawn into the network because of the collective interest in controlling problems that emanate from individual members' territories.

- Partnerships of the future will not be confined to state actors. The economic and social opening up of societies has unleashed the forces of the business sector, civil society, professional groups, and others. The communications revolution is making it possible for these participants to work together in real time, at close to zero cost, from anywhere on the globe. Exclusion is difficult to practice and impossible to justify.

Thus, despite their name, public goods need not be supplied exclusively by the public sector. Such pure public goods as military protection or peacekeeping are typically provided by governments. Club goods are increasingly expected to be supplied by the private sector under concession agreements. Examples of regional and global club goods are regional power grids, satellite communications, and global cultural and ecological attractions that can be made accessible on a fee basis, such as through tourism. Other public goods and common pools may be supplied by public agencies, public-private mixes, and not-for-profit private entities, such as nongovernmental organizations (NGOs). An example of the growing scope for public-private partnerships in solving problems of transnational public policy is the public-private partnership to develop and market new malaria drugs (Box 12.4).

In such mixed arrangements, the responsibility of public sector entities would include the articulation of goals, standards, and processes. Together with foundations and private philanthropists, the public sector may be the only viable source of venture capital for the development of products with little commercial prospect, such as drugs and vaccines for diseases that disproportionately afflict the poor. The for-profit private sector (for example, pharmaceutical companies) would supply research and development (R&D), marketing, and distribution services. NGOs would have a role in standards setting, review, and advocacy. Examples are the analytical and standards-setting work of Transparency International and the advocacy work of international human rights, health, and environmental groups.

Transnational Governance

Issue-oriented transboundary networks are an emerging answer to the quest for transnational forms of governance, since the theoretical alternative of world government is neither feasible nor (in this author's view) desirable. Such partnerships are already stepping in to fill the governance vacuum for policy issues beyond the reach of individual governments or intergovernmental agreements. In theory, they are applicable to many transboundary policy concerns. The Global Corporate Governance Forum, launched in 1999, is an example. A partnership of multilateral agencies and private associations such as the International Accounting Standards Committee and the International Organization of Securities Commissions, the forum builds on the Principles

---

Box 12.4
Medicines for Malaria—An Innovative Public-Private Partnership

---

Malaria continues to contribute massively to the disease burden in the regions affected. The malaria control situation is worsening owing to the spread of drug resistance. New drugs are needed but, because of inadequate commercial prospects, the pharmaceutical industry has almost completely withdrawn from malaria drug development. The public sector has increased basic science funding but lacks the expertise and the mechanisms to discover, develop, register, and commercialize products. Public-private cooperation is needed—the New Medicines for Malaria Venture (MMV).

The MMV not-for-profit initiative is a partnership between the pharmaceutical industry and the public sector. This effort will operate under the umbrella of the World Health Organization's Roll Back Malaria Initiative. Also backing this scheme are the World Bank and several charitable foundations such as the Rockefeller Foundation. Integral to the formulation of the MMV has been a significant industrial input, notably from the International Federation of Pharmaceutical Manufacturers Associations and the Association of British Pharmaceutical Industries.

MMV's goal is to achieve a sustainable portfolio of drug discovery and development projects that would result in the registration of one new affordable antimalarial every five years. Drug discovery partnerships between academic groups and industry will be established and funded at a level sufficient to ensure a real chance of success. Development candidates will be passed on to a virtual development unit that will take projects through to registration and seek industrial partners for manufacture and commercialization. Any royalty income obtained through outlicensing will feed back into MMV to provide a degree of financial sustainability.

Several pharmaceutical companies have agreed to partner drug discovery projects, primarily by providing gifts in kind such as access to their chemical libraries and high throughput screening facilities, as well as access to more general expertise, a commitment worth several million dollars per year. In addition, a funding commitment of $15 million per year, rising to $30 million per year, is being sought, primarily from the public sector.

Sufficient initial funding through Roll Back Malaria and other agencies was obtained to start the initiative in 1999 and fund the first one or two research projects. Efforts are ongoing to achieve extra funds to facilitate the full establishment of MMV and establish the legal framework under which MMV will operate.

Note: Further information on MMV can be obtained from www.malaria medicines.org of Corporate Governance of the Organization for Economic Cooperation and Development that were agreed on in 1998. Its role is to monitor corporate governance issues (seen to have been a factor in the 1997/1998 global financial crisis) and to marshal the best expertise available to support individual countries' regulatory and voluntary efforts in this field.

Slaughter (1997) calls this approach "transgovernmentalism." As she describes it, the state is not disappearing in the global era but disaggregating into its separate, functionally distinct, parts. These parts are networking with their counterparts abroad and creating dense webs of relationship that constitute a new transgovernmental order. Governance thus denotes cooperative problem solving by a changing and often uncertain cast.

Transgovernmentalism is often at work when international public goods are created (Slaughter looks into mechanisms of international law enforcement). The term can be usefully extended to cooperative problem solving (or partnerships) involving nonstate actors, such as NGOs, the private sector, special interest groups, and so on, in line with the analysis and examples presented here (see Box 12.5 on the riverblindness control effort). A model for addressing the transnational public policy challenges of the global era appears to be coming into view.

The Aid Effectiveness Link

How is all this related to aid (and development) effectiveness? As discussed, a shift from a country focus to multicountry collaboration is called for when cross-border spillover is present (for example, vector-borne diseases and financial contagion), when systemic risk or global commons issues are being addressed (requiring collective action involving all societies), and when knowledge sharing leads to a leveraging of resources and economies of scale in country-level applications. International research programs that make their results available to developing countries are a case in point (for example, international agricultural research). Clearly, in these cases, an international public goods approach adds value over and above a purely country-focused approach.

In addition, greater attention to international public goods is likely to improve development effectiveness by strengthening partnership and cooperation. To see this, it is necessary to recall the debate about aid effectiveness of recent years.

Foreign assistance strategies and processes have undergone a fundamental reassessment. The old consensus on development strategy—state-led in the 1960s and market-led in the 1980s—has evaporated. Instead, there is consensus that agreement on the particulars of a strategy for sustained growth and poverty reduction in developing countries is unlikely. But there is agreement

---

Box 12.5
Progress in Controlling Riverblindness

Riverblindness is a painful and debilitating disease caused by a parasite worm transmitted by a black fly. Twenty million people are estimated to be infected in Sub-Saharan Africa, 120 million people are at risk in thirty countries, and 99 percent of the world's cases of riverblindness are in Africa.

A multipartner Onchocerciasis Control Program (OCP) has been in operation in West Africa for twenty-seven years. The partners include African governments, local communities, international organizations, bilateral donors, private corporations, foundations, and NGOs. Intervention has focused on vector control, distribution of the drug Ivermectin (supplied gratis by the Merck Corporation), and capacity building in national health programs. The program has been highly successful: 34 million people protected, 600,000 cases of blindness prevented, 5 million years of productive labor added over the life of the program, 25 million hectares of land freed up, 12 million children spared the disease, and an overall economic rate of return of 20 percent. A separate program, the African Program for Onchocerciasis Control (APOC), was started in 1996 to cover the nineteen oncho-endemic African countries not covered by OCP.

OCP is a global partnership devoted to a regional problem. Lessons learned include the following:

- Partnerships have tremendous potential but are complex to form and maintain, particularly given the mix of corporate cultures that may be a constant source of tension.
- It is important to identify the comparative advantages that each partner brings to the table and to allocate the division of responsibilities in the partnership according to these assets.
- Personal relationships and trust count heavily, particularly when difficulties are encountered.
- Precisely defined objectives are critical, with all participants "keeping their eyes on the prize."
- Flexibility and compromise are fundamental to partnership.
- All partners need to be clear regarding the payoff to their participation. Altruism is an inadequate base for sustainability.
- Leadership is crucial for holding the coalition together.

Source: Presentational material developed by the Onchocerciasis Coordination Unit at the World Bank.

on certain fundamentals, including openness to trade and the flow of ideas, macroeconomic stability, investment in human capital, a transparent legal framework, well-regulated financial systems, and appropriately decentralized decision making. The list of fundamentals evolves as experience accumulates.

The Learning Dimension Neglected

But an understanding of fundamentals can never inform decision-makers and practitioners about specific actions for specific settings. Specific action is a matter of judgment and political process, and by definition not amenable to generalization. There is best practice, but it needs to be adapted to particular circumstances. Development is about learning what works in individual situations, as Hirschman (1958) noted more than forty years ago. Evaluation plays a critical role in this context.

Foreign aid can support this process, though it has not so far done enough to facilitate the participatory learning that fosters self-reliance. The debate about aid effectiveness points to several defects in the mainstream aid delivery pattern:

- a tendency toward top-down and spending-oriented approaches at the expense of local capacity building and ownership;
- fragmented aid delivery, with large numbers of insufficiently coordinated sources of assistance and projects relative to absorption capacity;
- questionable aid allocation patterns and sobering experience with conditionality.

While there have always been voices in aid agencies advocating a decentralized, bottom-up approach, the reality seems to have been that aid agencies offered preconceived solutions more often than they promoted dialogue with stakeholders. An approval and disbursement culture has prevailed over a quality-first focus on institution building in consultation with beneficiaries. Common answers to the lack of local capacity were the creation of donor-staffed project implementation units and the hiring away (at multiples of going rates) of competent civil servants from their government jobs. This perpetuated the lack of local capacity and prevented donor-funded activities from being "owned" by local stakeholders. Continuing aid dependency was the outcome (OECD 1998).

Fragmented aid delivery mechanisms have led to other insufficiencies. Recipient governments, particularly in the poorest countries, must respond to a proliferation of projects and a multiplicity of donors, each with its own procedures, reporting requirements, financing terms, inclination to undertake sector studies, and methods of evaluation and tracking expenditure. Coordination is the answer, but the history of aid coordination is not, by and large, a happy one. Borrowing governments have been caught in a vicious circle of passivity bred by lack of capacity and supply-driven donor methods that led to a lack of ownership and more passivity. We now recognize that a successful aid relationship requires beneficiary governments to take the lead in coordination. The key to better coordination appears to lie in strategic selectivity based on comparative advantage. Recipient governments should be given the opportunity to show how they propose to select donor-supplied resources in addition to their own in pursuing specified policies. At the same time they must be held accountable for their choices and spending patterns. Capacity building for accountability is, then, as important as capacity building for planning and execution.

Foreign aid has also been faulted for the way it has been allocated. A central conclusion of the World Bank's *Assessing Aid* (1998) and other recent literature on aid effectiveness is that aid works only in a conducive institutional and policy environment—an environment capable of promoting growth and poverty reduction. To the extent that bilateral aid is a tool of foreign policy, it is understandable that in selecting recipient countries, donors may use criteria other than the quality of the policy framework. A recent study of the aid allocation patterns of European Union member states confirms this reality (ODI 1998).

Researchers based at the World Bank have similarly concluded that the suitability of the environment for aid in terms of poverty reduction is not the only—or even the main—criterion for donors' country allocation decisions (Collier and Dollar 1998). Aid has the broadest scope for contributing to poverty reduction in countries with deep poverty and a proven willingness to introduce virtuous policies. The study found that aid tends to be poorly synchronized with promising reform episodes, coming late and going out too early. It has often been made available in the absence of a proven willingness to reform and has been "tapered out" when needed most, just as difficult reforms were in process and before a climate of confidence capable of bringing in private flows was created. The study does not discuss how to recognize an honest reform effort early on or how to use aid to cultivate initial good will (for example, in the early period of a new administration) so that intentions can flower into a fully fledged and ultimately successful reform program.

The notion and practice of conditionality are the subject of much debate. Killick, Gunatilaka, and Marr (1998) dismiss the belief that aid tied to conditionality can "buy" better policies. The acceptance of policy conditions is poor when donor and government objectives differ. Domestic politics usually prevail over donor pressure. For political and institutional reasons, donors cannot offer adequate incentives for compliance. One reason is that they operate under what might be called a "spending imperative" related to their budget cycle. And defensive allocations of new money are sometimes made to stave off arrears or defaults on old loans. For multilateral institutions, an additional reason is the difficulty of disciplining shareholders (see also Collier 1997 and Gaddy and Ickes 1998).

But aid without conditionality is unthinkable. While some practices in the design and the administration of conditionality have not withstood the test of time, donors will always (and with good reason) insist on a value-driven direction of the use of funds from official sources. A corollary is that the credibility of foreign aid might be enhanced by carefully considered, case-by-case denials of funds to noncomplying governments. The reasons militating against this in the post–Cold War world seem to be more institutional and bureaucratic than political.

Conditionality is an expression of the compact of mutual obligations of lenders and borrowers. The spirit of partnership in which it is crafted and negotiated is important. Conditionality can play a role in promoting the convergence of policy standards—an international public good. Today's widespread acceptance of macroeconomic stability as a necessary condition for sustainable growth and poverty reduction (in Latin America, for example) came only when the electorates began to demand it at the polls. But the conditionality that accompanied earlier multilateral loans may have been helpful in preparing the ground. It had an educational effect. The views and advice of outsiders can sometimes make a difference when domestic agents of change are thwarted in their endeavors.

The Comprehensive Development Framework (CDF) addresses these grievances at the country level. The CDF provides for improved partnership and coordination among development actors, the recipient government, and key stakeholders in the basic sectoral pillars of development. The CDF could be extended to cover international public goods, such as the multicountry and multistakeholder programs that are needed in the situations identified above, when development objectives at the country level cannot be achieved without them.

International Public Goods and the Process of Development Cooperation

International public goods partnerships hold the potential to relieve many of the process-related foreign aid shortcomings in cases where mission-oriented, multiactor networks can be called to life. Public goods pursued in individual ventures would serve as a rallying device for the coordination of the network of contributing partners. Fragmented behavior would have little place in the partnership, where its undermining of the very sense of purpose from which the network originated would be immediately apparent. Motivation and coordination among donors and partners would appear to be easier to achieve in the case of issue-oriented partnerships than in multisector, multiobjective country assistance programs. There would also seem to be less scope for politics to interfere with technical integrity.

The funding requirements of the partnerships could be calculated on a reasonably objective basis, given agreed-on program goals and phasing. (Maintaining adequate funding over the long term can be challenging, as the Consultative Group on International Agricultural Research—CGIAR—has demonstrated in recent years.) Selectivity would be ensured by the choice of public goods to be created. Shared learning would occur as a matter of course under the kinds of inclusive partnerships envisioned. And conditionality and the allocation of donor funds would not appear to be as contentious as in the case of country-based assistance.

As the domestic and the international dimensions of the development challenge become increasingly interrelated, issue-focused international partnerships can potentially go a long way toward securing ownership for domestic reform. Filling the policy gap at the regional and global levels means that reform becomes less dependent on intrusive conditionality. It is easier to encourage voluntary compliance with generally accepted international standards than to introduce top-down conditionality. But this presupposes both that developing countries are adequately represented in the partnerships that develop the standards and that coordinated national capacity and institution building take place to strengthen the ability to implement sectoral reform. There is a deficit on both counts.

The CDF provides a setting to address this. Its key tenets of inclusiveness and wholeness should be respected when partnerships at the regional and global levels are being established. Prioritization at the national level under the umbrella of the CDF can help identify areas where international programs are needed to supplement national efforts. Capacity building in national and local institutions (state and nonstate) is critical to the effective implementation of the resulting integrated endeavors.

Empirical Evidence

These predictions regarding the partnership and aid effectiveness merits of efforts to create international public goods need to be tested empirically. What can be said on the basis of partial evidence, while awaiting the conclusions of more formal analytical work?

Two long-standing international public goods ventures, the Onchocerciasis Control Program (OCP) in West Africa (Box 12.5) and the CGIAR appear to confirm our favorable hypothesis regarding the aid effectiveness boost of multicountry, multiactor sectoral partnerships. Both programs date from the early 1970s, and both display exceptionally high rates of return to investment. A key lesson of OCP is precisely that with the right kind of leadership, issue-oriented international campaigns can be highly effective. The vision underlying the program to eradicate riverblindness appears to have engendered a disciplined process and to have motivated participants to persevere. This is an important aspect because many development problems take a generation or more to solve. That perseverance contrasts virtuously with the sometimes observed proclivity of country-focused external assistance to succumb to the development fashion of the day.

An assessment of the CGIAR reached similar conclusions (Anderson and Dalrymple 1999).[2] A partnership of governments, multilateral institutions, and foundations, the CGIAR has catalyzed international collective action in the service of world food security. The program is devoted to sustainable crop improvement with a concentration on staple foods consumed by the poor. There is little incentive for private research for the crops of interest, which are mostly low-income-elasticity commodities. The CGIAR has generated impressive global externalities, and the partnership that it represents is a model of transnational standard-setting and governance in its field. It has often been suggested that something similar be created for tropical diseases or, more specifically, the underresearched "orphan" diseases that account for the bulk of the disease burden in poor countries. A recent move in that direction is the Global Forum for Health Research, established in 1997 as an independent, multiactor foundation hosted by the World Health Organization to correct the "10/90 disequilibrium"—the fact that only 10 percent of annual global spending on health research in the private and public sectors is devoted to the health needs of 90 percent of the world's population.

Other examples of successful regional and global public policy in development cooperation include the Special Program of Assistance for Africa (SPA) and the Global Environment Facility (see Box 12.3 and UNDP, UNEP, and the World Bank 1994). SPA is an association of donors aiming to support the adjustment and development process of Sub-Saharan African countries. Established in 1987, it has played an important role in aid coordination and consensus building among donors regarding the policies to be pursued. An independent evaluation by the World Bank's Operations Evaluation Department nevertheless identifies a number of recommendations for improved performance and stresses the need to involve African policymakers more closely (OED 1998).

Despite the documented merits of these and other instances of international collective action in development cooperation, two questions arise. First, beyond creating international public goods, have these programs successfully contributed to improvements in the corresponding sectors or policy domains in developing countries? And second, what of the doubtlessly numerous attempts at international public goods programs that have failed?

The National and International Public Goods Interface

The provision of international public goods may be ineffectual if unaccompanied by appropriate domestic action in developing countries. There may be a few international public goods provided by rich countries on which poor countries can free-ride—G7 (or United States) buyer-of-last-resort growth policies to support the world economy can be cited as an example. Poor countries benefit passively in this case. More often, however, international public goods—irrespective of who produces them—will benefit developing countries only if the countries invest in the corresponding national-level applications. Naturally, the converse is often (and probably increasingly) true: investment in national public goods without supporting international public goods may yield suboptimal returns.

Take the example of health research to serve the needs of the world's poor. The requirement for more international research and development should not mask the fact that responsibility for improved health outcomes lies primarily with poor countries themselves. Adequate national spending and policy reform to accommodate new health technology are critical. International partnerships can help set standards and generate energy for domestic reform. They can strengthen the hand of policy reformers in the domestic political context. Thus, for best results, international and national efforts should go forward in concert.

This is an important aspect to consider when examining the full contribution of these and other transnational public policy programs. The record on international public goods appears to be stellar in the case of, for example, the CGIAR. Is it comparably outstanding on building national capacity in the sector concerned and promoting domestic sectoral reform? Not necessarily. The CGIAR has done a remarkable job of generating spillover in the form of international public research goods capable of supporting the development of technology by national institutions in developing countries (Byerlee and Alex 1998; Purcell and Anderson 1997). But there is still a great need to strengthen national agricultural research programs in the poorest developing countries. SPA has made an enormous contribution in setting norms and standards for adjustment lending, among other aspects. But its interaction with decision makers on the ground and its impact on the performance of African economies have been modest at best. The GEF is the key instrument of the international community for funding programs relevant to the protection of the global environment. But its impact on country policies and programs has so far been limited (World Bank 1994).

Thus, more thought needs to be given to the interface between national and international public goods. Transnational public policy should be concerned with the question of synergy between investments in development resources at the national and supranational levels—a new dimension of aid coordination. The implication is not that investments in international public goods should wait until conditions are right for their application in most countries, but that conditions on the ground may need to be nurtured to speed the process of putting the international development goods to use.

This appears to have been recognized in the case of OCP. Ensuring the continuation of control activities after 2002, when the international partnership will cease to function, has long been a primary goal of the program. The program's primary control system (as well as that of the African Program for Onchocerciasis Control, or APOC) is currently community-directed treatment with Ivermectin, a process of active community participation in drug delivery and reporting. The approach recognizes decision-making and problem-solving by communities and health services as crucial to the installation of sustainable Ivermectin treatment. It is anticipated that this will help ensure the continuation of treatment and monitoring after 2002.

Both OCP and APOC are also concerned with capacity building. The staff of both programs is essentially local, and the training they receive ensures that the participating countries will be well equipped to take over ochocerciasis control when the programs end. In the OCP countries alone, more than 500 epidemiologists, entomologists, and other specialists have been trained, and 60 percent of them now work for the national ministries of health. More than 30,000 community drug distributors have also been trained. As a result of this preparation, countries will order Ivermectin directly and will soon take over all residual spraying, distribution of Ivermectin, and epidemiological surveillance. Additional surveillance will be provided by the regional multidisease surveillance center being established for West Africa. These measures should ensure that the progress made since 1975 will be safeguarded well into the future.[3]

The Promise and Challenge of International Public Goods Partnerships

International public goods partnerships hold both promises and challenges. The potential benefits to developing countries include solutions to transnational externalities affecting development prospects, more rapid progress in implementing domestic sectoral reform and in generating national public goods, and more advantageous integration into the global economy. But the challenges of implementation remain formidable. The development community needs to focus on new ways of cooperating to overcome practical and institutional hurdles in the area of international public goods.

Two kinds of hurdles are briefly addressed in concluding this paper—the motivation and ability of sovereign members of the international community to contribute to the supply of international public goods and the architectural issue of interinstitutional collaboration and multilateral leadership for the same purpose.

The motivation to contribute depends on the geographic reach of the transnational externalities to be controlled (public bads) or engendered (public goods). Unaffected countries are unlikely to be concerned, but interdependence means, first, that many transnational public policy themes have far-reaching (if not global) repercussions and, second, that global constituencies interested in the outcome of local and regional issues may be found half a world away. Remaining disengaged is frequently not an option.

But motivation is conditioned by the ability to act. Not all participants are equally capable of contributing to specified international public goods. Kanbur, Sandler, and Morrison (1999) have suggested different aggregation technologies to characterize the manner in which individual contributions to a particular public good help determine the total quantity of the good available for consumption. Their analysis speaks to the role of developing countries and donor countries in public goods partnerships.

According to their analysis, the overall supply of "best shot" international public goods is determined by the largest individual contribution toward the creation of the good. Efficiency considerations suggest that products of this kind be developed where the chance of success is greatest. In the case of highly knowledge-intensive ventures such as vaccine development, this means research institutions in donor countries. Once generated, the resources should be made available to developing countries.

The overall supply of "weakest link" international public goods is determined by the smallest individual contribution. Infectious disease control comes to mind. Within a given spillover community, the spread of disease is a function of the weakest effort undertaken by a member of that community.

Best shot goods thus tend to require investment in donor countries or wherever they are most efficiently produced. The work design should ensure that the products to be created respond to the needs of developing countries. As argued above, national capacity building efforts may be needed to enable these countries to take advantage of the international public goods. Weakest link goods require capacity-building in developing countries to create the goods—not the same as the capacity-building needed to get the most out of best shot goods created elsewhere. Developing countries may be able to bring considerable bargaining power to bear on negotiations with donors eager to see progress in the realization of "weakest link" goods, such as biodiversity preservation or controlling the spread of infectious or vector-borne disease.

In short, not all international public goods are alike when viewed from the point of view of generation technology and the roles and demands placed on different types of actors, in this case recipient and donor countries. This is an area for further reflection in the context of efforts to prioritize investments in international public goods.

On the role of multilateral institutions and interagency collaboration, it should be recalled that many agencies, in particular multilateral development banks, operate on a one-on-one country basis. Their lending programs will continue to operate on that basis. At the same time, if there is merit to the arguments advanced in this paper, multilateral agencies need to reinvent themselves with a view to responding to transnational public policy challenges. Their role as providers of knowledge, information, standards, and expertise and their role as honest brokers (Martin 1999) will be critical in fostering an international public goods approach to cooperation.

Institutional economics shows the need for a mixture of leadership and participation in creating public goods (Picciotto 1995, 1998). In the case of international public goods, leadership responsibility falls disproportionately on multilateral institutions—they are credible in ways that national governments and special interest groups such as NGOs and global corporations are not.

The important role that reverts to multilateral institutions in the area of international public goods suggests an architectural problem: the multiplicity of international agencies is not necessarily coherently employed in the face of this challenge. While discussion of that issue is beyond the scope of this paper, the international public goods agenda may yield food for thought on interinstitutional collaboration and the comparative advantage of, for example, the United Nations agencies (many with clear global or regional mandates) and the international financial institutions. Unresolved aspects of this discussion include the organizational implications of the evolving (knowledge-intensive and collective action promoting) role of multilateral institutions, the future shape of the bilateral-multilateral binomial in its many expressions, and new kinds of nondependency-inducing partnerships with developing countries in the creation of key international public goods. The subsidiarity issue in multilateral cooperation—devolution of responsibility according to the comparative advantage of different actors—is another worthy topic of debate. If the time is right for the international community to consider devoting greater attention to transnational problem solving, then a case can be made for exploring the implications for multilateralism.

Notes

1. Foreign aid is defined as official development finance from bilateral and multilateral sources. It includes grants and concessional and nonconcessional loans.
2. This study cautioned, however, that "in reporting research accomplishments, the basic problems are aggregation and attribution" (p. 51).
3. I am grateful to Bruce Benton and Chris Dragisic of the Onchocerciasis Control Unit at the World Bank for these data on OCP.

References

Anderson, J. R., and D. G. Dalrymple. 1999. *The World Bank, the Grant Program, and the CGIAR: A Retrospective Review*. World Bank–OED Working Paper Series, No. 1. Washington, D.C.: Operations Evaluation Department.

Byerlee, D., and G. E. Alex. 1998. *Strengthening National Agricultural Research Systems: Policy Issues and Good Practice*. Environmentally and Socially Sustainable Development Series, Rural Development. Washington, D.C.: World Bank.
Chen, L. C., T. G. Evans, and R. A. Cash. 1999. "Health as a Global Public Good." In I. Kaul, I. Grunberg, and M. A. Stern, eds., *Global Public Goods: International Cooperation in the 21st Century*. New York: Oxford University Press for the United Nations Development Programme.
Collier, P. 1997. "The Failure of Conditionality." In C. Gwin and J. Nelson, eds., *Perspectives on Aid and Development*. Washington, D.C.: Overseas Development Council, ODC Policy Essay No. 22.
Collier, P., and D. Dollar. 1998. "Aid Allocation and Poverty Reduction." Washington, D.C.: World Bank, Development Research Group.
Gaddy, C., and B. Ickes. 1998. "Russia's Virtual Economy." *Foreign Affairs* 77: pp. 53–67.
Gwin, C. 1999. "The New Development Cooperation Paradigm." *ODC Viewpoint*. Washington, D.C.: Overseas Development Council.
Hirschman, A.O. 1958. *The Strategy of Economic Development*. New Haven, CT: Yale University Press.
Jayaraman, R., and R. Kanbur. 1999. "International Public Goods and the Case for Foreign Aid." In I. Kaul, I. Grunberg, and M. A. Stern, eds., *Global Public Goods: International Cooperation in the 21st Century*. New York: Oxford University Press for the United Nations Development Programme.
Kanbur, R., T. Sandler, and K. M. Morrison. 1999. *The Future of Development Assistance: Common Pools and International Public Goods*. Washington, D.C.: Overseas Development Council, Policy Essay No. 25.
Kaul, I., I. Grunberg, and M. A. Stern eds. 1999. *Global Public Goods: International Cooperation in the 21st Century*. New York: Oxford University Press for the UNDP.
Killick, T., R. Gunatilaka, and A. Marr. 1998. *Aid and the Political Economy of Policy Change*. New York: Routledge.
Martin, L. I. 1999. "The Political Economy of International Cooperation." In I. Kaul, I. Grunberg, and M. A. Stern, eds., *Global Public Goods: International Cooperation in the 21st Century*. New York: Oxford University Press for the UNDP.
ODI (Overseas Development Institute). 1998. "Promises to the Poor: The Record of European Development Agencies." *ODI Poverty Briefing*, No. 1.
OECD (Organisation for Economic Co-operation and Development). 1998. *A Review of the International Aid System in Mali: A Synthesis*. Paris, France.
OED (Operations Evaluations Department). 1998. *The Special Program of Assistance for Africa (SPA): An Independent Evaluation*. Washington, D.C.: World Bank.
Picciotto, R. 1995. *Putting Institutional Economics to Work*. World Bank Discussion Paper 304. Washington, D.C.
———. 1998. "The Logic of Partnership." Washington, D.C.: World Bank, Operations Evaluations Department.
Porter, G., R. Clemencon, W. Ofosu-Amaah, and M. Philips, eds. 1998. *Study of GEF's Overall Performance*. Washington, D.C.: Global Environment Facility Secretariat.
Purcell, D. L., and J. R. Anderson. 1997. *Agricultural Extension and Research: Achievements and Problems in National Systems*. Washington, D.C.: Operations Evaluations Department.
Reinicke, W. H. *1998. Global Public Policy: Governing without Government?* Washington, D.C.: Brookings Institution Press.

Sandler, T. 1998. "Global and Regional Public Goods: A Prognosis for Collective Action." *Fiscal Studies* 19: p. 3.

Sjoberg, Helen. 1994. *From Idea to Reality: the Creation of the Global Environment Facility*. GEF Working Paper 10. Washington, D.C: Global Environment Facility.

Slaughter, A.-M. 1997. "The Real New World Order." *Foreign Affairs* 76: pp. 183–97.

Stiglitz, J. E. 1998. "Towards a New Paradigm for Development: Strategies, Policies, Processes." The 1998 Prebisch lecture, UNCTAD, Geneva, Switzerland, October 19.

UNDP (United Nations Development Program), UNEP (United Nations Environment Program), and World Bank. 1994. *Global Environment Facility: Independent Evaluation of the World Bank Pilot Phase*. Washington, D.C.: World Bank.

World Bank. 1998. *Assessing Aid: What Works, What Doesn't and Why*. New York: Oxford University Press for the World Bank.

Part 5

Synthesis

13

Promising Approaches
to Development Challenges

Nagy Hanna

The previous chapters have illuminated many of the challenges inherent in the Comprehensive Development Framework (CDF)—the emerging development compact between donors, aid agencies, and the governments and people of developing countries. These chapters have looked at the basic principles of the CDF, the implications of country ownership for conditionality and participation, new multisectoral and integrated approaches to development planning, the transformation of tools and instruments used by aid agencies, and new modes of partnership. They demonstrate the need to respond to a changing environment for development as donors and countries move beyond the current short-term, project-based development framework to one that emphasizes interactions among policies, investments, and institutions and their dynamics over the long term. They have shown that aid agencies need to promote more effective development assistance through national processes and institutions that address and manage the new challenges and opportunities arising from the global environment.

The new approach to development rests on transferring ownership to the aid recipient, focusing development plans and aid management on results, and broadening partnerships and addressing the global dimensions of development. However, key to each of these is allowing for greater flexibility in relationships and employing instruments that allow for adaptation by aid agency and recipient. Such "learning for comprehensive development" will be central to further progress in development effectiveness.

This chapter sums up the challenges that emerge from this analysis at the sectoral and country levels and their implications for implementation of the CDF and the new Poverty Reduction Strategy Papers (see Box 13.1). It draws on the findings of the Operations Evaluation Department (OED) of the World Bank to underline that much learning and experimentation will be needed to practice the CDF principles. It also outlines promising approaches for addressing these challenges, since resolving such dilemmas is key to effective management of aid in development. Finally, it explores the implications of the CDF principles for aid agencies, which will need to transform their institutional processes and instruments, taking a learning-oriented approach to development activities. A "one-size-fits-all" mindset will have to be replaced by an adaptable approach that is compatible with country autonomy and learning. Such change will take time, but as the preceding chapters have shown, the development climate today seems especially receptive to such a transformation.

Challenges in Sectoral and Thematic Programs

Many of the challenges at the sectoral and thematic levels are a result of tensions that need to be managed, taking into account country-specific factors: short- and long-term perspectives, comprehensiveness and selectivity, speed and broad-based ownership, partnership and country capacity and transaction costs, and accountability for results and local capacity.

Development efforts tend to have a short-term orientation, but only a longer-term perspective can deal with the structural dimensions of development. The more comprehensive approaches needed for sustainable development can lead to greater complexity and reduced selectivity. Speed in implementation, which accompanies the short-term perspective of aid agencies, often compromises ownership. The governance reforms needed to institutionalize participation may take decades to complete, while achieving full participation by all stakeholders requires time to build sustained commitment from reformers and donors alike. Partnerships with external partners and aid coordination increase development effectiveness and reduce demands on government capacity, but they can also increase transaction costs. Finally, while decentralization, privatization, and weak regulation have raised new challenges for monitoring and evaluation, local capacity constraints and inadequate indicators still impede the ability to track the development impact of lending, especially the impact on poverty.

Box 13.1 Challenges and Promising Approaches	
Challenges and Tensions	**Promising Approaches**
• Short- versus long-term	• Learning process, not blueprints • Use of sequencing to manage complexity
• Comprehensiveness versus selectivity	• Comprehensive analysis and selective actions • Programmatic approaches tailored to countries and sectors
• Ownership versus conditionality • Speed versus broad-based ownership	• Adaptable conditionality for a mutual commitment process • Time for building consensus • Broadening of participation
• Accountability for results versus local capacity • Poor accountability record versus scaling up	• Information for accountability and learning • Capacity building to manage for results
• Partnership versus country capacity and transaction costs • Country focus versus globalization and global goals	• From aid coordination to development partnership • Linking global to local

Short- versus Long-Term Perspective

Many factors contribute to the short-term orientation of development efforts: the project approach, financial crises, political instability, the election cycle, and the incentive systems of the civil service, as well as the incentives and planning processes of aid agencies. Yet fundamental issues of development, such as institutional development and governance, require long-term strategies and sustained efforts (Chap. 1).

A long-term perspective is especially important in dealing with the structural dimensions of development. Among recent failures to take the long view are privatization in transition economies, civil service reform, and deregulation of the financial sector (World Bank 1998b; Stiglitz 1998). Privatization increases inequality without contributing to growth if the appropriate regulatory framework and environment for private sector development are missing. In transition economies the rush to mass privatization, without establishing the underpinnings of capitalism, led to corrupt sales, asset stripping, lack of restructuring, insider-dominated transactions, and failure to induce domestic and foreign investment.

The more ambitious the reform, the more time and resources that are needed to prepare the way. A long-term commitment is essential. A World Bank evaluation study of financial sector operations found that they are more likely to succeed in a country when pursued over time through a series of operations. Equally, resettlement operations call for involvement of affected communities many years before the infrastructure investments take place (OED 1998b).

Comprehensiveness versus Selectivity

More comprehensive approaches frequently imply greater complexity and implementation difficulties for sectorwide and multisectoral programs (Chap. 2). Thematic, cross-sectoral, and structural dimensions are particularly challenging for sector-bound aid agencies and government ministries and are often ignored. For example, it took decades of external pressure and top management leadership to bring environmental considerations into the Bank's operations. Gender, public sector management, and private sector development issues raise similar challenges (OED 1997b).

Following the debt crisis of the 1980s, the Bank broadened its view to address systemic financial sector problems. But with increased comprehensiveness, the success rate of financial sector operations dropped to 50 percent (OED 1997b).[1] A World Bank review of recently closed operations supporting financial sector reforms found that success is often attributable to government ownership and commitment, consensus building, favorable political climate, and good policy dialogue (OED 1997b). Similarly, comprehensive multisectoral technical assistance operations have overtaxed borrower's management capacity, sacrificed focus and specialization, and persisted with increasingly detailed but irrelevant blueprints; these operations have been rated the lowest in the World Bank's portfolio (World Bank. 1997).

A focus on discrete investments under the control of independent project implementation units rather than integrated programs under existing ministries or local governments has been common in multisectoral projects (World Bank 1998a; Chap. 2). Working around ministries has advantages, but sustainability often suffers. Services provided through social fund agencies are particularly vulnerable because of weak links to existing government structures. The Bolivia Social Fund's emphasis on speed and autonomy from line ministries worked against fitting projects into sectoral plans. The assessments for social funds in Armenia, Ecuador, and Peru highlighted the need for complementary actions, such as funding educational material and other inputs along with infrastructure in school projects or including training in water and sanitation projects. Inattention to complementary requirements can put the impact of the project at risk, not to mention the satisfaction with use and maintenance of projects.

Multisectoral programs have been difficult to sustain without good coordination with ongoing programs of sectoral ministries. In Mali's Integrated Health, Population, and Rural Water Supply Program, implemented by several line agencies, the population and water supply components were not always well coordinated with the health component. Involvement of many agencies made programs difficult to monitor and implement. The challenges of managing multisectoral, multiagency programs were compounded by weak incentives and mechanisms for intersectoral coordination within countries and within the Bank (OED 1999b).

Integrated programs may also generate tensions between line agencies and ministries of finance or other oversight bodies. Activities requiring recurrent funding can create ownership conflicts between central and local governments, especially in non-revenue earning operations such as highways. Implementation of a Thailand highways project, an integrated intervention designed to address cross-sectoral issues, was marred by conflicts among different agencies. Implementing agencies were strongly committed to the physical works but less committed to policy reforms, in part because policymaking rested elsewhere in the government (OED 1997b). Similarly, urban development projects involving multiple sectors have provoked detrimental competition among oversight agencies, making them unmanageable.

Sectorwide approaches are necessarily ambitious, complex, and demanding, especially of supervision time and skills mix. In the energy sector, for example, the global move from public monopolies toward privatization and deregulation has required tackling a much broader range of issues: sector unbundling, private participation, regulation, competition, interregional trade, resettlement, environment, access by the poor, and renewable energy sources, among others. A wholesale movement toward programmatic lending is likely to increase these challenges.

Operationalizing a sectorwide approach through program lending has had mixed results so far. World Bank energy sector loans to Pakistan, the Philippines, and Turkey fell short of objectives because they were too complex — the fiscal 1989 Pakistan energy sector adjustment loan had more than forty conditions. Phased or incremental approaches have been more successful. In China a succession of incrementally more policy-intensive power sector operations succeeded because of a realistic assessment of institutional capacity, judicious use of technical assistance loans to build greater capacity, and effective use of analytical and advisory services. But a phased, sequenced, and sustained mode of assistance is not the preferred option for episodic, short-term oriented aid agencies.

Speed versus Broad-Based Ownership

The lack of government ownership of reforms or community ownership of local projects has undermined development efforts (Chaps. 3 and 4). Evaluations show that ownership is difficult to achieve in sectors that have a broad array of stakeholders with different interests, such as health and education; in thematic and structural areas, such as environment, rural development, and civil service reform; and in sectors where resources provided through state channels are under pressure, such as agriculture. Partners may have different views of the roles of the state, the private sector, and civil society. Coalition building and media campaigns to overcome vested interests or hold the bureaucracy to account may not be feasible. Thus governance reforms may be required to institutionalize participation, and this may take decades to accomplish.

Speed often compromises ownership. In a spirit of priority setting and capacity building, the World Bank has helped a number of governments address environmental issues through national environmental action plans and programs for strengthening national and local environmental institutions. But a 1996 review reveals that, for the most part, the environmental plans had not elicited local ownership. Many of the plans were prepared in haste and driven by deadlines that left little time for participation.[2] Making the plans a requirement for lending further eroded country support.

The interests of different ministries (and the priorities of center and districts) can vary and even conflict. Uneven stakeholder commitment and weak capacity can pose risks. World Bank evaluators found that the success of health sector projects was significantly correlated with how well program designers had assessed ownership by key stakeholders, including concrete evidence of commitment (OED 1999a).

In education, too, the number of stakeholders is very large, with many agencies and institutions involved in executing policies. Responsibility for selecting policy reforms and deciding on mechanisms to encourage support must come from within the country and be grounded in broad-based support for reform. The clear implication is that borrowers should be encouraged to take a leadership role in the preparation of projects and that all stakeholders, including women and the poor, should be fully engaged. But this takes time and sustained commitment from reformers and donors.

Thematic strategies of cross-cutting areas like environment or rural development have a better chance of being successfully implemented when a range of public and private stakeholders participate. Lessons from The Gambia, Ghana, Madagascar, and Mauritius suggest this for the environment. In Madagascar and Mauritius, national environmental action plans were able to increase local environmental capacity more than in some other countries because of substantial local ownership (Margulis and Bernstein 1995). The more participatory plans were also successful in information gathering and public education.

Accountability for Results versus Local Capacity

Tracking the development impact of policy-based and investment lending has been weak almost across the board (OED 1998a). Key factors contributing to a weak focus on results are the blueprint approach to policy and investment planning and the poor accountability for results among aid agencies and client governments. Monitoring and evaluation for results has been easier to achieve in infrastructure lending than in structural (public and private sector development), social (health, education), and thematic (environment, rural development) lending.

Monitoring and evaluation have also been weak in newer development dimensions, such as gender and knowledge. Aid agency evaluators have consistently identified weak monitoring and evaluation capacity (even for tracking inputs and outputs) and the need for greater attention to learning from results through sectorwide and thematic efforts.

Decentralization, privatization, and weak regulation have raised new challenges for monitoring and evaluation. Chile's power sector is typical: the combination of unbundling, privatization, and weak regulation led to deterioration in monitoring and evaluation (OED 1996). A clear lesson is that aid agencies should focus on sectorwide monitoring and evaluation as an integral part of their assistance in setting up regulatory frameworks.

Identification of relevant indicators has been a technical and negotiating challenge (balancing process with outcome indicators, ensuring coverage of key issues, and agreeing on a manageable numbers of indicators among key stakeholders). A concern expressed in Ghana's health sector program was that the indicators emphasized the priorities of donors more than those of national stakeholders or consumers. In addition, institutional mechanisms have rarely been created for improving performance incentives at district and facility levels. Too much emphasis on process indicators (decentralization, budget allocations) may compromise achievement of outcomes, as in health projects in Zambia (OED 1999b).

Perhaps the most serious shortcoming is the failure of aid agencies to monitor the impact of development programs on poverty and to build capacity to evaluate such programs. The World Bank, for example, has rarely used its lending portfolio to systematically collect evidence on what works in reducing poverty, what does not, and why (Evans 2000). Few rural projects have supported those who work with the poor or enhanced the monitoring of resource allocations to the poor. Indicators used were generally input measures, such as the number of personnel trained or wage expenditures rather than outcomes. Project completion and evaluation reports have often lacked a focus on poverty outcomes.

Partnership versus Country Capacity and Transaction Costs

Partnerships with external partners may be essential for coordinating development programs, reducing demands on government capacity, and enhancing selectivity and comparative advantage among aid agencies (Chap. 11; OED 1999b). Evaluations have highlighted examples of effective coordination with donors in transport, telecommunications, and energy. In many other areas, however, partnerships have a long way to go, especially in health, education, and other currently active areas of development assistance.

While aid coordination can reduce demands on government capacity, a lack of implementation capacity can still undermine reform. A World Bank Operations Evaluation Department (OED) evaluation of the Ghana Private Sector Adjustment Project concluded that "required expertise should be on board before the process begins, and potential legal issues, like land transfers, which proved problematic in Ghana, should be carefully reviewed in advance." An evaluation of Jamaica's Private Sector Development Adjustment loan highlighted the need to assess borrower capacity to implement reforms as well as borrower commitment. The borrower's own evaluation was highly critical of unrealistic demands by the Bank on Jamaica's weak implementation capacity.

Partnership and aid coordination may increase transaction costs. A Ghana health operation that adopted a sectorwide approach provided only marginally higher supervision resources than for a conventional investment project (OED 1999a). This limited the ability to establish a local presence, include appropriate technical expertise in supervision missions, or adequately participate in coordination meetings.

A better approach may be to promote strategic selectivity by sharing responsibility for sectorwide assistance among donors, relying more on pooled technical assistance support under government control, and resisting the inclination by any single aid agency to take on all tasks and cover all bases.[3] More intense supervision of increasingly complex projects will undoubtedly boost their effectiveness, but complex projects also involve opportunity and transaction costs for governments: senior officials' attention is directed to supervising missions at the cost of neglecting other, possibly more pressing issues.

Donor pressure also diverts a disproportionate share of scarce local budgets and staff to service a bewildering number of donor projects.

Challenges at the Country Level

At the country level, the CDF principles of comprehensive, country-led development pose important challenges as well. Here the tensions that need to be managed include ownership and conditionality, accountability and country-led partnerships and commitment, poor accountability record and scaling up, and country focus and globalization.

New forms of reciprocal and adaptive conditionality can help to resolve conflicts between country ownership and donor conditionality. Similarly, reconciling donor needs for accountability for aid effectiveness with client-led partnership and ownership will require country commitment to sound policies and institutional capacity to manage aid. The CDF emphasizes accountability for results at all levels, well beyond projects, yet efforts to build monitoring and evaluation capacity have focused mainly on project-level inputs, with predictably poor impact on sustainable domestic capacity for broad-based monitoring and evaluation. As globalization intensifies, the number of development problems requiring supranational policy responses and stronger links between national strategies and international programs also grows. Adapting global solutions to national conditions remains a major challenge for aid agencies.

Ownership versus Conditionality

How should the apparent conflict between country ownership and donor interest in performance and accountability (often enforced through conditionality) be resolved? How should the need for ownership be reconciled with the need for policy reform and sound development priorities?

Conditionality is widely viewed as a crude attempt to generate policy reform in exchange for grants or loans. Research and evaluation findings have shown that when applied as a one-sided, coercive instrument, conditionality can be counterproductive and incompatible with ownership (Chaps. 3 and 6). Some observers have rushed to declare all forms of conditionality a failure, a conclusion unsupported by the evidence. But the principles of ownership and partnership clearly call for reconciling the accountability of donors and countries through new forms of conditionality that are reciprocal and adaptive.

Poor Accountability Record versus Scaling Up

Despite evaluation evidence of the importance of monitoring and evaluation for learning and accountability, the record remains far from satisfactory.

The International Development Goals and recent attention to governance reinforce the need for enhanced accountability for results.

Past activities to build monitoring and evaluation capacity have focused on the project level, and mainly on inputs or volumes of lending, to satisfy donor requirements. The resulting lack of domestic ownership of monitoring and evaluation has undermined the use of its findings and the acceptance of performance measurement for sound governance (OED 1994). The limited capacity created through donor-driven, project-based monitoring and evaluation has been dissipated at project completion. The CDF raises the bar by emphasizing learning and accountability for results at all levels—well beyond projects.

Accountability for Results versus Country-Led Partnership and Commitment

How should donor demands for accountability be reconciled with client-led partnership, particularly when countries lack capacity for aid coordination or commitment to reforms? How can having the country in the driver's seat be reconciled with donors' accountability for aid effectiveness?

Two enabling conditions for country-led partnership are often missing: country commitment to sound policies and development priorities, and institutional capacity to manage and coordinate aid (Chap. 11; OED 1999b). Donor-related barriers to country-led coordination are donors' onerous and varied administrative procedures, continued reliance on independent project implementation units, and the numerous missions that countries must accommodate. For highly aid-dependent countries, these burdens can add up to thousands of reports and missions each year. These practices also undermine capacity development, public sector reform, and local accountability.

Country Focus versus Globalization and Global Goals

With globalization, development problems increasingly require multicountry efforts and strengthened links between national strategies and international policies and programs. Global forces (including technological change) are creating not only far-reaching growth opportunities, but also a host of potential problems—capital flight, financial contagion, illicit drug trade, cross-border environmental problems, the spread of disease, waves of migrants and refugees, and loss of biodiversity and cultural heritage. These cross-border challenges arise from a combination of market failure, government failure, and systemic failure.

The challenge of overcoming such failures creates a new role for development assistance. The country focus remains critical, but official development finance also must help meet the rising deficit in the supply of international public goods and global policies and standards. How can international efforts aimed at global public goods complement national efforts? How can aid agencies make globalization work for developing countries, particularly for the poor?

There is a growing drive to set and meet International Development Goals for poverty reduction. These targets are important to facilitate global action, to mobilize political commitment and resources, and to facilitate partnerships among donors. But this drive must avoid the pitfalls of target-based planning (Chap. 2) and conditionality (Chap. 3). Adapting global prescriptions to local conditions and engendering broad ownership remain major challenges to aid agencies.

Promising Approaches

While the challenges and tensions at the project, sector, and country levels are substantial and long-standing, promising approaches are being identified for addressing them (see Box 13.1), synthesized from the lessons of experience of developing countries and evaluative evidence of aid agencies. These are a good beginning, but more systematic learning is needed to enrich the toolkit and assess the strengths and limits of these approaches.

Learning Process, Not Blueprints

The blueprint approach has been a common pitfall—it seems to simplify decision-making and reduce uncertainties, particularly for aid agencies. But it imposes standard solutions on poorly understood sociopolitical issues and varied local realities and ignores social capital and local institutions, sustainability and learning, and the capacity to adapt during implementation. It also imposes rigid plans and conditions and thus ignores the uncertainties and volatility of global and local environments and their impact on growth and the poor.

OED lessons indicate that adaptive experimentation and sustainable learning through multiple rapid-results initiatives give better outcomes than a one-size-fits-all, "best practice" comprehensive blueprint (World Bank 1993, 1994). A learning process means starting small, building in a bias for action, and avoiding new bureaucracies. It emphasizes flexible, evolutionary, participatory, results-oriented, and client-driven processes. It calls for thinking thematically and managing across sectors without undercutting professional rigor and accountability. Building capacity to learn and act strategically and to manage risk and uncertainty is at least as important as preparing plans (Chaps. 2 and 7).

There are inevitably tradeoffs between detailed analysis and up-front design on the one hand and adaptation during implementation on the other. The new approach implied by the CDF requires a significant shift of resources from program design to implementation support and participatory monitoring and evaluation. A fundamental lesson from both development planning and corporate experience is that strategies emerge from continuous interactions of top-down and bottom-up learning processes (Chaps. 5 and 7). Top-down and upfront design approaches are best combined with bottom-up and learning process approaches to enable local initiatives, identify and scale up successes, promote stakeholder commitment, and ensure adaptation over time.

Adaptable program lending embodies some aspects of the learning process approach—agreement on long-term objectives and broad directions, with design limited to startup processes and capacity building. A learning process was embedded in Brazil's Water and Sanitation Program for Low-Income Settlements (PROSANEAR). Design was demand-based and iterative, shaped during implementation by beneficiary participation, feedback, and learning (OED 1999d). The program developed partnerships among residents for the selection and management of water and sanitation systems. Community mobilization and group decision-making were carried out differently in each community, depending on levels of social cohesion and other factors. The program encouraged ongoing evaluation of each community's experience for rapid feedback to the next subproject in an adaptive learning approach. Evaluation of Brazil's Northeast Rural Development Program reaches similar conclusions (OED 2000).

Use of Sequencing to Manage Complexity

Projects have become more complex since the early 1990s, along with Bank thinking about development. Managing the tradeoffs between comprehensiveness and selectivity requires an understanding of the sources of complexity. Insufficient upstream sector work before project preparation and appraisal leads to inadequate selectivity and mismatch with local capacity. Fiduciary requirements are becoming more demanding. There is pressure to add components to deal with the Bank's expanding agenda and survive the internal approval process. Career and budgetary incentives encourage the design of large projects and discourage priority-setting (OED 1997a). At the country level there is often a desire for large resource transfers, full-scale national coverage, and empire building by the implementing agency.

One way out of the complexity trap is the long-term view, sequencing a series of projects within a long-term strategy that builds on past learning. The real issue is often *premature* complexity. Projects that build on past learning and are integrated into existing practices can be complex and yet successful, as the Bangladesh Population Project and the Brazil Health Program show (OED 1997a). Repeater projects have higher rates of success, especially when carried out within a strategic and long-term framework. But repeater projects should not distract from the need for innovation and high-impact projects. The search for long-term strategies should not distract from timely investment in targets of opportunity (Chaps. 2, 7, and 10).

Another promising approach is to phase in coverage and expand geographical scope in line with government capacity to manage policy reform and implement the program. Accordingly, growth and poverty alleviation interventions should be piloted regionally and then progressively broadened and tailored to local contexts. This regional-focus approach is enhanced by explicit attention to capacity-building and progressive decentralization. Learning and innovation loans offer a suitable tool for managing complexity by starting small. There are often tradeoffs between innovation and scaling up. Adequate implementation support and monitoring and evaluation resources should be available to ensure learning during implementation and to build the basis for scaling up and managing complexity.

Comprehensive Analysis and Selective Actions

Comprehensive analysis should be combined with focused and selective actions. Comprehensive analysis is best conducted with key partners with a view to exercising selectivity in interventions in line with donor comparative advantage, country capacity and commitment, and the likely impact of such interventions. But donor selectivity—in terms of which countries, sectors and services to support—must move beyond the currently static and superficial definitions to more dynamic and strategic approaches that take account of needs, scale, nature of service, initial conditions, and the long-term comparative advantages of donor and partner institutions (Chap. 11).

Selectivity—in terms of focus, prioritization, and sequencing of national development and poverty reduction programs—should be primarily exercised by the country, the local community, and the poor. Through participatory approaches, poor people can express their priorities, choices, and tradeoffs, improving selectivity and results. The participatory poverty assessment process holds promise, as evidenced in Ghana and Uganda, where it brought the realities and priorities of the poor to the attention of national policymakers (Chap. 4). For participatory approaches to lead to superior selectivity and results, participants need access to information, options, and learning experience, as social fund and community-driven development programs have shown (World Bank 1998a). However, ensuring effective participation presents additional challenges. Experience suggests that the community does not demand some types of social fund projects, such as family planning, although these activities may have high social returns. The poor in a community do not come forward with proposals because of limited voice and capacity to propose projects.

The sustainable livelihoods approach provides an analytical structure for understanding the factors influencing poverty and identifying where interventions might best be made (DFID 1998). It emphasizes people-centered development in a holistic framework. This approach has been adopted by the UK Department for International Development, the United Nations Development Programme, and CARE, among others. It proposes an integrated and dynamic way of understanding poverty and thinking about poor people's livelihoods—the capabilities, assets (human, natural, financial, social, and physical), and activities required to earn a living. The approach builds on what people have and how they live their lives to add to their accumulation of assets and remove barriers to the realization of their own livelihood choices.

Central to this approach is a recognition of people's diverse livelihood goals—such as health, income, and reduced vulnerability—and the complex household strategies adopted to meet them. Strategies are driven by preferences and priorities shaped by vulnerability to shocks and seasonal variations. Options are also influenced by structures (the form and organization of government and the private sector) and processes (policies, laws, institutions). Selectivity is thus exercised by the community and is based on a broad understanding of poor people's diverse livelihood strategies.

Programmatic and Sectorwide Approaches

A programmatic approach provides an opportunity to shift attention from inputs to monitoring against agreed intermediate and outcome indicators (Chaps. 8 and 9). The Bangladesh and Ghana sectorwide approaches are good examples. They have been supported by two programmatic investment instruments: sector investment and maintenance loans, and adaptable program loans.

The sector investment and maintenance loan is intended to bring sectoral investments, policies, and performance in line with economic priorities and to ensure efficient operation and maintenance of investments. The focus is on institutional capacity to plan, implement, and monitor investments. Adaptable program loans are especially well suited to the support of sectorwide approaches that require embodying flexibility in what is financed. A recent review concluded that several operations would probably not have been brought to the approval stage without this new instrument because of the difficulty predicting costs, implementation arrangements, and results beyond three or four years.

Moving from projects to a full-scale programmatic or sectorwide approach (with pooling of donor finances) is risky if done prematurely (Chaps. 8 and 9). Proper implementation takes time and systematic capacity building. Its pace should vary with the quality of macroeconomic and public expenditure management, sector policies and resources, quality of sector management, degree of aid dependence, and other country- and sector-specific factors. Because sectorwide approaches add to program complexity for donors, more resources are required for implementation assistance, and effective partnerships become essential. Risks should be addressed and managed by supporting capacity building, setting clear performance targets and safeguards, strengthening financial accountability, and emphasizing monitoring and evaluation.

The fiduciary risks for donors are likely to be higher for sectorwide or programmatic lending than for project lending, since more fungible forms of financing are included. But these risks should be balanced against the costs to recipients of doing "business as usual." The proliferation of projects and project implementation units puts an enormous burden on weak administrations, undermining local capacity-building and sustainability. Balancing the fiduciary risk against current costs of doing business is therefore critical to the adoption, phasing, and adaptation of programmatic assistance.

As the development community moves to address interdependencies across sectors through programmatic lending and comprehensive analysis, a word of caution is due. Such broad, crosscutting approaches inevitably sacrifice depth in favor of breadth of advisory and financial assistance. Programmatic adjustment and investment lending will require staff skills and partnerships with client countries that will span many sectors and institutions. This approach may not adequately address complex reforms and interdependencies within sectors, where long-term, intensive, and in-depth assistance would be needed, and where broad-brush analysis and general knowledge would be inadequate. A wholesale shift towards programmatic lending is therefore ill-advised. A balance between comprehensive and in-depth assistance is necessary. This balance would involve a mix of instruments ranging from pilot and sector-based projects to sectorwide and multisectoral programmatic lending and comprehensive analyses, such as the Poverty Reduction Strategy Papers. This mix must match country conditions, local institutional capabilities, budget management, governance systems, and policy performance (Chaps. 7 and 8).

Adaptable Conditionality for a Mutual Commitment Process

Conditionality should be understood as a credible indicator of commitment, not an attempt to force externally designed policy changes on unwilling governments. Aid agencies act as enabling agencies to support the country's motivation for a reform process that is guided by genuine learning from successes and failures. This type of conditionality is agreed and consensual. It represents a policy compact based on mutual commitment.

Support for conditionality as a commitment process comes from a recent study on high-impact adjustment lending, a reevaluation of the *Assessing Aid* data using the country as the unit of observation, and a set of case studies on *Aid and Reform in Africa* (Chap. 3). In both studies, past success is shown to be a highly significant predictor of future success. This result supports the view of conditionality as a process of mutual commitment, since the Bank can refer to lending history in formulating future conditionality. Such conditionality is adapted as a country increases its ownership of reform, assisted by capacity-building to achieve parity in the relationship. Ongoing reformers can be offered the option of ex-post conditionality, while credible new reformers might choose to adopt floating tranche loans, as in the high-impact adjustment loan approach in Africa. Furthermore, policy reform conditions should take more flexible and adaptable forms than is currently practiced, to allow room for local learning, adaptation, and innovation. Blueprint approaches to institutional reform, in particular, are unlikely to be helpful or sustainable.

Conditionality should be part of a policy reform compact: the Bank and the borrower develop and then nurture mutual trust and commitment as reform proceeds. Conditionality is the Bank's side of a continuing relationship, while ownership is the country's side. A model for this approach is the relationship between a commercial bank and its customers: as long as the customer projects a credible path of earnings, lending continues.

Assessing ownership should lead to the use of selectivity to time and shape support for reform. For example, taking advantage of India's decentralized decisionmaking to demonstrate the benefits of reform, the World Bank shifted its policy dialogue from the federal to the state level and engaged only reforming states. Ownership and partnership were strengthened by waiting until the political economy for reform was right. The Bank halted lending to the power sector in India for three years until it found evidence of real ownership of policy reform in selected states. With other partners, it then engaged in capacity-building to nurture local ownership and commitment. Subsequent lending produced more sustainable results than the earlier approach.

Donors must remain engaged, not just "pick winners." They can be reform "shapers," not only reform "takers" (to paraphrase Hirschman). Although reforms are primarily shaped by domestic political forces, aid agencies can play a critical role by designing their engagement to support policy learning and strengthen the forces of change. They need to reshape their tools, modalities, and scope of conditionalities to remain proactive external partners throughout all phases of the reform process and supportive to poor countries at all levels of policy performance.

Time for Building and Institutionalizing Consensus

Mobilizing the support of beneficiaries cannot start early enough. Pilot projects do not always proceed smoothly, even with strong community support. Flexibility is essential, along with a willingness to listen and develop a program incrementally in light of lessons learned (Chap. 4).

Recent World Bank-financed irrigation operations in India, the Philippines, and Turkey show the importance of allowing time for interventions to take effect on a socially appropriate scale:

- In Andhra Pradesh, India, in the early 1990s irrigator groups were formed around pipe committees of twenty to one hundred farmers. This group size allowed the local elite to continue to dominate and led to water allocation disputes between pipe committees. The democratic election of much larger groups in the late 1990s overcame this problem.
- In the Philippines, large national irrigation schemes were effectively no more than fee collection groups for the government agency and had limited responsibility for operations and maintenance. Water user groups were more successful in small communal irrigation projects that had more autonomy.
- In Turkey, these lessons were taken into account. Efforts were made to build a consensus among stakeholders—a process greatly facilitated by the World Bank Institute—before irrigation systems were turned over to water user groups. Larger groups were also more likely to be financially viable and could be built around existing institutions, such as municipalities.

A key challenge to aid agencies is to find ways to localize and institutionalize the processes of consensus-building and beneficiary participation. These processes should not be viewed as on-off or donor-driven. They should be anchored in local institutions and democratic processes (Chap. 5). A related challenge is to find ways to deepen consensus and broaden participation beyond government, without undermining the often-fragile public institutions and home-grown democratic processes. Much more needs to be known about promoting democratic decentralization and building coalitions to initiate and sustain reforms and development programs for poverty reduction—the political will and social consensus to alleviate poverty cannot be taken for granted.

Broadening of Participation

How should participation be broadened across various interest groups and scaled up to the national level? Extensive evaluation and research findings point to several lessons (Chaps. 4 and 5).

Integrate a Learning Process. A well-known success in broadening participation in a government bureaucracy is the Philippines National Irrigation Administration, which adopted a step-by-step approach to building user associations' capacity to manage local irrigation systems.

Beware of Procedural Inflexibility. Changing organizational systems and procedures to facilitate participatory development is complex. But the costs of not changing can be heavy, as in the government of Uttar Pradesh's Doon Valley Project in the Himalayas (Shepherd 1999).

Allow Enough Time. Participation cannot be rushed—and the larger the scale, the greater the risk. When the Indonesian government tried to institute nationwide village development planning in less than a year in 1995–96, there was little or no ownership of the process at the village level. Too little time was spent building partnerships with nongovernmental organizations (NGOs), whose skills might have enabled the government to do a better job.

Persevere. The district-level Rural Integrated Project Support Program in the Lindi and Mtwara regions of Tanzania has evolved over time into a holistic program involving local government, agriculture, natural resource management, transport and marketing, education, savings and credit, health, and water components. This broad participation emerged from the accumulated experience of repeated mistakes and learning over twenty-five years.

Identify a Champion. A pronounced shift toward participation by government or NGOs can often be traced to a single leader or strong alliance of supporters. Taking the lead, these champions have often battled against institutional inertia and political pressures from wealthy elites.

Change Attitudes and Behavior. For participatory approaches to work, attitudes and behavior need to change among all actors and at all levels (Blackburn and Holland 1998). The bottom line in participatory change is individual and personal.

The CDF challenges the ability to better deal with difficult governance issues that often involve stakeholders other than government. For example, the Bank's concerns for honest government and improved public financial accountability extend well beyond government to other elements of the state, such as the watchdog agencies charged with monitoring and protecting the public interest, civil society, and media. The judiciary and legislature also take on new emphasis in capacity-building.

A recent World Bank study finds mixed results for efforts to broaden NGO interventions (Gibbs and Fumo 1998). Many NGOs are reluctant to increase the scope of their operations or to enter large-scale partnerships. Scaling up can pose a challenge to an NGO's management capacity and create obligations to members that are difficult to sustain. Thus, any scaling up initiative must be preceded by an assessment of capacities and commitment of partners. A critical step is to involve all stakeholders in developing performance indicators, a process that clarifies expectations and priorities.

While the World Bank is a leader in policy formulation, it is often a laggard in attitude and behavior. Unless changes in attitude and behavior become a priority in the Bank, the CDF could be perceived as an exercise in domination rather than a move toward principled partnership.

Information for Accountability and Learning

Targets for monitoring progress are effective tools for guiding decisionmakers during implementation. For example, recent Bank-financed education projects have invested heavily in setting and monitoring targets. The Mozambique Second Education Program used indicators to help sustain the operation after the credit closed. It used targets set at appraisal and added new ones to establish a five year plan agreed with the borrower. The project also identified outstanding policy and implementation issues, leading to agreement on remedial actions.

Experience in health, nutrition, and population projects also shows the importance of effective monitoring and evaluation designs. Selecting a limited number of well-chosen outcome indicators and paying attention to capacity for data collection and analysis increase the focus on results and the likelihood of achieving development impact. Strengthening borrower systems for collecting, analyzing, and using health information in policymaking takes time. It requires devoting adequate attention and resources during program design and implementation and strengthening incentives for achieving results and using information.

The Poverty Reduction Strategy Papers and the International Development Goals (IDGs) are likely to heighten the need for better monitoring and statistical improvements of poverty indicators and development results. Public actions and expenditure management systems should be increasingly linked to poverty outcomes. Carrying out social impact assessments is a difficult task, and aid agencies need to pilot such assessments and provide analytical assistance to countries in assessing the social impact of policies and public expenditure programs and in building local information systems to enhance accountability and learning. The International Development Goals could further reinforce results-based management within countries and aid agencies. But care should be taken not to have the IDGs lead to unintended distortions in country or aid policies, thus repeating the mistakes of target-based planning (Chap. 2). In particular, the primary focus of the IDGs on social goals should not lead to a mechanistic focus on social expenditures or targeted programs and to the neglect of a broad-based growth agenda.

Capacity Building to Manage for Results

Developing results-oriented public management is a key challenge in many developing countries. An initial focus on performance monitoring in particular sectors or ministries can create a demonstration effect. This would prepare the way for a more comprehensive public evaluation program (Marcel 1999), for results-based conditionality, and for more extensive use of programmatic approaches to lending (Chaps. 8 and 9).

The emphasis on managing performance for projects and programs is being complemented by a wider focus on governance. Dissemination of monitoring and evaluation information on government performance can support civil society involvement in assessing government performance. Civil society also has a role to play in influencing the evaluation agenda. Key stakeholders, such as NGOs, the media, and parliaments—particularly those representing and empowering the poor—gradually learn how to use performance concepts and tools and to understand their limitations. Donors and governments can help build such capacities among these stakeholders.

Participatory monitoring and evaluation is one step toward building the capacity to learn and manage for results (Gaventa and Estrella 1998). As various stakeholders work together to develop indicators of success, their differing expectations and priorities are brought into the open. Stakeholders must then negotiate to develop a more common framework, building ownership in outcomes and reflecting partnership in the assessment itself. Participatory monitoring and evaluation also allows for tracking holistic goals, both tangible and intangible. Developing large-scale participatory monitoring and evaluation requires different skills from those needed for traditional evaluation. Stakeholders need help to acquire skills in indicator development, monitoring, facilitation, and conflict resolution (Van Wicklin 2001).

From Aid Coordination to Development Partnership

Effective aid coordination guides countries and donors toward agreement to accept mutual responsibility and distinct accountability for development outcomes. For countries, this requires a commitment to developing sound policies and effective institutions. For donors, this requires adopting a development orientation, being selective in ways that reflect comparative advantage, accommodating country-led efforts to achieve coherence and selectivity, and providing effective capacity-building assistance to create a level playing field among partners (Chaps. 6 and 11; OED 1999b).

Although many countries have expressed a strong desire to take the lead in aid coordination, only a few, such as the Republic of Korea, Malaysia, and Thailand, can be said to have fully assumed the role. Many countries lack the capacity to take the lead, and some still lack the commitment and resolve. A critical step is for aid agencies—in consultation with countries—to make country-led aid coordination a reality. The chief role of aid agencies should be to support country leadership and help build the capacity to exercise that leadership effectively. Giving countries room to exert leadership also better positions aid agencies to assist in building long-term capacity, in line with CDF principles.

The costs of poor partnership and inefficient aid coordination—poor use of decision-makers' time, gaps in assistance, and distortions in country priorities—are borne primarily by developing countries. For aid agencies, the tensions between practicing partnership and reducing the reputational risks and transaction costs involved may be high in the short term. These up-front costs should be viewed as long-term investments in building the infrastructure of partnership and creating the necessary skills, trust, and learning. And the costs are likely to decline if partnerships among donors are pursued selectively and strategically at the institutional level. The monitoring and evaluation of partnership and coordination can be strengthened to assess the cost-effectiveness of different approaches and accelerate learning about creating and managing strategic alliances. Much can be learned from private firms' experience in selecting and building strategic alliances (Chaps. 7 and 11; Doz and Hamel 1998).

Linking Global to Local

Mission-oriented transnational networks addressing highly visible and urgent human priorities—such as the Onchocerciasis Control Program and the Consultative Group on International Agricultural Research—can help to rally contributing partners. Selectivity is ensured up-front by the choice of public goods to be created. Shared learning occurs as a matter of course. Motivation and coordination among donors and partners may be achieved more readily than in multisectoral national programs (Chap. 12).

Attention needs to be given to the interface between international and national public goods—a new dimension of aid coordination. The implication is not that investments in international public goods should wait until conditions are right in most countries. It is that conditions need to be nurtured through transnational collaboration programs. Leadership and results orientation will be also critical to avoid the risks of settling on the least common dominator approaches (Chap. 10).

The CDF provides guidance. Efforts to build regional and global partnerships should follow its key tenets of inclusiveness and ownership. Priority-setting at the national level can identify areas where international programs are needed to supplement national efforts. And capacity-building in national and local institutions (government and nongovernment) will be critical for achieving the development goals of global programs.

Adapting global targets and prescriptions to country conditions and local contexts will remain a major challenge to development assistance, particularly among the large and highly centralized aid agencies. Economic and sector work and country-focused assessments should help, especially when local experts and think tanks are involved (Chap. 7). The experience of USAID suggests that decentralization of authority to local resident missions can facilitate adaptation of programs to local conditions (Chap. 10).

Implications for Aid Agencies

The CDF principles call on aid agencies to move into uncharted territory. To equip themselves to implement the framework effectively, they will have to jointly and continuously examine the results of ongoing CDF experiments. An independent, learning-oriented evaluation of these experiments is critical to practicing these challenging principles. Rapid integration of lessons learned can make these principles "a way of life" for development assistance.

A holistic, long-term, locally owned, and knowledge-driven strategy for development calls for a new research agenda (Stern, 2001). Much needs to be learned about linking development visions to building a climate for sustainable growth, and empowering poor people to participate. Much needs to be learned about development as a process, defined by ex ante freedoms and capabilities, rather than ex post outcomes and blueprints (Sen 1999, Hirschman 1958). How can countries create enabling environments that support pro-poor dynamic growth? How can learning capabilities be built within small and medium enterprises, poor communities, and public institutions? We need to understand how governments can facilitate firms and individuals to acquire the needed tools for success, and empower them to fulfill their potential (Stern 2001).

A process-conscious development assistance strategy raises many research issues about how aid agencies should act as catalysts of change (Stern 2001). Becoming a change agent requires some understanding of the dynamic process being influenced. Even if there were ready-made models for reforms and institutions for all circumstances, they cannot be imposed. Development agencies such as the Bank have for a long time espoused financing projects as "privileged particles" of development, and most recently argued for projects with powerful demonstration effects. But, this often led to creating enclaves and separate project implementation units, with little diffusion and learning effects. Similarly, prepackaged conditionalities and shock therapies have backfired, and successful and sustainable reforms remain the exception. So, what have the aid agencies learned about diffusing innovation, inducing reforms, and accelerating learning? How can the external partners help people help themselves? How can partners help build and sustain local broad-based coalitions for reform? How can they be in tune with the dynamics of reforms? How can they remain open to support countries to travel on a number of possible paths, without succumbing to familiar terrains and fixed blueprints? And what measures of progress should guide this journey?

The CDF principles and their implementation through the Poverty Reduction Strategy Paper (PRSP) call for new development assistance practices with major institutional implications for aid agencies. A "one-size-fits-all" mentality should be replaced by a customization mindset. Blueprints should be blended with or replaced by experimentation and local knowledge. Aid agencies should differentiate and adapt their approaches to countries at different levels of development, and should be prepared to question current orthodoxies and blend best practices with local innovations and local learning (Rodrik 1999). Every effort should also be made to ensure that the CDF does not become another blueprint, repeating the pattern of the planning and adjustment eras (Chaps. 1, 2, and 7). And the framework will have to be continually adapted. Rigidity is a real implementation risk.[4]

Assistance should be compatible with autonomy and learning. Too often in the planning and adjustment eras, donors and central governments adopted a hegemonic planning mentality that excluded vital local knowledge and practical know-how (Scott 1998). Similarly, in the adjustment era it was assumed that the Bretton Woods institutions or the big donor agencies had all the answers. The only problem was to sell those answers to developing countries through conditionality or training (Chaps. 6 and 7). Under the CDF, these institutions can no longer pretend that they are a storehouse of universally applicable knowledge. Instead, their staff should work to empower their country counterparts to experiment and adapt from expanded menus, and in the process enhance mutual learning and knowledge sharing.

The CDF will also increase the demand for nonlending tools and advisory services—to engender ownership, partnership, and long-term holistic thinking (Chap. 7). Depending on the skills and attitudes of users, these tools can either empower clients or lead to their cognitive dependency. Tendencies toward bureaucratization and excessive documentation—the pitfalls of the planning era—need to be overcome by participatory and creative approaches to strategy development. Donor-led economic and sector reviews and policy prescriptions—the hallmarks of the adjustment era—will increasingly be displaced by country-led approaches that build on local processes and experience and develop commitment for policy reforms. Advances in information and communication technologies offer new opportunities to share knowledge, to reach out to broader and diverse constituencies, to build new style knowledge partnerships, and to strengthen local learning capabilities.

The processes and instruments of aid agencies have been attuned to a different paradigm and will have to change to implement the CDF and the Poverty Reduction Strategy Papers. A survey of World Bank staff (and local donor representatives) found that more than half did not consider an active government role a prerequisite for effective in-country aid coordination (OED 1999b). Institutional changes within aid agencies, both subtle and demanding, will be necessary to fulfill the potential of the espoused new principles of development assistance. If aid agencies are asking developing countries to be open to reform and learning, then they should ask the same of themselves. A fundamental change in donors' attitude toward partnership, risk-taking, and mutual learning should drive other changes in instruments and modalities of assistance.

Aid agencies ultimately respond to the demands of their authorizing environments, and given the stakes involved, developing countries should help shape these environments to support the principles of ownership and partnership. Agencies such as the World Bank are facing accelerating demands, particularly from major shareholders and international advocacy NGOs. In turn, these agencies translate these demands into conditionalities, safeguards, and standards that must be met by all clients—regardless of their local practices and capabilities. Such universal standards are set at little cost to the advocates but high cost to the intended "beneficiaries"—in terms of eclipsed learning, diminished ownership, and increased dependency on outside expertise. To avoid having such rigid and unrealistic standards imposed, developing countries must organize and strengthen their voice at and beyond the governing boards of the international aid organizations.

Notes

1. A 1998 review of World Bank assistance to financial sector reform found that of twenty-three countries to which the Bank had provided support since 1985, only twelve had satisfactory performance (OED 1998d). The East Asian crisis is thought to have affected the performance ratings of three of the twenty-three countries found to have satisfactory overall ratings.
2. The donors urged that National Environmental Action Plans be completed for all International Development Association (IDA) recipients by June 30, 1991, or at the latest before the end of the IDA–9 period, with priority given to countries where major problems have been identified, and that the results be incorporated into country lending strategies.
3. Other partners perceive a tendency for the Bank to send large missions for too short a time, to produce bulky aide-memoirs and then disappear, leaving a shell-shocked local government to make sense of the contents and action plans. Rather than facilitating partnership, this increases the transaction costs for clients and partners.
4. The Bank, International Monetary Fund, United Nations Development Programme, and others should exercise caution in introducing too many planning and programming instruments. Developing countries should have a voice in shaping and harmonizing the design and use of these tools.

References

Blackburn, J., with Holland, J., eds. 1998. *Who Changes? Institutionalizing Partnership and Development*. London, U.K.: Intermediate Technologies.

Dollar, David, and Jakob Svensson. 1998. "What Explains the Success or Failure of Structural Adjustment Programs?" Policy Research Working Paper 1938. Washington, D.C.: World Bank, Development Research Group.

DFID. 1998. "Sustainable Rural Livelihoods: What Contribution Can We Make?" Paper presented at the DFID National Resources Advisors' Conference, July 1998. London.

Doz, Yves, and Gary Hamel. 1998. *Alliance Advantage: The Art of Creating Value through Partnering*. Cambridge, MA: Harvard Business School.

Evans, Alison. 2000. *Poverty Reduction in the 1990s: An Evaluation of Strategy and Performance*. Washington, D.C.: World Bank.

Gaventa, John, and Marisol Estrella. 1998. "Who Counts Reality? Participatory Monitoring and Evaluation: A Literature Review." IDS Working Paper 70. Brighton.

Gibbs, Chris, and Claudia Fumo. 1998. "Non-governmental Organizations in Bank-supported Projects." An OED Report. Washington D.C.: World Bank.

Hirschman, Albert O. 1958. *The Strategy of Economic Development*. New Haven, CT: Yale University Press.

Marcel, M. 1999. "Effectiveness of the State and Development Lessons from the Chilean Experience." In G. Perry and D. M. Leipziger, eds., *Chile: Recent Policy Lessons and Emerging Challenges*. Washington, D.C.: World Bank.

Margulis, S., and J. Bernstein. 1995. "National Environmental Strategies: Learning from Experience." Environment Dissemination Note 30. Washington, D. C.: World Bank.

OED (Operations Evaluation Department). 1994. "Report of the Evaluation Capacity Task Force." Washington, D.C.: World Bank.

———. 1996. "Chile: Pehuenche Hydroelectric and Alto Jahuel-Polpaico Transmission." (Loans 2832-CH, 2833-CH), OED Project Performance Audit Report. Washington, D.C.: World Bank.

———. 1997a. "The Effectiveness of the Bank's Appraisal Process." Washington, D.C.: World Bank.

———. 1997b. "Second Provincial Roads Project (Loan 2311-TH), Highway Sector project (Loan 2894-TH), Second Highway Sector Project (Loan 3008-TH), Third Highway Sector Project (Loan 3220-TH), and Railway Efficiency Improvement Project (Loan 2872-TH)." OED Project Performance Audit Report 16733. Washington, D.C.: World Bank.

———. 1998a. "Annual Review of Operations Evaluation." Washington, D.C.: World Bank.

———. 1998b. "Civil Service Reform: A Review of World Bank Assistance." Washington, D.C.: World Bank.

———. 1998c. "The Effectiveness of the Bank's Appraisal Process: An OED Study." World Bank, Washington, D.C

———. 1998d. "Financial Sector Reform: A Review of World Bank Assistance." Washington, D.C.: World Bank.

———. 1999a. *Development Effectiveness in Health, Nutrition, and Population: Lessons from World Bank Experience*. World Bank, Washington, D.C

———. 1999b. *Review of Aid Coordination and the Role of the World Bank*. Washington, D.C.: World Bank.

———. 1999c. "Higher Impact Adjustment Lending (HIAL): Initial Evaluation." Washington, D.C.: World Bank.

———. 1999d. "Brazil: Water Project for Municipalities and Low-Income Areas." OED Project Performance Audit Report. Washington, D.C.: World Bank.

———. 2000. "Brazil: Northeast Rural Development Program: OED Project Performance Audit." Washington, D.C.: World Bank.

Rodrik, Dani. 1999. "Institutions for High Quality Growth: What they are and how to acquire them." Paper prepared by the International Monetary Fund on Second-Generation Reforms, Washington, D.C., November 8–9, 1999.

Scott, James C. 1998. *Seeing Like a State: How Certain Schemes to Improve Human Conditions Have Failed.* New Haven, CT: Yale University Press.

Sen, Amartya. 1999. *Development as Freedom.* Oxford, U.K.: Oxford University Press.

Shepherd, A. 1999. "Evaluation of DFID Support to Poverty Reduction: Lessons from the Evaluation of a Bilateral Program." Working Paper for a World Bank Conference on Evaluation and Poverty Reduction, June 14–15, University of Birmingham.

Stern, N. 2001. "Strategy for Development." Annual Bank Conference on Development Economics. Washington, D.C.: World Bank.

Stiglitz, Joseph E. 1998. "Towards a New Paradigm for Development Strategies, Policies, and Processes." 1998 Prebisch Leture, UNCTAD, October 19, Geneva, Switzerland.

— — —. 1999. "Whither Reform? Ten Years of the Transition." In Boris Pleskovic and Joseph E. Stiglitz, eds., *Annual Conference on Development Economics.* Washington, D.C.: World Bank.

Sweden, Ministry of Foreign Affairs. "Making Partnerships Work on the Ground." Workshop Report, August 30–31, 1999.

Van Wicklin, Warren. 2001. *Participation Process Review.* Washington D.C.: World Bank.

World Bank, 1993. *New Lessons from Old Projects: The Workings of Rural Development in Northeast Brazil.* Washington, D.C.: World Bank.

— — —. 1994. *Twenty Years of Lending for Urban Development, 1972–92.* Washington, D.C.: World Bank.

— — —. 1998a. "Getting an Earful: A Review of Beneficiary Assessments of Social Funds." Social Protection Discussion Paper 9816. Washington, D.C.

— — —. 1998b. "Mainstreaming Gender in World Bank Lending: An Update." Washington, D.C.

— — —. 1998c. "Recent Experience with Involuntary Resettlement: Overview." Washington, D.C.

Contributors

Ramgopal Agarwala is the chairman of a development research company called International Development Policy Institute in New Delhi, India. He has twenty-five years of experience with the World Bank.

James Blackburn is an independent consultant, Institute of Development Studies, Sussex, United Kingdom.

William Branson is professor of Economics and International Affairs at Princeton University, NJ, USA.

Robert Chambers is a research fellow at the Institute of Development Studies, Sussex, United Kingdom.

Tim Conway is a research assistant at the Overseas Development Institute, United Kingdom.

Richard Crook is a research fellow at the Institute of Development Studies, Sussex, United Kingdom.

David Ellerman is economic advisor to the chief economist, World Bank, Washington, D.C.

Marco Ferroni is currently the principal evaluation officer at Inter-American Development Bank. At the time of this writing, he was senior adviser for the Resource Mobilization and Co-Financing Department at the World Bank.

Mick Foster is the head for the Center for Aid and Public Expenditure at the Overseas Development Institute, United Kingdom.

James Fox is an independent consultant. He was formerly lead economist at the USAID evaluation office.

John Gaventa is a research fellow at the Institute of Development Studies, Sussex, United Kingdom.

Nagy Hanna is lead corporate strategist and evaluation officer in the Operations Evaluation Department of the World Bank, Washington, D.C.

Stephen Jones is the economic policy program manager at Oxford Policy Management, United Kingdom.

Andrew Lawson is public finance and management program manager at Oxford Policy Management, United Kingdom.

James Mano is a research fellow at the Institute of Development Studies, Sussex, United Kingdom.

Simon Maxwell is the director of the Overseas Development Institute, United Kingdom

Felix Naschold is a research assistant in the Center for Aid and Public Expenditure at the Overseas Development Institute, United Kingdom

Robert Picciotto is the director general of the operations evaluation department of the World Bank, Washington, D.C.

Index